Diary of a Dinosaur

Memoirs of a larrikin geoscientist

Warwick Newton

Diary of a Dinosaur © 2025 Warwick Newton

All Rights Reserved.

No part of this book may be reproduced in any format by any electronic or mechanical means including information storage and retrieval systems, without permission in writing from the author. The only exception is by a reviewer, who may quote short excerpts in a review.

No generative artificial intelligence (AI) was used in the writing of this work. Without in any way limiting the author's exclusive rights under copyright, any use of this publication to 'train' generative artificial intelligence technologies to generate text is expressly prohibited.

Cover Design by Teneille Newton

Typography and Formatting by K E Barden

Paperback ISBN 978-1-7642649-0-7

eBook ISBN 978-1-7642649-1-4

Distributed by LightningsourceGlobal

To Kitty and Harold Newton
my parents, who created and raised the larrikin

To my sisters Ann and Wendy
who ran around the Wishing Tree hoping for a brother

To Deb
who weathered some of the extremes of the larrikin behavior

To Babs
who has managed to somewhat tame the beast

Finally, to my daughters Teneille and Emma
who have helped to moderate the larrikin behavior but in doing so have inherited
some of the same

Contents

Foreword	VII
1. Bad Habits	1
2. A Public Caning	15
3. Mastering The Art	37
4. The Finishing Touches	53
5. Welcome to the Real World	69
6. Another Planet	85
7. The Wild West	101
8. Going Bush Happy	111
9. Breaks in the Big Smoke	130
10. What Possessed Me	138
11. The Top End of Down Under	153
12. Cyclone Tracy	164
13. Fieldies, Drillers and Prospectors	177
14. The Hump Sign and Other Top End Misadventures	192
15. Marriage, Birth and Meanderings	206
16. Swimming with Crocodiles	221
17. The City of Churches	237

18.	The Second Mine that Saved South Australia	253
19.	Replete with Wine, Surf and Safaris	270
20.	Always Face Your Swag Away from the Campfire	283
21.	A Dingo Took My Boots	299
22.	Talking to Traditional Owners	313
23.	Spruiking and Romance	325
24.	Last Dance in the Rain with Jethro Tull	334
25.	Diamonds are a Boy's Best Friend	348
26.	A Bridge-Playing Grandad; Never a Queenslander	356
Reflections		365
Acknowledgements		379
Bibliography		381

Foreword

My dear daughters Teneille and Emma provided the stimulus for writing these somewhat dubious memoirs. At many a family dinner after good food and copious amounts of red wine, stories of past adventures tend to arise and for some reason my tales have often proved to be a little more outrageous than most. The girls' response invariably has been "Dad for goodness sake write these stories down" (or words to that effect).

On one of my last bush trips in South Australia over 20 years ago I was sitting in the Marla pub with a work colleague, Mark Flintoft, bemoaning the fact that you don't meet the characters you once did in outback pubs. Mark could not have summed things up better when he came up with the response "I hate to tell you this old mate but these days we are the characters". It was a bit of a shock but on reflection it was spot on. Sadly, with the advent of breathalysers, nonsensical OH&S standards and the lobby that thinks alcohol is bad for everyone we may never again encounter such people.

Another stimulus to writing this book was a road trip from Adelaide to Alice Springs and Uluru that I did with my wife Babs in 2010. As soon as we reached the Territory border, I introduced her to Ted Egan and Slim Dusty albums so she could fully take in the ambience of the occasion. On listening once again to two Ted Egan classics about drinkers and characters of the Northern Territory I realised that I either knew or knew of, all the people mentioned in these songs.

This book was supposed to be about characters I've met over the past 70 years with mention of a few of my own exploits. Unfortunately, I fear that I've been far too introspective in looking into what makes a larrikin and have also been overindulgent in giving my opinions on some of my pet likes and dislikes.

I love a good red wine and nearly all food and revel in the way alcohol serves to decrease our inhibitions. I've always enjoyed backing the underdog and love to unsettle the establishment wherever possible and believe the lyrics of Slim Dusty's classic "Big Frogs in Little Puddles" aptly reflect my attitudes to bureaucracy, pedantry and pomposity in all their lifeforms.

These yarns are based on memories from a long time ago. In most cases characters are mentioned by their real names with one or two exceptions, and no harm or offence is meant to any of them. I'm acutely aware that memories can become somewhat clouded and old memories even more so. Certainly, some of the characters may dispute the events as recorded here and who knows which version if any would be correct. Certain stories may be marginally embellished but all contain more than an element of truth.

1
Bad Habits

Connells Point, NSW 1947–57

I was born in Hurstville, NSW, in the heart of the St George district, in 1947. Earliest memories are of living in a very loving family situation at 71 Queens Road, Connells Point. My two big sisters were both pre–World War 2 arrivals, Ann in 1936 and Wendy in 1938. Post-war they were deluded enough to run around a wishing tree in some park hoping for the birth of a baby brother, an action they may have wondered about in later life. It was also a brave decision on my Mum, Kitty's part to have me, as she had previously been critically ill in childbirth.

My earliest memory is sitting on my mother's lap with her fur coat draped snugly around me in the front seat of the old Vauxhall Velox, heading home after Sunday dinner at Grandma Emma Newton's home at Mortdale. The feeling of security and love being safe with family in the car on a dark, cold night still lingers. For years I loved car travel at night because of this feeling of protection from the outside elements. Today I can't stand night driving because of poor night vision and the risks of hitting wildlife and cattle on country roads.

In the early 1950s my Dad, Harold, ran a successful grocery business, Newtons Cash Stores, with four shops at Mortdale, South Hurstville, Carlton and Sutherland in the southern suburbs of Sydney. He did most of the stock buying for the stores and I was lucky enough to accompany him on occasional trips to the PDF factory. Here bite-sized chunks of cheese were drawn from large blocks for tasting and assessment and I always got to try them, leading to a lifetime love of good mature cheddar cheeses.

Dad being a grocer had its benefits and occasional disadvantages. He would always bring home stock that wasn't moving too well and when it was exotic like pineapple-flavoured iced vovos or honey jumbles with green icing it felt like Christmas had come again. The tinned broccoli was another matter: it was one of the most disgusting products I have ever tasted and he seemingly had cartons of it; most was discreetly put aside but there was always a family rule that you must at least have a taste of everything on your plate. I think I was in my 30s before I could bring myself to eat fresh cooked broccoli after this experience.

Dad would sometimes get waylaid on his stock buying trips and one of his favourite stops was a visit to his oyster farmer mates at Oatley Bay. This entailed consuming many oysters and for some reason the oysters always needed to be washed down with a few longnecks of beer. As a three or four-year-old I could barely stand the sight of a fresh oyster let alone eat one and a sip of beer was also met with a degree of ambivalence. Despite this it was apparent to me that these men were deriving great pleasure from eating oysters and drinking beer: it is one of life's lessons that I learnt well and came to embrace with gusto.

Another regular stop on the way home was the South Hurstville pub, where Dad would often get caught up with his old cricket and lawn bowls mates, Ralph Kable and Charlie Coogan. I spent considerable time on my own in the car but received regular lemon squashes for my patience. In today's world Dad would probably be locked up for child abuse but back then no one worried, and the car windows were always open. These stops reinforced my growing idea that there must be a clear link between beer, mates and having a good time.

Christmas Days at Grandma Newton's are another fond memory. Dad had two brothers and four sisters so with children in tow it was a big roll-up and everyone had to be seated for Christmas dinner. In the early years everybody brought presents for everyone else; it was a bit of a bonanza but sanity prevailed and in later years each person brought one present to be given to someone in their equivalent age group. After presents were distributed each younger grandchild had to perform some Christmassy act for the assembled audience. For several years I did "If you knew Susie" as performed by Eddie Cantor but then graduated to "Mary's Boychild" à la Harry Belafonte. These performances must have been somewhat galling for some to endure to the extent that my cousin Jean refers to me as Mary's boychild to this day.

Grandma had a lovely big backyard with plenty of trees and a tennis court, and a cricket game was a family favourite to work off Christmas lunch. There was also a paddock full of beagles immediately behind and some of us took delight in encouraging them to break out into howling, which provided a kind of Christmas melody. Grandma who came from Lancashire, was a bit of a temperance lady so there was never any alcohol on the Christmas dinner table. Strange then that her sons and sons-in-law used to congregate in the outside laundry. From the laughter coming from within they were obviously having a good time. When I was finally old enough to have a peek into the laundry, you guessed it, there was the beer supply iced down in Grandma's laundry sinks. When I think back, Grandma probably knew exactly what was going on – the beery breath would have been a giveaway – but she chose not to recognise it.

For a time second cousin Harry Mayer lived with us at Connell's Point. Harry had just arrived from Lancashire after serving in the British Navy during the war and had commenced work with Qantas. Dad and he were known to like a beer or two and I was always in awe of the number of empty brown beer bottles that emerged from under our house when the local bottle collector made his six-monthly rounds. Surely you couldn't drink that much beer in a lifetime? I know better now.

Early school days

Primary school days at Connells Point Public School evoke lots of good memories. It was about a kilometre walk there and home each day. Best friends on and off were Brian Ashley and Terry Foreman. I caught up with Terry again much later at Sydney University where he went on to represent Australia in rugby union but then with four other players refused to play against the all-white Springbok team when they toured Australia. Memories of teachers are a bit of a blur except for one Mr Rose who at the time seemed positively ancient. He was forever digressing from lessons to recite poetry and lines like "Go to the ant thou sluggard, consider her ways and be wise ..." or "Abu Ben Adam may his tribe increase awoke one night from a deep dream of peace ...". His words remain deeply imprinted to this day.

Primary school food could be interesting and thick slices of bread with vegemite and golden syrup were a perennial after-school favourite of most of the young boys on Queens Road. My Mum used to make school sandwiches with a fruit mince filling, which became known as squashed fly sandwiches. I don't know whether it was the thought of eating squashed flies or that they tasted so good, but I always had mates at school wanting to swap their lunches for squashed fly sandwiches. Another great treat for the local Queens Road kids was Miss Bushell's annual Christmas party. Miss Bushell was an heir to the Bushell's Tea empire and enjoyed spoiling the kids in her street with presents, great food and amusements. A further lasting memory of Queens Road is the gangs of wild dogs which would occasionally come roving by; they were quite savage and any pets, particularly any bitches, needed to be locked away for their own safety. Dogs seemed to be generally more aggressive in those days.

I think the naughtiness began to show itself at primary school: I have vague memories of pushing Peter Brady into the urinal in the first few days of school. By far the greatest mischief, however, occurred when you got the job of milk monitor. In those days all children were provided with a small bottle of milk each for morning recess; the bottles were sealed with a soft aluminium lid. On Friday afternoons it was the milk monitor's job to empty, clean and stack up the week's used bottles and distribute any refrigerated leftover milk around the classes. At the back of the school were rocky cliffs which looked over the suburb of Blakehurst. The temptation was great, such that several bottles, both full and empty, found their way over the cliffs each Friday. Worse still, concoctions of old and new milk and other ingredients (but always chilled with some fresh milk) were made up and lids were straightened to look like new. These along with untainted milk were then distributed around the school. I'm not aware that there were any reported food poisonings – kids must have been tougher back then.

Walking home from school could also entail some mischief. There was a little corner shop below the school and pinching toothpaste from there was an occasional pastime – why toothpaste I don't know. Just beyond the shop was a house with a high fence all round; it was like a red rag to a bull for young boys, who ensured that the gate was always left ajar and always found a pressing need to lob a few rocks into the yard as they walked by.

For as long as I could remember Dad had driven a black Vauxhall Velox with his initials HN002 on the number plate, so imagine my surprise as I was walking home with mates one day when a big black Humber Super Snipe pulls up, the door opens and a voice says, "Hop in." Yes, it was Dad's new car and riding home with my mates I must have been the proudest boy in Connells Point.

The Humber provided great pleasure to the family: it was roomy and well-appointed with leather seats and wooden trim. There were day trips out Penrith way to collect mushrooms and blackberries, trips to the Blue Mountains and regular holidays to Bermagui on the Far South Coast. Around this time my sister Ann was learning to drive, and this is where the Humber failed us, not once, but at least twice when Ann was driving, the Humber had either total brake or steering failure, once on very steep roads in the Blue Mountains. We survived these experiences, none of which could be attributed to Ann's driving; however, from then on, I would always be howling for Dad to drive and even today I tend to be a bit dismissive of Ann's driving skills.

Not long after starting school I fell off a log in the driveway between our place and next door and managed to break my leg. Ann, who by then had commenced studying medicine, heard the break and was out attending to me in a flash; an ambulance was called, and I was off to St George District Hospital at Kogarah. As luck would have it, Dr Webb, a Macquarie Street specialist, was at the hospital that day so I got the very best medical attention. I still remember having the most vivid of dreams during the operation: there was a bright blue background, and skeletons were pulling at me from all directions. In fact, the doctors were pulling my leg out straight to set the fracture correctly and I can only now surmise that I was partially conscious during that part of the operation.

There followed ten weeks in Lower C ward, much of the time with my left leg dangling in a metal splint because the fracture was too high up for plaster. In those days visiting hours were only twice a week, Tuesday evening and a few hours on Sunday. For a six-year-old this was a traumatic experience and probably had a lasting impact. The nurses were for the most part caring but it wasn't the same as having your parents and family around looking after you. I quickly learned that sometimes you have no choice but to look after yourself, and I've carried that through life by being reluctant to confide in or seek help from others. This is rather sad because there are so many benefits to be gained by working with others, but unfortunately old habits die hard. During that period there were a lot of children in the hospital having their tonsils removed and although it was obvious that they suffered somewhat post-operation I was always envious because they were on a diet of ice cream and jelly. We longer-term patients on the other hand usually got junket for sweets, so much so that I have rarely eaten it since.

Fishing, sport and mortality

Dad loved fishing and together with his good mate Bruce Wilson purchased a ten-metre fishing boat, *Kath*, which was permanently moored at Dolans Bay. Bruce spent much of his time working as a diesel mechanic in NSW's Riverina district, but when he was home the fishing was on for young and old. Many was the story of staying out too long when the fishing was good then getting hit by the huge waves of a southerly buster on the way home. Unlike the boats of today, *Kath* with her Lister diesel motor had a top speed of about eight knots so there was no outrunning the storm. Some of this weather must have been horrendous, so much so that one of their mates Mack Cormack got so sick on the rough trip home one day that whenever he went fishing after that he would be seasick as soon as the anchor was raised, even in sheltered waters.

I never got to go on any offshore fishing trips but would often board when Dad and Bruce were undertaking maintenance in Dolans Bay, which was great fun. Maintenance also involved several longnecks for the maintainers. For one of my last birthdays at Connells Point I was allowed to have a pirate party on board with a few of my schoolmates. At the time the film "Treasure Island" was popular, so Dad, who scored the role of supervising us, was christened Captain Blackbeard for the day. Luckily none of us had to walk the plank and we all stayed relatively dry.

My Dad was a heavy smoker in the days when heavy smoking was the norm, and at least two packets of "Craven A" was his daily quota; he would also occasionally smoke a cigar or two with Uncle George or other mates, and the smell of cigar smoke seemed quite luxurious at the time. Inevitably in his mid-forties Dad had his first heart attack: he spent the entire day at home feeling crook before Mum finally said enough is enough and called the family doctor, Dr Everingham, that night. The diagnosis was swift and he was immediately admitted to hospital. At the time he must have had a lot of business worries as well, as the change from grocery stores to self-service supermarkets was just beginning and he had missed out on the opportunity to sell the grocery holdings while still relatively profitable. After a few days in hospital, he was home again, but he wasn't quite the same: he had lost interest in running the business and was generally lethargic, which today would probably be diagnosed as depression. I think this was my introduction to mortality and while he was recuperating, if he fell asleep in his lounge chair I would always check to make sure he was still breathing.

Around this time Dad arrived home one day with a beautiful little Alsatian puppy which had been rescued from a litter. "Lucky", as he was christened initially, had to be hand-fed with a bottle and after nine or ten months was growing into a great dog until one day he started having fits and frothing at the mouth. The vet confirmed that he had distemper and needed to be put down as there was no chance of recovery. As my first introduction to death and dying this was a rather horrible experience.

By this time Dad had cut his losses with the grocery business and sold what he could and had decided on a sea change by moving to Bermagui and taking up professional fishing with his good mate Bruce Wilson. About an acre of land was bought in Murrah Street, Bermagui and construction of a new house by his brother Alan and Mum's nephew Bernard was underway.

Two other experiences come to mind from that last year at Connells Point. The first was attending my first St George rugby league match at Jubilee Oval with Dad. I was absolutely awestruck to see my heroes in the flesh at their home ground. On the day Brian Graham starred at fullback but I was also particularly taken by the stocky bald bloke at five-eight, Brian "Poppa" Clay. Before moving to Bermagui I was also told that I must learn to swim; I had attended heaps of school learn-to-swim classes but just didn't have the confidence to take off. So, it was off to regular swimming lessons at Ramsgate Baths near Botany Bay. The instructor, who was a brother of an Olympic swimmer/coach (Frank Guthrie rings a bell), had a novel technique of tying a rectangular tin can to your back to give confidence with flotation, it obviously worked because when it was removed a week or so later, I immediately swam about 400 metres non-stop. It took me another 30 years to learn to breathe properly, but that is another story.

As I first remember Connells Point, we had no houses behind us so you could walk right down to the water of Oatley Bay. Paddling through the mud flats at low tide was an adventure but there were also beautiful sandstone caves along the water's edge which provided hours of entertainment, I wonder whether I unconsciously developed an early interest in rocks and the outdoors from these experiences. Once houses were built in this area we had a funny experience with a neighbor who had to access this area via the laneway next to our house.

For years a very large prickly pear grew on our block and overhung the lane; although officially a noxious weed it caused little problem but one day council workers arrived to cut it down. What we found out some time later was that they were acting on the complaint of a new neighbor, Chicka Bullock, who by then lived behind us. Chicka was bald and apparently a section of the tree fell on his head as he was walking by. Thoughts of Mrs Bullock painstakingly pulling prickles out of Chicka's bald head provided us with many laughs and more than compensated for the loss of the prickly pear.

Early characters

So, who were the characters I got to meet in those early years at Connells Point? My Dad is the first one that comes to mind.

Harold Newton arrived in Australia in mid-1911 as a four-year-old having travelled with his parents and younger brother Alan from Stockport, England to Sydney via Durban in South Africa. His prime memory from the trip was that a black man stole the pie he was eating in Durban. The family loved their sport. Alfred his father had played soccer for Stockport, trialled with either Manchester United or City and played for NSW when he arrived in Australia until his boots wore out, at which time he retired. Harold was a good cricketer who represented NSW as a junior but never fulfilled his potential at the senior level. This may in part have been due to business commitments but in his own words he was far too impetuous as a batsman. He loved his cricket, however, and was an exquisite stroke player and played through the golden years of the St George District Cricket Club when the club was graced by the names of Don Bradman and Bill O'Reilly, and later Arthur Morris and Ray Lindwall, to name just a few.

Harold only played with Don Bradman once, opening the batting with him in an exhibition match at the Gosford Boys Home: Harold got a duck, Bradman a century. As a young kid what I found fascinating was his stories about some of the players, for instance he always maintained that Bradman was the first player he encountered who played for and/or looked after his interests before those of the team. He also maintained that Bradman was not a classic stroke player like Stan McCabe, but rather had magnificent anticipation, timing and footwork skills. Ray Lindwall was another: he was a great all-round sportsman, also playing fullback in first grade for St George in rugby league, but in his early years had troubles looking after his money, to the extent Harold had to prop him up on occasions.

Harold was determined that I was going to be a good cricketer. I think I may have let him down there, and we practised together from a very early age. As he had been too impetuous as a batsman, he taught me to say to myself "This bloke can't get me out" before each and every delivery, which resulted in a very dour batsman indeed until much later in life. I was a right-handed batsman but a left arm bowler. Harold decided that I should bowl slow leg spin as Hedley Verity had done. Verity was an English bowler who Harold felt had contained and troubled Bradman more than anyone else. Unfortunately, he died in action during the Second World War and perhaps didn't reach his full potential. While he was as Australian as the next man, Harold never formally sought Australian citizenship and of course he never stopped barracking for the Poms in cricket.

Harold often took me to the cricket at the Sydney Cricket Ground as a young boy; we always sat in the M A Noble stand so we could observe how the ball was moving and I still remember the first game we went to, South Australia vs NSW in the Sheffield Shield, where Les Favell, an ex–St George player who had moved to SA, scored a brilliant 160 or so.

The Second World War must have been a period of mixed emotions for the Newton family. Harold's Uncle, another Harry Mayer, had also migrated to Australia but sadly he enlisted in World War 1 and was killed in the Battle of Fromelles at the age of 21. Grandma Newton, Harry's sister, must have been most concerned about any of her sons joining the war effort. Harold was exempted from service during World War 2 because his grocery businesses were deemed essential to the war effort, but both his brothers, Alan and Stan, his sister Lucy and brother-in-law George Mollet enlisted. It must have been a very hard time and both my sisters attended boarding school at a very early age so that Mum and Harold could devote their time to the business. I think it hardened Harold quite a lot and I always took notice of one of his later gems of advice to me which probably had its origins in the war effort.

Harold's advice was: "Don't go getting into fights son but if you have to, always make sure you give the other bloke at least half a hiding while you are copping one yourself." Although I have never seriously had to put his advice into action, it has certainly always given me a degree of confidence in approaching and handling other people.

My Mum, Kitty, was not so much a character as a huge influence in my life for almost 60 years. She was born in Leichhardt, NSW, very much the youngest in a family of eight children and lived a happy childhood first at Croydon, then the family moved to Sans Souci when she was twelve. The delightful family home "Osprey" sat by the water's edge where the Taren Point bridge is now. Put simply, Mum was just a very caring person.

The newly arrived Harry Mayer was another notable character in my early life. During World War 2 he served as a signalman on several ships in the North Sea, the Mediterranean, Atlantic and Pacific Oceans. The last two years of the war he spent on Manus Island, off New Guinea, at the British Naval Base at Pityiou. Harry migrated to Australia as a 24-year-old in 1948. He lived with Grandma

Newton at Mortdale but had periods staying at Connells Point with us, possibly to escape the strict temperance conditions at Mortdale. Harry initially worked for Harold in his South Hurstville grocery shop before joining Qantas Airways in 1951, the start of a life-long career. As well as enjoying a drink or two with Harold, Harry was always the life of the party, telling marvellous jokes in his broad Lancashire accent, and often he was the butt of his own jokes. He always laughed at his own jokes which created much mirth among his extended family.

Harry had a public relations role with Qantas and initially worked with the early flying boats in Rose Bay. He spent time with Qantas in Darwin, Perth, Fiji, Indonesia and Manilla. His Darwin escapades and love of the newly introduced Super Constellation were what impressed me as a young boy. He was involved in the Petrov affair, in which a Russian diplomat and his wife were being forcefully repatriated to Russia by the KGB and were finally removed from the Qantas plane in Darwin. Another story was of a forced landing of a Constellation at Daly Waters, about 600 kilometres south of Darwin, with a full load of international passengers. Harry was instructed to get down to Daly Waters ASAP and to keep these passengers happy while Qantas engineers worked out how they were going to get the plane airborne again. To anyone who has been to Daly Waters recently he had a gargantuan task and that was back in the early 1950s. Serious as these events must have been Harry could always bring out the humorous side of such adventures.

As a young lad Harry was always bringing me little mementoes on his regular trips back to Sydney. I especially remember him arriving at St George hospital when I had my broken leg and proceeding to produce several Aboriginal spears and other artefacts which he had acquired on a recent trip to either Bathurst or Melville Island. To say I was impressed would be a mild understatement and I treasure them to this day, although they did cop a bit of rough treatment when I got out of hospital and decided to do a bit of spear throwing.

Uncle George Mollet was another character., He lived at Penshurst not far from Connells Point, so there were regular family visits and they were always great fun. George suffered from bad asthma so the house always smelt from a combination of his asthma inhalant and cigars, which he enjoyed smoking with Dad. He was strongly into charity work with the Rotary Club but always combined this with a wicked sense of humour which was enhanced by his comic artistic skills, honed through being a professional signwriter. Bonfire night was always a memorable event: George and Dad competed to see who could buy the most firecrackers so the night always seemed to go on forever. George's son Graham was about ten years older than me and had wonderful big boy toys like train sets and Meccano, which again always added to visits. One year Uncle George entered a float in the annual Festival of Flowers at Hurstville: it was an open horse-drawn wagon filled to the brim with flowers. One of his apprentices outfitted in cowboy gear led the horse while I, also dressed as a cowboy, rode in the wagon among all the flowers. I was never quite sure whether I was grateful to Uncle George for this opportunity.

George ran his business from a huge shed in his backyard and like all signwriters' premises the walls were daubed in all sorts of excess paint. One year he cut a section out, framed it and entered it in the Royal Easter Show art competition. You guessed it: he won first prize in the modern art section and was never brave enough to reveal the origin of his artwork to the judges.

Dad's mate Bruce Wilson was another character of note. Of Scottish descent, he spent most of his year travelling the Riverina district servicing and repairing vital refrigeration equipment on many of the big sheep stations. To listen to Bruce, he was mates with most of the squattocracy and particularly with the legendary McCaugheys on "Boonoke" station. Bruce would always tell me these great yarns of encountering a big tiger snake while boiling his billy by various rivers. According to Bruce he would quietly throw his hat to the ground, whereupon the snake would take shelter under the hat. At this point Bruce would get his shotgun from his trusty old Chev ute and proceed to shoot both hat and snake. I now suspect it probably only really happened once, but it made for a good, if expensive story.

Finally, there was Jimmy Meldrum, an old Scotchman who visited us at Connells Point every Christmas morning. Jimmy always arrived with a bottle of the best Scotch whiskey and he and Dad would proceed to have two or three glasses together; where Jimmy came from or where Dad knew him from has always remained a mystery. My lasting memory of Jimmy is his huge, red, bulbous nose.

2

A Public Caning

Bermagui-Bega 1958–64

In 1958 the sleepy fishing village of Bermagui on the Far South Coast of NSW had to be a ten-year-old schoolboy's dream, with beautiful beaches that ran for miles and fishing to die for. In earlier times Bermagui was promoted by world-renowned Western writer and big game fisherman Zane Grey, who established many game fishing world records while at Bermagui. Another Australian author, Arthur Upfield, who wrote the Boney series of detective stories, was resident in Bermagui in the early years of my family's time there until 1964, and one of his Boney novels is set on that coast, "The Mystery of Swordfish Reef".

The Newton family, Mum, Dad and me, arrived from Sydney via the train to Bomaderry then the bus to Bermagui. Bathroom tiling hadn't been finished at the new house in Murrah Street so poor old Dad had to lug a case full of tiles all the way with us – it must have nearly dislocated his shoulder. Sadly, the Humber had been sold before this to finance the new house.

Dad's planned venture into professional fishing with Bruce Wilson using their boat *Kath* didn't last long. *Kath* really required modifications to be a professional fishing boat and Dad and Bruce, while the best of mates when fishing was for fun, didn't see eye to eye when the fishing was to earn a living. Fortunately, Dad was offered a job as the secretary/manager of the Bermagui Fishermen's Cooperative. While the pay was average and the office at the end of the old wharf was spartan he had a wonderful view from his office of the harbour entrance with the magnificent backdrop of Mount Dromedary (now Gulaga) as well as ready access to fresh fish, prawns and oysters including the incomparable John Dory. Dad spent eighteen years at "the Co-op" until his retirement in 1976 and during that time he, along with Co-op committee members, was instrumental in persuading the State government to undertake major harbour works including the construction of new wharves – something today's hordes of recreational anglers must greatly appreciate.

Enrolling at Bermagui Central School was a bit of a shock, as it was a much smaller school than Connells Point Primary. I was suddenly considered a bit of a brain because I was consistently getting 100 per cent in Maths. The kids were friendly but bullying and fighting to settle arguments was the norm. One of the then bullies Morris Williams, got his come-uppance one day: he had been terrorising Arthur Cotterill on the way home from school for days but on this day Mr Cotterill, also Morris's uncle, pulled up in his ute and proceeded to summarily bash Morris. It stopped that bullying but certainly wasn't what we were used to witnessing in the big smoke.

At Bermagui Central I was also pushed to learn to write with my right hand, which had never occurred at Connells Point. Lessons went on for at least six months and even today I can still write quite well with my right hand. Fortunately, I was allowed to revert to left-hand writing.

As I'd only learnt to swim the year before coming to Bermagui, Dad was intent that I should improve. To this end he managed to coopt a travelling salesman who had also been a champion surf swimmer to give me occasional lessons at Bermagui's Blue Pool. At the end of this I was reasonably fast but still a thrasher who couldn't breathe properly. However, it was good enough for me to win the twelve-year-old sprint and come second in the junior championship at the 1959 interschool swimming carnival at the Blue Pool, which did wonders for my popularity at school.

Weekends at Bermagui were wonderful. In summer honing the skills of body-surfing at Horseshoe Bay together with hours of swimming at the Blue Pool. The water at Bermagui can be cool right up until Christmas but in those days, it didn't seem to matter. Soon after our arrival at Bermagui I was on the beach at Horseshoe Bay with Mum and challenged her to a race along the beach; she was 46, I was 10. I was quite devastated when she beat me easily, Mums aren't supposed to do that.

Fishing was another great love in those days. You could always get a good feed of fish just fishing from the wharf, especially if you dropped your line into the fisherman's live bait traps under the wharf. River fishing was always good for bream, flathead and blackfish. I remember fishing in the Bermagui River with Harry Mayer who was down on holiday. He had left his line by the water's edge for a nature call when suddenly line and reel disappeared into the middle of the river. Harry thought about swimming out to get it but then borrowed my rod and began casting to try and jag his reel. After perhaps half an hour and about a kilometre upstream he jagged the reel and hauled it to shore to find a very respectable snapper on the end of his line. Harry lifted his line to show me the fish and at that moment it fell off the hook and proceeded to escape to the deep through only a few inches of water.

Fishing was so good that on a few days a year you didn't even need a fishing line. Frigate mackerel or "leadenall" as they were locally known would invade the harbour; all you had to do was chase them through the shallows and they'd beach themselves. In fact, fishing was so good at Bermagui in those days that I've never been really excited by fishing since, save for some rare occasions.

The other great fishing event was the tuna season, from about October to January. It was so exciting to see the boats both big and small return from a good day's fishing with only inches of freeboard because of their massive load of tuna. Unloading onto the old wharf could often take most of the night.

The annual boating event of note was the Sydney to Hobart Yacht Race. As the race headed to Hobart all you got was a glimpse of white sails on the horizon, but on the way home many of the boats dropped into Bermagui for a day or two and the crews partied on. The 1959 handicap winner, *Cherana*, was one of these and the photo opportunities weren't lost on an impressionable twelve-year-old. Whale sightings were also very common in the season despite whaling still being in full swing. Sunday afternoons also saw the regular journey of the passenger ship *Kanimbla* heading up the coast from Melbourne to Sydney. For some reason at Bermagui, she only sailed a kilometre or so offshore, which made for a great spectacle. With the aid of binoculars, you could see the passengers on deck.

The other great joy at Bermagui was just walking around the rocky coastline for hours marvelling at the rocks, the ocean, the birds and the rugged scenery. Little did I know then that those rocky outcrops would be used to teach structural geology to budding students because the outcrops graphically display the various phases of folding and distortion of the geological strata.

Not long after we moved to Bermagui, I experienced my first Tuna Festival. Uncle George had come down to design and construct a big tuna float for the Co-op and my sister Wendy was also down for the weekend having a few days off from nursing at St George Hospital. I was allowed to attend the festival ball on Friday night and Wendy somewhat reluctantly came along in a red-and-white dress with an unsewn hem. Regardless and to my sheer delight, Wendy was crowned the Queen of the Green Seas and given a beautiful green winner's sash which I believe her daughters treasure to this day. After this the rest of the Tuna Festival, which included a parade down the main street, side shows and sporting events, seemed wonderful.

Dad bought me a high-powered BSA air rifle to protect his veggie garden and any fruit trees in our backyard from parrots. Over several years I hate to think how many beautiful parrots and other birds I destroyed, even some magnificent hawks that were foolish enough to perch on the top of next door's flagpole. Occasionally there were also parrot massacres in sweet corn paddocks that local growers wanted protected. What finally caused me to have second thoughts about all this slaughter was a wonga pigeon–shooting expedition to Mount Dromedary that I went on with Jack Payne, a local bushie and Wallaga Lake fisherman. With Jack and me seated on the ground holding shotgun and air rifle respectively, Jack would whistle up the pigeons. The doomed birds, thinking they were meeting a mate, would appear from the bush and waddle up to our feet, if I didn't get them with the first shot then Jack made short work of them with his shotgun. Although they were reputed to be somewhat of a delicacy, I didn't think they tasted all that good.

The other schoolboy shooting pastime was to wander along the banks of the river and shoot toadfish in the shallows. Some limitations were put on unsupervised shooting expeditions after my mate next door, Brian Mead, was accidently shot by his cousin, Barry Smith, with a .22 rifle. Though seriously injured and hospitalised, he survived.

Orchards and fruit trees were another new experience after coming from the city. Old Jack Warn and his wife had an apple orchard beside the Bermagui River, just a short walk from school. It was standard after-school practice to wander up and raid the orchard and run. The stolen apples seemed to have a flavour all of their own. Another time two of my older cousins, Andrew and Graham, were staying with us. After school I headed off with Brian Mead to pick apricots at an abandoned orchard not far from home. We got back with bags of apricots just before dinner but must have eaten at least as many while picking. Once home the apricots hit: I was so bloated I could do nothing but lie on the lounge and moan; dinner was out of the question. When the others had finished dinner Dad, and my cousins decided a game of backyard cricket was in order and I was literally dragged out to join in. It was probably the least enjoyable game of cricket ever and I've never again gorged on apricots like that.

Another brief encounter with fruit and vegetables was an attempt at growing them, leading to an entry in the Bermagui Country Women's Association cookery and gardening competition where I won first prize for "one table pumpkin". I treasure this certificate and have displayed it in many offices over the years as my most prized qualification.

Further shocks coming from the city were the size of the backyard – about an acre – and the fact that we had a wood stove for cooking and hot water. As a result, I learned how to use a mower and got a lot of satisfaction from mowing, especially in keeping the cricket pitch in the backyard in top shape. Likewise, I quickly became adept at chopping wood, something I still enjoy. As an aside, when I went off to uni in 1965 Dad bought Mum an axe for her birthday, I still have the axe, but I don't think Mum ever took the hint.

Religion had never been a big thing in the family although my sisters attended SCEGGS (the Anglican girls grammar school) at Darlinghurst in Sydney. However, Mum became a Sunday school teacher at Bermagui's Anglican church and from there I did my confirmation and became an altar boy. (I know this may be hard to believe.) Apart from sneaky sips of red wine these events caused me to contemplate eternal life and infinity at an early age. The more I contemplated the less I liked the idea of eternal life, and I started to wonder whether these ministers were all they were cracked up to be. Talking about contemplating infinity, about that time I went to the Bermagui picture theatre with Mum to see "Earth versus The Flying Saucers". I don't think I've ever been so scared in my life as I was on the walk home in the dark.

We had regular visits for tea and scones from the local minister, Mr Brassington, and it was during one of these visits that I realised what a potent force the power of suggestion is. I pretended I had put salt instead of sugar in Mr Brassington's tea and sure enough he convinced himself that there was salt in his tea. My disillusion with organised religion has only grown stronger with age and back then led to some heated discussions with the clergy during high school religious lessons. How can organised religion perpetuate such utter myths and horror stories with impressionable young people in the modern age and still retain such power in the community?

High school days

The year 1960 saw me start at Bega High School, living away from home Monday to Thursday nights at the Bega Boys Hostel. When I went to Bega with Mum to enrol I noticed one teacher who appeared particularly sour and thought, I hope he won't be teaching me. First day in class 1A and in walks the sour-faced teacher, Mr Barry Thode, who announced he'd be both our maths teacher and class teacher. It was a lesson in don't judge a book by its cover: he turned out to be a wonderful teacher with a great sense of humour. Unbeknown to me, my reputation for maths prowess had preceded me to Bega, but it was assumed the local Bega Primary maths whiz kid would put things right. That idea was put to rest at the first half-yearly exams.

The Bega Boys Hostel was another matter: bullying was rife and first-year students were the lowest of the low. While some of the lads made alliances with older boys or relatives, I quickly realised that the best form of protection was to be as invisible as possible; in other words, don't rock the boat if you want to avoid "Royal Flushes", "greasing" and "muscle-grinders". Luckily, I was quite strong and fit so if ordered to do twenty chin-ups I could usually complete the task. However, you couldn't always avoid run-ins, and I copped it one day after giving a fifth-year boy a bit of lip; he was also from Bermagui. Despite round after round of "muscle-grinders" and many tears I kept telling him he was a "dickhead". He gave up in the end.

The first year of school was generally good fun but there were some disappointments like starting first term cricket in D Grade, where the pitch was a rutted dirt track running around the main oval, making it truly impossible to show any skills with bat or ball. This was where coming from the hostel had its advantages. The senior boys noticed I was very hard to get out in afternoon cricket at the hostel so when cricket recommenced in term four, I suddenly found myself in A grade playing on the central oval.

Another teacher who left a lasting impression in first year was Henry Plunkett, the French teacher, who was always dressed to a tee in a designer suit with flamboyant tie, shirt and handkerchief and with unmasculine mannerisms to match. He was quickly dubbed a poof – "gay" still meant "happy" in those days. Henry although Australian also had the classic continental temperament, at best highly strung, at worst shockingly bad tempered. If French lessons didn't go strictly to plan missiles including chalk, books and chairs would fly in every direction and it's a wonder no-one was ever seriously injured. He often had to walk out of class for a five-minute break to calm down. However, Henry was an excellent teacher who engendered a real interest in the French language and culture and, just to prove all the students wrong, a couple of years later he announced that he'd got married; his wife turned out to be an absolute stunner.

High school just got better with time, particularly in second year when the boys hostel was relocated from central Bega to the old hospital about two kilometres south of Bega, which also formed part of the school dairy farm. The hospital was a magnificent old building complete with a morgue, which was somewhat intriguing to schoolboys, and it was situated in spacious grounds which allowed for cricket and rugby league games.

New herringbone bails had been constructed for the farm dairy and local farmers had donated about 30 head of dairy cattle together with "Scholar", the prize bull. Some enterprising soul in their wisdom had decided that the hostel boys would be responsible for milking the cattle, and a weekly roster of usually four boys at a time was set up. A good producing herd needs to be milked properly, twice a day, but this herd definitely wasn't. In winter in below freezing morning temperatures, if a cow or two were missing they weren't rounded up. Consequently, in less than twelve months the whole herd had gone dry and to top it off "Scholar" died of cancer. A farm manager was employed from that time on to look after the dairy.

In retrospect I wonder about the donated cattle and whether it was all the fault of the hostel boys. The cynic in me suggests that some if not all the cattle may not have been among the best in the donor farmers' herds.

The hostel boys either came from the Coast like me or from the Monaro, which included some then very isolated little townships like Wyndham and Bibbenluke. Today these places are little more than an hour's drive from Bega, but back then the trip could take most of the day. There was a real rivalry between the two groups and a few times each year there were State of Origin–like cricket and rugby league matches which were very serious affairs. Particularly in rugby league it was a disadvantage to be an older member of these teams, as hostel rules meant that older players had to go a bit easier on tackling whereas anything went for younger players, including kicking and punching. I think the younger players thought it was payback time and took full advantage. Games were played with a win-at-all-costs mentality that wasn't usually present in normal school sport.

Bullying at the hostel was as rife as ever and one gradually progressed from bullied to bully. However, some got their come-uppances such as when one night I walked outside after dinner to find Michael Love buried with just his head above ground. Michael, a big bloke, had avoided early bullying because he got into the First Thirteen rugby league team at an early age and thus had the protection of senior boys. However, by this time many of these seniors had left school and on this occasion many of the younger boys had had enough and banded together for the burial. It worked, as he was a changed man from then on.

Other hijinks at the hostel included inducing new kids to piss on the electric fence, with someone strategically located by the on/off switch so that older boys could demonstrate that it was a harmless exercise; also, on one occasion hoisting a boy, bed and all, about five metres up a tree where he slept the night. Dennis Whiffen was a notorious snorer and heavy sleeper, so the boys carried his bed, with him in it, out of the hostel and then proceeded to hoist the package up a convenient tree. He was well roped in so that he couldn't fall out. However, the joke was on us, as when he hadn't re-appeared inside by early the next morning, we had to check on him and indeed wake him up. He slept through the whole exercise. Short sheeting of beds and regular night-time raids of other dormitories were the norm, with some of the protective measures against these raids being rather brutal. It wasn't uncommon to have doors booby-trapped, and there was always a liberal coating of drawing pins on the floor for unsuspecting raiders who were silly enough to come in bare feet.

We had one apparently gay fellow at the hostel, for whom you had to take precautions to ensure that he didn't try to hop into your bed. Interestingly he was well tolerated and liked both at the hostel and at school, perhaps because he was a bit of a novelty back then. In order that the boys didn't loiter too long in Bega after school, a local barber was engaged to give haircuts at the hostel once every three weeks or so. What a rogue he turned out to be as the main supplier of cigarettes and other contraband, including of course "French letters", 99 per cent of which ended up as water bombs.

I was somewhat disappointed during my final year at the hostel when a paper chase was organised. Three senior boys were to set the trails through the school farm. I must have spent at least an hour setting my trail, running through dams, swamps and clumps of blackberries as well as having a brief confrontation with a large and angry, red-bellied black snake. I was chuckling all the way at the thought of what the following boys would have to go through. When I got back to the hostel everybody was there – no-one had been silly enough to follow my trail.

Back to high school itself: second year progressed well academically and as I managed to get into the school Second Eleven in cricket I had the opportunity to go on my first interschool visit to Cooma, where we were billeted with Cooma High School pupils and parents. What an adventure it was. One of Plumb's Tathra-Bega buses transported us there and when we got near the top of Brown Mountain all the passengers had to disembark and walk for a bit so that the bus could get over the summit. Also, by second year there was a realisation that girls might be of more than passing interest, but sadly even first-year girls wanted nothing to do with immature second-year boys.

By the final year of high school I had managed to make the First Eleven in cricket, First Thirteen in rugby league and the debating team, but after being dux of the school in first through fourth years my marks were slipping, probably due to more involvement in life's social aspects. There were interschool visits to and from Cooma and also from Nowra. We had played cricket in Cooma the previous year when Steve Liebmann, of Channel 9 fame, was one of Cooma's opening batsmen and was belting Bega all over the place until John Armstrong, who hailed from Eden, felled him with a bouncer; after that Bega went on to win convincingly. The roles were reversed in rugby league in the final year, where Cooma thrashed us in a year where they went on to either win or be runners-up in the NSW State High School competition.

A public caning

The best story from that final year, 1964, came from the annual sports day. A tradition had built up over several years whereby during the lunch break on that day, senior students had free rein to duck younger male teachers under taps or with hoses. As normal, several teachers copped a drenching and at least some of these activities were observed by the Deputy Headmaster, Mr Nethery, with a degree of mirth. One teacher, Mr Reynolds, took exception to the ducking and assembled some of the perpetrators in his classroom afterwards, where he proceeded to inflict some rough justice. Matters could have ended there but Mr Reynolds then decided to take his grievances to the Headmaster, Charles "Acka" Anderson. At which point the shit hit the proverbial fan.

Next day the whole school was assembled in the school hall and twelve identified perpetrators of the teacher duckings were named and ordered to join Acka on the stage: the group included almost all senior prefects and myself as school captain. The only exception was Darryl Berry, the school vice-captain, who had wagged school on the sports day. Despite being a gifted athlete, he wasn't prepared to carry the school flag and lead the march down Carp Street, Bega's main street, before the athletic events started.

Acka proceeded to give us a dressing down, dismissed us from office and announced that each of us would receive six of the best in front of the assembled school, at which screams were heard from some of the girls in the audience. He also called on any others involved to show the courage to come forward but was somewhat shocked when a further eleven senior boys joined us. He had badly miscalculated, in that the assembled perpetrators were near-adult males who weren't about to show any emotion and being in his sixties he was lacking the fitness to carry out the task. As the canings proceeded at least two girls in the audience fainted, the perpetrators remained impassive and Acka got progressively redder and more breathless. One boy, Colin Sinclair, who was a gifted pianist, provided some light entertainment when he offered his backside for punishment to protect his hands. Acka refused the offer and just about went apoplectic.

One can only conclude that Acka was unaware of Mr Reynolds's initial physical punishment of some of the boys and of Mr Nethery's and other teachers' tacit approval of the duckings, before he rashly decided to undertake the public canings. The ramifications of the public canings were swift and far-reaching. As soon as pupils got back to class, they spontaneously refused to do any work, effectively going on strike. This was no five-minute statement but continued until the end of the school week and then at least two days into the following week. Meanwhile several parents were threatening legal action against the school for forcing their children to witness the canings and then of course the Sydney press got hold of the story and Bega High School was front page news in the *Sydney Morning Herald* and *Daily Telegraph*. The press came out very much in support of the establishment and as someone directly involved in this event it was an eye-opener to see how little factual information they included in their articles.

The upshot, by about Wednesday the following week, was that, although we heard nothing from Acka, Mr Nethery called the perpetrators into his office, muttered "sorry boys," and proceeded to return our prefects' and captain's badges. I only recently learned that all the female prefects were ready to resign if their male counterparts weren't reinstated. The school returned to normal and classes immediately resumed once a general announcement was made; but things would never be quite the same. Mr Reynolds was transferred to Broken Hill at the end of the year. Acka soldiered on for a time but then took retirement.

With the wisdom of years, I feel quite sorry for Acka. He'd enjoyed a long and distinguished career until one poor decision where he probably wasn't appraised of all the facts resulted in a major and lasting blemish. Mr Reynolds's ego probably got the better of him: he was a short but very muscly man who was a formidable forward in the Bega first grade rugby league team; as an art teacher he also had a quite urbane character. One wonders if he felt his manliness was threatened by the impromptu ducking leading him to both physically retaliate and lodge the formal complaint with "Acka".

The Griffith "Mafia" connection

About 1960 our Griffith relatives Peter Payne and Sav Salvestro and families began making regular Easter trips to Bermagui. Little did we know then that these would become a family tradition at Bermagui for the next 20 years and then be transferred up the coast to Narrawallee, near Ulladulla, for a further 30 years. Sav, who had a fruit farm at Griffith, would arrive with boxes of fruit and watermelons and a plentiful supply of local wine; Bill Smith, my sister Wendy's husband, who was a butcher, would arrive from Sydney with ample stocks of steak and sausages for barbeques; and Dad would source the fish, prawns and oysters locally as well as providing vegies from his backyard garden.

In the early days Sav and Peter loved their deep-sea fishing, and Dad was just the bloke to well and truly stitch them up. They would put in long Saturdays at Kitty (later Bill) O'Shea's Bermagui Hotel, knowing full well that they needed to be up before daylight the next morning to go fishing with one of the local fishermen – but not just any fisherman: Dad would usually line them up with Jack

Christiansen, a Dane, who always went fishing regardless of the weather. Despite some horrendous tales of rough seas and seasickness Sav and Peter kept coming back for more year after year

No Easter was complete without a big barbeque at the southern end of Cuttagee Beach, a few kilometres south of Bermagui. Dad would head down early to claim the only barbie and start opening oysters. The mob would follow, and a great lunch would ensue, washed down with copious quantities of red wine. Observing the best in occupational health and safety, the obligatory body-surf would follow, and here Sav initiated a somewhat novel tradition. As soon as he was hit by the first big wave Sav would have a big chunder. The first time it happened Sav maintained he was simply burleying for flathead, a comment he was never allowed to forget. Sadly, Sav is no longer with us and the family group is desperately trying to recruit a new burley master from the younger generation.

As a result of the Griffith connection, I was allowed to visit Griffith on my own during early high school years, first on a 20-hour train trip and later, on my first air flight in a Fokker Friendship from Sydney It was on one of these trips with Sav's son Larry that we made the acquaintance of a group of Spanish fruit pickers on Sav's farm. After a day of helping with fruit picking the Spaniards invited us back to their quarters for a feast of suckling pig. Sav and his wife Jill (my cousin) didn't see any problem with this and allowed us to go.

What we didn't realise was that we had to help in first dispatching or at least observing the dispatch of the piglet. Until then I didn't have any idea just how haunting the squeal of a pig having its throat cut can be. Then of course there was the long delay while the pig was cooked. The Spaniards fed us various bits of antipasto, which were a revelation to young palates, and then they produced a goat skin replete with red wine. They were very generous and urged us to join in as the goat skin was passed around and refilled several times. As an introduction to red wine Larry and I thoroughly enjoyed ourselves and the Spaniards convinced us that at least one of them had been a renowned bullfighter. By the time the suckling pig was served we had had a wonderful time; unfortunately the red wine splashed all over the front of our clothes was a dead giveaway when we returned home.

Country sport

During the years at Bermagui there were regular trips to Sydney and whenever possible Dad would take me to the SCG for cricket test matches and St George rugby league grand final games in their golden era when they won eleven premierships in a row. The 1963 grand final played between St George and Western Suburbs in the mud, where the two captains, Norm Provan and Arthur Summons were immortalised in their mud-soaked photo at the end of the game, was particularly memorable, not only for Johnny King's heroics on the wing but also for the fact that St George won the premiership in all three grades. However, there was a price to pay for these attendances because, like South Hurstville earlier on, Dad had cultivated a good mate, Keith Merrin, who ran a boating and fishing supply business in Wooloomooloo. They would meet at the local pub while I sat languishing in the car with a lemon squash or two. It always felt as though we'd be late for the game, but as in earlier years we always arrived on time, usually just as the starting whistle was being blown. They were great times.

In my last year at high school Dad also taught me to drive on weekends. He had a novel approach, first showing me the rudiments of the clutch and gear changing in our one-acre backyard. From there we headed to a maze of dirt tracks out the back of Bermagui with some very steep inclines. Dad's approach was to get me to drive down one of these tracks and drop him off with his fishing rod on the Bermagui River. I was instructed then to drive round the dirt tracks and practise hill starts on the steepest incline. It probably saved him a lot of pain and suffering and I did manage to get my licence in Cobargo, late in 1964. What it didn't prepare me for was driving in traffic, and when next year I first ventured down Broadway in Sydney my first impulse was simply to stop and abandon my sister Ann's Datsun Bluebird and walk home. Luckily, I stuck with the vehicle and finally negotiated this ordeal safely.

In 1964 I was in the Cobargo under-17 rugby league team and opened the batting for the Cobargo senior cricket team. We were lucky enough to win the Far South Coast premierships in both, particularly going through the season undefeated in the under-17s. We had a trump card in rugby league, Anthony Allen from Cobargo, who attended Waverley College in Sydney but often came home on weekends to play for Cobargo. He was a fearsome tackler who took no prisoners. I remember a game at Candelo where one of the opposition players needed medical attention after one of Anthony's crash tackles. The ambulance officer turned out to be the victim's father, who started abusing Anthony. Anthony's response: "Hurry up and get off the field or you'll get some of the same.". The ambulance officer took the hint. Later in life Tony Allen went on to play first grade for Bega and represented NSW Country; he also held the office of Mayor of the Bega District for many years.

Playing in these country competitions was a wonderful experience, travelling many hours up and down the picturesque Far South Coast then playing games at many idyllic locations. Locals were very proud of their sporting venues in those days and maintained them in top condition. Playing senior cricket, however, was a bit of an eye-opener. I had been brought up to walk if I knew I was out and admit it if a catch was dropped or if a ball hit the boundary. I found some of the best senior players in the competition appeared to have problems with either their eyesight or hearing or both.

A big impact on my life was the arrival of eight nieces and nephews in the period October 1960 to June 1967. What's more, both my sisters had twins in this period. Over the years I learned to tease them all mercilessly but also came to love them dearly. They still remind me of ordeals like being put head-first into a sleeping bag then being locked in the boot of the car (for all of five seconds); and of having to put youngest niece Kristena, then four, under the shower after she drank too much beer from a flower vase while I was the responsible baby-sitter. I showed some responsibility by offering them $100 each on their 21st birthdays if they never smoked. Most got the payout, but I suspect in some cases under false pretences. Things turned out all right, however, and today I regard them all as some of my best friends.

My eldest niece, Kathy, lived with us at Bermagui for a time while her mother Ann was attempting to complete her medical residential qualifications in Sydney and cope with a failed marriage at the same time. To me it was a most joyful time and felt like having a baby sister in the household, and it was heart-wrenching for us all when the time came for her to return to her mother.

Fishermen and other locals

Memories of Bermagui wouldn't be complete without describing some of the characters encountered during this period.

Sam Sinclair was a classic. Sam apparently arrived in Bermagui in 1904, after the Boer War, and established himself as the village blacksmith, wheelwright and coachmaker. He was also a very strong man who featured in Toohey's beer ads for half a century although reputedly he rarely drank. He featured as a blacksmith holding up a beer with the classic toast "Here's too 'ee" in a picture which graced many NSW pubs. His outline from this picture was later used as a logo on many of Toohey's beer products before being replaced with the Toohey's "deer". In his time at Bermagui, according to the Bermagui Historical Society he was variously dentist, undertaker, boat-builder, fisherman, big game fishing weighmaster, boxer, champion strongman and emergency midwife. He was also a mentor to renowned strongman of the era, Don Athaldo. Don Athaldo may have worked in Sam's blacksmith shop at some stage and in his waning years graced one of the early Bermagui Tuna Festivals with his strongman act.

When I first met Sam, he ran a hardware and petrol shop in Lamont Street where the Bermagui Motor Inn is now situated. He must have been in his mid-70s by then. The little shop was fascinating: not only did it contain every bit of imaginable hardware but also fishing gear, shark's teeth, old signs, paintings, photos, etc. If he couldn't find it in his shop he'd rummage through his shed out the back and his house next door where he would invariably come up with the required product (much better than Bunnings's service today).

He was still clearly a powerful man, but with a soft voice and a kindly smile he would entertain young customers like myself with stories of his early adventures in Bermagui. One of his then projects was hand-building a rock retaining wall at the back of the beach at Horseshoe Bay as a service to the community, and he must have moved tonnes of rock by hand to complete the project. Today the sea has obliterated all signs of those endeavours. By the time I met Sam his wife had died, and he was left to care for his adopted Downs syndrome daughter, Violey, who must have been at least in her forties. He always looked after her with love and affection. Sam died on 21 August 1964, aged 82, from injuries sustained falling off his roof.

The professional fishermen at Bermagui were a very diverse bunch of characters, some well-educated, some astute businessmen, many of whom were very capable in their profession; combined with some of questionable character and the occasional out-and-out drunk. While the majority were of Australian or British background, there was also a mix of Europeans and the Italian trawler fishermen who visited regularly from Ulladulla.

When the seas were rough the fishermen tended to congregate on the old wharf while effecting repairs to their boats and fishing equipment. At lunchtime they'd dine on their favourite fish dish. Fat sea mullet would be cooked whole on a fish trap over an open fire until they were charred black. The blackened skin and scales were torn off one side and copious quantities of butter, pepper and salt were added to the milky white flesh. The result was delicious and rivalled the more fancied snapper and john dory, but you did need to look out for bones.

When no other fisherman would venture beyond the harbour, Jack Christiansen would be in his element way out to sea, on his own, beyond the continental shelf, in fact in his time as a professional fisherman at Bermagui and later

Eden, Jack managed to sink at least three boats. Jack eventually realised that his luck on the water was going to run out one day, sold his boat and bought a cattle property out of Rockhampton, a sea change indeed.

Harry Jubb was a fisherman who stood out from the crowd. He never wore shoes (well maybe to church on Sunday) and looked like a bit of a derelict. Harry was a devout churchgoer, and I think he needed to be, as his boat, *The Star of the Sea* was not only ancient but at about six metres long was the smallest in the fleet and looked as if it could sink at any time. Despite this Harry was a successful fisherman and died of old age. Johnny Jubb his son wisely stuck to larger, more seaworthy boats and eventually transitioned from professional fisherman to be the first of the modern big game fishing guides, who now greatly outnumber professional fishermen.

George Trafford was another interesting character who got into professional fishing late in life and always went to sea alone. George was very protective of his near shore fishing spots and if another boat followed him, he'd steer clear of these spots. He only fished with handlines and would regularly return with two or three boxes of flathead, which was enough to earn a comfortable living. No doubt the amateur GPS cowboys of today have now depleted George's fishing spots.

Docky Franks was another barefoot fisherman who always sported a well-worn ship's captain's cap. He knew his fishing but was also seen as the town drunk. I went to school with his boys for two years at Bermagui Central. Lloyd the oldest was a lovely bloke but sadly went the way of his father; Johnny and Danny, the younger brothers, were never very interested in school but became successful fishermen and Danny (or both) established a slipway business in the harbour.

Trawlers from Ulladulla were regular visitors to the port, particularly those of Tony Lavalle and Tory and Joe Pugliesi. They were greeted with mixed feelings by the local fisherman as their trawling methods damaged the in-shore fishing reefs. Dad developed a liking for spaghetti bolognese after dining and sharing a few red wines on their boats.

There are so many other fishermen from that era who deserve a mention: Jock Dinse on *Edith*, Tom Paddon and his son-in-law Ron Keating on *Vida*, Ron Taylor on *Gladiator*, Frank Broder on *Fair Venture*, John Gray and Ted Luscombe (the odd couple), Ray Went, Bob Loring and Gordon Simpson. There were also oyster farmers like Ivan Wills and Wallaga Lake fishermen like that old bushie, Jack Payne.

The only purpose-built big game fishing boat in Bermagui at that time was *Boy David*, owned by the redoubtable Colonel John Mansel Bruce-Steer. *Boy David* was moored away from the wharf and people could only come aboard if they wore white-soled shoes. Despite this the Colonel was an affable old sea captain and I imagine stiff gins may have been served up before venturing out to sea. He had served in India and personified the Raj.

I visited his home several times mainly because of Mrs Bruce-Steer's and Mum's involvement in the Country Women's Association and once when the Colonel gave a civil defence presentation on the perils of atomic warfare, which was pretty scary at the time. The home was full of Indian memorabilia, an umbrella stand made from the lower leg and foot of an elephant, a tiger head and skin on the floor, elephant foot ashtrays, ivory in many forms, several animal heads adorning the walls and of course the overwhelming aroma of cigars.

Two characters who mustn't go unmentioned in the Bermagui period are my Griffith relations, Silvio "Sav" Salvestro and Peter Payne, who lived life to the full and have both recently passed away. They figured prominently in family Easter get-togethers, firstly at Bermagui and later at Narrawallee over a 50-year period.

Sav was born in Cavaso del Tomba in northern Italy in 1927 and moved to Australia with most of his family, establishing large fruit farms at Griffith in NSW. Although he always retained a slight accent he was more Australian than most, excelling at rugby league, cricket and later lawn bowls. He was passionate about life and that passion rubbed off on everyone around him, and he always told a good story. If you believe him, he claimed to have once burst the football while tackling a player in the local rugby league competition.

Sav was friends with and seemed to know everyone, I remember walking into the Mollymook Golf Club with him and there was Johnny Raper, St. George and Australian rugby league immortal. Sav simply said "Gooday, John" and Raper responded in kind to his mate Sav. Another time on a European trip Sav stayed with the legendary French rugby league fullback Puig Aubert (who generally only took one step to kick goals up to 60 metres distance). Sav had played against him when the French touring side had played a country game in Griffith, and they formed a lifetime friendship.

He also loved to play up to his Italian heritage and often claimed to be the Griffith mafia godfather, even owning a vehicle with rego number starting in GDF, and when my Dad died our immediate family claimed him as our godfather. He did at one stage have a run-in with the real Griffith mafia. He and his son wanted to purchase a certain citrus orchard and had put a deposit on it; however, via the local grapevine he received a message from a certain Mr Sergi suggesting he not go through with the purchase. He did the wise thing and withdrew; I'm not sure but I think that orchard property may now house either the massive Yellowtail or Warburn Estate winery complex.

Peter Payne – what can I say, was my cousin and my idol, but like my relationship with Sav it grew into a mates relationship which I very much cherished as I got older. Peter was born in Sans Souci in 1937 and moved to Griffith when he was four. He was a gifted all-round sportsman, from diving to athletics, rugby league and aussie rules. In 1955, still a teenager, he scored most points in a season and scored the winning try to win the Premiership for the Griffith Black and Whites after a long time out of the finals, although he was happy to acknowledge that it was Brian Clay, later to become a St George rugby league legend, who set up the try. His rugby league career was sadly cut short after he sustained a badly broken leg on the field.

Peter joined the Griffith Leagues Club at its foundation and was very proud of his membership number, 007. He served on the board for 26 years in various capacities including many years as president and must have been delighted in the local institution that it has become today. However, Peter's greater attribute was his humanity and empathy: when you socialised with him he made you feel special and always like his best mate. A classic tale about Peter related to one night when he was carrying a tray of beers back to the table in the pub at Bermagui when someone thought it would be funny to pull down Peter's shorts, but there was no way Payney was going to drop those beers, so he just kept on walking and didn't spill a drop.

The Bermagui of today is somewhat different. Only two or three professional fishing boats remain, replaced by up-market big game charter boats and literally hundreds of small but sleek and fast amateur fishing boats. Horror of horrors, the two upright goalposts at each end of Bermagui oval have been replaced by four to cater for the wants of the ongoing Mexican invasion. In 1989 Bermagui featured in the television series *Body Surfer*, while in 2001 director Mark Joffe brought the town into world focus with the movie *The Man Who Sued God*, starring Billy Connolly.

I can't help feeling that, as always, history is decided by the last man standing. In the flash, new shopping and restaurant precinct by the harbour, which also houses the current Bermagui Fisherman's Cooperative, there's a statue to one of the Pugliesi family for his contribution to the Bermagui fishing industry. While not denying his legacy, many others who probably contributed far more, go unnoticed.

3

Mastering The Art

Sydney University 1965–68

To a lad of seventeen who had become somewhat countrified over the past seven years, Sydney University was a whole new world. Clive James and other well-known characters had by then departed for London but there were still plenty left.

Now a noted commentator and lawyer, Geoffrey Robertson was then President of the Students Representative Council and delivered some spellbinding speeches welcoming new students during Orientation Week. That first week there was a debate between Eric Baume (the original shock jock before the term existed, when John Laws and Alan Jones were still in nappies) and a recent law graduate Michael Kirby, on the topic "Is the RSL still relevant?". Baume of course took the side of the RSL, delivered a caustic and withering oration and his cause appeared irrefutable. However, the young law graduate proceeded quietly but quite brutally to cut both Baume and his arguments to shreds. Little wonder that the young law student went on to become the Chief Justice of the High Court of Australia. I learned one thing that week from Robertson and Kirby and that was the incredible power of the spoken word.

The other thing learned in Orientation Week was the true meaning of a "boat race" at the nearby Forest Lodge hotel. The race didn't in fact involve boats but a team of four, each downing a pint of beer in relay in the shortest possible time.

Having come from a relatively small country high school where one could usually expect to be dux of the year and to get into most sporting teams, it was somewhat overwhelming to suddenly be a very small fish in a very large pond. It was also quite lonely at first; most of the Sydney people had well-established networks of friends and supporters, especially those from the "Great Public Schools" (GPS) and inner-city public schools.

I was planning to do a science degree and back then subject choice was limited: everyone did physics, chemistry and mathematics, and the choice for a fourth subject was biology or geology. Not wanting to cut up frogs I chose the latter, little knowing what it entailed or where it might lead. I thought I'd probably end up as an industrial chemist or metallurgist.

I was able to live with my sister Ann at Burwood during first-year Uni. This was rather fortunate as it not only meant cheap board and lodgings for a student on a meagre scholarship but also easy access to rail and bus transport, and a family environment with Ann and her three young daughters. There were also regular visits to my other sister Wendy, husband Bill Smith, and their growing young family at Forestville on weekends.

Lectures for maths, physics and chemistry involved literally hundreds of students, so it was a little difficult to strike up quick friendships, but the geology group was much smaller, making it easier to get to know people. Consequently, early socialising tended to be with old schoolmates who had moved to Sydney. Included in these was Kerry Cochrane from Candelo, who was the only other male from Bega High to start at Sydney Uni that year. Kerry had enrolled in agricultural science, and I probably got to know more Ag. science than science students in the early days, including making reacquaintance with Terry Foreman, an old mate from primary school days.

Early entertainment was limited to on-campus movies, regular visits to the Forest Lodge, the ubiquitous "sherry party" (these seemed to occur with regularity across campus probably because it was the cheapest form of alcohol) and weekend visits to Jim Buckley's Newcastle Hotel in George Street followed by music at the nearby Jazz Club, where many of Australia's jazz greats started out. With no money for taxis and often having missed the last train, I regularly walked home to Burwood from the city; it took two to three hours but ensured that there was little or no hangover the next day.

Sport was a great way to get to know people and Kerry and I both joined the Sydney Uni rugby league club when the season commenced. The A and B teams back then played in the NSW second division comp. We could only manage C grade, which played in the Newtown junior league, and what a competition it was. Most other teams hailed from the rougher parts of inner Sydney and viewed our team as the Sydney Uni "poofters". There was often more fighting than football but our team had a firm rule; no retaliation (well at least not from twelve of the team). We had one enforcer, Leon Horsnell, a front rower and Ag. student who noted any attacks on our players and efficiently delivered retribution as and when required.

I had personal experience of this when I took the ball from the kick-off one day and was immediately held on two sides by opposition players when a third came in with a haymaker which fortunately only grazed me. However, Leon had taken note, and shortly after, the haymaker man lay prostrate on the ground. Despite the rough and tumble, the season was enjoyable and good friendships were made.

I was the team utility man and played in every position from front row to fullback, though the coach confided that he regretted playing me on the wing one day when I got the ball from 50 metres out with a clear run to the line – to his amazement I just made it.

One of my first new mates was Phil McSharry. I don't know why we hit it off – possibly because neither of us knew many people, Phil having moved up from Melbourne. We were both very anti-establishment at that time, so greatly enjoyed a bit of stirring. Phil was very bright, he instantly understood new concepts as lectures were given while the bulk of us took time to come to grips with them, if we ever did. Phil had this habit of seating himself in the front row of lecture theatres and promptly falling fast asleep. The lecturers would seize the opportunity to wake him and ask him some question from the day's lecture – to which he would always give a lucid and accurate response, how I'll never know. They finally gave up and left him to sleep uninterrupted.

Probably inspired by the early James Bond movies, Phil and I decided to join the Sydney Uni judo club. What an interesting establishment it was, and at that time boasted several Australian champions as members. The story went that in past years the members would wander into Kings Cross on a Friday night to get first-hand experience with willing but often drink or drug-affected combatants. We were rather pleased that practice (if it ever really happened) had ceased by the time we joined, but the club was awash with larger-than-life characters.

One of the first lessons in judo is how to fall, or "breakfall", and mastering this skill led to a compulsion to do impromptu breakfalls anywhere around campus and in fact randomly at social events for many years to come right up to the Clare Valley wine festival in 2008. One thing I mastered early was holding people down, which earned me a bit of a battering from Peter Page, the then Australian middleweight champion. Peter was demonstrating a hold release to us one evening and asked me to hold him down. After struggling for several minutes he couldn't break free and was rather grumpy that a yellow belt could do this to him. Once I released him he proceeded to throw me all round the dojo to vent his frustrations.

Another bit of a pyrrhic victory came about because of lessons from a Pom/Scotchman by the name of Chapman. His training regime was jumping round the dojo in a squatting position; it was brutal but certainly boosted fitness levels. His other forte was ren-raken-wasa or feinting one throw then moving in a different direction with a second throw. I tried this in practice with Alex Bykirk, another Australian champ, and threw him with the fundamental and rarely used hiza-guruma throw. Unlike Peter, Alex could see the funny side of the situation.

The other lasting memory of judo is taking on Ted Boronovski in practice along with about 20 other martyrs. Ted, a large and very strong individual, had won a bronze medal at the Tokyo Olympics; in doing so he had defeated several opponents with much higher gradings using either superior skills, brute strength or a combination of both. This particular evening he had come in to get some practice before a tournament. He was irresistible, the moment after you came in contact you were flying through the air. It was good breakfall practice but there was an expectation that you kept coming back for more to assist with his training.

The judo social events were also a tad spectacular. I vaguely remember one where we were unable to crack the keg and had to resort to spirits instead. It was my first introduction to "bloody marys" and by the end of proceedings most participants were crawling around the floor. Amazingly I was as good as gold by the time I had walked home and fit as a fiddle next day.

The annual Uni "Commem" day was another eye-opener to new students with some of the hijinks that more senior students got up to. I believe my first Commem was the year some students gatecrashed the ABC and flour-bombed James Dibble as he was reading the evening television news. I also experienced my first harbour cruise. These cruises had only just been reinstated after some past ones had seen some fairly drastic police intervention, and the ferry master this night was taking no prisoners. Two or three people running late jumped for the ferry and missed; they were left to find their own way out of the water at Circular Quay. Later in the evening on the other side of the harbour some others fell overboard near shore. There was no rescue; the ferry master trained a spotlight on them until they reached shore, after which they were similarly left to their own devices to find a way home.

I could only afford a flagon of rosé (then about 50 cents) for the cruise and after we got going some character kept geeing me up to chug the rosé, which I obligingly demolished in a fairly short time frame. Not too long after I was spectacularly sick all over the geer-upper, which people watching the activity saw as poetic justice.

Campus was full of characters in those days, among them the long-haired and eccentric Professor of Italian, Fred May, who always seemed to be giving public discourses on anything of a controversial nature; there was Charles Perkins, the Aboriginal activist; there was the bearded Canadian Professor of Physics, Harry Messel, who around that time decided he would become the flagbearer for saving crocodiles from extinction in northern Australia; and there were of course mysterious characters like Serge Matiche-Ostermann, the karate expert, who acted as bouncer at many Uni functions.

In the last term of first year I went to training with the Sydney Uni cricket club, which fielded about four teams, with the hope of getting a game. I had no hope. With the ingrained GPS influence back then, you had to be an outstanding cricketer to make the cut (which I wasn't).

My sister Ann had a reasonable selection of classical music and I honed the skill of being able to recognise the first few lines of many well-known and some less well-known pieces. This skill went down well when conversing with female arts students, and surprisingly the cultural illusion was rarely exposed.

I believe there was a little study done during first year but I was (and am) an exponent of last-minute cramming for exams, which isn't a particularly great way to learn your trade. I managed a meagre three Passes and a Conditional Pass in physics, which Ann is still amazed at. By comparison my mate Phil McSharry achieved two Distinctions and two High Distinctions in the same subjects.

Around the end of the year Ann, battling with custody and separation issues, decided on a major sea change and moved with her daughters to Derby in the Kimberley region of WA to work as a flying doctor. Consequently, I was homeless and spent the summer break back with my parents at Bermagui.

Dad lined me up a bit of work at the Fishermans Co-op, and I remember one particularly big night when the local fleet must have come in with about 100 tonnes of bluefin tuna. There were no conveyor belts; in those days it was all manual handling, first from boat to a trolley on rails on the wharf; once loaded the trolley was hand-pushed to a waiting truck at the end of the wharf and the tuna were thrown onto the truck. Then back for the next load, and the next and the next. The tuna were generally under 20 kilos, so most loading could be done by one person, a few 30-plus kilograms tuna certainly slowed progress. I finally got home very weary and covered in tuna blood and goo in the early hours of the morning. It was nice to earn a bit of money, but the biggest disappointment was that Mum refused to wash my treasured Bega High footy jersey, along with the rest of my work clothes, and they were summarily binned.

Sister Wendy and husband Bill managed to find me a room with shared bathroom, cooking and laundry facilities in a heritage-listed old three-storey building adjacent to North Sydney station on the Sydney harbourside, so there was a harbour view of sorts from my bedroom window. Wendy had stayed here while nursing in Sydney and they had first met here as a result of Bill and the owner Neville Smith both playing cricket for North Sydney. The late-night walking time was consequently reduced to a quick stroll or stagger across the Sydney Harbour bridge. Bill also managed to get me a game of cricket with North Sydney's City and Suburban side, and I played there for the rest of my time at Uni.

The art and science of geophysics

Orientation week took on a whole new meaning in second year: as a now seasoned student I was bold enough to interrupt one of Geoffrey Robertson's introductory speeches and take the stage to announce that the Ag Science team had just won the boat race. Having just witnessed the event at the Forest Lodge it was the way it was won that really impressed. As the second pint glass was slammed on the table the next competitor's glass shattered internally. Jack Frost, undeterred, grabbed the glass and gulped it down (he was an exponent of the no-swallow, open-throat method) to set up a memorable victory for the Ag team. Amazingly Jack suffered no ill effects from the experience.

My romance with geoscience was almost over when I enrolled in maths, chemistry and mathematical statistics in second year; however, after attending the first chemistry practical I had a quick about-face and dumped chemistry for geology, which most of my friends had enrolled in.

One of the most memorable moments of second year was the first lecture in geophysics from Don Emerson, at which he promised to teach us the science of geophysics during lectures and the art of geophysics post-lecture at the Forest Lodge Hotel. This made a lasting impression on many of us. Many years later in Adelaide Don was awarded life membership of the Australian Society of Exploration Geophysicists at a conference dinner. After Don had concluded his acceptance speech, I couldn't help myself and rose to relate to the large audience Don's introductory promise to students, I then asked Don whether he was accepting his award as a scientist or as an artist. His laconic response: "The phoenix has risen." His later one-on-one response was a little more expletive-laden.

Don was a larger-than-life character and a very large man to boot. He apparently pondered becoming a Jesuit monk before he found his life vocation in geophysics. An active amateur wrestler in those early days, Don related how he once took on Killer Kowalski in a practice match. Kowalski was a world-renowned baddie of television wrestling in North America and Australia and was the only man to have held down Andre the Giant. Despite the crazy antics of television wrestling, Don was surprised that Kowalski was not only a very competent wrestler but in real life he was a quietly spoken man who had taken up wrestling to help pay his way through an electrical engineering degree. So, in the latter area they had a lot in common. Most of all Don was an inspiring educator who instilled his life-long love of geoscience in most of his students.

Another lecturer who left a lasting impression was Ian Threadgold, whose specialty was crystallography: that is, the study of the crystal structure of various minerals as an aid to their identification. "Threddie" had a rather stentorian or sergeant-major-like approach to education and at one stage failed the entire class in practical crystallography just a few weeks out from second-year final exams. He really had the interests of students at heart and helped to infuse a strong work ethic in them and scared us enough to get most of us across the line.

The Forest Lodge Hotel became a bit of a second home, especially on a Friday night, and post–decimal currency (14 February 1966) you could get nicely plastered for two dollars, which at that time bought ten (fifteen-ounce) schooners. Lots of looney left-wingers also frequented the Lodge, among them one Meredith Burgemann. Meredith delighted in her image as a dirty, untidy woman who frequently appeared to be quite inebriated. She went on to become a respected senior NSW Labor politician. Appearances can indeed be deceptive. At one stage after hurling a few items into the backyard of a house next to the beer garden on a Friday night I entered the bar the following week to find my photo along with others plastered behind the bar. When I ordered a beer, the barmen compared me with the photo and informed me that I was banned for life. Apparently, the next-door neighbour had wisely taken photos rather than confronting us on the night. About a week later I decided to test the ban and found the photos had been removed, the life ban had been short-lived and service had resumed.

Another regular haunt was the old Taiping Restaurant in the Haymarket, reputed to serve the best Chinese meals in Sydney, but in basic surroundings. It was also a favourite of Labor Party cronies and ABC afficionados like Bill Peach of "This Day Tonight" and "Four Corners" fame. Michael Luey, the restaurant manager, was the perfect host, greeting the high end of town and the low end (rowdy Uni students) with equanimity. His regular greeting to me was, "Hello Newton, I hope you will behave yourself tonight." Despite our untiring efforts Michael never reached the stage of ejecting our group though it must have been perilously close on many occasions. In later years Michael opened the Four Seasons Hotel in nearby Redfern and the Taiping Restaurant moved to those premises.

Several years later, when I was living in Darwin, Michael's hotel was my residence of choice when visiting Sydney. As students we always speculated about Michael's background and it was only recently when doing research for this book that I found out that he was recruited from New Zealand and married to the daughter of Stanley Wong, who in those days was arguably the most influential person in Sydney's Chinese community. The other interesting fact is that the

Four Seasons later became Sydney's Chinese Embassy. Who knows what machinations went on behind the scenes with the inscrutable Michael and family.

Another tradition which I was initiated into in second year was the annual pub crawl down Broadway and George Street, from Sydney Uni to Circular Quay. The crawl always coincided with celebrations of the anniversary of the Battle of the Coral Sea, and as a result there was no shortage of American and Australian sailors and veterans in each pub along the route. This caused real problems in completing the crawl. All would go well up to Town Hall, but it was literally and figuratively all downhill from there. We were always respectful to the sailors and veterans and as a result many drinks were shouted, particularly by the Yanks; inevitably this led to mission failure. I cannot recollect ever completing the crawl as a student.

After finishing Uni, I attempted the crawl again with Peter Cockcroft, an old colleague, not only did we complete the crawl with ease, but we got a taxi out to Doyles at Watsons Bay for a seafood lunch and a few wines midway through the proceedings.

Second year also saw my mate McSharry acquire a high-powered Triumph motorbike which became the stuff of legends. How he survived that bike is beyond me – particularly his racing round the narrow streets near the Forest Lodge at breakneck speeds. I managed to fall off the back as we accelerated away from the toll gates on the Harbour Bridge one night, but the judo breakfall training worked and there was no damage. McSharry just did a U-ey in front of the traffic and collected me.

Another night the same scenario played out with his future brother-in-law Mick McManus, who did lose a bit of bark in falling. A party ensued around Cammeray where Mick attempted the five dollar note burn-through trick on his arm with a cigarette. Mick won the five dollars but had some horrendous burns on his arm to show for it. Later in the evening he was getting sore from the earlier bike fall and a belated decision was made to get him to Royal North Shore casualty. Apparently, the doctor treated Mick for the bike grazes but was a little reluctant when Mick asked if he could also help with the cigarette burns. The doctor was pontificating when Mick came up with the classic question, "Have you taken the Hippocratic oath?" When the answer was yes, Mick responded with, "Well fix me, I'm buggered."

Poor old Mick was misbehaving at another party and started firing a .22 loaded with blanks directly at partygoers. I was incensed, having been brought up with the maxim that you never point a gun at anyone (loaded or unloaded). I took the gun off him and got him in a headlock. After a brief struggle Mick was unconscious on the floor, possibly from hitting his head on a door while we were tussling. He died of an early heart attack some years later and I can't help feeling this episode may have been an early warning sign of a serious heart condition.

After the ritual big Friday night at the Forest Lodge, weekends usually involved cricket or rugby league on Saturday, then camping at Wendy's and Bill's Forestville home on Saturday and Sunday nights, which included some solid steak meals (Bill had a butcher's shop at Pymble at the time). In those days my Uni scholarship paid about $36 per fortnight, which had to cover rent, meals, transport and entertainment, so a few free steaks on the weekend came in handy.

The summer schedule entailed cricket on Saturday afternoon then rendezvousing with Bill at Claude Fays Hotel at North Sydney, ample schooners, then home to Forestville. Sunday often saw bodysurfing at Collaroy and much backyard cricket. I'd accompany Bill to the Homebush meat markets (now the Olympic stadium) at about 4.00 a.m. on Monday morning, after which he would drop me off at Pymble railway station. Keeping up with Bill at the markets meant jogging behind him the whole way while he made his meat purchases, and the markets were extensive: we probably covered four or five kilometres on these mornings.

Through my North Sydney landlord Neville Smith's contacts, I managed to get vacation work at Cedric Williams Bayview marina, which led to some interesting experiences. The basic work involved scraping and painting boat hulls on the slipway. Occasionally you scored the task of taking a dinghy round many of the moored boats and ensuring that they were pumped dry. Some of these boats were owned by TV personalities of that era and had well-stocked bars, so a perk of the pumping task was access to these bars.

A TV crew doing an Eveready battery ad featuring Tony Bonner of "Skippy" fame, hired a pair of Halvorsen cruisers from the marina, and I was assigned as the skipper/driver of one of these boats. My experience handling a boat of that size was zilch. The ad producer was a cantankerous old foreigner nicknamed "the Baron", whose main claim to fame was producing a series of Colgate soap ads featuring well-known Hollywood actresses. Once we were near Lion Island he insisted that we got as close to the rocks as possible to enhance the visual impact. I was a nervous wreck by the end of shooting, often expecting the boat would founder on the rocks, but we survived. To compensate, ample drinks were provided on the cruise back and some of the Baron's younger female offsiders were quite friendly. When I later saw the ad on TV it was darkened to night-time shadows (it was a battery ad after all) with absolutely no sign of the rocky shorelines.

Second year ended with me again scraping through with three Passes. My mate Phil McSharry's decline was more spectacular: after his first-year Distinctions I think he managed a Credit and two Passes.

Linga-ing Longa

Third year started with a bang with the annual combined Sydney and Uni of NSW geological excursion to Glenbawn Dam near Scone. I travelled there with Dave Sargeant, Pete Spraggon and Ned Overton in Sarge's father's 1929 Dodge. How we got there I will never know; we had to walk occasionally to get the Dodge over the steepest parts of the Blue Mountains, with numerous watering hole stops along the way.

The first night in camp Sarge decided that we needed to do a grog supply run into Scone, so orders and cash were collected from quite a few students and off we headed. After collecting the supplies and a few quiet beers in Scone, we headed back to camp. It was a balmy, moonlit night and Sarge suddenly stopped the Dodge on a shallow river crossing and suggested it was the perfect spot for a party. We all thought it was a great idea and attacked the booze supplies with gusto. For light entertainment we watched another car fast approaching with some consternation as we knew there was a 90-degree bend it needed to negotiate, the headlights suddenly did a full 450-degree spin and continued toward us. When it arrived, we realised it was the Broken Hill contingent of students who had also gone to town for supplies. When asked, the driver had no recollection of his spectacular spin, but one of his passengers suggested it had been a rather hairy moment. The Broken Hill crew joined the party and a good time was had by all until the wee hours.

We finally arrived back in camp and realised we had drunk most of the supplies. Someone had a brainwave, so we went round the tents of those that had ordered grog and offered them their order from the limited supplies remaining. As it was about 3.00 a.m. most responded with a "Fuck off" or words to that effect, which we took to mean that they didn't want what they ordered. This worked a treat; only Phil Cremer insisted on accepting his order there and then. We collapsed for the night thinking it was all sorted.

Not surprisingly there were many unhappy campers the next morning and word of the party quickly got back to the powers that be. As a result, we were banned from alcohol and from leaving camp for the rest of the excursion. This was something of an imposition as it deprived us from visiting a wonderful waterhole, the Linga Longa Inn at nearby Gundy, after a hot day in the field, though we did manage to sample its wares before returning to Sydney. Booze debts were slowly paid back over the ensuing months.

Our banishment had unexpected benefits as we were allotted Ken Glasson as our mapping supervisor (seen as the best person to keep us in check). Ken was the lecturer in economic geology and was probably the most practical geologist in the department, so we gained a lot from his mentoring and experience. Ken had worked for many years in industry and related some wonderful stories over the next few days. At one stage Ken had worked at the Captains Flat mine near Canberra and two tales he related from that time warrant mention.

The first was the major collapse of the Keatings lode section of the mine workings. Back in the 1950s the mine was not run on a 24/7 basis like today's mining operations; in fact there was just one eight-hour shift per day. This was very fortunate as on a Saturday night (28th October, 1961) when all the miners were either in the pub or otherwise occupied, this section of the mine totally collapsed from the surface downwards. One can only speculate on the loss of life that could have happened. The collapsed section of the mine was never re-opened.

The second tale involved the big strike (circa 1954-55) where about 115 miners affiliated with the AWU wanted to break the strike and return to work while about 110 miners from the MWU wished to continue the strike in a bid for an increased lead allowance. Pragmatically they decided there was only one way to resolve the issue, so the two opposing groups met on the Captains Flat footy oval to fight it out. Ken was sitting back in the grandstand (probably sipping on a beer or two), and told us the battle was an amazing spectacle after which the proponents all adjourned to the pub. For the record I understand the AWU was victorious.

Back at the Glenbawn Dam excursion there was some concern when "McShaggers" didn't join us, particularly as he had just added a sidecar to his Triumph expressly for the trip. Two days later he turned up in camp somewhat battered and bruised. He had befriended a group of bikies at some watering hole in the Blue Mountains and joined them in the next leg of their ride, where the lead rider failed to negotiate a bend and the following riders managed to do the same. Fortunately, there were no serious injuries.

With the start of Uni for the year I had made a firm commitment to geoscience as a career and was specialising in Geophysics, probably based on Don Emerson's inspiring lectures. The other career attraction of geoscience was the opportunity to travel within and beyond Australia while getting paid to do so.

Geophysical field excursions back then might be construed today as basic terrorist training, with handling and firing detonators and gelignite for various seismic surveys as well as learning to use and maintain sophisticated electronic devices, some involving high voltage. Many a tree stump and an occasional tree were vaporised on these excursions.

The Forest Lodge Hotel was again the focus of many activities and two incidents that year readily come to mind. Articles began appearing in the student newspaper *Honi Soit* written by disaffected arts students who complained that the ambiance of the Forest Lodge was being destroyed by the boorish behaviour of engineering students. Aggrieved engineers wrote back to the paper proclaiming their innocence, and so it went on for several weeks with claims and counter-claims. Geoscience students chose to remain tight-lipped during these ongoing exchanges (I wonder why).

With Australia's involvement in the Vietnam War rapidly escalating, conscription of twenty-year-olds had been introduced to swell Australia's armed forces. I arrived at the Forest Lodge after lectures one day to find old rugby league teammate and Ag student Leon Horsnell more than a little worse for wear and shouting drinks for everybody. It took a while for the penny to drop: Leon and I shared the same birthday and results of the conscription draft based on drawing a few birthdates from a ballot were due to be posted out any day. Much to my relief I realised that Leon had received his letter advising him that he had missed the draft. What to do but buy drinks as well. I found a similar letter waiting for me when I finally got home that night.

Social rugby matches also became a feature of third-year activities with annual geology versus geography and past versus present geology matches. The latter instilled some fierce rivalry. The past included younger faculty staff members, PhD students and some past students drawn from industry. The past team were physically much larger but the present team had youth and fitness on their side. At the time the staff kept reminding the students that they had a trump card, Dr Robin Helby, up their sleeve. Robin went on to become well known in his field of palynology but had in an earlier life been a very aggressive breakaway for the Drummoyne Rugby Union Club. Apparently, he would sit in the change rooms on his own before the match and hate the opposition, or so the story went. It certainly put the wind up us, but when the first scrum of the match was set Robin came reeling out of it with a tooth protruding through his top lip. It slowed him down and the students took full advantage until he came back with some crushing tackles late in the game, but by then it was too late. What happened in that scrum we will never know, but the present students had a gentle giant in their front row, Phil Cremer, who wouldn't hurt a fly – but on the other hand he was very protective of his mates. The matches were always very willing affairs and probably due to a lack of match fitness some player always ended up visiting Casualty at the Royal Prince Alfred Hospital, which was adjacent to the various rugby ovals, usually for something like a broken collarbone.

Barry Humphries and his alter ego Barry MacKenzie reigned supreme with Sydney Uni geoscience students at that time and in their honour we acted out and photographed the ditty *'Chunder Down Under* in The Old Pacific Sea' for inclusion in the student yearbook. With prawns and chunder in abundance the Manly locals must have wondered what was going on.

4

The Finishing Touches

Sydney University 1967-1968

By the end of third year and after sitting exams I was off as a vacation student to the legendary goldmining city of Kalgoorlie (Kal) in Western Australia. The flight to Perth in a Boeing 727, my first jet flight, was a great experience especially when I realised the drinks were free. The next leg back to Kalgoorlie in a DC3 (also a first) was a little less comfortable with late summer afternoon turbulence and the sight of oil pouring out across the wing. When I asked the hostie about it she was unconcerned, saying that was normal for a DC3, but she kindly brought me more beers to settle my nerves.

The job in the Kalgoorlie region was with a large Canadian company, International Nickel (INCO), and senior staff were mainly Canadian with little concept of working in arid Australian conditions. There was no such thing as induction and training in those days and after a couple of days in the office with other students we were handed maps, a vehicle, a caravan, an order book and a marginally experienced offsider and instructed to get out there and undertake various surveys and come back into Kal for a break every ten days or so.

After stocking up with essential food and fuel supplies including the luscious Canadian frozen strawberries which INCO had induced the local supermarket to stock, we headed out to Karonie, about 100 kilometres east of Kal. My offsider Paul Southam, a rather sardonic English traveller, must have had all of two months experience working in the Kalgoorlie region, so we were a rather green team taking on the great Australian bush. Problem one; we soon realised that we had taken a secondary track on the wrong side of the Transcontinental railway line. We could see the smoother track on the other side of the line but how to get to it with a large caravan in tow? After about 50 kilometres of rough track we finally found a clear spot where we thought we could cross, but of course we had no idea of the Indian Pacific timetable.

The Land Rover got across the line no trouble, but sure enough the caravan got stuck, and just then in the distance we noticed the Indian Pacific train bearing down from the west. The next few minutes seemed like an eternity as we frantically tried to build up gravel and rocks against the rails. With about 100 metres to spare and the train's horn blaring, the Land Rover, in low range four-wheel drive, gave a mighty heave and the caravan was clear of the line. The rest of the trip to camp was uneventful and we could only speculate on what the Kal newspaper headlines might have been had the van remained stuck.

After finding a campsite we proceeded to set up, and this is where I got taken hook, line and sinker. Paul suggested that I might dig a rubbish pit, so away I went in 40-degree heat. Paul kept coming back to inspect my work and saying the pit needed to be a bit bigger. After an hour or two he declared the pit just big enough, by which time our Land Rover could have been buried in it. When we departed that site about a month later our rubbish took up about five percent of the space, but at least Paul helped to fill it in.

Learning to identify relatively fresh rocks in NSW in no way prepared us for the highly weathered and altered rocks encountered in the WA goldfields, another trap awaiting unsuspecting students. So-called ultramafic rocks which host much of the nickel mineralisation have a characteristic "spinifex structure", but dried kangaroo poo exhibits a similar structure. The old hands were adept at getting new chums to try to identify the kangaroo poo.

Back at our Karonie camp the task was to put in a baseline and then run perpendicular lines off this, along which we took readings and samples at regular intervals. The baseline with pegs about every thirty metres formed a very sandy slalom track, and it was a great way to hone four-wheel driving skills going to and from camp each day in the same time even though the distance was increasing as the baseline expanded. Likewise, by trial and error the skills of extracting a vehicle from a salt lake and how to negotiate a way round salt lakes were quickly learned. The fancy new six-cylinder long wheelbase Land Rovers that we were provided with were woefully inadequate for these bush conditions (no wonder Toyota cornered the market when they introduced a rugged vehicle designed for Australian conditions), so learning bush mechanics on the run was also a necessity.

The first weekend's break in Kal was a bit of an eye-opener and coincided with Harold Holt's mysterious disappearance in Victoria. Kal still had a myriad of pubs then, although just as many had closed since the gold rush era. A major pub crawl was obligatory as was a tour (outside only) down Hay Street and its red-light district with the various brothels already adorned with Christmas decorations. A visit to the two-up school was also a necessary part of an induction for any new arrival to the city. Having practised bush slaloms at Karonie, Hannan Street, the main Kal thoroughfare with a line of telegraph poles along the centre, presented a challenge on future visits to town.

There was one topless bar in Kal back then, but the era of the infamous "Skimpy" bar was more a product of the 1980s. The concept of the Skimpy bar was that you tossed any leftover gold coin change with the barmaid. If she won, she kept the coin, if you won the barmaid flashed her boobs. The reality was the barmaid always ended up with the coin. Many Uni students financed their way through Uni and likewise overseas backpackers financed their travel with a stint in a Skimpy bar.

After Karonie, field activities were centred around Widgemooltha, where INCO had quite a large field camp; however, for some reason we were housed in the Widgiemooltha pub. The Widgiemooltha region boasted the discovery in 1926 of the largest gold nugget found on any WA goldfield, the Golden Eagle, weighing in at 32.2 kilograms, sparking a significant goldrush. By 1968 the rush had well and truly petered out and "Widgie" comprised a pub and not much else. Owned by an old local character, George Napier, the watering hole was a major attraction to young nickel explorers after long, hot days in the field. Adding to the attraction at that time was George's pretty daughter, who was studying nursing in Perth but was then home on holidays. A dip in the cool depths of the large water tank (ex–railway water supply), with a cold Hannan's lager in hand and George's daughter for company, was a wonderful diversion from hot fieldwork, but unfortunately there was always lots of company as every young man within 50 kilometres of Widgie had the same idea.

As it was midsummer and very hot, many of our Land Rovers had been stripped of their upper canopies to make for a cooler ride; there was no car airconditioning back then. This was fine driving round the bush but a bit interesting on the 100-kilometre drive to Kalgoorlie, when driver and passenger sat on the top of the front seats, the driver having put the vehicle in a crude mechanical cruise control and leaning forward to handle the steering vehicle. Fortunately, we never encountered any highway patrols but I believe today's OH&S Nazis would take a rather dim view of such practices. The other popular bush activity was Land Rover jousts, where the winner was the vehicle that pushed the other backwards, it took a lot of steely nerve to keep your foot flat to the floor, so the other didn't get the upper hand. What this game did to the vehicle transmission is anyone's guess.

An attempt at vehicle jousting in one of Kalgoorlie's caravan parks while on a field break was not well received by long-term park patrons. Field breaks also saw most of us do the Hannan Street slalom at one time or another, although care had to be taken with the timing of such events to avoid the local constabulary.

An ex–British army INCO employee managed to organise a pub crawl along Hannan Street one weekend which was open to all comers. There were about seventeen pubs, and the object as always was to reach the finish line first with two provisos: minimal spillage and all fluids had to be retained in the stomach. The early race leaders failed miserably as one by one they were violently ill. The organiser, who had done it all before and ran/drank a steady race, was unsurprisingly declared the winner.

At one point I was directed to mark and peg out a mining lease application for INCO about halfway between Kal and Widgie. The WA Mines Department in their wisdom had recently decreed that there must be a cleared line along each lease boundary. INCO liked to do things big and had hired a D9 bulldozer to clear the boundary lines. Never having carried out such an exercise I was told to walk ahead of the bulldozer with a compass to ensure the line was straight. After we'd completed about 400 metres of clearing, a look back revealed that the line in fact ran in a broad curve. It turned out that the compass was deviating due to the highly magnetic rock in the area. When we changed to backsighting each line the result was much straighter. Regardless, a huge scar was left across the countryside by this extreme form of line clearing, which would have drawn the ire of the modern-day greenie. The Mines Department amended their regulations soon after so that only minimal clearing with axe and small chainsaw was permitted for such activities.

The highlight and lasting memory of Kal was witnessing and experiencing my one and only all-in bar room brawl at the Albion Hotel in Boulder. As background to this event, Sunday drinking back then was limited to a late morning and late afternoon two-hour guzzling session; also there was a degree of animosity from the long-established miners to the newly arrived, upstart nickel explorers who seemed to be taking over the town (including some of the girlfriends). The afternoon session was proceeding as normal with the band playing, some dancing and plenty of drinks all round when there was a minor altercation. The Albion's Greek manager had come in to break it up, when he was summarily belted on the back of the head with a chair, and then the place erupted into one big brawl. Seizing the opportunity, I headed behind the now-unattended bar and proceeded to pour myself drinks while observing the mayhem from an almost safe distance. After ten minutes or so the scream of numerous sirens approaching was heard:

the Kal riot squad arrived and the brawling miners and explorers as one now saw the police as their enemy. The Albion was an old-style pub with an overhanging balcony at the front supported by a series of posts. The police were handcuffing combatants to these posts but as fast as they did it hacksaws and bolt cutters materialised to help free them. Our group wisely decided it was time to beat a hasty retreat.

The upshot of the brawl next day in the Kal court was that about a dozen people were sentenced to up to a year's gaol. The whole event had an atmosphere like the final scene in the *Casino Royale* film starring Peter Sellers, but thankfully there were no knives involved nor were there any major injuries.

While in Kal I received third-year Uni results where I obtained my first ever Credit in Geology and Geophysics and just scraped a Pass in my other subject, Applied Mathematics. With a lot of persuasion from lecturer Don Emerson (to whom I am forever grateful), I was allowed to return to Uni by the powers that be to undertake an honours year in Geophysics. So, a further year of partying awaited before I finally had to try and earn a crust.

Derby diversion

Before I returned to Sydney my sister Ann, who was now the flying doctor in Derby, invited me to stay with her for a few days. Little did I realise then that the 1800-kilometre flight to Derby by Fokker Friendship, with several stops along the way, took about twice as long as the 3300-kilometre return flight from Perth to Sydney. The trip was well worth it, however, allowing me to catch up with Ann and her three young daughters and see a lot of new country for the first time.

Ann organised a free flight to inspect the iron ore mining operations on Cockatoo Island in Yampi Sound for me. It was my first flight in a light plane, and landing on the short, sloping airstrip on the island was certainly an experience. The beauty and grandeur of the Kimberley coastline and offshore islands made for a memorable day.

It was approaching the end of the wet season in Derby and in those days most of the perishable supplies arrived once a month by boat from Perth. The boat was due in and as Ann was working she asked me to get down to the local supermarket and stock up with supplies of fresh fruit and vegetables. Once loaded up I headed home and, in my wisdom, put all the fresh supplies in the deep freeze. Although we managed to rescue some when Ann arrived home most of the fresh supplies were ruined and Ann had to wait another month for the next boatload.

During my stay I met Lawson Holman, the surgeon at the Derby Hospital. Lawson had arrived in Derby as a young doctor and had become something of a legend in his own lifetime. As well as being a flying doctor and surgeon he variously took on roles as cattle station owner and mayor of Derby. Apparently, he was known to sometimes tote a six-gun in his belt when out in the bush, but his dedication to patient care was unchallenged as evidenced when he once volunteered to parachute into a remote coastal community with a cyclone brewing. A young boy was stuck with his broken leg bone impaled in a palm tree. Fortunately, the locals finally freed him (or he fell) and he received treatment locally until he was evacuated when weather conditions abated, and Lawson's parachute jump was averted.

Lawson was a skilled surgeon. Ann tells a story of a young geologist who walked into the tail rotor of a helicopter somewhere in the Kimberley and was evacuated to Derby Hospital. Brain damage appeared severe, and emergency surgery was vital: applying the anaesthetic, Ann watched as Lawson proceeded to slice off large sections of damaged brain. The patient not only survived but, after a lengthy rehabilitation in Perth, had minimal long-term damage. Many years later I met the patient at a mining conference: apart from a distinct furrow in the centre of his forehead he was doing well.

Lawson and my sister Ann both went on to hold senior positions in the WA Department of Public Health and Lawson is credited with pioneering preventative medical procedures in many remote WA communities, I would like to think Ann also provided significant input.

Another story of an earlier Kimberley flying doctor is of note: he was an old Scotchman who loved a drop or two of his native spirit. He also later rose to a position of authority in WA Health and one of his official duties was to set the level of alcohol permitted in all licensed spirits in WA. Unsurprisingly for many years WA spirits contained several percent more alcohol than those of the other states. It was the early 1980s before WA came into line with the rest of Australia.

Before leaving Derby to return to Perth and Sydney, Ann kindly washed my clothes, which included my airline tickets. Unlike computerised bookings of today with your ticket on your mobile phone, in those days your ticket was your official booking confirmation. There were some anxious moments and extended calls to Perth before new tickets could be obtained.

Honours hardships

Back in Sydney my honours year began. The course was more about learning to do independent research rather than formal lectures and practical sessions as in past years and involved undertaking a research project over the three semesters together with assignments on specific subjects, some study of the philosophy of science and researching papers in a foreign language (in my case scientific Russian). McSharry and I were the only two doing Geophysics honours, with about ten others who were doing Geology honours. We formed a close-knit group within the Department of Geology and Geophysics.

Most students partied hard and idled along on their research/mapping projects in semester one, then suddenly realised the enormity of undertaking such a project in semester two and then frantically worked through semester three to get their thesis written and submitted by the due date. The pressure was intense, and I had nightmares of failing to submit my thesis on time for many years after finishing Uni.

Of course, occasionally there's an exception to the rule: in our year it was a red-headed character by the name of Ned Overton. Ned worked like a navvy through semester one and had virtually completed the course and his thesis by the end of semester two; he was effectively antisocial during this period. Then he became a serial pest urging us all to party with him at every opportunity during semester three when our thoughts were elsewhere.

My research project was on the electrical properties of the Captains Flat copper-lead-zinc ore deposits, an abandoned mine site not too far from Canberra. My initial research revealed that a geophysicist in the Commonwealth Bureau of Mineral Resources (BMR) (today Geoscience Australia) in Canberra had done similar work at Captains Flat about eight years earlier, which I was keen to have a look at.

So off I headed to Captains Flat and Canberra; site reconnaissance and collection of representative samples of drill core from Captains Flat went without a hitch, but when I met the BMR geophysicist it was a different story. Despite having done the work years before with Commonwealth funding, he still hadn't published the results, so was unwilling to release any information. I was gobsmacked, but in retrospect was probably better off without his results.

While in Canberra/Captains Flat I stayed in the Commonwealth single quarters with some honours students from the previous year who had all recently joined the BMR. Bob Whitely, Mike Smith, Jeff Weissel and Dave Pratt all went on to distinguished geophysical careers. I was a bit taken by the blue lighting in some of their units and upon inquiry was told we could possibly go on a sortie later in the evening. On arrival at the outskirts of Canberra airport I realised we were heading for the main runway, the source of the blue lights. Unfortunately, there were a few too many RAAF security guards and dogs around that night and the mission was aborted.

The boys also had a story of climbing Black Mountain in the dark in the days when it boasted a tower only. During their wanderings they came across an unattended shed with a generator humming away inside. Being inquisitive, someone switched the generator off and they were in total darkness, not only was the shed light turned off but the red aircraft warning lights on the tower had also been extinguished. There was a frantic attempt to restart the generator, which roared back to life, and the lads rapidly decamped. At that point in time the death penalty was still in place in the ACT for endangering aircraft safety.

Back in Sydney, McSharry and I were allocated our own office on campus in the Carslaw Building, some distance away from the main geological building; a large geophysical laboratory was also located in Carslaw and we were allocated keys giving us 24/7 access. You could easily sleep there, and we occasionally did.

The lab was well equipped and contained several large perspex water tanks in which electrical geophysical modelling was undertaken. One of the tanks was being used by an American PhD student, Tom Johnson, who like so many Yanks was extremely gullible. One evening after a few drinks at the Forest Lodge, McSharry and I returned to undertake some more work in the lab and before long nature called. It was a long walk down the corridor to the toilets, so Tom's water tank experiment seemed the logical choice to relieve ourselves. We thought no more about it but a few days later Tom was getting quite excited by his discovery that the Sydney tapwater in his tank was turning acidic due to Sydney's atmospheric pollution. He was so excited in fact that he was preparing to head off on a tangent with his research to better understand the effects of atmospheric pollution. Don Emerson, his research supervisor, had to go to some lengths to convince him not to be sidetracked. Don asked us if we had used the lab recently, and while he didn't say anything, he instinctively knew the source of the unexpected acidity.

At one stage during the year, probably the end of semester one, I invited McSharry and Phil Cremer for a few days' stay at Bermagui. Joining us was Ross Moore, one of our third-year colleagues who was now working as an engineering geologist with the Department of Main Roads, based in Bega. A fishing trip was to be part of the weekend agenda and I somewhat ill-advisedly left my Dad to organise this.

After wandering around the scenic coastland, which hosts some of the most stunning structural geological features, our crew had a night at the Bermagui pub and later at the country club but managed to get home at a reasonable time in anticipation of an early start for fishing the following day. Sometime after midnight the howl of a southerly buster working its way up the coast could be heard, after a fine and calm day.

As we assembled in the gloom on the Bermagui wharf the next morning, the wind was screaming and the ocean beyond the bar was all foam. Surely no sane fisherman would take us out in this. Dad had booked us with that Danish fisherman, Jack Christianson, who was never deterred by a bit of weather. Jack welcomed us aboard his fifteen-metre trawler, and off we went with Jack as solo captain and crew. Jack decided that we might get a bit of calmer water for fishing in the lee of Montague Island, so we headed there.

While the seas were mountainous the wind was behind us on the way out, so in retrospect the voyage was tolerable. We reached Montague in about an hour, found some calmer water and caught a few snapper. When we headed back to Bermagui the wind had eased a little but the trip back was head on into the gale, Jack spent half his time up the mast looking for the shoreline with the boat on autopilot; the two Phils spent most of the time hanging over the side and were violently sick; I think I was too frightened to be sick; and Ross sat very quietly in the cabin not saying much. There was no thought of sampling the beers we had brought along. Jack had no fear of the sea and was clearly enjoying himself. About two hours later we started to catch glimpses of the big pines along one side of Bermagui harbour, and Jack had delivered us safely home.

After a string of motorbike accidents, McSharry had acquired an old red MG TF to improve his chances of survival. Mid-year we were having the usual Friday night beers when Ned Overton (who had pretty much completed his honours year work already) came up with the wonderful idea that we should head off and visit Dick England, who was doing his honours mapping project in the Tumut region. It seemed like a good idea at the time, so off we headed in the MG around 9.00 p.m. Three adults crammed into an MG for a 400-kilometre drive in cold and wet conditions wasn't such a great idea, but we eventually arrived in Tumut in the wee hours of the morning and located Dick's lodgings. Of course, we'd brought no camping gear nor anything else for that matter. With the sparse bedding Dick was able to put together, the rest of the night was rather cold and unsettled at the base of the Snowy Mountains.

We were able to spend most of the next day in Dick's mapping area, and after it warmed up it turned out quite a pleasant day, which was fortunate given we had neither warm clothes nor appropriate field gear. That evening Dick entertained us with dinner and a few drinks at his favourite watering hole, the local RSL club. That we were admitted was something of a miracle, as Dick a few weeks earlier had "accidentally" extinguished the eternal flame in the club and had used all his powers of persuasion to avoid ejection and banishment from it. After another coolish night we headed home on Sunday morning, resolving to be a little more circumspect next time Ned came up with a great idea.

A Meeting with the Vice-Chancellor

Another Friday night at the Forest Lodge late in semester two ended up with some unexpected consequences. McSharry and I after a solid session decided we needed to pick up gear in the office before heading home. On the way through campus one or other of us decided to also pick up some programming we had been doing on the Uni's massive computer. As we left the computing building we spotted a hand truck loaded with unused reams of computer paper. For whatever reason we decided to commandeer this and head back to the office in the Carslaw building. After a few drinks back at the office the computer paper was unravelled with great gusto, eventually filling the office with paper to a height of about 1.5 metres. After a few swallow dives off desks and a few more drinks we collapsed in our paper bedding.

Waking early the next morning we had a problem: how to get rid of all this paper undetected. In truth I think our antics had already been well and truly detected the previous night. The weekend was spent ferrying many loads of paper out of the office and into McSharry's MG and my sister Wendy's Datsun

Bluebird. Having completed our task successfully by late Sunday we went home well satisfied.

Monday morning, we had Don Emerson at our office soon after nine wanting to know what had gone on and to tell us that we had an appointment with Charlie Marshall, the head of the department, at 10.00 a.m. After a serious dressing-down from a furious Charlie, he told us that the matter had gone beyond a departmental issue and that we would be dealt with in due course. A day or two later we were summoned to a meeting with the Vice-Chancellor – could this be the end of our Uni careers?

Bruce Rodda Williams, the Welsh Vice-Chancellor, gave us a summary rap over the knuckles for all of two minutes, then asked if we'd like tea or coffee. For almost an hour we then discussed our aims and aspirations in the field of geoscience with Bruce, who seemed genuinely interested and happily threw in some advice of his own. I really wonder how many students ever get to have the experience of an extended tete-a-tete with the Vice-Chancellor, and feel we were privileged to get the opportunity, if for all the wrong reasons.

The main upshot from the computer paper incident was that we were booted out of our office in the Carslaw building and relegated to an 8.00 a.m.-6.00 p.m. office in the Geology Department with no out-of-hours key access. This change couldn't have been better timed as it meant we really had to concentrate on our research and thesis writing efforts.

Jobs a-plenty

By 1968 the so-called nickel boom was in full swing following the discovery of the large Kambalda nickel deposits by Western Mining Corporation (WMC) in 1964. This coincided with an oil and gas boom following on from significant discoveries of gas and oil on the Northwest Shelf off northern WA. Job prospects for geoscience graduates were at an all-time high and students could really pick and choose. I had several job interviews including one with Western Australian

Petroleum (WAPET), then both McSharry and I headed to Melbourne on separate flights for interviews with Conzinc Riotinto of Australia (CRA) in the afternoon and morning respectively. We were jointly shouted to lunch by the Chief Geophysicist and Exploration Director, Don Carruthers.

I got the better end of the deal with the morning interview as I had a free afternoon to spend in Melbourne until a flight back to Sydney at about 6.00 p.m. As I wandered into the nearest pub after lunch I became aware that our visit to Melbourne coincided with the launch of Powers beer in that fair city. All pubs involved in the Powers promotion were providing a free schooner of Powers, so the afternoon turned into a free pub crawl and I met McSharry at the airport a little worse for wear. Later we were both offered jobs with CRA. McSharry accepted their offer and worked with them for a year or two after graduation. I on the other hand accepted the WAPET offer.

Final Uni days

Before we knew it the year was over, and the day of thesis submission had arrived. Ned Overton, of course, was first to submit and arrived at the Forest Lodge as the doors were opening. After a day of frantic last-minute activity, I finally managed to submit at about 4.00 p.m., just an hour before shut-off (but I wasn't the last). Arriving at the Lodge it was clear that Ned and several others were quite advanced in celebrating the end of Uni. I suffered one last indignity when they chained me to a chair and would only hand-feed me beers if I was very polite to them. It was a relief to be unchained a couple of hours later and celebrate the end of Uni in a more relaxed fashion.

Most people traditionally dedicated their theses to people who had helped them get there, but not McSharry: his thesis was dedicated to King Kong, the recently deceased gorilla who had for many years been the star attraction at Sydney's Taronga Park zoo.

Two characters deserve further mention before closing this chapter of the story. Dave Sergeant's city driving skills amaze me to this day. Sarge drove a small Renault wagon around town and he wasn't exactly blessed with the best of eyesight. However, he had a theory that if you signalled to change lanes, space would miraculously appear to allow you to do so. He was scary in the extreme to drive with, as he would head for the nonexistent space in the next lane, and every time it opened up so that he negotiated the manoeuvre safely. Sarge had a big let-off driving home from the Forest Lodge one Friday night. On approaching the toll gates on the Harbour Bridge, he noticed a somewhat dishevelled but nattily suited man walking with some difficulty as he had a ball and chain attached to one leg. Ever the good Samaritan, Sarge pulled up and offered him a lift which he readily accepted. As they negotiated the bridge Sarge learned that it was the gentlemen's "bucks" night and that his good friends had simply dumped him at the toll gates to find his own way home. Just as he was coming off the bridge Sarge heard the shrill of a siren and was directed to turn off the bridge at Milsons Point. A belligerent police officer appeared by Sarge's window and suggested that his driving was somewhat erratic. The situation didn't look promising.

His passenger began digging in his pockets, produced his wallet, leant across to the police officer and introduced himself as Detective Sergeant Johnson of the Fraud Squad and let him know that the kind gentleman, Sarge, was giving him a lift home. The policeman's demeanour towards Sarge changed immediately. The outcome: Sarge drove his passenger safely home and then drove home to Pymble, all this time with his personal police escort.

John Davis or JD is the other character who in retrospect was way ahead of his time and his mates. JD liked to party as much as the next man and was heavily into sport, so much so that he had to repeat second year. What we didn't recognise was that JD was networking way back then: mainly through sport he cultivated friendships with law and accounting students, something anathema to the rest of us (unless they were female of course), and he also fostered early stockbroking and company director contacts. The fruits of his labours were realised within a few short years when he and a colleague, Terry Fern, took over a penny-dreadful oil exploration company, which within weeks was involved in a major discovery on the Northwest Shelf. They were written up in the Sydney finance papers as the $50 million men. Yes, luck always plays a role, but the spadework JD put in improved the odds of success immeasurably. To rub salt in the wounds JD also married arguably the best-looking blonde in the Department of Geology and Geophysics. Sue Davis was model material, intelligent and just an all-round nice person, with the added ability to drink most students under the table, including JD. I think every male in the faculty was secretly in love with her. What a woman.

JD and Terry Fern some years later managed to pull off another major oil discovery in the Gulf of Mexico. JD's major interest, however, was always wine, and he subsequently established three successful winemaking ventures in the Hunter Valley together with vineyards on the Limestone Coast of South Australia. Then working in South Australia, I managed to provide JD with some published but little-known soil/surface geology maps which may have helped him to acquire land and establish vineyards on undervalued "terra rossa" soils, so prized in the nearby Coonawarra wine district.

5

Welcome to the Real World

Placer-Darwin, 1968–69

Although I'd accepted a job with WAPET I still wasn't sure if my career should be in the minerals or the petroleum exploration industry so, to give myself a bit of breathing space, I took a vacation job in Darwin with Sydney-based Placer Development Ltd (Placer). Soon after my honours year results came through Placer offered me permanent employment as a geophysicist at the princely sum of $5200 per annum and my career in the minerals industry was locked in.

Placer was a Canadian company, the brainchild of an Australian corporate lawyer and a New Zealand mining engineer back in 1926, which developed an amazing gold mining operation near Bulolo in New Guinea in the 1930s. With no roads into the mountainous terrain, three Junkers aircraft lifted 35,758 tonnes of freight from 1927 (until they were destroyed by Japanese fighters in 1942) for the massive alluvial dredging operation which ensued, in what was at that point the greatest peacetime airlift ever undertaken. The Bulolo alluvial gold mining project produced more than 2 million ounces of gold before it ceased production in 1965.

Placer's mineral exploration operations in Australia and Papua New Guinea were jointly funded by US mining giant Kaiser Aluminium. In 1968 Canada was arguably at the forefront of innovative mineral exploration techniques and many of Placer's Australian-based exploration management executives were Canadian. Kaiser also had a smattering of US staff representing its interests. This led to regular misunderstandings with Australian personnel, as operating and ground conditions in Australia are nothing like those in Canada. The words "now this is the way we do it in beautiful British Columbia" at times became somewhat irritating.

To an industry novice it was also puzzling to me the way the Canadian executives were so revered and I am still not sure what they had achieved to attain this status. The Yanks on the other hand, showed a bit more Aussie humour. Ed Schulz the Exploration Director for Kaiser was reputed to get an erection whenever he stood atop an undiscovered ore deposit, fortunately or unfortunately as the case may be, I never witnessed this phenomenal skill.

As a geophysicist with Placer I was Sydney based and moved from project to project as required spending terms from two weeks up to three months on any one project. It was like being on one big paid holiday touring remote parts of Australia and Papua New Guinea. Some of the field camps were alcohol free by decree and others by choice but it was generally easier to get work done in an alcohol-free environment while in the bush. This of course led to great thirsts and binge drinking when field crews got to the next town or indeed to Sydney head office. As there was nothing to spend money on while in the field it meant cash reserves were substantial by the time you got back to town. The whole system was a recipe for disaster and the lifestyle was truly frenetic. The lifestyle also wasn't great for establishing long-term relationships: for instance, three times I booked to see the musical "Hair" with some young lady and three times the booking was cancelled as I was summoned to the next "urgent" field assignment. I never did get to see "Hair". Sport was another thing that languished.

The climate in mineral exploration at the time was also the stuff of legends with the Poseidon boom in November 1969, the false Tasminex boom of January 1970 and the overly optimistic announcement of a major uranium discovery at Nabarlek (NT) also in 1970. By the time I departed Placer in 1972 this boom had deteriorated into a major slump with very limited employment opportunities. My whole career has seen a series of booms and busts, which need to be weathered as best we can. One of the benefits of the boom days was that employers were regularly upgrading salaries to counter the demand and the somewhat outrageous salaries being offered by newly floated companies.

Darwin

Val LeRoy (Lee) Furlong, Placer's senior geophysicist, was the guy who interviewed and subsequently employed me and after a few hours in head office the following day, he told me to pack my bags as I would be heading to Darwin. A couple of days later I was off, and Lee advised me to enjoy the first-class air travel and free drinks as I would be heading bush on arrival in Darwin. As I came to learn, plans often change when you reach your destination and, arriving a little the worse for wear, I was met by Lee at the airport, who said that there had been a slight change of plans which meant an overnight stay in Darwin.

After finding a bed for the night and freshening up at Placer's Darwin office it was off to the Fanny Bay Hotel for the evening with Lee, Bill Barber, John Sandy, Burge Brown and John Gallo; I had been ambushed. The old Fanny Bay Hotel was everything you would expect in the tropics in those days, and sunset over the ocean was spectacular. The wet season humidity was also something else when experienced for the first time. By the end of the evening I was ready to collapse into bed but boy had I met a few characters.

Lee Furlong was an East Coast American who had graduated in Geoscience and Music from Washington State Uni, which made for a somewhat eclectic combination. Lee, a giant of a man, was not a big drinker but he loved his food, especially long business lunches. He was a great innovator and entrepreneur working within a conservative company. During the three years I worked for Lee he must have tried just about every new geophysical technique that came on the market and he had designs for setting up our own company geophysical survey plane. Placer to its credit strongly supported his innovation although the survey plane idea was a little beyond the budget of a then mid-sized exploration company.

Lee was instrumental in establishing the Australian Society of Exploration Geophysicists (ASEG) in 1970 and served as Treasurer, Vice-President and ultimately President in 1974–75. Ultimately Lee's enthusiasm could not be contained and he joined the stable of the irrepressible North American entrepreneur, Ike Shulman, in late 1971. He went on to manage and chair mid-size and junior Australian companies over his career in the mineral exploration industry. I am indebted to him for the variety of mineral exploration experiences he introduced me to over a brief period.

Bill Barber was a tough and weatherbeaten prospector, but also a lovely old gentleman from Cairns. At that time Placer valued prospectors' expertise and employed several of them around Australia as a supplement to its geoscientific staff. Bill, with no formal training, was arguably one of the best when it came to alluvial gold and tin prospecting/mining, who honed his skills on the fabulous Palmer River goldfield in North Queensland. Bill's story of survival on the Palmer River as a youngster during the Great Depression left a lasting impression. He and his mates, with little money and not finding much gold, apparently survived on a diet of porridge and home brew beer for about nine months, with no ill-effects.

John Sandy was the geologist in charge of the Darwin office and a Kaiser employee. John was the archetypal Yank: he hailed from the deep south, was tanned and blond with a crew cut and relatively loud. I was immediately on the defensive but how wrong I turned out to be. John was probably the nicest American I've met and we remained good friends until his death a few years ago. John understood the Australian psyche that what you say is often exactly the opposite of what you mean, and he loved Australia so much that he was a regular visitor over a thirty-year period. He also loved a drink, or fifty, and his passion was the music of New Orleans although I believe his favourite performer was Arkansas-born Jimmy Driftwood. Jimmy, a guitarist also renowned as a maestro of the mouth bow, wrote and composed "The Battle of New Orleans", a song made famous by the late Johnny Horton.

John's other passion was sailing, at the tender age of sixteen he crewed in the Florida to Havana yacht race when the dictator, Battista, was still in power. His arrival in Cuba must have been an eye-opener for an impressionable young man. He told of his yacht being met in the harbour by a Cuban gunboat which pulled alongside, at which sailors presented each member of the crew with a bottle of 50-year-old Cuban rum just to get them warmed up before docking. At the docks they were greeted by a bevy of gorgeous, young, scantily dressed Cuban ladies who were also clearly at the crew's disposal. The next night there was a state reception in Battista's palace and pre-dinner they were treated to more aged rum served in elegant crystal glasses. John said he was a little shocked when he realised that etiquette demanded that on emptying each glass it had to be hurled into a huge brick fireplace. It's little wonder that Fidel Castro deposed Battista some months later.

Despite the shenanigans John became an accomplished sailor and I was fortunate enough to sail on Sydney Harbour with him on several occasions, albeit in docile trailer-sailers. John sailed out of the Drummoyne Sailing club and had purchased a secondhand boat from one of the board members who had bought a brand new and supposedly better boat at considerable cost. John just seemed to sense the little wind changes around the edges of Sydney Harbour and consistently finished in front of the chap he bought his boat off.

Whenever I sailed with John we always managed to consume a few tinnies (perhaps a dozen between us) on the legs when we had the wind behind us and we stowed the empties at the back of the boat to the chagrin of other yacht club members who could never understand how we finished in the top placings – believe me, it was all due to John's yachting skills. The last two sails with John were memorable, the penultimate on Botany Bay when we were leading and got hit by a southerly buster which we weathered and still won the race. It must have been an omen of the incident a few weeks later when we were sailing in the Australian (or maybe NSW) championships on Lake Macquarie. We were leading the first race when a big thunderstorm blew up and it was a bit scary as we watched the twenty-odd yachts behind us capsized one by one. There was a fleeting moment when we thought about and had time to pull down the sails, but no one wants to surrender the lead. The result, the leading seven yachts, including ours, not only capsized but had their masts snapped, it was a brief but frightening experience. We then had to endure an hour sitting on an upturned hull in a severe thunderstorm before the rescue boat got to us, all the while observing three other title races for different class yachts continuing on different parts of the lake with little or no impact from the storm. John just had time to repair and sell his yacht before returning to the USA; I've never sailed since.

Burge and Ida

Now I come to the inimitable Burge Dawson Brown, probably the greatest bullshit artist that I've encountered in my lifetime, but an absolute master of that trade. Like all good bullshit artists Burge led an amazing life but he just had to exaggerate somewhat to enhance each story. To his credit I believe he always knew when he was having you on and there was (nearly) always an element of truth to his various tales. In undertaking research for this book I came across an NT Archives oral history interview with Burge from 1981. By the end of the interview, it's apparent that the interviewer had been overwhelmed by Burge and could no longer distinguish Burge's truth from his fiction.

Burge was born in Rochester in the Goulburn Valley of Victoria in 1922. According to Burge's oral interview one great-great-grandfather was John Brown of Glasgow, whose shipbuilding company built the "Queen Mary" and "Queen Elizabeth" among many other vessels; his maternal great-great-grandfather was

George Dawson, a geologist who pioneered the development of the legendary Klondike goldfield in the Yukon territory of Canada and after whom the city of Dawson is named.

Burge was brought up in a farming family in the Goulburn Valley and at age 17, in 1939, applied to join the RAAF at the start of World War II. He served in northern Australia and the South Pacific as a mechanic and gunner on Beaufort surveillance planes throughout the war. In 1945, after the war's end, he married the lovely Ida and they returned to farming in the Goulburn Valley. In 1949, supposedly with the encouragement of the then Deputy Prime Minister "Black Jack" McEwen, he purchased and moved to the semi-abandoned Murray Downs station in the remote Hatches Creek area of the Northern Territory with Ida and their young family.

Burge and Ida battled to make Murray Downs a viable operation between 1949 and 1959, but eventually a prolonged drought forced them to sell up. Primary Industry records indicate that Burge was quite an innovator and one of the first graziers to introduce buffel grass to the region. Ida and Burge were also instrumental in having the first school established on a pastoral lease in the NT. When they first arrived at the abandoned station there were no indigenous residents on-site but within a few years as they re-established the property several hundred indigenous people had returned.

Living with the indigenous people Burge and Ida learned much of their lore and tradition and Burge had a particular fascination with the Kadaitcha Men who featured in many of, his yarns. The Kadaitcha were feared as indigenous hitmen with supernatural powers who stalked their victims while walking backwards shod in emu-feathered footwear. Some of Burge's yarns implied that the Kadaitcha were not averse to other means such as rifles to achieve their outcomes.

From Murray Downs, Burge and Ida with an expanded family moved to Banyan Farm, a plantation near Batchelor where they grew bananas, pawpaw and pineapple with mixed success. There was also an attempt to domesticate a buffalo herd which was well before its time in the Top End. To supplement their income

Burge also took to feral buffalo shooting, for which the barefoot Burge and his several very attractive daughters gained a reputation as very effective shooters.

In the mid-1960s Burge seems to have changed his focus from farming to mineral exploration and mining with a base at the old RAAF camp near Darwin River and a move to Darwin so that the younger daughters could complete their education. He was somehow involved in the discovery and development of the Mt Bundey iron ore deposit, which produced iron ore from 1968 to 1972 (after Burge had divested his interest in the project). Placer's involvement at Darwin River was through a joint venture agreement with Nevsam, who held several exploration tenements there; Burge's role was as manager of Nevsam's mineral exploration interests.

In 1973, sometime after Placer's interest in the Darwin River tenements had waned, Burge and Ida moved to and built a remote tropical home at Bynoe Harbour, southwest of Darwin, where Burge promoted some further mining projects with limited success. Burge had many fantastic project ideas for the Top End, but unfortunately none ever reached the scale he envisaged, although boy did he provide some entertainment along the way.

Burge and another man were awarded the British Empire Medal for gallantry after they rescued an unconscious pilot from a crashed helicopter just minutes before it exploded on 21 January 1966. When he first related this rescue story in camp, we were all a bit sceptical; how wrong we were.

The other attendee at that fateful dinner at the Fanny Bay hotel was John Gallo, John, a recent Geology graduate hailing from far north Queensland, had been with Placer for about a year and was more prepared for nights like this than I was. John, who came over as a somewhat gruff individual, became a good friend in my time at Placer.

The Darwin River camp

The next morning, we were off to the Darwin River camp. It was quite a safari heading down the Stuart Highway as unbeknown to me the entire crew had been in town for a weekend field break. The old RAAF camp was just that, comprising somewhat dilapidated, corrugated iron mess, office, ablution and single sleeping quarters, but there was power and hot water and it kept us dry. The area we were exploring was interesting in that most of it was proposed to become catchment for the planned Darwin River Dam, with quite an extent to be inundated. It was very high-risk exploration where only the discovery of a world class ore deposit, like Broken Hill or Mt Isa, could have prevented dam construction. Today, with the dam long since completed, the area provides a wonderful recreational facility for Darwin and Palmerston.

With a field crew of about twelve our exploration activities included drilling, mapping and sampling and in my case conducting magnetic and radioactive geophysical surveys together with supervising an electrical geophysical survey crew and interpretation of all geophysical data. Up until Christmas we had regular and spectacular late afternoon thunderstorms, but ground access was still good; then we all headed off for a week's Christmas–New Year break in Darwin.

I chose to visit my sister Ann and her three daughters in Derby over Christmas as it only seemed a short hop from Darwin (about 800 kilometres by air) and had a pleasant time catching up there. As I went to board the Viscount aircraft for the return journey Ann, who was the flying doctor, recognised the pilot, Brian Bayly, a WWII bomber pilot, and assured me that I was in good hands as he was one of MacRobertson Miller Airlines most experienced pilots. The flight back to Darwin was smooth and uneventful with fine weather all the way and I remember reassuring the somewhat nervous young lady sitting next to me that we couldn't be safer (what a pick-up line).

On New Years Eve, sitting in the Green Room of the Darwin Hotel and enjoying a beer or two, I was shocked when John Gallo walked in and said, "Have you heard about the plane crash in WA?" It was the same Viscount and the same Brian Bayly as captain: the plane had returned to Perth, then on its next flight its left wing had detached as it was descending to land at Port Hedland. Everybody on board was killed. Brian Bayly was a last-minute replacement for the pilot scheduled to fly that day. I can only speculate on what might have been if there had been a turbulent thunderstorm around Darwin two days earlier.

The Wet Sets In

There were a few changes when we headed back to the bush in the New Year: half the crew moved to the Harts Range in central Australia while the rest of us headed back to Darwin River. Looking back on things, why any of us were out in the field at that time of the year is beyond me. At Darwin River the humidity dropped your working efficiency by at least sixty percent, while the heat at Harts Range led to tragedy for our crew. At least in Central Australia the nights were cool.

We had an Alice Springs-based prospector at Harts Range who insisted on working independently and one day he headed off from camp on a motorbike leaving no details of where he was going and didn't return. A search party was quickly organised with a female indigenous tracker. Sadly, the prospector left his broken-down bike and started walking; the crew later told me that the tracker was on his trail but when his tracks led into the hills she announced, "Im bugger up bigtime." The search party found him alive but lying on his back and blinded by the sun; he died shortly afterwards. It did bring home the risks of working in the outback summer.

Back at Darwin River it was still very humid, but the wet season had arrived. We continued with the geophysical surveys and drilling along accessible tracks, but the weather played havoc with us. If there was lightning nearby the electrical geophysical surveys had to be abandoned and the continual rain meant that we often spent hours extracting ourselves from bogs.

I'll always remember the problems with high-tech Canadian instruments in the tropics. There was one swampy area that I was told to survey that involved walking through about three kilometres of knee-deep water. Each time I'd get about halfway through the survey the state-of-the-art Canadian scintillometer would malfunction (a scintillometer measures radioactivity). So, it would be back to Darwin to check the instrument in John Zeroni's lab, where it worked like a charm, then back to the bush where it would fail yet again. I must have walked that swampy line at least four times without completing it successfully, but at least there were no snake encounters. High-tech Canadian geophysical instruments which functioned beautifully in cold weather conditions were "ratshit" in Darwin River.

I should briefly mention John Zeroni, who was a technical officer with the Commonwealth Bureau of Mineral Resources but did some electronic repair work on the side. John constructed probably the world's smallest Geiger counter (radioactivity measurer) housed in a Kodak slide box, which he sold for about $20 a pop, he was also very liberal with drinks while he was undertaking repairs.

Back at Darwin River I was bogged one day but returned to camp pleased that I had got myself out of trouble, I was telling Burge Brown about this and mentioned that I had uprooted a tree in winching myself out. When I explained where it had happened Burge got grumpy and said, "You put the winch rope up too high and have buggered up my winching tree." I took this as normal Burge bullshit but when I snuck back to have a look a few days later there were several low winching marks on the tree from Burge's earlier use of it.

We had two Canadian police officers on long service leave working with us and in retrospect I now think they were partners although it never crossed my mind at the time. These two were like the odd couple and just hadn't adapted to Aussie conditions, I remember advising them to drive through the middle of a flooded patch of track as I had walked through it and knew it had a solid base, they ignored the advice, detoured off the side of the road and got hopelessly bogged. It was mean but I just abandoned them and headed back to Darwin River camp for a beer and dinner; they finally arrived about midnight.

Camp characters

I met two wonderful young characters at the Darwin River Camp. Jack Schubert was all of eighteen or nineteen. Jack had left his large family in Taree at age sixteen and headed north. John Sandy gave him a job as a driller's offsider and he never looked back: that was to be his vocation. To speak to, Jack sounded like a fifty-year-old with his many words of wisdom and if you shook hands with the man his word was his bond. However hard the going got at Darwin River or elsewhere, "Placer Jack" as he was affectionately known would put a positive spin on things and he'll feature in a couple of later stories.

Two stories need to be told here, however: the first, his legendary trip from Darwin to Perth. Jack innocently got on a Fokker Friendship in Darwin expecting a long but straightforward trip to Perth. All went well until Port Hedland when with minimal passengers on the plane he was advised that it had been diverted to the "mail route" but he was assured he would be well looked after on the extended flight. The plane went north again to Halls Creek and then proceeded south with many stops through inland WA. Jack finally arrived in Perth 27 hours after departing Darwin. He was indeed looked after but is the only person I know who swears he was seeing pink elephants when he finally lay down in his motel in Perth.

The other story comes much later but epitomises the man. At about age 40 Placer Jack had finally acquired his own drilling company in Mount Isa and soon after was married. He and his new wife headed off on one of those expensive and exclusive Kimberley cruises. When they got to the halfway point at Broome, Jack and his new wife got off the boat. Jack didn't seek a refund but simply said, "The scenery and facilities are fine but I can't put up with the other tossers you have on this cruise." I think this says it all about "Placer Jack". Sadly, Jack was killed in a helicopter crash a year or two later when a sling under the chopper he was flying in got snagged by a tree.

Peter Dreverman was a young geophysics student working with the electrical geophysics crew when I met him at Darwin River. We hit it off well, probably because of a liking for the brown ale. Peter went on to complete his geophysics degree and returned to the Territory to work at the Nobles Knob gold mine near Tennant Creek, one of Australia's richest. Peter moved from geophysics into mine management and became a bit of a local legend. He was always a rather excitable and ebullient character and it's been a pleasure occasionally to catch up in Perth where he moved to after Nobles Knob closed.

After a very protracted and wet period our electrical geophysical crew finally finished the surveys at Darwin River. Many celebratory drinks were had in the Darwin River camp but stupidly the contract crew and I decided we should head back to Darwin later that evening. At the corner of Bagot Road and the Stuart Highway for some reason I thought I should run over a road sign with the Landrover I was driving, but at that moment I noticed a cop car on Bagot Road and aborted the mission. Next thing I am pulled over and asked what I am up to. I was quick to get out and lean on the Landrover to avoid any wobbles but once the police ascertained that the Landrover had Queensland plates, and I had a NSW licence it was all in the too hard basket for officers near the end of their shift. They asked me where our office was and told me to follow them there, then advised no more driving until the morning.

Just a few further recollections of Burge Brown and Darwin River. Burge was adamant that we should always walk across any flooded creek before attempting to cross it in a vehicle, which was a commonsense approach from a safety aspect. I didn't witness the event but in a hurry one day Burge ignored his own advice. Into the water he went in the trusty Nissan Patrol and deeper he went until he was completely submerged, then miraculously the Nissan started to emerge from the creek on the far bank but at that moment the engine died and Burge was left sitting in the vehicle with about a foot of the top of the vehicle clear of the water. The drilling crew following in a much higher vehicle managed to winch the Nissan to safety. More than a little teasing took place in camp that night.

Another of Burge's stories related to lightning jumping along railway tracks, and I was a bit sceptical. The Darwin River camp was right beside the old Darwin-Larrimah railway line and sure enough I got to witness this spectacle on more than one occasion. Burge's son-in-law Ross Anictomatis was another budding young Territory character who wandered everywhere through the bush in bare feet and, with his dogs and a solid stick as a weapon, was known to run down wild pigs, Ross went on to become a very successful Darwin businessman.

When we were having a break in Darwin Burge often had the whole crew round to his home where he was a most generous host. I still remember some of the excellent barramundi he served up (well, Ida probably cooked it). Before the electrical geophysical crew and I headed back to Sydney in late February we had a meeting to do a bit of a review of the geophysical surveys with John Sandy, John Gallo and Burge in Nevsam's office in Darwin. After the serious stuff was concluded a few drinks were introduced and as the evening wore on Burge felt he needed to say a few words of thanks and stood on the (non-too flash) conference table to deliver an oration which just went on and on. Finally tiring of this and knowing Burge was a bushie who forsook jocks in the tropical heat, I snuck up behind him and dacked him. It was a futile exercise as with everything exposed to the masses Burge just continued with his oration as if nothing had happened. He was a man not to be underestimated.

Flying High

Returning to Sydney in late February I had an interesting flight, after quite a sendoff in Darwin and free drinks on the plane. I was "flying high" as the Boeing 727 made its descent into Mt Isa but I was also busting. Despite the seatbelt sign being on I pleaded with one of the hosties to make one quick visit to the toilet at the front of the plane. She could sense my desperation and demurred to my request but said be quick. I noticed a couple of bumps while relieving myself and then speedily (I thought) made my way back to my seat, but other passengers were staring. What was wrong? Nothing really, except on looking out of the plane window I realised that we were taxi-ing along the runway after landing. After a brief stop in Isa, as I reboarded the plane the same hostie very politely said, "Please, Mr Newton, let's not have a repeat on the next leg." I assured her it wouldn't happen again and wisely chose to sleep most of the way on the ensuing Brisbane and Sydney legs of the flight.

Back in Sydney I had my first proper introduction to head office. The Placer office was in Goldfields House at Circular Quay. In those days business lunches were the norm so a strict dress code of collar and tie with a suit or sportscoat was adhered to. This was not to meet any internal office standards but simply to ensure entry to all restaurants for lunch, as dining dress codes back then were rigid.

Lee Furlong was dead keen on Placer buying its own geophysical survey plane and during this first short stay in Sydney I helped him compile specifications for the required aircraft. The critical features, a long range and high load capacity coupled with the ability to fly low (fifty metres) and slow (less than 140kph), and highly manoeuverable in order quickly to turn around and start the next survey line possibly only 100 metres from the previous one. The newly released British-built Britten-Norman Islander met these specifications and a test flight out of Bankstown was arranged.

Imagine my concern when Lee rang me the night before the test flight to say he was crook so I would have to take the test flight on my own, a twenty-one-year-old with minimal flying experience. To his credit Lee provided me with a list of questions and details of manoeuvres he wished the plane to undertake so that I didn't look like a total idiot. Arriving the next day I was greeted by the pilot, who had about forty years experience, and an equally experienced salesperson. The flight went smoothly and the pilot took the plane through its paces, which was something of an experience; however, he was a little hesitant when I asked him to fly at just 100kph (as requested by Lee), as the plane had a stall speed of 75kph. At that speed it felt like the plane was barely moving but at least we were flying above 1000 metres and not operating at survey height of 50 metres. The plane passed with flying colours as far as I was concerned but Lee failed to convince the Placer Board to go ahead with the purchase.

6

Another Planet

Placer - Queensland, 1969–72

I had vaguely heard that Queenslanders were a bit different from other Australians and I was about to find out in a hurry. In 1969 Mt Isa was a bustling city with a population of about 40,000, with many pubs and clubs and several restaurants which reflected the ethnic origins of many of the miners who had made "the Isa" their home. The copper and lead-zinc mining operations on the city's doorstep were booming and the bitter industrial disputes of 1964–65 led by Pat Mackie were a thing of the past. I was to have many visits to the region over the next few years and unlike Kalgoorlie there wasn't the same depth of animosity between miners and upstart mineral explorers. Air access was probably better back then than it is today with both Ansett and TAA running daily Boeing 727 jet services between Brisbane and Darwin which stopped over in Isa on both the outgoing and return legs.

Lady Annie Field Camp

My initial destination was the Lady Annie field camp about 130 kilometres by road north-northwest of Isa. Here Placer was drilling to prove up copper reserves at the old Lady Annie copper mine and exploring for lead-zinc deposits to the east of Lady Annie. My involvement was with the lead-zinc exploration, conducting and interpreting geophysical surveys. Within two years Placer discovered the medium-sized but high-grade Lady Loretta lead-zinc-silver deposit, which was eventually mined by Glencore. The discovery was a geochemical sampling success story, the geophysical surveys were of only minor use in definition of the deposit.

The field camp was basic but comfortable and the countryside was rugged, so it was handy having a permanent camp cook after working up an appetite from a solid day wandering through the scrub. The first camp cook was an old Queensland bushie named Bill. He was a bit of a rogue and what he got up to during the day when we were all absent was often speculated on. His limited menu of bush tucker never lacked for quantity, but it was very predictable. However, he always had a big pot of coffee percolating away on the wood stove, which was greatly appreciated by all. The camp was officially dry at the time but Bill often reeked of rum. I remember travelling back to Isa with Bill on one occasion, where he was flinging lighted matches into the bush as we travelled and was cackling away to himself. The reason: the camp manager was following in a separate vehicle and Bill thought he would make things a little uncomfortable for him by starting a few fires. Bill was eventually replaced by an ex-Navy cook who negotiated a full catering package deal for the camp, and suddenly barramundi, good steak and crayfish were regularly on the menu. In providing this he was also saving money for the company – it's amazing what a bit of coordination can achieve. This cook would occasionally invite people round to his caravan to share a bottle or two of vino from the profits (so much for a dry camp).

The two terrors in the camp were Mango and Muncher, who spent most of their days in the repair workshop but also helped with some exploration activities. Often strange vehicles would turn up at the workshop late at night. It turned out the boys were selling off mine machinery and parts from earlier mining operations for cash plus always a carton of beer. It was quite an enterprising operation as the superseded equipment was of no real value to Placer. At some point, however, they ran out of beer supplies and there was Mango in the camp kitchen making up a cocktail in a two-litre container, he offered me a sip which I foolishly tried and quickly spat out. It was the old standard bush recipe of metho and vanilla essence with a dash of lemon juice.

Mango was finally leaving Isa and as we were having a farewell beer at the airport he confided in me about his soil geochemical sampling at Lady Loretta. The results showed a consistent pattern except across one line of sampling where similar high results were recorded over half of the line (about a kilometre). This had the exploration crew puzzled but Mango's confession explained all. It had been a very hot day and rather than taking samples at fifty-metre intervals, Mango sat under a shady tree and collected them all from one spot where unknown to him the lead and zinc values were high. I never let on about his confession but people had a fair idea what had happened once the line was resampled.

The mining stock market boom was in full swing round this time and we used to have a bit of fun making bogus requests for share purchases during daily radio schedules on our call sign "8QKQ Paradise Valley". Everybody in the district could listen in and more than once these bogus orders led to a flurry of mining share purchases by other parties on the bush radio.

Drillers in those days had a reputation as rough, tough individuals who were prone to throwing tools in all directions when drilling problems occurred. This often resulted in the loss of expensive equipment. There were stories of one driller who had resolved this problem and alleviated his temper tantrums by biting a drill rig tyre whenever a major breakdown occurred. It seemed a bit of a tall story but right on cue there was said driller at Lady Loretta. As I approached the drill rig one day, there was a lot of swearing and kerfuffle, then this individual ran up to the tyre and bit it with vigour. He may have saved on equipment loss, but I still wonder what his dental bill was like.

After work a few of us would often go for a jog and, if in camp, Cliff Rennie, a Canadian mining engineer, would accompany us. Cliff was fortyish and fairly fit but he could never be convinced to wear a hat and he paid the price for this practice. One day, traversing the hills on his own Cliff failed to return to camp, a search party set out and he was found dazed and disoriented. It took about six months in head office for his recovery. It certainly convinced me that a broad hat is vital when working in the Australian bush.

The Lady Loretta deposit was named after entrepreneur Ike Schulman's wife, as Ike had a carried interest in the property through his company Triako. However, the executive was in an uproar when a young geologist, Dick Lewis, had the temerity to christen another newly discovered prospect Lady Brenda, after his infant niece. Despite the executive indignation the name has survived to this day.

Just a few kilometres east of our camp, Broken Hill South Ltd had another exploration camp where they were evaluating the Lady Annie phosphate deposit. Two of my Sydney Uni colleagues, Dave Sargeant and Chris Brown, were working there and there were occasional evening camp visits to swap a few yarns. Unfortunately, our fortnightly weekend breaks in Isa never seemed to coincide.

Mt Isa escapades

These weekend breaks in the big smoke were highly anticipated. On one such break I scored the dubious task of driving the camp manager's Land Rover into town for a pre-arranged trade-in. It could barely manage 50kph when we started off as he must have coked up the engine by constantly driving so slowly around the campsite. The vehicle kept overheating and our drum of water was soon exhausted. We had on board both an esky of cold beers and a carton of hot Fourex. There was only one option, so we kept filling the radiator up with Fourex (which is about all it was good for). Miraculously the vehicle went faster with each top up of Fourex and by Isa it was almost running normally. I was very quick to deliver it to the car yard next morning.

The Barkly Hotel was owned by the Theiss brothers, who dined there regularly, and was the centre of entertainment (today it's a rather sleazy, gambling pub). It boasted a fine dining area upstairs with a grand piano playing in the background and a huge bar and entertainment area downstairs. Downstairs was packed to the rafters on Friday and Saturday nights, especially for the two-hour sessions eleven to one and four to six on Sundays. The resident band at the time was an NZ group, the Tikiwis, who were great musicians and entertainers. The Concordia Club also regularly hosted top performers, including Johnny O'Keefe, who I was lucky enough to share a drink and yarn with out the back of the club; while I downed a stubbie he knocked over half a bottle of whiskey but what a performance he gave.

One driller from our camp had a novel approach to clothing on these weekends in town – he maintained it was quite cost-effective. On arrival in town he would head to the upmarket clothing store in West Street (which is still there today) and purchase an expensive casual outfit. On Friday night he looked a million dollars. On Saturday he still usually looked reasonably dapper but by the afternoon session on Sunday he was starting to look a little tatty. He then proceeded to wear the same outfit drilling in the bush for the next fortnight (I hope he occasionally changed his jocks) then discarded the entire outfit on his next visit to Isa.

There were a few interesting tales relating to the "Barkly". On my first visit to Isa I left my mates at the Barkly to buy some takeaway in town. On the way there I tooted some vehicle that I felt was driving erratically and thought no more about it. Alighting in Miles Street I just caught a glimpse of this fellow jumping out of a vehicle and heading my way. Luckily, he only caught me a glancing blow and I was able to throw him rather heavily using his momentum. That was lucky as his mate had a similar idea but backed off. From then on, I decided tooting vehicles à la Sydney was not an option in Isa. I was a little surprised when I returned to the Barkly and one of the boys asked me how I got blood over my left eye.

On one weekend trip Roman Daskiew and I foolishly volunteered to undertake a short sampling program on a prospect about fifty kilometres north of Isa on the Sunday. After a solid session at the Barkly on Saturday night neither of us felt up to the task on arrival on site the next day. A quick sleep in a shady dry riverbed seemed appropriate. Refreshed somewhat after an hour or so's sleep we realised the place was teeming with scorpions which were crawling all over us. We both escaped without a bite and got on with the job in hand.

After another late Saturday night at the Barkly I decided to souvenir the "Seeing Eye" dog at the entrance which had fortunately just been emptied of cash. The dog accompanied us to a huge party in town the next day, where the mass of people took a liking to it to such an extent that it was full of cash by the end of the day. When I returned the dog to the Barkly next morning the manager's first thought was to call the constabulary but the realisation that the dog was full of cash tempered his reaction to "Please don't do it again."

One weekend at the Barkly I managed to wine and dine a young lady named Barbara, who was a librarian at Mount Isa Mines. Both in the restaurant and the downstairs area a lady used to come round during the evening selling roses and taking instant photos, both at five dollars a pop – she must have made a fortune back then. Returning to camp I caught up with Sarge and some of the Broken Hill South mob a few days later. Relating the weekend's activity, I pulled out the photo of me and Barbara. Sarge looked but made no comment, but then one of his mates piped up: "That's your Barbara, isn't it, Sarge." It's a small world.

Another regular weekend activity was the drive-in. I was a little obsessed with vehicle winches at that stage so decided to attach the winch cable to the small car in front in which a couple were clearly having a good time. With the winch put into gear the car commenced its backwards journey; brakes were frantically applied but to no avail. Eventually the winch was stopped and the cable disconnected, but the couple neither said anything nor got out of the car. They either thought it was aliens or were just having too good a time.

In 1971 I was lucky enough to have a weekend in town when the Isa Rodeo was on. It was quite a surreal experience. The town was abuzz with ringers, black, white and brindle, who apart from the rodeo were in town for the three F's, a fight, a feed and a fuck, generally in that order. I'm sure many didn't get beyond the first F, which was the priority. One had to be careful, particularly at the rodeo where you had to take care not to stare too long at anyone, otherwise they would come up and want to fight you. On Friday night at the Barkly, I unintentionally got into the rodeo vibe. Drinking with workmates, I bought everyone a cigar for the occasion and inadvertently failed to get one for one of the drillers' offsiders. He was insulted and invited me outside to settle the score. Buoyed by several drinks I wandered out with him where I realised he was a big lump of a lad. Luckily, I ducked his haymaker, moved in close, threw him down and got him in a judo hold. When he realised he couldn't free himself he agreed to come back inside where I would buy him a drink and a cigar. Getting up he couldn't resist throwing another punch but this time his work crew intervened and gave him a few thumps for good measure. When we returned to the bar all was forgiven and a great night ensued.

The weekend activity was all held at the old rodeo ground near the airport. The rodeo itself was superb but adding to the atmosphere was Slim Dusty singing live between each event with so many of his songs about northwest Queensland. Of course, one still had to treat the ringers with extreme caution. Returning to the Isa Rodeo at the flash new venue of Buchanan Park in 2017 I was underwhelmed; it was a very choreographed affair by comparison with 1971.

Classic Queensland Pubs – Quamby and Malbon

As well as Lady Annie/Loretta I also worked in the Quamby region to the north of Cloncurry and at Placer's other major project at Pegmont, about 150 kilometres south of Cloncurry, which meant getting familiar with a couple of classic Queensland pubs.

The Quamby Hotel, about fifty kilometres north of Cloncurry, was then owned by Billy Keyes, an Irishman who was apparently a talented jockey in his day and post-retirement was a keen racehorse owner and trainer as well as a publican. The key to the popularity of the Quamby pub was not the beer or the atmosphere but the fact that Billy and his wife raised very attractive daughters who acted as a magnet for the ringers (and mineral explorers) for miles around. Quamby was also the last beer and fuel stop before Normanton, a 350 kilometre dirt road in those days. The advent of the breathalyser and construction of the Burke and

Wills Roadhouse (about half-way between Cloncurry and Normanton), together with most of the Keyes daughters marrying or leaving, saw the slow demise of the pub. It closed then had a brief reincarnation in the early 2000s. Sadly the old pub seemed doomed to permanent closure and deterioration. Great news, in 2023, the pub was rejuvenated and opened once again by two likely lads from the Gold Coast. Apart from the colour, the front looks very much like its 1970 version.

The Pegmont lead-zinc deposit, which was discovered by Placer during this period, lies about 150 kilometres south of Cloncurry on Cuckadoo station. To get there in the 1970s you travelled via dirt track through the old township of Malbon and then past the abandoned and once booming mining towns of Kuridala and Selwyn. Late last century Malbon was a stopover point on the way to the bustling township of Kuridala and boasted four pubs with regular Saturday race meetings. By 1971 all that was left was one pub and a few scattered houses. The beauty of Malbon was that it was bounded by the Cloncurry and Malbon rivers, which meant you could get stuck there on the very rare occasions when the rivers were in flood, which happened in 1971 with the breaking of a fifteen-year drought.

The Malbon publican was Phil Ruse, a tough and wiry old character who was a legend in northwest Queensland. Part of the legend was based on his time as publican at Kajabbi, further north, where the story goes that he once locked the local policeman up in his own cells overnight until he sobered up. Phil had a son Phil Junior who was almost equally as rough and tough as his old man. The story goes that Phil Junior at one stage brought his young fiancé/girlfriend home to meet Dad and Dad took a real liking to her. So much so that a huge fight ensued, with Dad the eventual winner, claiming the prize and marrying her in what turned out to be a lasting relationship. By 1971 Phil Junior worked as a barman at Malbon beside his Dad and step-mum in what appeared to be an amicable relationship. Phil Junior attempted to emulate his Dad's relationships with the local constabulary, on a lost weekend in the Isa he hit the front page of the local news after biting a hunk out of a policeman's calf while officers were trying to deposit him in the paddy wagon. This led to an extended stay at Her Majesty's pleasure somewhere else in Queensland.

While you could always book a room at the Malbon pub, allocation of beds was a little haphazard. On retiring from the bar it was not uncommon to enter your room to find the bed already occupied, you just wandered down the hallway until you found a room with an empty bed. If desperate, you could escape the clutches of Malbon in flood by driving across the railway bridge to the north, a somewhat hazardous venture given the random nature of train schedules. Today there's just an empty block where the pub once stood, burnt down, it was never rebuilt.

Rainwater and aftershave

A few kilometres from our Pegmont field camp was Cuckadoo Station homestead. Before the drought broke, I've never encountered a more dismal place, not a blade of grass in sight, a few bony cattle, homestead and outbuildings in a state of disrepair and of course no airconditioning to counter the blazing summer heat. The owner, Mrs Murphy, ran the place, her only assistance from her companion Mac, an emaciated old Scottish-born ringer. Despite the unbelievable hardships they seemed to love the property and the lifestyle with a passion.

In February 1971, while we were in the Pegmont field camp, the fifteen-year drought broke with a vengeance. After an afternoon and night of teeming rain it was obvious that we were driving nowhere for at least a week. An emergency camp meeting was convened. We had plenty of food, good radio communication, were all safe and healthy, but the booze supply was clearly limited. The big question was, do we ration it out or have one big party? The answer was obvious as we planned for a big night. One of the drillers took it to the extreme, confiscating everybody's aftershave so he could prepare one powerful after dinner cocktail. We were all a little the worse for wear the next day but the transformation in the country over the next few days was a sheer delight: pan-sized fish suddenly appeared out of nowhere in the flowing creeks and birds came from everywhere, especially flocks of budgerigars in their thousands. We eventually got back to the Isa but not before getting stranded overnight at the Malbon pub.

Another quirky little driller story comes to mind from Pegmont days. One night I was following about an hour behind three drillers heading to camp after a supply run into Cloncurry when I noticed three empty Fourex cans left beside the track. Having nothing better to do I checked the tachometer and then noted it was exactly seven miles to the next can dump, and so it went on all the way back to camp at exactly seven-mile intervals. When I asked them about this back in camp they denied all knowledge of timing their beer stops. I'm not convinced.

A Shot in the Dark

I mentioned earlier that Lee Furlong was such a good salesman to the powers that be that in a three-year period he managed to get them to try out almost every available new geophysical technique. This included false colour and thermal infra-red surveys over most of Placer's Australian and PNG prospects.

The colour infra-red surveys involved bringing out two North American photographic experts and flying surveys at up to 4500 metres altitude. I was to act as an observer on the Mt Isa leg of these surveys and innocently set out from Sydney. At Mascot airport I ran into my old Geophysics lecturer, Don Emerson, who was also heading to Isa to do some consulting work for a French exploration company. As soon as we boarded Don coopted the seat next to me and proceeded to order a beer immediately after take-off (about 8.00 am). I was a bit reluctant as I knew I'd be heading off in the survey plane on landing in Isa; coupled with that we would be using oxygen masks on the survey plane to allow us to operate at the altitudes required in an unpressurised aircraft. Don on the other hand was expecting to have drinks and dinner with his clients and a good night's sleep in Mt Isa before heading bush.

As it turned out we managed to share several beers on both the Sydney-Brisbane and Brisbane-Mt Isa flights. Needless to say we were both in high spirits on landing in Isa. After baggage collection I headed for the survey plane, a twin engine Italian Piaggio P-166. What was somewhat disturbing was that the prop engines were mounted backwards, but despite my misgivings the surveys went smoothly. Don, however encountered a bit of karma: instead of a chauffeured ride into Isa, the French company rep who met him led him out to a little single engine plane for the two-hour flight to their project area. After a bumpy flight, Don said the French did lavish him with gourmet food and wine on arrival in camp.

The thermal infra-red survey was a totally separate exercise run in conjunction with researchers from the University of Newcastle. These surveys attempt to measure any heat naturally radiating from rock formations and possibly ore bodies, necessitating that surveys are undertaken pre- and post-dawn and pre- and post-sunset for comparative purposes. I happened to be the bunny who knew how to reach all the prospect areas on the ground (within a 200-kilometre radius of Isa). So, I was allocated the task of setting up and picking up all the survey lights on the ground, which allowed the aircraft to navigate in the dark.

Finding one's way through the bush in the dark turned out to be a literal nightmare but the cycle of moving from one prospect to the next was an absolute killer. After minimal sleep between overnight survey flights the task would be to pick up the lights and head to the next prospect area. This usually entailed a drive back to Isa, a lunch and quick beer with the survey crew, then off to the next survey area to set up, either alone or with an offsider. At the end of three days with little or no sleep, I was exhausted but still headed out from Isa at dusk to set up lights at Pegmont for a pre-dawn flight run. I was falling to sleep on the highway to Cloncurry, realising I wasn't going to make it to Pegmont I passed the turn-off and drove on to Cloncurry. I bought a carton of beer there and started to drink them once I got off the bitumen. Amazingly, on my own, with several gates to open and close, the beers gave me a new lease of life and I reached the Pegmont camp at about 1.00 am, just in time to rouse the others in camp who then helped to set up the survey lights. The crew didn't find me until about 10.00 am the next day, sound asleep slumped over the steering wheel. So much for OH&S back in those days.

King Prawns in Karumba

Two short weekend trips while on the fortnightly break in Isa were memorable. The first was with Jack Schubert, a flying trip to the prawn port of Karumba on the Gulf of Carpentaria. Arriving at Isa at about 4.00pm on a Friday for a weekend break, Jack announced that he had to pick up his new car, a brand-spanking new blue and white Holden Kingswood. After a brief test run our crew adjourned for the normal Friday evening of dinner and drinks at the Barkly Hotel. In the latter part of the evening Jack decided he needed to cover the full run-in mileage of 1000 kilometres over the weekend, and the small prawn fishing town of Karumba was randomly selected as the destination. I was the only one silly enough to join Jack in his little adventure.

We were off early the next morning with an esky full of cold beer and a change of clothes. First stop, just on opening time was the Quamby Hotel. After a couple of refreshing ales there we headed off on the 350-kilometre all dirt trek to Normanton. The Kingswood was running like a bird and Jack was dutifully sticking to no more than 100kph, but about halfway into the journey Jack noticed the fuel gauge was dropping at an alarming rate. On inspection we discovered that petrol was trickling out of the fuel tank, which must have scored a lose stone. With no repair kit on board some very temporary repairs were made with chewing gum at which Jack decided that he may as well use the fuel rather than lose it. The speed for the rest of way into Normanton was more like 150kph, not an ideal running-in speed.

On arrival in Normanton about 3.00pm we were amazed and delighted to find an open garage with a mechanic on duty. He advised us to adjourn to the nearby (now purple) pub as he needed to let the fuel tank drain completely before effecting welding repairs. On our arrival back after a well-spent ninety minutes at the pub he advised us that the repairs had only taken fifteen minutes because when he inspected the tank with the car up on a hoist it was bone-dry. The rest of the trip to Karumba was uneventful and we managed to book overnight accommodation at the pub. Bitter disappointment came, however, when we breasted the bar and asked one of the locals where we could buy king prawns to take back to Isa. There weren't any to be had as it was the prawn fishing shutdown period. This blow ensured a rather heavy drinking night which flowed through the remainder of the weekend, but we were able to have a few non-local prawns in a prawn cocktail for dinner.

As the night wore on we gravitated to the pool room and bar almost beside the crocodile-infested Norman River. A group of prawn fishermen were enjoying their holiday time and had "adjusted" the pool table so no coinage was required. We had a great evening in their company. When last drinks were called they grabbed all the pool cues and balls and ceremoniously dumped them in the Norman River. After a big sleep and a little the worse for wear we decided after breakfast to stay for the 10.00 am to noon session at the pub before heading back to Isa. To our surprise the pool table was fully operational with cues and ball., Where they came from is unexplained to this day but I'm sure no one went diving for them in the Norman River.

As soon as the Sunday session finished we made a b-line for Quamby in the hope we might make the closing stages of the four to six afternoon session there. This meant that the Kingswood running-in speed needed to be exceeded once again. Arriving at about 5.30pm, we needn't have worried: Billy Keyes took a somewhat liberal approach to the 6.00pm closing time. There was a minor mishap on leaving Quamby when Jack ran off the road and neither of us could remember which side. In the pitch-dark Jack had to drive in increasingly expanding circles through the bush until we encountered the road. We arrived in Isa about midnight and I believe the Kingswood was by then most definitely run in.

Easter Celebrations

The second trip started a bit like the first, a very quiet Good Friday in Isa had us wondering what we could do in such a dead hole for the remainder of the weekend. After a few drinks someone suggested, let's head to the bright lights of Townsville, so first thing Saturday five of us set off in Jack's by now trusty Kingswood. Apart from Jack and me our party included then lab assistant Geoff Handley, roly-poley Malaysian-Chinese geologist Lee Mun Kit and surveyor Bob Ward. Geoff after gaining a geology degree went on to become worldwide exploration director for Placer Dome while Lee was later instrumental in the discovery and development of (I think) the massive Lihir gold deposit on one of New Guinea's islands.

Once again, we were equipped with a change of clothes and a beer-filled esky. The journey to Townsville was uneventful but on reaching there we realised it was Easter and accommodation was at a premium. After much searching, we found a family room in an old motel with a double bed and three singles, Jack and I drew the short straws and ended up sharing the double bed. The room was available for one night only. Wanting to make the most of our stay we headed for the nearest pub with a band as recommended by the motel owner. We had been warned that the locals liked an occasional fight or two but, on this night, Lee saved the day. Seated next to a few locals it was apparent they were looking for some action, when Lee lit a big cigar one of them took exception saying he didn't like the smoke and demanded Lee put it out. Lee's reaction was to take a big puff and blow it directly in the complainant's face and commence to loudly crack his knuckles, I still don't know if Lee had any martial arts skills but his oriental demeanour was enough to carry the bluff. By the end of the night we were quite pally with the other party. After closing time our crew headed down to the then largely undeveloped Esplanade and decided to harvest some coconuts. With a bit of Dutch courage climbing the coconut trees presented little problem but getting down was another matter and we all suffered from some severe leg chafing and lacerations the next day.

With no further accommodation and heavy overnight rain that night, all the way from Mt Isa to Townsville, we needed a plan of action for the rest of Easter. Firstly, we took in the Sunday session at a local hotel after which Lee managed to jag flights back to Isa that afternoon while Geoff, Bob, Jack and I, ever optimistic, decided we could make it back to Isa in the trusty Kingswood despite the rain and hundreds of kilometres of dirt road.

Arriving in Charters Towers that afternoon we decided to stay as there was accommodation available, then attempt to get to Isa the following day. So off we headed for the afternoon session at a local pub where we heard of a dance at the local Catholic Hall that evening. From being an altar boy at age twelve I had over the years developed a deep aversion for organised religion, so it seemed quite logical during the dance evening to enter the adjacent church and souvenir the crucifix off the altar. The crucifix was extremely heavy and being in Charters Towers, an early gold boom town, there is a good chance it was of considerable metal value.

On reflection the next morning, before our early start, we transported the crucifix to a phone box at the post office where a call was made to the local priest advising of its whereabouts, after which there was a somewhat hasty departure from the Towers. The Kingswood behaved admirably, sliding around in the mud and slush, but by Hughenden it was apparent we could go no further, particularly as there were now signs up saying the road was closed. There was some urgency in getting back to work on Tuesday, so after leaving the Kingswood safely at a local garage we boarded a freight train with a single passenger carriage bound for Isa at about 10.00am.

What a trip it was. The carriage was chock-a-block with other stranded travellers and apart from a water dispenser there was no food or other drinks to be had and no toilet facilities. As a result when the train stopped in each little town there was a frantic rush for booze, food and relief. The men on board were a little more fortunate in that they could stand at the railings outside the back of the carriage to relieve themselves but one desperate simply relieved himself from an open carriage window. We were lucky enough to contact a colleague in Isa at one of the stops who drove to Cloncurry to pick us up at 11.00 pm. The 400-kilometre trip from Hughenden to Cloncurry took a total thirteen hours.

As an aftermath to the weekend, when we had returned to our project area at Pegmont, Bob the surveyor erected a very large wooden crucifix on a small rise at the project area and named the feature Crucifix Hill. Over fifty years later, the Pegmont lead-zinc deposit still hasn't been mined, and I sometimes wonder whether Crucifix Hill still features on current project maps although the white ants would have long ago destroyed the crucifix. After the crucifix weekend I for many years avoided being outside in thunderstorms just in case there was a god. Jack many years later told me he received a summons about three years after that weekend regarding the borrowing of the crucifix because somehow the Kingswood was traced back to the event. He didn't attend court and received an arbitrary fifty-dollar fine. The church was clearly not forgiving.

7

The Wild West

Placer - Western Australia, 1969–72

The bulk of my work in the West was around the little township of Yalgoo, 200 kilometres inland from Geraldton, but there were also shorter work trips to Kalgoorlie, Shaw River near Marble Bar and Lansdowne Station in the Kimberley region.

Yalgoo Yokels

Yalgoo was and is a little one-horse town that had its origins in sheep grazing and gold mining and was deemed too far inland to grow grain crops. It had a pub, shire office and general store with a smattering of old houses. The local policeman was largely a law unto himself and the publican, Frank Sabbatini, and the pub were vital to local entertainment. The policeman would often come into the pub just before closing time at 10.00pm and declare the pub shut at which time Frank would oust a few stragglers and lock the front door; the cop would then take off his badge and order a drink, at which drinks continued all round until he was ready to leave, often several hours later. We were warned early on never to cross the local JP, a tiny, wizened, white-haired old fellow who was notorious for handing out maximum sentences for the most minor of offences when he sat as the local magistrate.

The country around Yalgoo is mainly flat and featureless although some of the low laterite ridges are quite scenic and in spring when the wildflowers bloom the countryside is transformed overnight into floral splendour. Flying into and out of Yalgoo, Mount Magnet and Meekatharra could be a bit interesting. The flights took off from Jandakot, Perth's second airport, and were usually modern ten-seat twin prop Cessnas but you were never quite sure. One day all passengers boarded this strange plane in the hanger; the pilot then reversed the plane out of the hanger under its own power, which was a bit of a first. The plane turned out to be an Irish-built Short Skyvan, a very squat aircraft that allowed you to drive a large four-wheel drive vehicle into the rear compartment. (Short Brothers PLC had its origins in the shipbuilding industry in London, around 1850. then became the first company in the world to build production aircraft. It moved its main production to Belfast in 1948.) Another day as we were cruising at about 3000 metres in a Cessna on the way to Yalgoo, a wedge-tailed eagle whizzed past the front windscreen, a quite uncomfortable experience.

Our crew in Yalgoo stayed in Mrs Willis's general store, which doubled as a guesthouse. Once again there were some interesting characters among them. Adrian Vanderplank, the geologist in charge of the project area, was South African and somewhat eccentric but easy to get along with. He concerned us a bit, however, when he found an initialled old g-pick along with what he claimed were some human bones while prospecting, but steadfastly refused to report the find to the police because he didn't wish to be involved in all the paperwork such a report would entail. Another young geologist, Ian Lewis, was a very average poker player who consistently lost in our low-stakes poker games; however, he was far more astute as an investor and bought 1000 Poseidon nickel shares at one dollar, which he subsequently sold for more than $100 each. Ian went on to set up a winery in Margaret River with his winnings.

Bala Param was a most affable, dark-skinned Malaysian Indian, who was a quite committed Hindu devotee. Bala was a scary bush driver, racing around the countryside at breakneck speed, which resulted in at least two collisions with the local wildlife. The first time he hit and killed a sheep, and steadfastly refused to drive any further, because the poor animal would have cursed him; we were about fifty kilometres from Yalgoo. Eventually he allowed me to drive the rest of the journey. The second collision was far more traumatic for poor Bala; he hit a fox and, in its death throes it appeared to sit up and stare directly at him. He believed that he had received the "evil eye" and was truly petrified. On that occasion it must have taken at least an hour to convince him to get back in the car and let me drive back to town. Bala with his Indian background was also very caste conscious and was somewhat mortified in the pub one day when some of the local indigenous residents decided to claim him as one of their own. His workmates of course did nothing to help him extract himself from the situation.

I first met Fred Bichard in Yalgoo; he had worked with Placer as a technical assistant for several years and his reputation had proceeded him to the West. Fred was born in Guernsey in the Channel Islands and after completing his tertiary education worked as an English teacher. He was well spoken and erudite. For whatever reason the lure of the Australian bush got to Fred and he migrated to Australia and joined a mineral exploration company, Placer, as his meal ticket to seeing Australia. Fred wasn't a stunning physical specimen but he sure had the gift of the gab. The story goes that on his first Australian assignment to Cloncurry in northwest Queensland he immediately sought and invited out the best-looking single female in the town for a platonic dinner even though she was already spoken for. When he told her his motive, she gladly accepted the invitation. His ploy was simple, be seen with the best-looking lady and surely the rest of the town's young ladies will come looking. I never asked him if it worked.

That was Fred, a first-class storyteller (it seems too crude to label him a great bullshit artist). He lived up to his reputation in Yalgoo on many occasions, but the incident I remember best was the local snooker competition, which was promoted by Frank Sabbadini. The event was eagerly anticipated by the town and Fred did his best to extol his snooker prowess to all who would listen. The big night came, and it was Fred's turn to break. A complete miscue saw the white ball rise high in the air and land in the middle of the other balls, three "big ones" went straight in the pockets. Fred proceeded to sink the rest of the "big ones" and then the black ball without his opponent getting a single shot, the Yalgoo pub was in stunned silence. Fred didn't win another game in the competition – it really was a miscue followed by some very lucky shots, but he had us all convinced for a fleeting moment. A year or two later while having a Sunday off in the New Guinea bush, I was listening to "Family Favourites" on ABC radio when a Mrs Bichard from Guernsey requested a song for her favourite son Adolphus working in the wilds of Australia. Fred had a few problems living that one down. He eventually went back to university and graduated in geology at a quite mature age; there followed a successful career in the Australian mineral exploration industry.

One of the contract geophysical crew, Cedric Johnson, merits a brief mention. Cedric was a big lump of a bloke who I think played a couple of rugby league games for North Sydney. When sober, Cedric was shy and polite, but when inebriated he was a raving lunatic. The story I like best about Cedric is second hand and happened sometime after Yalgoo. Cedric was working with a crew in remote country in the Keep River area near the border between the Northern Territory and Western Australia. With the wet season fast approaching, the crew had decided to decamp for the summer. When the plane arrived to pick them up, they realised it was a seat short. Cedric was nominated to stay and catch another charter the next day if the weather held up. Not wanting to be stranded on his own for the wet season Cedric objected rather strongly and after some heated exchanges demanded to be flown in the nose baggage compartment. The pilot was very reluctant, but Cedric was adamant and survived the short flight to Kununurra.

To have a break from Yalgoo we would head down to Geraldton on the coast for a weekend every fortnight. The break as always was somewhat boozy especially because like Mt Isa there were then two two-hour drinking sessions on a Sunday. One of these I remember as a great escape. I had been dancing with a young lady quite a bit on Saturday night and we caught up again on the dance floor at the Sunday morning session. While dancing she suddenly stiffened up a bit and suggested that when the current song ended, I might move to the opposite side of the dance floor. Hear was I wondering what I had done so wrong when she offered an explanation. "My husband has just walked in, he's a professional fisherman and has come back early." I followed her instructions to the letter and after a brief discussion our crew decided it was in our interests to move to another pub as far from this one as possible.

The final departure from Yalgoo just before Christmas led to some more interesting flights. Our crew was a bit the worse for wear after our last night in town. About ten of us boarded the Cessna and I happened to get the seat beside the pilot, who quickly summed up our parlous state and kindly flew at maximum altitude to reduce cabin oxygen, twenty minutes into the flight he suggested I look around to check on my mates: they all slept like babies for the entire flight to Perth. Those of us continuing east found a new lease of life in the Perth airport bar and were well away again by the time we boarded the "drunk flight" to Melbourne just after midnight. I fell asleep as we were heading for takeoff in Perth and woke as we were on our final descent into Melbourne; I rate it my best ever flight.

I travelled back to the midwest of Western Australia in about 2008 to attend an Aboriginal heritage meeting with native title claimants in Mount Magnet. My daughter Emma, who was working in Perth at the time, took a few days off and came on the trip with me. We decided to drive back to Perth via Geraldton rather than the inland route. I suggested a beer in Yalgoo for old times' sake, but on entering the bar we found that the surroundings and patrons looked like something out of *Deliverance*. Emma was quick to drag me out saying she was totally spooked, so I was only able to grab a quick six-pack for the road. It's so sad to see the demise of once vibrant and friendly little hamlets and towns. Mullewa further towards Geraldton has also gone backwards, here farming families have moved to Geraldton and the farmers just come to Mullewa to work their properties during the week, with fewer children the once top-class educational institutions are in steep decline and the fabric of the town has suffered.

An introduction to underground etiquette

While in the west I managed a work trip back to the old stamping ground, Kalgoorlie, in company with Garth Wilson, the geologist in charge of Placer's WA office. Garth was a bit prickly and old school, although a companionable enough bloke, and his manner led to a less than enjoyable first experience of an underground mining operation. We had arranged to visit a small nickel mine not far from Kambalda. In those days miners were paid by the amount of ore they could move in a shift, so were keen to extract as much as possible. The mine manager gave us a good tour underground and left us with this miner at a working face which the miner was preparing to blast; we were to meet the mine manager back at the shaft as he had some other work underground to attend to. After about ten minutes of our examination of the rock face the miner was ready to blast, but Garth persisted in perusing every minute geological feature for the next half hour while the miner became more progressively and visibly agitated. Garth eventually relented and he and I headed back down the drive to the shaft. As soon as we turned a corner and were out of the direct blast path, the miner set off the blast. The noise and the rush of wind we experienced in that drive was horrendous for a first-timer like me. When we finally got back to Kalgoorlie later that afternoon, I insisted that Garth shout me several beers at the Palace Hotel to settle my nerves.

A taste of the Pilbara

A trip to Shaw River in the Pilbara region then to Lansdowne Station in the Kimberleys in the warmer months of October and November provided more memorable moments in the West. The trip started out badly: I had just returned to Sydney after an extended time in Isa and was anticipating a bit of social life in the big smoke. That wasn't to be as I was told to get on a plane to Perth ASAP as there was urgent work pending at Shaw River. Arriving in Perth the following day I was informed that the trip had been postponed for a week (they hadn't bothered to inform head office), so I spent a leisurely week at a motel and on the beach at Scarborough in the days before Bondy constructed his monstrosity there. This I admit wasn't too shabby, but I would have preferred to stay in Sydney.

A week later, four of us plus the pilot spent about five hours cooped up in a tiny single engine plane on a charter flight to Shaw River. Unable to fly above the summer turbulence, it was a very bumpy ride with only a brief fuel and toilet stop in Meekatharra. The Shaw River tin mining operation had declined by that time to just a two to three-man operation, but the camp, built for a much larger operation, was more than adequate if somewhat spartan. The camp drinking water was the worst I've ever encountered in Australia and made conditions unpleasant in temperatures hovering around the old century mark.

Our assessment crew comprised American consultant Tom Murphy and his wife, Irish field assistant Mike and me. Tom was to assess the current mining operations and potential for expansion while Mike and I undertook hammer seismic surveys to define any buried river channels in the immediate area.

Tom, a most affable fellow, then about 65, was a silica sand expert contracted by Kaiser to assess the potential for specialty metal minerals (tin, tantalite, rare earths) in beach sand and alluvial deposits throughout Australia and New Zealand. Nothing, however, quite prepared Tom for the heat, dust, flies and rotten water at Shaw River, so his assessment was brief. His wife found conditions even worse; it must have been an over-the-top culture shock for her, which was exacerbated by the local miners who, sensing her discomfort, proceeded to behave like polite pigs, for instance drinking the communal milk direct from the jug, or scooping ice cream out of containers using very dirty hands. The poor lady was quite appalled.

Mike and I got on with the hammer seismic survey, which was largely unsuccessful in locating buried river channels. Instead of the more normal use of explosives to send a sound wave into the ground, in this technique a large metal plate on the ground is hit with a sledgehammer to create the sound wave. As the sledgehammer operator, poor old Mike was exhausted most days while I sat back and operated the recording instruments.

A Kimberley legend

We finished with Shaw River after about ten days and I then caught up with Fred Bichard in Port Hedland before heading on to the Kimberley region. After an extended dinner in Hedland Fred and I caught MacRobertson Miller's Fokker Friendship service to Derby at 3.30am the next morning. From there it was on to Halls Creek in a Twin Otter; the landing at Halls Creek was a bit bumpy as we hit a willy-willy just as we were landing. After collecting a hire vehicle and buying supplies we were off to Lansdowne Station in the heart of the Kimberley region. Arriving there late afternoon we met and got directions from Rod Quilty, the station owner, then headed on for an hour or so to our campsite for the next ten days.

As we were limited in supplies and logistical back up, Fred and I decided to rough it and get out of the oppressive November heat ASAP. There was no washing or changes of clothes, no refrigeration or ice, just eat, drink, work and sleep. Our brief was to do an assessment of narrow uranium-bearing beds within the massive, spectacular cliff-forming King Leopold Sandstone. This required walking into canyons in the formation to gain access. Nearing the end of the trip we had one rather long traverse to undertake and realised carrying enough water could be a problem so our drink supply comprised a can of pineapple juice each plus whatever water remained in the creek bed we were following. We reached the end of the traverse after about two and a half hours, sat down to have our juice and a snack, then headed back. The afternoon sun was a killer, the return journey took double the time and for the last two hours we had no water. Fred, who was about ten years older than me, desperately wanted to sit down several times and was physically sick but we just kept on walking. On reaching our vehicle we both took a full water bag off the front of the vehicle and gulped it down. At the time I didn't think much about it but in retrospect I think we could have perished if we had sat down to rest. It was a lesson well learnt and never again did I attempt such a long trek in hot Outback weather without water.

On finishing our work we headed into Lansdowne to see if we could have a shower and clean up before heading off the next day. In talking to Rod Quilty, I mentioned that my sister Ann was a flying doctor in Derby; Rod of course knew her well. Anyway, Fred and I had long showers in the stockmen's quarters, disposed of our ten days wear clothes in the nearest bin and were having a quiet and cool rum and ice with Jim Ruck, the head stockman, when this apparition appeared out of the darkness: it was Rod with a carton of red-hot Swan longnecks. He proceeded to hand them around and, in an hour or so we had polished off the carton. I now understood the meaning of "Kimberley cool" but can't say they were the best beers I've ever tasted, although Rod downed them with relish. As we chatted then and later talking to sister Ann in Derby we learned something of the legend of Rod Quilty. Rod was the son of the stockman, grazier and poet Tom Quilty, who was a pioneer of the Kimberley beef industry. Rod, with his young wife Edna from Julia Creek in Queensland, purchased Lansdowne around 1952 and over the next 30 years of trial and tribulation developed the million-acre property into a profitable beef production enterprise.

Rod suffered badly from asthma and other health issues, especially in the wet season, and to alleviate his suffering he had bottles of whiskey (he didn't like rum) stashed at stockyards and gates all over Lansdowne. Often the grog was locked up by Edna and indeed he had raided the same shed to provide us with those longnecks. Ann told the story of being on the flying doctor radio schedule one morning when Rod took over the airwaves (Edna and the children were on holidays in Perth at the time) and proceeded to discuss the lineage of many of the Kimberley cattlemen. Ann tried to get him off the air but not before the entire region had heard most of the monologue. The story goes that there were a few big fights at the ensuing Halls Creek races that year. On departing Lansdowne the next morning, a little ill from the warmish longnecks, Fred and I decided to search around a gate some ten kilometres down the track, sure enough there was a half-full bottle of Johnnie Walker stashed in a shady spot.

8
Going Bush Happy

Placer- Papua New Guinea, 1970–71

When told my next job would be in Papua New Guinea (PNG) I was very excited both to be going overseas for the first time and to be going to such an exotic place. The "Tasminex" nickel share boom had just happened and the day before leaving I tried all day to ring a stockbroker but with no luck. After the stock exchange had closed I finally got onto a broker and asked to buy a quantity of Metal Investment Holdings shares at best the next day and to sell them in two days' time. The company held ground adjacent to Tasminex at Mt Venn in Western Australia. The broker was a bit reluctant to do this but when I told him that I might have little if any communication once in New Guinea he agreed to the transaction. Finishing work that afternoon, it was off to the Newcastle Hotel for pre-flight drinks with geophysical colleagues Ian Lilly and Pat Hillsdon before heading off to Mascot airport.

Flying in a Different World

The flight headed off from Sydney at about 9.00pm in an old Ansett Lockheed Electra (same plane as the Orion surveillance planes flown by the RAAF). After a stop in Brisbane we headed off just before midnight and of course there were free drinks on an international flight, an opportunity I wasn't about to miss. After I ordered my second beer the lady sitting next to me who was trying to sleep asked if I intended to drink all night. When I replied in the affirmative, she switched on her passenger light and said, "Well I might as well join you." She was thirty to forty-ish and a resident of Rabaul in New Britain, and over the next few hours I got a potted history and a rundown on what to do and not to do in PNG over numerous drinks. We arrived in Port Moresby just on sunrise and after a short stop proceeded on to Lae on the north coast in the same plane. It was my first taste of the spectacular and rugged terrain that is Papua New Guinea.

After bidding farewell to my newfound Rabaul friend I headed out to an old DC3 for the short flight to Bulolo. The flight followed the Markham Valley, but what I didn't expect were the towering mountains on either side of the plane. It was quite an experience flying between these majestic citadels, especially after the previous night's antics. After greetings at the airport I spent a brief time in the local office before heading to the single men's quarters, where I was able to rest for the remainder of the day. As always there had been a change of plans and instead of heading to New Britain the following day it was instead a short drive to the old gold mining area at Edie Creek.

Gold by the Pan Full

The drive to Edie Creek was an eye-opener, very scenic between Bulolo and Wau with a chance to catch glimpses of the massive old dredges that had been used for previous alluvial mining operations. Wau itself was a rather idyllic little town in those days. The ten-plus-kilometre trip on to Edie Creek was both spectacular and scary: in the short distance the road gains another kilometre in altitude. Blue Point was particularly inspiring: sitting on the steep slopes of Mt Kaindi the narrow one lane road drops away near vertically for about 300 metres, a point where there have been numerous landslides. The bulldozer driver who maintained the road had constant nightmares about going over the edge when he had to rebuild the road after each landslide. There wasn't much left of the mining operations at

Edie Creek, just a wooden house, large shed and old mine workings. The scenery was sensational and, as Edie Creek was above 2000 metres, a similar height to Mt Kosciuszko, the climate was delightful with warm days, cold nights and no humidity, unlike the coastal areas.

The region was originally inhabited by the Kukuku tribe, who had a reputation as fierce warriors who disposed of many an early gold prospector, and rumour had it that there were still some tribesmen in the area. My work at Edie Creek was running magnetic surveys along all the tracks in the region. One day on the old "Bulldog Track", an area of legendary World War II warfare, on my own, kilometres away from camp, I had the distinct feeling I was being watched but never saw anyone. It was probably only one of two times I felt threatened by or at least apprehensive of bush natives. I early on learned that a native advising that it was "lic lic long way" (meaning not far) to some destination had to be taken with a grain of salt, with such distances varying anywhere from ten minutes to two days walk. There was plenty of wildlife around and, again on my own, I steered clear of what was the largest python I have ever seen – at least six metres. Venomous snakes like Australian varieties and cassowaries were to be avoided too, but if you were accompanied by natives, it was never a worry as they scattered frantically into the bush if any were sighted leaving you looking around for where the danger was.

Our timber house accommodation at Edie Creek was spartan but had an open fireplace, which was delightful in the cold evenings. The nearby native boys' shed was crowded and much more basic; sounds of merriment emanated from the so-called "haus banana" during the evenings. We shared our house on Tuesday and Wednesday nights with gold miner Tony Herriot. Tony had been a patrol officer for many years before he acquired a very profitable small-scale gold mining operation at Edie Creek and seemed to have the best job in the world. He lived in an idyllic setting in the township of Wau and had several natives working his mine all week, pressure hosing down the established working rock face to expose the gold-rich quartz veins. His working week commenced with a late Tuesday afternoon drive to Edie Creek followed by a sociable evening with our work crew.

The next morning, armed with his mining equipment – a large screwdriver and gold pan – he would set off on a one-hour walk to his mine site. Once there and having paid his miners, he would spend most of his day levering out the gold-rich quartz before returning to the house on sunset with his pan laden with twenty or thirty troy ounces of gold. He returned to Wau the next day to process the gold.

At that time Tony could only earn $50,000 per annum in gold production (equivalent to at least $500,000 today) without paying any tax. So he earned exactly that amount. When he finally decided to sell his mine and move back to Australia, his stereo equipment and other furnishings were all surprisingly heavy: perhaps you could say they were lined with gold. Rumour had it that much of his windfall was quickly lost on the stockmarket during the mining share collapse of that era.

Back in Bulolo I was to meet another legendary character, Tom Lega, who was Placer's advisor on all things PNG. Tom, working in Sydney in 1939, tried to enlist when World War II broke out, but was told to come back when he turned twenty-one. Not wanting to wait, Tom joined his brother in Bulolo working on the gold dredges and immediately enlisted in the New Guinea Volunteer Rifles. After the Japanese invaded, he was heavily involved in what was largely guerilla warfare in the Lae-Wau-Salamau regions in northeast New Guinea. He later moved further west along the north coast of New Guinea, and was based in Saidor, Madang and Wewak, where he led native patrols into the hinterlands, which the Japanese had heavily infiltrated. On one of these patrols Tom's small group engaged and defeated a much larger Japanese party, Tom was wounded but managed to get back to Madang unassisted. He was awarded the Military Medal for this action. At one point he also received a bullet wound to the knee from American friendly fire. Stories go that few Japanese prisoners were ever taken during New Guinea actions and that any support for the Japanese from the native population wasn't tolerated, with extreme deterrent measures used, such as forced exits from aeroplanes in flight. Tom, by then in his fifties, still looked as tough as teak and had a rigid approach to dealing with natives, insisting that we always deal with them in a "masta-boi" relationship with minimal social interaction. This went against the grain but thanks to Tom's instructions we never had any issues with some of the more remote tribes.

After finishing the work at Edie Creek there were a few days R&R in Bulolo before setting off for New Britain. The Bulolo pub was a dream, lazing beside the pool with native boys regularly bringing South Pacific lagers to your lounge-chair. Back to the single men's quarters for a sleep I was amazed the next morning to find the previous night's dirty clothes washed and ironed. Each of us paid a native boy one dollar a week to look after our rooms; given there were about a dozen of us, he was earning a top wage, and when you consider we stayed in the bush for six-week stints and then arrived back in Bulolo in dribs and drabs, he was on a very good wicket, so he looked after us very well. The tropical fruits on offer with breakfast at the adjacent mess were also sensational. The other great pleasure on the late-night walk home from the Bulolo pub was to call into the bakery and grab a loaf of freshly baked bread for an early morning snack.

A tropical paradise

Finally, we were off to New Britain; the charter flight left Lae travelling across the crystal blue waters of the Solomon Sea to the north coast of New Britain flanked by quite incredible coral reefs. Palm trees were everywhere as we landed at Hoskins airport and the view northwest across the water to Talasea with its magnificent smoking volcano made the place look like an island paradise. Later, working in the Central Highlands, we were exposed to some less pleasant aspects of New Britain like regular downpours, leeches, scorpions, centipedes, tropical ulcers, foot rot, malaria and ceaseless clambering up and down mountains.

After a brief break at Hoskins, it was a 50-kilometre Jet Ranger helicopter flight to Placer's Plesyumi project near the head of the Metelen River in Central New Britain. The flight was uneventful but provided a close-up look at the rugged terrain we'd be working in. The camp, nestled beside the Metelen River, occupied a cleared area about the size of a football field with half a dozen typical bush buildings constructed of small timber tied or wired together, with a covering of clear plastic on the roof and walls to keep the rain out. The buildings were raised half a metre or so off the ground to avoid the mud. Apart from sleeping quarters there was a large kitchen/mess/recreation building, a small trade store and a long-drop toilet with a great view of the river.

Many of the local natives had never seen a white person, but were friendly, and most spoke some pidgin English. Placer had established the trade store to allow the native population to spend their wages on staple foods and goods like lamps, torches, axes and radios, which were otherwise only available to them by undertaking an arduous two to three-day walk to the north coast. They were paid one dollar per day, which was above the going rate in larger towns, but were only permitted by the company to work three weeks at a time before returning to their villages for at least a week to tend their food crops.

We initially tried to run geophysical surveys by clearing straight lines to run the surveys along as done in Australia. The lines were cleared by a gang of natives with axes. I am amazed there was never a fatality as very large trees continually came crashing down, but there were plenty of axe cuts and it was a new experience to sew up a leathery native foot. The natives' feet were so tough they didn't appear to feel any pain during such procedures. Another hazard for the natives was our generating large and potentially fatal electric currents through the ground via an electrode which consisted of a large shallow hole, lined with Alfoil and soaked with salt and water to achieve a good electrical contact. Despite our warnings to avoid them, some natives still managed to step on/in these holes and received quite a jolt, but their tough feet seemed to save them. Back in Australia the same type of electrodes have been known to kill straying cattle. Battling the terrain along these straight survey lines was exhausting and on each trip to New Guinea I lost at least six kilograms in the first week of field work. Eventually we modified our survey procedures and subsequent calculations by working along curved contour lines wherever practicable.

During the first few days at Plesyumi I developed tropical ear because of swimming in the Bulolo public pool, which I had been warned against; the Bulolo pub pool was safe, however. My ears and one side of my face were swollen; when Lee Furlong arrived by helicopter, he took one look at me and ordered me to get on the return helicopter flight to Hoskins/Kwalakesi for treatment. Treatment was by medically trained nuns at the nearby mission and I still remember my concern at having peroxide injected into my ears with a large syringe, but then the joy and relief, as my ears were drained with the same syringe. The best part was I had to spend a few days recuperating on the coast lazing on beautiful beaches all day then heading to the local club for evening drinks.

Returning to Plesyumi, day-to-day life was never dull; there were regular earth tremors, probably caused by the pending major volcanic eruption at Mt Ulawun about 150 kilometres to the northeast; we walked everywhere and our feet were always wet, leading to foot rot after about two weeks. Good quality waterproof boots were useless in these conditions, and we were issued with green canvas "Japanese jungle boots", which at least drained quickly. These boots had a maximum life of about six weeks in these conditions. As our immunity wore down after about four weeks, tropical ulcers also became a concern, especially from leech bites. A day rarely went by without suddenly feeling a machete wielded by one of the natives sliding down your arm or leg to remove a bloated leech. Due to this reduced immunity and in order not to go "bush happy", shifts in the bush were usually limited to six weeks. This didn't always happen and at one stage two work colleagues, Bill Hodgson and Ian Ward, were somehow into their fourteenth week straight. They had indeed gone "bush happy" and were working in bare feet. They refused instructions to take a break until they finally acceded under threat of being sacked.

The local natives considered flying foxes ("blak bocis") a delicacy, and one day asked to use the camp shotgun to shoot a few. They were duly issued with the gun and three cartridges and headed off. We heard the three shots fired but then another three and yet another three. Shortly after, a young native boy of about five came back with the shotgun, but no adults were to be seen. He was sent back to get the original borrowers, who about an hour later skulked back into the camp. The excitement of bagging a huge meal had got the better of their judgement and they had apparently acquired the extra cartridges from the trade store when no-one was around. They were sent back to their village for a week as punishment.

One of our geologists, Peter Atherton, had decided to spend a day in camp compiling geological map data. At some stage during the morning he was enjoying the river vistas from the throne in the long-drop toilet when it suddenly collapsed and next thing he was four metres down, uninjured, but standing waist deep in it. With everyone out in the bush for the day he was literally in deep shit. He then remembered the cook should be in camp so yelled his lungs out until the cook came running. Once out, Peter headed for the river and sat shoulder-deep in there for the rest of the day though he said the memory of the stench stayed with him for weeks afterwards.

Scorpions were another camp hazard and at one time or another we all got bitten. The pain was quite intense and would extend all the way up the bitten limb to the torso and last for a few hours. Before heading for bed, you would always check blankets to ensure they were not fly blown and check bedding for scorpions; likewise in the morning you would check all clothes and boots for scorpions. Charles, a young Englishman, for some reason chose bright coloured overalls as his field attire and one morning, forgetting the scorpion check, he got himself tightly in the overalls when he began yelling and going into the craziest of spasms. He was attempting to get out of the overalls and all the rest of us could do was roll about laughing. When he finally divested himself of the overalls he was covered in bites from not one but three scorpions. He was very sore, feverish and quite ill for several days after.

Tom Smith, an older Canadian, was the Placer geologist in charge of PNG operations and was slowly winding down into retirement. He ran a radio schedule with all field crews at 7.00 each morning. He had one radio transmitter by his bedside and another more powerful one in the adjacent office back in Bulolo.

Taking the view that if we were up and about then Tom should be too, we always pretended we couldn't receive his initial signals from his bedside, so after a few minutes he would grudgingly tell us to hold on and ten minutes later the signal would boom through from the office transmitter. I feel sure Tom knew what we were up to.

A fair exchange

After Plesyumi, our crew moved on to another prospect, Yau Yau, about seventy kilometres to the northeast. One of the pleasures here was our regular trade with the natives, bags of coarse salt used for electrodes as previously mentioned, in exchange for freshly caught river prawns. The bush natives had a salt deficiency and would sit round gorging on handfuls of coarse salt while we thoroughly enjoyed the prawns; it was a good deal all round.

Regarding food, our choices were severely limited because of helicopter availability and costs. There was no refrigeration in camp, so no point in having beer or other alcohol, and any fresh meat was hung in a bush safe, so had a very short shelf-life. After a few days it was just variations on bully beef and tinned fish and vegies, and maybe some occasional taro from the native gardens. I think we must have suffered a sugar deficiency as when the chopper arrived with supplies we would each grab a block of chocolate as a priority and immediately munch it down.

While at Yau Yau there was a major eruption at Mt Ulawun. There were no safety risks at Yau Yau apart from the odd earth tremor but our chopper was seconded to the volcano site to carry out local evacuations. The skills of our helicopter pilots were often the subject of discussion. The long-term PNG employees favoured a couple of ex–British RAF pilots who always took the shortest, fastest route. I preferred an older American who had a long history in crop dusting and was still alive. He tended to follow rivers wherever possible and was forever looking out for emergency landing sites, although he had a disconcerting habit of smoking a cigar while checking the fuel tank. I later learnt that Avgas does not exude the very inflammable fumes that petrol does. The pilot none of us particularly liked to travel with was ex–Australian army and ex-Vietnam. He had suffered some traumas in Vietnam and was visibly nervous. On one flight encountering turbulence he panicked and ejected a net loaded with expensive geophysical gear hooked underneath the chopper. Amazingly a native party recovered the gear, but it was well beyond repair. Chopper flying was always an uncertain affair because once rain clouds set in on most afternoons flying was impossible.

Burning the toast in Bulolo

Steve Dawe was a young character who really found his feet in PNG. I first met him at the Pegmont project south of Mt Isa. Steve had been schooled at one of the more elite Brisbane high schools but on completion he had just one ambition, to become an outback ringer, so he headed west. By the time he joined Placer he had learnt his trade well and could turn his hand to just about anything. In PNG his keen ear gave him wonderful linguistic skills: he could encounter tribes with little or no Pidgin English and converse in their language within two or three days. There may have been an ulterior motive for honing these skills, as he did fancy the native ladies. He eventually left Placer and ran his own trading vessel around the PNG islands.

On an R&R break in Bulolo, Steve and some workmates decided to have a day out at a local dam above Bulolo. Floating on lilos and sipping on an occasional South Pacific Lager, the boys were having a relaxing day when Steve and his lilo disappeared, sucked down into an unobserved whirlpool and then a concrete pipe running through the dam. Steve fully considered the fact that his time was up as these pipes usually have a grid across them at the outlet. His luck was in that day – no grid, and he came spewing out of the pipe with a short tumble down the dam wall and into a lower pool of water. When he recovered from the shock and extracted himself from the water, Steve decided a bender was in order, to celebrate his incredible luck. There were more beers at the dam before venturing back to the Bulolo pub to continue the bender. By midnight he was suitably inebriated but his night wasn't quite over. Staggering back to the single men's quarters he decided to pick up a freshly baked loaf at the bakery. He nor anyone else knows exactly what went on at the bakery, but he managed to scare all the native bakers off the premises, proceeded to try to run the ovens himself and ultimately flaked on the bakery floor. Bulolo smelt of very burnt toast the next morning and there was no bread to be had for at least a day until ovens were checked and cleaned. Being a small town, word got around quickly and Steve's name was mud. However, when the full story of Steve's lucky escape came to light all was forgiven.

A smoking time bomb

When I had finished my stint in New Britain, the first stop was the mission clinic at Hoskins for a shot of penicillin to counter the tropical ulcers. The native medico produced a huge and very rusty syringe which he wanted to plunge into my backside, I was having none of that and insisted it went into my arm while reasoning the penicillin would hopefully counter any effects from the rusty needle. Instead of the usual charter I took the commercial flight in a Twin Otter to Rabaul. It was a roundabout trip but well worth it for the spectacular scenery on a surprisingly clear afternoon. From Hoskins we travelled due south to Gasmata on the southern coast, flying directly over the Plesyumi camp on the way. From Gasmata the plane headed east for Pomio, another idyllic little hamlet on the coast, then north again to the then splendid capital of New Britain at Rabaul. On descent into Rabaul the plane flew over the smoking Vulcan volcanic vent.

Rabaul was a tropical paradise and its coastal people were generally taller and healthier looking. Blond hair was in vogue at the time, particularly popular with the ladies, but also adopted by many native men. After a congenial night of luxury at the Rabaul Travelodge I had a morning to kill before the flight back to Lae in the late afternoon. As luck would have it Placer were in the process of commissioning a new landing barge to assist with their island mineral investigations. I managed to get a ride and spent a most pleasant time cruising the splendid harbour around Rabaul and nearby Kokopo.

In 1994 the volcanic vents of Vulcan and Tavurvur erupted simultaneously, the subsequent ash effectively destroyed the picturesque Rabaul and eruptions of the Tavurvur volcanic vent have continued on a regular basis to the present day. Out of a total population of 17,000 in 1994 only about 4,000 have remained in the immediate Rabaul area; the remaining population relocated about twenty kilometres west along the coast to Kokopo, which is now the administrative capital of Eastern New Britain.

The prime exploration use of the new coastal barge was to drop usually one but occasionally two Placer exploration personnel at the mouth of each river. Natives from the nearest village would then be employed as porters and over a two to three–week period the field party would trek to the headwaters of each river in the mountains, sampling sediments from every tributary of the river encountered on the trek. This proved a most effective technique for initially defining copper occurrences for later follow-up. At the end of the trek the natives would clear an area to allow helicopter access. A helicopter would subsequently pick up the Placer personnel, the samples and any equipment, leaving the natives to make their own way back to the coast.

The beat of the kundu

By the time of my second trip to New Guinea in mid-1971 Ansett were flying Boeing 727 jets into Port Moresby and Lae, so the trip was considerably shorter and a little more sober. John Sandy had replaced Tom Smith in charge of New Guinea operations, so instead of heading straight for the bush there was an extended afternoon reunion at the Bulolo pub. Next day it was off to the project area in the Finisterre Range to the north of Lae and inland from Saidor.

As we flew in and out of Saidor to refuel the chopper, the smoking volcanic peaks of the offshore Long Island were visible and the peaks of the Finisterre Range, averaging about 4,000 metres elevation, made for some rather rugged and spectacular terrain.

There were just four or five of us in camp at any one time, with a native village on the next plateau maybe 800 metres away, with the magnificent backdrop of the high peaks of the Finisterre Ranges. Luckily, we didn't have to scale them; the highest peak Mt Boising (4,150 metres) was only officially recorded as climbed in June 2014. Every evening in camp we were treated to several hours of kundu drumming across the valleys and ranges, which was initially rather eerie but came to be a rather reassuring evening sound. Nobody could have moved through the area without every village being aware.

Most of the natives in this area had had some contact with Europeans and spoke pidgin English, so communication was quite easy. The area inland from Saidor had been the subject of heavy fighting between the Americans and Japanese during World War II, but whether it reached as far into the Finisterre Range as our project area is unclear. The villagers invited us to a big feast one day when they were roasting a large pig. Whether they like their pig cooked a bit rare or whether they were just very hungry and couldn't wait I'm not sure, but the pork we received was soft and barely cooked. We all pretended to enjoy it but didn't rush back for seconds.

The natives had a lend of us with bush kangaroos: they would always have one caged and supposedly ready to eat, and we would purchase it off them to release back into the wild. In retrospect I think it was just one pet that always returned to the village, which we paid for repeatedly. While we were in camp the fourth manned moon landing by the Apollo 15 crew took place; it was being broadcast live in pidgin by Radio Australia, and it was fascinating to watch the reactions of the natives as the broadcast unfolded. It happened to be a rare clear night and the natives were staring up at the moon in disbelief – I somehow think they may have thought the white fellas were trying to have a big lend of them. They certainly didn't appear convinced.

We always took Sunday off when working in the New Guinea bush, not for any religious observance but simply to wash our clothes, attempt to dry out our boots, write some letters and just generally recover a little from the rigours of the harsh terrain. Apart from our own cassette music, entertainment was limited to *Family Favourites* on Radio Australia in the days before *Macca on Sunday*. To relieve the boredom, we did some strange things including the taping of a World Championship farting contest, which was narrated superbly by Steve Dawe with his Western Queensland ringer's twang. We had prepared well, eating copious quantities of onions and baked beans the previous evening but it was Steve's sparkling commentary which made it into a classic. Every now and then he would burst out laughing as he became more inventive with the narrative. It ended with one of the contestants, Big Blurt, disgracing himself and being disqualified. That memorable scene from Mel Brooks's *Blazing Saddles* had nothing on this production. I treasured my only tape copy but lost it during the mayhem of Cyclone Tracy in Darwin some years later.

The Mount Hagan Show

On our first break from the Finisterre Range four of us, including Steve Dawe, geologist John Poole and I, made a spur of the moment decision to head up to the Mount Hagen show for the weekend, after all it was merely a tad over a 500 kilometre drive each way and we had John's trusty old Holden station wagon housed back in Bulolo to get us there. We were offered two bits of advice by the locals: one, don't stop if you hit a pedestrian, but head as fast as you can for the nearest kiap shop (police station), as the locals are very strong on payback, and two, get right off the road (if you can) if there is a truck heading the other way, as they simply will not budge.

So off we headed after a big night in Lae with few spares or tools, an esky full of beer and as an afterthought some light sleeping bags in case there was no accommodation available. In those days the Highlands or Okuk Highway was mainly dirt and often no more than one lane wide up in the Highlands. The first flat stretch following the Markham Valley was relatively smooth and wide, but we copped a broken windscreen from a rock thrown up by a passing truck. Soon after, we reached the narrow Kassam Pass, which rises 1500 metres from the Markham Valley over a very narrow and precipitous ten kilometres. It wasn't long before we were forced into a deep gutter on the side of the road by a passing truck. After extricating ourselves from this hole with some difficulty, it was onwards and upwards to the mountain township of Kainantu. Through some stroke of luck the town mechanic was able to extract a windscreen from a local wreck and attach a windscreen, albeit held in place by much tape and a few dabs of araldite.

By that stage it was late afternoon, so we decided to stay in this beautiful little oasis, heading for the colonial-style pub, boasting fabulous views across the Highlands. We decided to head for the front, "natives" bar as we all looked like bulldozer drivers, covered in dust from the broken windscreen. The bar was congenial enough but by about 6.00pm it was getting rowdy and the barman urged us as Caucasians to move to the more conducive lounge bar reserved for the exclusive use of the local expats. The lounge bar was filled with well-attired ladies and safari suited men, but we were greeted cordially enough and were welcome to stay as long as we remained as unobtrusive as was possible under the circumstances.

It turned out to be the weekly bingo night and we were urged to join in, but as it turned out we couldn't stop winning, so one of the filthy "bulldozer drivers" would have to regularly step into the limelight to collect our winnings. Regardless it was a great night, we had a good feed, and the crowd dispersed fairly quickly when the game finished. We adjourned to the lounge bar with one native barman looking after us. We had earlier informally booked in for the night but had not gone through the booking procedure of paying or obtaining room keys let alone knowing where the rooms were located. A bit later we realised the bar waiter had disappeared and despite our best efforts we were unable to locate either the barman or any other staff. What to do? Simple really, we served ourselves at the bar for another couple of hours, leaving adequate payment on the bar, then let ourselves out of the building and slept on the lawn with our meagre sleeping bags. Fortunately, the late-night drinks shielded us somewhat from the cold mountain night air.

Waking early the next morning we decided that a rapid departure was in order as we still had about 250 kilometres of rough mountain roads to cover to reach Mount Hagen. The drive, which we completed without further incident, must be one of the world's more spectacular highways. Daulo Pass, which peaks at 2,478 metres, tested out the old Holden, but the previous incident on Kassam Pass had prepared us well for kamikaze truck drivers. On arrival in Mount Hagen, unsurprisingly there was no accommodation to be had. Steve, the language and networking guru of our party, made a few enquiries and met up with a native kiap he had previously befriended. We ended up camped under one of the local schools, which at least provided shelter and access to toilets and hot showers. The kiap also offered several "meris" (local native girls) at a cost, to keep us warm during the cold Highland nights, but we judiciously declined his hospitality.

The Mount Hagen Cultural Show was first staged in the early 1960s in order that the various tribal groups might share their cultural experiences and become a little less hostile to one another. Up to seventy-five Highlands tribal groups attend, some walking from tens to hundreds of kilometres through rugged mountain terrain, bringing many thousands of bush natives together in the Highlands capital. There are also usually a large group of expats and more adventurous overseas tourists in attendance.

The next two days of the show were spectacular to say the least, as we mingled with armed tribesmen and their families within the Mount Hagen showgrounds. Photographs were at a premium and at a cost. After paying some tribesman for photographs it was not unusual to be confronted by other tribesmen demanding a payment, who might have been standing 100 metres off in the background. The pidgin term "somting bilong you" (variously meaning *your problem* or basically *piss off*) proved to be the most appropriate response, though there were some uncomfortable moments. The modern world had also arrived with stunning Bird of Paradise plumed headdresses somewhat marred by sunglasses or plastic or cardboard backing.

The grand parade was the highlight each day, with thousands of tribesmen in their groups, and heavily armed with bows and arrows and axes, prancing round the oval. At this stage of the day most expats and tourists were confined to the fenced grandstand area. One felt very exposed, but the tribes were much more intent on doing harm to one another, and each group was accompanied by several "kiaps" to keep them apart. Ian Downs, a long-time Papua New Guinea patrol officer, administrator and farmer, published a novel, *The Stolen Land*, around that period, which included a native uprising at the Mount Hagen show, which I am so glad I hadn't read before attending.

A redolent chopper flight

After a gruelling two days of Highland culture, coupled with copious eating and drinking and some spartan accommodation, we headed back to Bulolo. Thankfully it was mainly downhill and went without incident though we did decide not to call in at the Kainantu pub. Another day or two in Bulolo and it was back to the bush, staying the last night in Lae for an early start to the next day's helicopter trip. As normal it was quite a night out in Lae.

With five passengers and a pilot plus personal gear, field equipment and food supplies, the French Alouette III chopper was loaded to capacity. Rather than flying round the coast to Saidor, the pilot decided to fly north directly over the Finisterre Range, reasoning that he wouldn't need to refuel at Saidor for the return trip. With the heavy load and a certain amount of turbulence, the chopper was struggling to gain sufficient altitude to fly over the 4000-metre range. After about twenty minutes of circling in an attempt to gain altitude, the pilot was getting visibly frustrated and concerned. With perfect timing Steve Dawe, with a silly grin, exuded a silent but very pungent fart reeking of the past week's spicy and boozy excesses. We were all just about retching, and the pilot went bananas; he was all for turning round and heading back to Lae, but after profuse apologies from Steve he was cajoled into continuing. Shortly after, the chopper managed to gain sufficient altitude, and we proceeded to camp, but due to the delays the pilot had to refuel at Saidor after all. All this, amid some of the most spectacular mountain scenery: it was indeed a most memorable chopper flight.

Paradise lost

In our field camps, especially in New Britain, we worked with tribes who had minimal contact with modern civilisation. Placer's policy was always to cause minimal disruption to their village activities, and it was policy that tribal natives working for the company should return to their villages for at least one week per month to tend to their native gardens. Even the opening of a small trade store at the Plesyumi camp was done with the best of intentions as a non-profit activity. I was therefore disappointed to hear that a party who visited the area a few years after the camp was closed found the tribal natives in an unhealthy state with many of their gardens, a major food source, quite run down. Our activities had created a dependence on outside goods.

Reflecting on my brief times in PNG over 50 years ago I'm somewhat saddened by a paradise lost. It could be one of the tourism capitals of the world with its tropical islands, vast coral reefs, volcanoes and magnificent mountain scenery, and it's superbly endowed with mineral riches. Prior to independence in 1975 you could walk the streets of Port Moresby or Lae any time of the night or day and feel safer than being on the streets of Sydney. Australia, by no means perfect as a long-term administrator, did its best to ensure that PNG had a fairly smooth path to independence, but something went terribly wrong, expectations were way too high and the cities and towns lapsed into a state of lawlessness, with corruption seemingly rife at all levels of government. Subsequently native forests have been ruthlessly destroyed to make way for China's voracious demand for palm oil. In New Britain alone a quarter of the lowland forest below 100 metres altitude disappeared between 1989 and 2000. If that rate of deforestation continues it's estimated that all forest below 200 metres in New Britain will be cleared by 2060. Likewise, some massive mineral resources have been developed with insufficient foresight, leading to major environmental issues and indeed civil war in the case of Bougainville (which had been in production before independence).

In 2001 I was personally tempted to return to a cushy position in Wau by way of an informal offer, until the proponents related that they had recently been waylaid by gun-toting *'raskals'* on the Lae to Wau road and left by the side of the road in just their underpants. No thank you. However, more recent and better-considered mineral developments such as the Hidden Valley gold mine and the sustainable pine forest industry at Bulolo bode well for a better future where PNG may yet reach its full potential as a modern tropical paradise.

9

Breaks in the Big Smoke

Placer/Esso-Sydney, 1969–73

Although the stays in Sydney between field trips were brief in the period 1969 to August 1973, there were a few notable occasions. Initially Phil McSharry and I rented a home due for demolition, very cheaply, located in the leafy surrounds of Pymble. Our paths rarely crossed although we both returned for graduation. In those days you could only get a drink on Sunday in NSW if you were a bona fide traveller, that is you must have travelled over eighty kilometres from your previous night's location. Phil and I had decided to catch up at the Newport Arms on Pittwater for a drink, but when we wrote in the visitors book that we had stayed in Kalgoorlie and Mt Isa respectively the night before, the doorman wasn't inclined to let us in. Fortunately, one of us still had his plane ticket, which gave credence to our claim and entry to the pub.

Enter the Bull

As 1969 went on Phil fell in love and married not too long after. He was less inclined to party, so I tended to spend more time with Peter Cockcroft plus a few others from my honours year, some of whom had remained at Sydney Uni to do postgraduate studies. Peter, "the Bull", or "Coey" as he was known, was something of an enigma; he was a year or two behind our group and was doing a

General Science degree which gave him more flexibility in subject choice, and he tried them all while taking the best part of ten years to complete his degree. Coey was renowned for his "animal acts", many of which I can't describe in these pages, but the character of the man comes through in a story from his high school days. Coey was a very good swimmer; he was the last person to beat Michael Wenden in a sprint before Wenden went on to claim Olympic gold. So, at a major interschool carnival the expectations of his whole school were on Coey's shoulders as he prepared to swim the final leg of the freestyle relay with his team then in the lead. Coey did a spectacular swallow dive and decided to swim breaststroke for that final lap, coming in a clear last. That same man some years later went to Indonesia with his oil exploration work, married into the Indonesian hierarchy, forged a career in the international oil industry and today, living in semi-retirement in Singapore, is a much sought-after motivational speaker.

After Pymble I sometimes stayed at the Wynyard or North Sydney Travelodge at company expense for brief Sydney stopovers, and later Coey and I rented another rundown house at Cremorne – well, I paid rent but only occasionally got to stay there. When I did, it was an absolute joy to travel by ferry to and from work to the office in Goldfields House at Circular Quay.

Jim Buckley's Hotel

Some of the regular haunts included once again Jim Buckley's Newcastle (Arms) Hotel on George Street. Jim Buckley was a legend, the original "mine host", who rarely served a beer but spent most nights immaculately dressed mingling with his various clients and working so hard to know each and every one by name. What a publican and gentleman. In his last years throat cancer had got to him but through one of those devices he still managed to communicate with his patrons. Jim was renowned for his patronage of budding artists, whose works adorned every spare space on the bar walls; Jim apparently bought many of the artworks himself (perhaps more than once). He also had a wonderful, more than full-size nude on one bar wall which rivalled the noted Young and Jackson Hotel's "Chloe" in Melbourne. Jim was also renowned for cashing a cheque regardless of your bona fides, I tried this myself one night (after many beers) and was presented with a cheque book to sign without further question. The cheque didn't bounce but today's cards and mobile phones destroy those times of real trust. I also remember the front bar of the Newcastle as the only place where I drank a pint of beer upside down, probably in suit and tie – not exactly sure what the bet was but I won it.

There were many other popular bars in the Rocks region, but another one that brings back memories is the News Bar at the Menzies Hotel. Its main patrons were journos, politicians and stockbrokers unless the cheeky mineral explorers of the 1970's invaded their space. What fun we had, starting a fantastic new discovery rumour in one corner of the bar and seeing it disseminated and expanded quickly round the bar and indeed onto the Sydney Stock Exchange the next day. I'm sure no profit was made as we often couldn't remember what bonanza discovery we'd invented.

The other very popular venue was the Island Trader bistro in the basement of Goldfields House. A great spot, for a year or so I drank cider down there at lunch time thinking it was non-alcoholic – wrong. There was also a late afternoon encounter down there with Placer's International MD. Several late lunching employees ran into him one afternoon when he had a rather stunning young lady in tow. We expected to be hauled across the coals the next day but never heard another word. It was probably his daughter and perhaps he was just a very tolerant MD. Another night at the Trader I learned the art of being obvious (and getting away with it). The Trader had spears and other artefacts on the restaurant walls; on this night Coey and I, in a larger group decided to very overtly take down a couple of the spears off the wall and walk out with them. We held the spears upright as we went past the checkout and as we paid our bill there was no attempt to challenge us. Once into George Street I challenged an oncoming double-decker bus with a war dance but quickly backed off. Coey and I then tested the spears on a couple of metal garbage bins, they worked so well we couldn't extract them from the bins, so adjourned to the Newcastle; on the next visit to the Island Trader we were welcome guests as usual.

A character I often ran into in Sydney was Joe Williams, a noted geophysicist hailing from Tasmania. Joe liked a tipple or two but he's the only person I know who reportedly received workers compensation for falling off a bar stool. Apparently, he was holding business discussions over lunch when he leaned back and subsequently fell off the stool, incurring some quite serious back injury.

Hunter Valley wine tasting

Hunter Valley wine trips also become part of our Sydney social fabric. JD, as usual, had befriended one of Murray Tyrell's senior winemakers and inveigled us into weekend tastings of Tyrells Private Bin Reds. The Saturday trips started with a few schooners of "Old" at Maitland amongst the many coal miners. The Old in the Hunter Valley was nothing like Sydney Old, more like a Sydney stout, but you couldn't back out with the local clientele. When we finally extracted ourselves, it was off to Tyrell's, where we tried to put on a sophisticated front. Over the years we ended up with some incredibly good reds, in fact a twenty-year-old private bin (maybe a No 6) from that era is the best red I can remember having drunk.

On these wine trips I often caught a lift with Bryan "Cheeky" Chenhall, then a PhD student at Sydney Uni. Cheeky owned an old Rover sedan which he treated more like a tank. In city traffic if Cheeky deemed that the car in front was not going at an acceptable pace, he would simply give it a rear end nudge with the trusty Rover – bumper bars actually did their job back then. The technique was much more effective than tooting the horn but was a little unnerving if you were a passenger or the other driver. After one long day of wine tasting in the Hunter, Cheeky and I for some stupid reason decided that we needed to return to Sydney that night. On the way home we picked up a hitchhiker who I suspect had a rather terrifying experience as Cheeky negotiated the newly built Newcastle Expressway with his usual aplomb while most of the way sucking on a Toohey's longneck (just to freshen the tastebuds after a hard day of red wine tasting).

Cheeky hailed from Carss Park and like myself was an avid St George rugby league supporter, and we attended many a game together at the Sydney Cricket Ground after a protracted mandatory stop at the "Coopton Cack" (Captain Cook) hotel before the game. After one of these outings Cheeky decided to go out for dinner at the St George Motorboat Club, a short distance from his home at Carss Park. Driving home he was apprehended by the constabulary and when questioned answered honestly that he must have had at least twenty-four beers over the day. The police were astounded, admitting that he appeared quite sober.

By 1972 Cheeky had completed his PhD and took a position as a lecturer in Geology at Wollongong University where he spent more than three decades. I got to know the "Gong" a little with occasional weekend visits, and Cheeky asked me to run a geophysical survey weekend for his students. The location was the Abercrombie River area inland from the Gong. The local Laggan pub was the Friday night meeting point, which meant the camp wasn't reached until late in the night and it was freezing to boot. Despite this, the excursion went really well. Two of the more dedicated drinkers of the students went on to forge notable careers in the mineral industry, Graham Carr as a research geoscientist with the CSIRO and Ted Ambler initially in the quarrying industry and later developing several small gold mines in NSW.

When back in Sydney I would also try to visit my parents at Bermagui and sister Wendy and family, who had by then moved to Bega. These were generally more quiet family get-togethers, but I do remember one Easter at Bermagui when the Griffith mafia of Sav Salvestro and Peter Payne, after many beers at O'Shea's pub, induced me and Sav's new son-in-law John McFadzean to streak down the main street. Off we headed with the barman Ira Shearing in hot pursuit. We had youth on our side and Ira gave it away after 100 metres or so. Ira was really quite a nice bloke but just a tad straight-laced. He had stopped working in the bar when next I visited, thank goodness.

Coming back from northern Australia in midwinter it was always nice to show off a good tan to the rest of the pale-skinned crowd on the Hill at the SCG. One event there wasn't so nice, however: that was the test match between South Africa and Australia on 10 July 1971 when apartheid protests were at their peak. The protesters had vowed to disrupt the game as much as possible and the rugby union stalwarts insisted the game would go on. When police apprehended protesters running onto the field, they weren't arrested but simply thrown back over the fence to be dealt with by irate rugby supporters – it was brutal to say the least. The protests worked and that was the last Springboks tour to Australia before apartheid ended in South Africa under the Mandela regime. My old schoolmate, Terry Foreman, was in the Australian rugby union team at the time but he and four other members refused to play against the Springboks, effectively ending their international careers.

A near death experience

Another not so well-known Sydney landmark, Collins Beach, also evokes fond memories. This secluded beauty spot lies within Sydney Harbour between Manly pier and North Head, and features a small waterfall at one end and a picture-perfect sandy beach. The serenity was broken whenever members of the Sydney Uni baseball club decided to use it as a venue for a keg and BBQ. Coey and JD were both club members and I got a gig as a hanger-on. Getting the 18-gallon keg, cooling and dispensing equipment, bbq, tables and food to the beach was a major undertaking. From a parking spot near where Collins Beach Road ends at the police training barracks, a rough bush track leads you to the beach. However, it proved easier to lower the heavy equipment down the sandstone cliffs than carrying it along the track. Once set up, Collins Beach was a delightful venue with the scenic waterfall, refreshing dips in Sydney Harbour and a few nudists to harass at the far end of the beach.

Collins Beach has one drawback: at high tide there is no beach, so we were barbequing and accessing the keg in knee to waist deep water. Late in the day I remember falling face down into the water and happily gurgling away with no feeling of anxiety. Luckily Coey saw me and possibly prevented a drowning when he dragged me out. Once the keg was exhausted, in complete darkness, getting all the gear back up to our vehicles was a major undertaking. When the task was completed most of us then wisely chose the rear seat of our respective vehicles to sleep off the effects of the keg. The next morning I noticed when urinating, that part of my anatomy was very tender. A nightmarish realisation then came back to me: at some stage of the afternoon Coey had either dared or somehow induced me to add another sausage to the BBQ. Fortunately, it was removed very quickly with no real damage done.

Working in the snow

From the Sydney head office there were occasional field trips in New South Wales around the Orange-Molong-Wellington and Singleton areas. Molong was the only place where I have ever undertaken field work in the snow, and back in Orange in the evening we would add a dab of snow to our beer or wine, though why we would wish to cool our drinks defies logic. Avis hire vehicles took a bit of a battering on some of these trips where a new Falcon sedan was used in preference to a company 4WD. On one evening, after a drink on a work colleague's property near Wellington, he warned me not to take the track through the creek on the way back to Orange as there had been a bit of rain falling. When I got the brand-new Avis Falcon stuck in the creek his words of advice came back to me – and he had also mentioned that there was occasional flash flooding. It was dark and wet, and I had no equipment to dig or winch the vehicle out. I had been told that if you rapidly change gears from forward to reverse and gun the accelerator you may break free of a bog. With no other option, that's what I did, and after ten minutes or so of this procedure the vehicle came roaring out of the creek. I did at least take it to a car wash before returning it to Avis, but what state the automatic transmission was in is anyone's guess.

Another time in Sydney I had ordered an Avis Falcon for a field trip, but when I went to pick it up there were none available. I was offered a brand-new Holden Monaro coupe at no extra cost, which I reluctantly accepted. I have never been a real fan of fast cars but must admit to a drag with a passing MG through the Blue Mountains on the way out to Orange. The MG driver was way too good through the bends, but the Monaro left it for dead on the straight stretches, and by luck I reached Orange safely. It was later in Orange that I got to appreciate the unbridled power of the beast when I pulled out of a parking spot, accelerated and was suddenly travelling sideways down the main street. However, this was mild compared to the next day when on heading up to Wellington on an icy road I gunned the Monaro to pass another vehicle. I don't know who was more surprised as I passed the other driver's window but with the Monaro pointing in the wrong direction. Luckily the Monaro slowed and I was able to correct the 180 degree spin but admit to stopping on the side of the road for ten minutes or so to calm the nerves. I believe these Monaros, first released in 1968, with huge power and less than adequate handling, were a death trap for inexperienced drivers. My dirt driving skills were probably all that saved me. After the field trip I returned the Monaro to Avis in Sydney vowing to never hire one again. In fact, I've avoided high powered vehicles ever since: they have no place on our busy roads.

10

What Possessed Me

Esso/McPhar, 1972–73

Looking back at my diaries I realise that I may not have been in the healthiest mental state by early 1972; I no longer had the support of my mentor Lee Furlong, who had moved onto new opportunities, I wasn't getting on with the American manager of the Mt Isa office, I was rankled by the Canadian exploration manager's constant harping on "this is the way we do it back in beautiful British Columbia" and I'd recently had a bit of a failed romance. My itinerant lifestyle essentially guaranteed that any long-term relationship was doomed. It was time for a change.

I should have and nearly did hop on a plane to London for a complete change of scenery but oh no, I took on another geophysical assignment contracting to Esso Australia Ltd through McPhar Geophysics, which involved 100 percent field work.

Esso was one of the world's largest oil producers and had decided to enter the minerals industry in a big way. With a massive budget they had employed a young American geoscientist, Fred Park, to go out and find them another Broken Hill or Mt Isa–sized deposit. Fred was the son of one of the doyens of the geology of the world's metallic mineral deposits, Charles F Park.

Fred had formulated a very technological, recipe book–based approach to making such a discovery. Large tracts of geologically suitable country across

Australia were firstly covered by airborne geophysical surveys which defined electrically conductive zones that could indicate areas of buried metallic minerals like copper, lead and zinc. Results were interpreted in the office, then the ground-truthing crew would conduct ground geophysical surveys along with some sampling and geological observations to better define the conductive zones on the ground. The final phase would involve drill testing of selected zones. All three phases of exploration were conducted by contractors who reported back to a small core of Esso project managers with effectively no interaction between the contracting groups. In hindsight, this lack of interaction and discussion was a fatal flaw in the exploration program, and no major ore deposits were discovered.

I was involved in the ground-truthing phase, responsible for interpretation of electrical geophysical surveys undertaken by the McPhar crew and for carrying out any additional geophysical surveys, sampling or geological observation. There were very occasional one or two-day head office visits between jobs to discuss results with the Esso geophysicist and project managers.

Yass

During the Esso period I must have spent a total of about six months undertaking exploration in the Yass region. Yass was a much-needed change of scenery because unlike living in bush camps in the Australian outback, here we were staying in a hotel on the main street. The town then had a population of about 10,000 and it was under an hour's drive to nearby Canberra, so life was quite civilised. Similarly, the surrounding farmland consisted of relatively small properties including very prosperous sheep studs owned by some of Australia's most wealthy, very different from the vast expanses of outback stations.

Undertaking mineral exploration in this region meant that extra care had to be taken not to disturb livestock and always to leave gates as found, either open or shut. We also became very adept at scaling the myriads of barb-wired fences in the region. Landowners were generally friendly and quite interested in our activity on their properties but working on Saturdays occasionally proved hazardous as rabbit shooting was a favourite local pastime. Yass can be a fairly chilly place, and we were witness to the tribulations faced by farmers when a cold snap decimated the newborn lamb population. It was pitiful to wander the paddocks and witness crows shredding the bodies and particularly the eyes of these helpless creatures. On the other hand, on a nice sunny day it was a joy to work in this climate and surroundings. We used to keep our pub supplied with mushrooms, regularly coming back with bucket loads after a day of field work.

The Australian Hotel was run by a very friendly Dutch-born couple with a young family. Because our crew was providing a regular source of accommodation income, we really had the run of the place. Our group comprised me and the McPhar IP crew of Brian Rau, Gary Colmer and Steve Jewitt. People were swapped around from time to time, but these were the main players.

Brian Rau was a chick magnet but was such a gentleman he rarely took advantage. At least twice in Yass he found the same barmaid in his bed and had to gently and politely get her to leave. With this ability to attract the opposite sex he was a good man to hang around with and over the stay in Yass we must have met many of the town's eligible young ladies. Brian was also a dedicated geophysical survey operator who must have spent the greater part of his life in the field. Together with his brother Graham he later formed Solo Geophysics, their own geophysical survey company, and their services were highly sought after in the mineral exploration industry. Due to the time they devoted to field work I believe they've seen more of remote regions of Australia than anyone else I know. I'm uncertain but I think they remained confirmed bachelors all their lives. Indeed, Graham often seemed uncomfortable in the company of women, but this may have changed later in his life. Despite time spent away from Adelaide they still managed to construct an oceangoing catamaran in their backyard and in later years Brian was an avid glider pilot in the brief periods he was at home. It was always a pleasure to run into both brothers.

Gary Colmer – now there was a man, just out of school and out of control, I suspect his parents pushed him out to see what the rest of the world looked like. You could never have doubted his work ethic nor his party ethic. For whatever reason, he was a mad gambler – where it came from, who knows? Suddenly experiencing pokies, which were nonexistent in South Australia, he was off the planet. At one stage his colleagues had to get him banned from the Yass Soldiers Club because he was losing a week's pay in the first night after payday on those horrible machines. The saving grace for Gary was that he fell in love with Therese, a local sheep farmer's daughter. All he ever said was that she had the most beautiful brown eyes, and yes, those brown eyes were spectacular and enticing. Gary, long after work had finished in Yass, went back and wooed and won the love of his life. He was very loud and boisterous but became a lifelong friend.

Steve Jewitt was a fast-talking individual who also enjoyed a drink and the odd bet or game of poker. He later found his forte as a salesman with Beaumont Tiles, rising through the ranks to become one of their senior management team.

At this time, I was earning $50 per day which based on a six-day week was a princely sum at a time when average weekly earnings were hovering around the $100 mark. On top of this, accommodation and meals were fully covered by McPhar. However, living in a pub and with the bright lights of Canberra not far away it was also a lot easier to spend money than when isolated in an outback bush camp. I remember one day walking into a local supermarket only to spy a pallet of Chilean red wine being offered at $15 per dozen. As luck would have it I had sampled these same wines at a tasting in Sydney with John Davis a few weeks earlier. They were quality wines that had been provided as part of a wheat trade deal with a very cash-strapped Chile. I couldn't help myself and immediately bought the whole 30 dozen pallet – after all it was only a week and a half's wage. Our publican host was only too happy to store the wine until I could deliver it to my brother-in-law Bill Smith at Bega, who bought a half share in the bounty. The magnificent "Vina San Pedro" and "Vina Underaga", which were both potent drops, later gained some notoriety in Bega by helping to stitch up the local cricket team and also several of the local constabulary when Bill was entertaining.

Despite Canberra's attraction, the weekend venue of choice was the Yass Soldiers Club. Poker machines were then illegal in the ACT so Canberra residents flocked to licensed clubs at Queanbeyan and Yass in neighbouring NSW. Early on, a barman at the club advised us never to play the pokies on a weekend as the odds were wound down for the Canberra influx. The story went that the odds were then wound back up for the locals on Monday to Wednesday. Regardless, the meals were excellent at the club, the local ladies flocked there in droves and then there was the dancing, old-style not rock and roll, where I realised the merits of the progressive barn dance in which you get to swap partners regularly as they proceed around the dance floor.

The progressive barn dance usually didn't come up until later in the evening when everyone was a little primed up. It drew young and old to the dance floor, and how better to utilise this social interaction than to put a little proposition to each partner as they passed along. The older partners got a bit of a laugh out of it while I can't recollect if it was ever truly successful with the younger partners, but no-one was ever offended. However, our bluff was often called by partners in the 40-50 age group, who were regularly and seriously keen to take up the proposal.

We did have a small problem in Yass when some of the local footy team took exception to the fact that the local ladies seemed to be spending too much time in our company. It turned into a heated discussion outside the front of the Australian Hotel. Luckily Bobby Welsh, the local team captain, intervened on our behalf and convinced his boys all was ok, at which we all returned to the bar for a few shared drinks. Bobby's girlfriend was another Australian Hotel barmaid, which probably helped our cause. During the discussion outside we noticed one of our crew, Paddy McHugh, briefly wander off and then return with one hand behind his back. Paddy, a little Irish gnome, had joined our crew about a week earlier; he arrived from Sydney battered and bruised after being beaten up in Kings Cross the night before departure. Later in the bar I asked Paddy what he held behind his back. He had grabbed a tyre lever from one of our vehicles – he wasn't about to be bashed up a second time.

One hot autumn Saturday we were working in the Binalong area about 35 kilometres northwest of Yass. We hadn't brought lunch along that day so Steve Jewitt and I headed into Binalong to buy some for the crew. It was a glorious day and the whole town was buzzing so we decided to join in at the delightful, sunny beer garden of the local hotel. About two hours later we remembered our errand and purchased the takeaway lunches but not before I bought three flagons of red wine. I thought I would provide the boys still working in the field with an after-work treat and emptied the water tank in the old Landrover and refilled it with the contents of the flagons. The intention was good, but the outcome fell a bit short of expectations. We drove straight back to where the crew were working, some distance from the other vehicle holding water supplies. After we'd fielded some questions as to why it took so long, Brian Rau announced he was parched, dived under the Landrover and turned the water tap full blast to both drink and to let the cool water run over him. Brian was not one to swear, but when he emerged from the vehicle covered in red wine a few choice words were said; in fact he called work off for the day after that and we all returned to Yass. After a shower and cool drink, all was forgiven if not forgotten.

Queensland

Work in the Sunshine State usually involved shorter two or three-week trips, in both the Rockhampton and Charters Towers regions. The McPhar IP crew changed from time to time but the core crew from Townsville were John Christie, his trusty old Arctic Samoyed dog Nero and his two offsiders George Sowerby and Geoff Brind. John was a dour Englishman in his early forties while George and Geoff were also Poms who could only be dubbed likeable rogues. George hailed from England's largest iron processing town of Scunthorpe and was an avid supporter of Scunthorpe United; he was into every sly lurk imaginable but did it with great humour. Brindy had previously driven the night cart in Charters Towers and his main claim to fame was emptying its contents onto the front lawn of his ex-girlfriend after a messy break-up – I think he needed to find a job out in the bush after that episode. Later, at a job in western NSW, George and Brindy on their Sunday off visited the local pub. Leaving a few hours later they stopped at a railway crossing within sight of the pub. However, they misjudged or forgot that the bull bar jutted out a long way: sure enough the passing train caught the bull bar and flipped their vehicle on its side. Patrons from the bar, having observed the collision, came running to their aid. When one asked if they were ok, Brindy, somewhat damaged, responded: "Yes you fool, we're bloody stuntmen," at which, after righting the vehicle, they all returned to the front bar. The train continued without stopping, its driver apparently oblivious to such a minor collision.

The most memorable character of the group was in fact the ageing dog Nero. It was horrendous to travel in the front seat of the Nissan Patrol with Nero as he was constantly dribbling saliva to keep cool and he wasn't too particular about how he shared it around. Nero also had an attraction to cane toads and would constantly catch and chew them in the bush leading to effusions of white froth as their poison took effect, but he wouldn't let them go. Nero suffered badly from arthritis, so much so that his back legs would regularly give way, but he was still a formidable canine when the need arose, as an errant motel owner in Biloela discovered. Nero was chained to the front wheel of the Nissan for the night when the motel owner decided to unleash his two Afghan hounds. They kept bowling Nero over but when he got his back braced firmly against the wheel, he bit both hounds on the leg leading to a massive vet bill for the owner to repair broken legs. To his credit the owner conceded that it was his own fault. John also told of Nero's genetic background regularly coming to the fore in the ocean back in Townsville where he would patiently stalk seagulls floating on the water with regular success, providing him with a quick snack.

The town of Charters Towers and hamlet of nearby Ravenswood were fascinating locations to work around. Gold was discovered at Charters Towers in

1871, and in the boom period between 1872 and 1899 the population rose to 30,000, then the second largest city in Queensland. The mines were incredibly rich, in fact it was by far Australia's richest major goldfield with over six million ounces (170 tonnes) of gold produced. It had its own stock exchange and locals referred to it as "the World" because it simply had everything a man could want. Today, with its population under 10,000, the legacy of the mining boom is seen everywhere, with many magnificent buildings still standing. What I especially liked back in 1972 were the pubs, with swinging half-doors as seen in Western movies – it made you want to go out and purchase a holster and six-gun.

Meandering home to the Irish pub where we were staying, in one of the back streets of the Towers after some big party, I came face to face with a gun-toting local when I decided to take a short-cut through his back paddock. He bailed me up and called the police. Back at the police station the arresting officer decided to slap me around the head a few times (he had apparently decided that I was on drugs) but after getting nowhere he escorted me out the door and pointed the way back to my hotel. Arriving back there, I related my experiences over the bar to Paddy, the Irish publican. What I didn't realise was that Paddy had it in for this cop, who had a bit of a name in town. Some days later when said police officer walked into the bar for a quiet drink, Paddy promptly kicked him out saying, "No-one who assaults my guests gets a drink in this bar." For the remainder of this particular field trip I determined to be as invisible as possible.

We also worked in the Ravenswood area but commuted from Charters Towers. Ravenswood had been a boom gold-mining town, where gold was discovered in 1868, three years before at the Towers. Many of the early miners moved to the higher-grade Towers mines but Ravenswood in its boom years, in the period 1868 until 1917, when the mines closed, had a population of 5,000 and, incredibly, 48 hotels. In my Placer days I stayed a night at the Imperial Hotel with John Sandy. This magnificent architect-designed building with red cedar bar area and stained-glass windows was built by James Delaney in 1902 after an earlier hotel built by him in 1901 burned down soon after opening. The Delaney family ran the hotel until 1994 when it was eventually sold. When John and I stayed there in 1971 the population would have been less than 200 and the pub was wholly run by Delaney's two remaining spinster daughters Tessa and Jo, both then at least in their 70s. Everything was done properly, tables formally set for dinner, but it was a bit surreal with only four of us in this large hotel with so much history. Unfortunately, the exquisite ceramic bar taps were out of action during our stay. Gold mining began again in the 1980s and today there's a major operation and resulting population of more than 500, with a thriving tourist trade for the Imperial Hotel and the nearby Railway Hotel of the same era.

Working out of Rockhampton, then a major Queensland city, was another interesting experience. The fieldwork was unremarkable but the city itself offered many distractions. George Sowerby and I had made a pact at the start of this trip, until the final night I wouldn't drink alcohol and George wouldn't smoke. That bet held until our first Sunday off when we all decided to take a day-trip to Great Keppell Island, George and I looked at one another and agreed to put our bet on hold for the day. It was a beautiful day and most of the morning boat trip out to the Island was spent in a net alongside the boat, luxuriating in the warm Great Barrier Reef waters.

On arrival we walked round easily accessible parts of the island and had another refreshing swim before making a beeline for the bar. With our bet deferred George and I decided to work our way through all the spirits on the shelves behind the bar, not a wise idea. By mid-afternoon we were a mess: he was violently ill and I headed to the beach, having decided to swim back to Yeppoon on the mainland, a mere 16 kilometres. I didn't get beyond splashing in the shallows, and my next conscious memory some hours later was walking into the bar of the hotel in Rockhampton where we were staying. I have shied away from spirits and cocktails ever since that experience.

At this same hotel bar on another evening Brindy suggested that I should turn my glass upside down on the bar when I had finished my beer. As a naïve Southerner I had no idea that in Queensland this action meant you were ready to fight anyone in the bar. I was quickly confronted by several willing participants. It took a lot of fast talking and the purchase of many beers to convince them that I had been conned by my mate Brindy.

The other Queensland project area was in the Theodore region about 200 kilometres south of Rockhampton, where we resided in the local hotel-motel. Theodore then as now is a friendly little town of about 500 where everyone seems to know everyone, and lies within the Shire of Banana, though I can't recall seeing too many banana trees. The scale of open pit coal-mining operations came as a revelation while I worked there. Navigating to our next worksite using a topgraphic map I was startled to see a mountain range in front of us that wasn't on the map. Approaching the "range" we realised it was topsoil and overburden from a coal mining operation. It was about 30 metres high and extended into the distance for kilometres. Deviating from our track we were able to drive right up to the edge of the pit to observe the massive scale of the mining. I doubt access like that would be possible today given the stringent OH&S rules in the mining industry.

The Pilbara

The final fieldwork that I undertook for Esso was in the Marble Bar–Port Hedland region of Western Australia, and once again it was in remote country with just a very large caravan with kitchen, dining area and bunk beds as our accommodation for the stay from May through August 1973. With no mobile phones, our daily communication with the outside world was a 7.00am radio schedule run through the Royal Flying Doctor Service in Port Hedland. Any messages from Esso in Sydney, McPhar in Adelaide or for that matter family and friends were communicated by telegram read out to the whole of the eastern Pilbara region over this service.

This part of the Pilbara region was both a spectacular and arduous area to work in. Daytime temperatures were pleasantly in the mid-thirties but many clear nights could be bitterly cold, particularly if the wind was blowing off the inland desert regions. The extensive iron-rich red hills were complemented by black dolerite ranges covered in bright yellow spinifex, and some of the sunsets tinged by the red dust of the region were a delight. Working on the plains was easy enough, but most of our target areas were in the hilly regions which while not particularly high were extremely rugged. I'd rate it as probably the roughest country I've worked in in Australia. Vehicle access in these areas was very limited so that much of the heavy survey equipment, including generators and reels of electric wire, often had to be hand carried over quite large distances; consequently, our crew quickly became quite fit.

Negotiating these hills, I had a couple of interesting wildlife encounters. Rounding a corner near the top of a sharp ridge I came face to face with a two-metre albino roo. I'm not sure who got the bigger shock but we both rapidly departed the scene in opposite directions. Another day, climbing a rocky hill, I encountered a big black python just sunning itself on a rock at my eye level – again a rapid retreat was in order.

Field breaks every fortnight or so were either a weekend in the "big smoke" of Port Hedland or a night or two at the friendly Ironclad Hotel in Marble Bar. We stayed at the modern Hedland Hotel, which sits by the shores of the Indian Ocean. Seafood meals were excellent and the beer was cold, but Port Hedland in those days had one major drawback: the ratio of single men to single women was about 10:1. Scenic outings round the town were uninspiring and one day after a few drinks I decided to have a big ocean swim in front of the hotel to relieve the boredom. As I emerged from the water about half an hour later one older local walked up to me saying "You're ******* mad, you bastard, this bay is full of sharks and the occasional croc." I didn't swim there again.

The Ironclad at Marble Bar, while still very light on in terms of younger members of the opposite sex, did offer some good entertainment when the local characters hit their straps on a Saturday night. Incredibly this tiny town had its own taxi service, and the driver backed up as the local JP and sitting magistrate, so he was a man to stay on the right side of. A swim and a few cold tinnies at the actual marble (jasper) bar a few kilometres out of town was a weekend highlight.

About once a week I scored the duty of doing the grocery supply run to Port Hedland. Leaving camp at 7.00am it should have been easy to do all the shopping and be back in camp before dark, but the watering holes on the way out of Port Hedland often proved a distraction. The last two stops before departure were the South Hedland post office to collect any mail and the airport to collect any air freight. Next to the airport was/is the wonderful Walkabout Motel, in those days boasting a welcoming bar, so a short stopover was always in order. The real hazard lay another 50 kilometres down the road where the Mt Newman railway and Great Northern Highway converge. Rio Tinto or BHP had established a field camp there for their railway construction and maintenance crews with another enticing bar, and better still the camp manager welcomed passers-by in the know to their establishment. Many an hour was whiled away there on the way back to camp, but I remember being a little envious when leaving late at night to find the maintenance crew that I had been enjoying an ale or two with simply drove their Toyota onto the railway line, lowered its railway wheels, set the vehicle on cruise control, opened a stubby and headed for their destination down the track. I might add they did keep in radio communication to warn them of any massive iron ore train heading their way. Meanwhile I had to negotiate another 50 to 100 kilometres of rough dirt road back to camp, although I'm sure that I also cracked a stubby or two along the dark, lonely way. After my first supply run our camp knew not to send out a search party before daylight the next day.

Before leaving South Hedland post office on one of these trips I just couldn't help myself. Back in camp Brian Rau had become aware that McPhar had a field program coming up in Fiji and he was very keen to be the crew leader for this. So I penned a telegram "Brian and Steve to finish up in the Pilbara on Friday, replacement crew on their way, tickets back to Adelaide at Hedland airport, you will depart for Fiji a week later, Ian Bishop". (Ian Bishop ("Bish") I knew was the logistics manager for McPhar, and we later became good mates.) I then returned to camp without too many stops along the way. As we sat down to breakfast the next morning the 7.00am radio schedule came on, and sure enough there was a telegram message for our camp, and the boys seemed to overlook that its source was South Hedland. There was immediate excitement in the camp when the message was read; Brian even started taking some malaria pills which he was still carrying from an earlier New Guinea program. By about 10.00am out in the field, with Brian and Steve highly excited by the prospect of a Fiji trip, I decided that I had better come clean. Not the most popular man in camp for a day or two.

The highlight of the Pilbara project was the Marble Bar Cup race weekend. We brought the field caravan into town and booked it into the caravan park on Friday evening. Saturday was the first race day, so after a heart starter at the Ironclad it was off to the racetrack. Like the Mt Isa rodeo, the ringers had come in from all the surrounding stations and the town population must have increased to three or four times its normal size. A big black horse, "Tunku", won the feature race in a canter and was clearly the odds-on favourite for Monday's cup. The "Gents" was a bit of a revelation: set well back from the track, it looked like a normal white painted corrugated iron structure but on reaching the other side proved to be only a screen, devoid of any facilities other than a large pipe in the ground with a toilet seat perched atop. Privacy wasn't a priority.

At the races and later in the evening back at the Ironclad we befriended some of the iron ore miners who had come in for the weekend from Shay Gap. They were a bunch of rough and tumble characters, and one introduced us to the term "white ant". Aside from the union type connotations of "white anting somebody" I loved its broader use as anything from a term of endearment to perhaps the worst insult you could give someone. From there I believe I helped spread its use widely in Darwin and indeed it's a term that I still rather favour today.

On Sunday afternoon there was an Aussie rules footy match scheduled between Marble Bar and miners from the newly constructed Shay Gap facility. Shay Gap had some good players, but they were short on numbers so sought a few volunteers over counter lunches at the Ironclad. From constant fieldwork plus running a few kilometres back to camp after work each day I was as fit as I've ever been, so I put my hand up, at the same time advising them I had never played a game of Aussie rules. As we lined up pre-match at the grassless oval the Marble Bar team looked resplendent in their uniforms while Shay Gap was rag-tag in any t-shirts and shorts they could lay their hands on. I had no idea how to kick or handball Aussie rules style but contributed with some solid if somewhat illegal Rugby tackles. After the game I was a bit nonplussed when told that I not only tackled the opposition but occasionally in a burst of enthusiasm tackled some Shay Gap team members as well. Amazingly Shay Gap won the contest by a narrow margin.

In the evening it was back to the Ironclad for the all-important Calcutta auction of horses in tomorrow's Cup. "Tunku" went for several hundred dollars and when they were getting down to the outsiders I got carried away and purchased a horse by the name of "New Pride" for $90. Whoever bought the winning horse received 50 percent of the auction funds, the remainder going to charity.

Wandering round town the next morning, a little dazed from the weekend celebrations, I ran into a chap I had met at the Shaw River mining camp when there with Placer a few years previously. Bill was now a Marble Bar resident and indeed advised that he was race steward for the weekend. Confidentially he advised me not to put any money on the favourite "Tunku" as the story was going around that poor old "Tunku" had been given the better part of a bottle of whiskey for breakfast.

Race day was as good as you can get at a small outback meeting with a string of Perth bookmakers in town for the big day. The time came for the running of the Marble Bar Cup, and sure enough "Tunku" completely missed the start and came a long last although he was gaining ground towards the finish. On the other hand, my horse "New Pride" ran a very creditable second, losing to the winner by a nose after leading most of the way. In my somewhat brain-addled state I decided that I should lodge a one-man protest because the favourite had apparently been nobbled. I was heading up the stairs of the stand towards the PA system to let everyone know about "Tunku" but I think some organisers or bookies realised what I was planning and I was intercepted by the local constabulary before I could reach my target. The next three hours until 6.00pm were spent in an old police cell back in Marble Bar. After 6.00pm all bets had been settled and the Perth bookies were on their way back to Port Hedland for a civilised evening. The police let me out and drove me back to the Ironclad where they joined me in a drink or two. I learned then that you never interfere with any goings-on at an outback race meeting.

There was one aftermath to the weekend: I had severe gravel rash all over my arms and legs from the footy match, and when this became infected a few days later I had to return to Marble Bar for a course of antibiotics. The attending sister, it turned out, had been a drinking mate at the Ironclad on the Saturday night so she was at least a little sympathetic.

11

The Top End of Down Under

Top End, 1973–80

In early 1973 I saw an ad for a geologist based in Darwin with the Northern Territory Mines Department (DM), which prior to Territory independence was a Commonwealth Public Service position. I didn't much like the idea of becoming a "public servant", but I did have good memories of Darwin and fancied the thought of a slightly more settled lifestyle, so I sent off a hastily prepared job application. Apart from an acknowledgement I heard no more for some time, then out of the blue received a communication asking if I was still interested. Next thing I received a telegram inviting me to an interview in Sydney the following Monday.

The previous Friday I had arranged to meet up at a hotel in the Rocks with some Sydney Uni colleagues who were then working with the NSW Mines Department. Among the group was a senior geologist with the Department, John Cramsie, whom I had met at earlier Friday night sessions. I was a little taken aback at the interview on Monday when I realised that John was one of the interview panel along with a retired surveyor from the Territory. The interview was relaxed and seemed to go okay, although neither John nor the surveyor could shed much light on what I might expect from the job.

Soon after, I left for Western Australia and the Esso project in the Pilbara. Not having heard anything about the job for some time I assumed that I had missed out, until a re-addressed letter of offer arrived belatedly at the South Hedland post office in late July. Suddenly I had to make a life-changing decision, but it was easy. The next planned contract with Esso was in northwest Tasmania, where we would be helicoptered into remote sites to carry out surveys. The arduous nature of the work and the hordes of snakes likely to be encountered in Tassie made Darwin seem positively enchanting.

Into the Unknown

At the end of August, I returned to Sydney for a final project review with Esso and brief catch-ups with family and friends, then headed off to Darwin on a Friday with a single suitcase. I was met at the airport by Peter Crohn, the Chief Geologist, and run back to the DM office for a brief induction on what I had let myself in for. I was then driven to my living quarters in the Commonwealth singles hostel at the Esplanade, in the heart of Darwin.

My room with overhead fan but no air conditioning was spartan but comfortable and caught any breeze wafting over the Darwin Peninsula. Good meals were provided in a large canteen area and the Esplanade was within walking distance of all the city pubs and restaurants. The room lacked one essential item for Darwin, a fridge, so the first item on the shopping agenda on Saturday morning was a bar fridge. The salesman must have seen me coming as he could quote the exact beer can capacity of each fridge, ensuring a sale was quickly transacted.

Wandering around Darwin's streets I ran into my old mate "Placer Jack" Schubert, so a counter lunch with him and his offsiders at the old "Vic" hotel ensued. Consequently, the rest of the weekend was spent in various watering holes with a visit to that other old Darwin character, Burge Brown, at Fannie Bay.

I signed on at work the next Monday, 3 September 1973, and met the small NT Geological Survey (NTGS) staff group comprising Peter Crohn, his deputy

John Shields, Malcolm Daly, John Willis, Berndt Weber, Geoff and Libby Lau and admin assistant Snowy Balfour. My first project was to undertake a shallow drilling assessment of the Palmerston region for sand, clay and gravel resources that might be used in the planned construction of the new city of Palmerston. That evening back at the Esplanade I decided to go for a run down to the Botanic Gardens and back, a mere 2.5 kilometres each way. Given the level of fitness attained in the Pilbara this should have been a stroll, but I was gasping for air by the time I reached the gardens. It was a stark introduction to how the torrid build-up to the "Wet" season totally saps your energy levels.

Before starting the Palmerston project, I went on a few short field trips with other staff to get the feel of the Top End. Geoff Lau was involved in a construction resources project for the Arnhem Highway, which was being extended about 225 kilometres east from Darwin to the still to be established township of Jabiru, deep in the heart of the yet to be proclaimed Kakadu National Park. We travelled along the Arnhem Highway as far as the South Alligator River, where the bridge was under construction and, despite the reduced numbers back then, spotted big crocs at both the Adelaide and South Alligator Rivers. From there we travelled via Jim Jim-Yellow Waters onto the East Alligator River, where we camped near Obiri Rock (now Ubirr). The rock paintings at Ubirr were amazing, and in those days you had it all to yourself, allowing you a full appreciation of the ambience of such an ancient site of human habitation. The mosquitoes at our camp-site were horrendous, and I believe it was very near to where park rangers in their wisdom later established the Mel camping ground for visitors to Ubirr. Having stayed there in more recent times, I can report that the mozzies are still horrendous.

After completing resource work, Geoff decided we should travel back via the South Alligator Valley and inspect some of the old uranium mines/prospects in the area. This entailed camping near UDP Falls (now Gunlom). UDP stands for Uranium Development Project, a name coined for the falls by the uranium miners and prospectors in the 1950s/1960s. What a delight the falls were, as we again had the place to ourselves, or so we thought. We climbed to the pools at the top of the falls and later to cool off swam out to the base of the falls. Noticing many beer cans in a crevasse and unable to carry them back to shore we decided to sink them. Suddenly a diver appeared, and he was a tad agitated. He had been laboriously free diving to the base of the falls all morning to retrieve the cans and suddenly near his last ascent for the day he meets them all descending back to the bottom. We helped him mount another rescue mission, and over a few beers that night all was forgiven. By the end of this trip, I was hooked on the Top End and knew that three essentials for any future field trips were a mosquito net, a fishing rod and a camera. Having said that, I never again encountered mozzies as fierce as those at the Ubirr camp.

Back in Darwin it was amazing how easily friendships could be made, probably because there were few long-term locals, and everyone was from somewhere else. The first Thursday evening, in the Zodiac bar of the old Darwin Hotel, I struck up a conversation with two likely lads, Lynton "Lumpy" Sherry, who hailed from Cockatoo-Gembrook in Victoria's Dandenong Ranges, and Alan "Neddy" Barden from Launceston in Tasmania. After the bar closed, we adjourned to one of our rooms at the Esplanade, where a carton of beer was demolished over the next hour or two. There were similar introductions over the next few weeks to characters like Mike Sanders, Jack "Hooley Dooley" Doughty, Ric "Tricky" Smith, Ron Brown, Bob "Creekie" Creek, Trevor "Tinkerbell" Bell and Joy, Jan and Debbie. Lumpy, Neddy, Mike and I have remained lifelong friends over what is now a 50-year period, while Tricky and I ended up marrying Jan and Debbie respectively.

In those days many public servants from the southern states moved short term to Darwin to gain rapid promotion and then return south. Despite this Lumpy, Ron Brown, Creekie and Tinkerbell remained in Darwin and forged successful careers with the fledgling NT Government, the last-named attaining the position of Officer-in-Charge, Southern Division for the NT Police Force. The Territory truly has an enchantment about it.

The Palmerston resource drilling project went smoothly apart from the driller's offsider nearly losing a finger when he tangled it up with an auger drilling rod. There were regular early finishes because of the afternoon thunderstorms that were part and parcel of the build-up to the Wet. A drilling rig with a tall mast and drill rods extending deep into the ground makes an excellent lightning conductor. When the program was completed within a month I was a bit taken aback when John Shields suggested that I was in the Territory now and needed to slow down to Top End pace.

Very soon the Christmas season was upon us, and the first office Christmas party proved interesting. With liberal amounts of alcohol being consumed, someone got hold of a "Received" stamp and many attendees were in turn stamped as "Received". Gordon Williams, then Deputy Director of DM, was an old school and very proper colonial administrator and on this day was in his tropical outfit of long white socks and immaculately pressed white shorts and shirt. I couldn't help myself and proceeded to stamp his ample rear end. Gordon went apoplectic, snatched the stamp from me and reciprocated multiple times. I was somewhat apprehensive when I returned to work in the New Year, but all was forgiven if not forgotten and Gordon and I got on extremely well after that incident.

Christmas dinner at the Esplanade was adequate but unremarkable, but my Mum had posted a Christmas fruit cake to which Dad had, unknown to her, added a double helping of rum. On cutting the cake after lunch the wonderful aroma took over the second floor of my block in the Esplanade and many guests were lured by this fragrance, ensuring a solid post-luncheon party.

The Hayes Creek Pub

Straight after Christmas two carloads of Esplanade and Zodiac bar mates headed off for a few days down the track as the wet season had not yet set in. In those days many of the locations down the track were known by their mileages from Darwin, probably a legacy of World War 2, when many strategic airstrips and camps were located adjacent to the then newly upgraded Stuart Highway. The first pub stop down the track was always known as Noonamah but after that you had the "78 mile" (Adelaide River), the "119 mile" (Hayes Creek) and the "133 mile" (Emerald Springs), after which the townships of Pine Creek and Katherine reverted to their proper names. This initial post-Christmas trip was the forerunner of many momentous weekend and Easter trips to the legendary Hayes Creek pub and the Rockhole (now known as the Moline Rockhole) about an hour northeast of Pine Creek.

The Hayes Creek pub was owned by Sir William Gunn of Australian Wool Board and political fame, who also held a large nearby pastoral lease. The publican Dave Kear was one of those laconic Territorians; tall and wiry, he wasn't someone to argue with, but he was a most agreeable publican. The pub is situated about halfway up a low rise about 100 metres from the old highway. As the fuel pumps were near the road and service could be slow, many motorists filled up and drove off without paying. Pub patrons were alert to this and would note the colour and make of any offending vehicle; this information was then relayed to Dave and then on to Graeme Browning, the Pine Creek police sergeant 60 kilometres down the road, who would in turn pull the vehicle over, extract the money owing and, to their chagrin, lock the offending motorist up for the day/night.

It wasn't unusual to arrive and find the bar unattended; one quickly learnt to serve yourself and leave payment on the bar. If other bar patrons or fuel purchasers arrived, there was an expectation that you'd man the bar and accept payments until Dave or one of his attractive barmaids appeared. There was many a boys' weekend at Hayes Creek where we would arrive on Friday night, book just four beds for six or more of us and then drink and sleep in rotation to ensure the bar stayed open continuously through to Sunday afternoon. Designated drivers were expected to sleep through Sunday to ensure a safe return to Darwin that evening.

If feeling the effects of too much time in the bar, the normal practice was to run across the beer garden and dive into the pool. There was a green-painted concrete dance floor in the beer garden area. One new attendee, Big Stewie, got a little confused and executed a graceful swallow dive into the dance floor, knocking himself cold. We truly thought he was dead, but he finally regained consciousness, was helped to his feet and returned to the bar to resume where he had left off. On one of the weekends, returning to the bar after an enervating dip in the pool, I was served by none other than Sir William, with just a palm leaf as my outfit.

Hayes Creek was a regular stop on many field trips and if you stayed overnight you could always guarantee to have a massive green tree frog residing under your toilet seat. Once I was lucky enough to break down at Hayes Creek and was devastated (not) when directed by head office to stay overnight rather than get a tow back to Darwin. At one time an old high school mate, Dennis McNulty, was working as a yardman there. He and another old timer somehow managed to catch a large dingo pup and had it in a hessian bag. They took it into their room and released it. Suddenly there were all sorts of wails, both human and dingo, emanating from the room. Next thing the door flew open, and the dingo came rushing out slowly followed by two very bloodied humans. Taking on a dingo in an enclosed space is not recommended. Dennis had moved to the Top End soon after high school and had been immediately enchanted by its charms, but he sampled a few too many and died in Katherine only a few years later.

Incidents with wildlife were common at Hayes Creek and I remember once lying on the bar floor and using all my 170-centimetre frame as a yardstick for measuring a cranky python that had been captured. It was being well held by several patrons while measurements took place, showing it was more than three times my height, which equates to over five metres. Another time I was having a conversation with this bloke at the bar when he took a sip of his VB stubby; a few seconds later he went berserk and was ejecting beer all over the bar. Two or three of us had to restrain him until he finally calmed down. What had happened? Amid the spilled beer lay the still kicking culprit, a single green ant. The ant had apparently dropped from the ceiling and landed directly in the VB stubby, so when the victim soon after took a swig of his beer the ant did what all good green ants do and bit him on the tongue.

I had a lucky escape there one day. Drilling Supervisor Fred Leonhardt and I were heading back to Darwin and decided to have a quick counter lunch. It was one of those horribly humid days during the build-up to the Wet so after lunch we decided to have a quick refreshing dip in the actual Hayes Creek. Shirtless and dressed in only shorts and thongs we hopped in the 4WD and proceeded down the roughly sealed road. One problem, I had forgotten to close the passenger door and at the first bend out I went. I seemed to have forever before I landed and realised that I needed to land as flat as possible to avoid serious injury (a legacy of judo). This strategy worked in that there was no serious injury, but I was missing a lot of bark off my chest and stomach including a torn nipple. Fred and I continued to the creek for what was a most enervating swim and clean-up and then returned to the bar to calm the senses before returning to Darwin.

It was early evening by the time we reached Darwin, and I had contacted my partner Debbie to tell her not to wait for me and head off to the barbeque we were scheduled to attend. At home I showered and cleaned up the best I could before catching a taxi to the barbeque, without thinking I put on a light-coloured shirt. The barbeque was in full swing when I arrived, and a good night was had by all. As the night wore on the humidity got to my many grazes and I ended up with a light shirt polka-dotted with drops of oozing blood, not a particularly pretty sight, and the tale of the Hayes Creek swim had to be revealed to all.

The Rockhole

The Moline Rockhole lies a few kilometres past the Mary River at the first jump-up on the Pine Creek to Jabiru Road. It's an idyllic spot on the edge of Kakadu National Park with a deep, 30 metres long pool below the falls, the waterfall itself and then for the more active, beautiful clear and cool pools above the falls, and best of all in those days, no crocs. It has featured in several NT tourism ads including one by Paul Hogan.

The Rockhole became a regular weekend camp spot, and it was rare to have to share the place with others. It was also a great base for day trips to other waterfalls in the South Alligator Valley. Our group would usually head off late Friday afternoon, stop for dinner and drinks at Hayes Creek and eventually arrive at the Rockhole anywhere between 9.00pm and midnight. Camp set-up often proved difficult after late night arrivals. The remaining weekend would be spent sunning ourselves on the rocks, sitting under the waterfall and swimming in the cool waters with the occasional beer and barbeque thrown in for good measure. Snakes both in the water and around the campsite led to a bit of excitement now and again.

One weekend we arrived late and were aware that there was another group camped closer to the falls because of their blazing fire and a bit of music. We didn't bother to socialise with them that night, instead putting in a solid session around our own campfire. Rising early the next morning, quite hungover and totally forgetful of our other guests, I wandered down to the falls for a refreshing swim. Dropping all my gear by the edge of the pool I swam out to the falls and then looked up. The rocks adjacent to the falls were occupied by several naked ladies. My first thought was that I had died overnight from an excess of alcohol and that I was indeed in heaven. A few casual waves and I then remembered this must be the other party from last night.

On another occasion, come Saturday morning I foolishly decided to chop down a dead tree for firewood clad only in budgie smugglers and thongs. Unknown to me there was a wasp's nest in the tree and when it was felled, I was assailed by hordes of angry wasps as my mates got a great laugh out of my frantic histrionics. The upshot, I received at least 20 stings and spent the rest of the weekend either in my swag or lazing in the water, with neither food or beer offering any attraction, while the rest of the sympathetic crew partied on as usual.

After my elder daughter Teneille was born in early 1978, she became a regular visitor to the Rockhole, even having a bright orange T-shirt proclaiming her as "The Rockhole Wriggler". Returning to the Top End in 1988 for a Kakadu trip, we called in to the National Park headquarters near Jabiru, where I enquired about the Rockhole only to be greeted with blank looks. Deciding to stop by regardless, we found it largely untouched, with some sections overgrown with spider webs. I doubt you'd still have such a wonderful place all to yourself today.

Darwin Lifestyle

After spending little time at home over the previous five years, Darwin was a boon for social and sporting activities. Nightlife revolved around pubs, restaurants and barbeques where people seemed to compete to make the hottest satays. I think I'd been in Darwin more than two years before being offered a cup of tea in preference to a beer. Concerts in the auditorium in the glorious botanic gardens were regular events and attracted big names. Two memorable performers were Donovan, who sat on the front of the stage unaccompanied and entertained the large crowd on his own for over two hours, and of course the incomparable Joe Cocker who really got into the Darwin spirit, arriving wobbly and at least half an hour late he proceeded to vomit off the front of the stage and then gave a dynamic performance. Donovan's appeal may have come in the form of marijuana: the gardens absolutely reeked of it, and I suspect the whole audience was high on pot regardless of whether they were smoking it or not.

I toyed with the idea of playing rugby league again, but after watching a couple of games decided there was just a little too much biff in the Darwin game. In the dry season (the southern winter) I played cricket again and very much enjoyed my Saturday afternoons. Not surprisingly, at the drinks break beers were provided in lieu of the customary cup of tea, then an accepted part of the game down south. A few years later our Nightcliff team appointed an Adelaide first-grader, Dennis Rebbeck, as captain coach as a move to a more professional approach that was being instigated in Top End cricket.

Playing in his first match Dennis was somewhat taken aback at the first drinks break when the beers were brought out. He uttered words to the effect of "You can't do that" – but of course we did. At the next Tuesday training session he decreed that there would be no more beers during drinks breaks in A and B grade, but C and D grade would be exempted. Nightcliff had a very good C grade team from then on and we in fact won the C grade competition in 1980. In later years Dennis went on to briefly become a test match umpire.

12
Cyclone Tracy

Top End, 1973—80

Over the years my work with DM took me to many unique and isolated spots throughout the Territory, but the bulk of my time was spent in the Top End, particularly in the Pine Creek–Mt Wells region. Pine Creek had seen a significant gold rush when gold was discovered there in 1871 during construction of the Overland Telegraph; this was followed in 1878 by the first tin discovery nearby. By the 1890s Pine Creek boasted fifteen active mines and had a population exceeding 3000. As a result, in the 1970s there was a plethora of old mines within 100 kilometres of Pine Creek, with active stamp batteries at Mt Wells and Mt Harris to treat the small parcels of gold and tin ore extracted by the small miners still residing in the region.

DM operated its own drilling section and offered free drilling services to prospectors and small miners whose properties were sufficiently prospective to justify one or more investigative drillholes. One of my tasks was to assess applications for drilling, which involved reviewing old mining and exploration data and visiting the various properties for mapping and sampling. If approval was granted, geological logging and sampling of subsequent drillholes was undertaken.

I spent a lot of time in the bush (but usually from Monday to Friday, given the relatively short distance to Darwin). Accommodation was basic: camp stove, esky, camp table and chair and a light swag with a mosquito net slung over the top. On wet nights the swag cover was slung over the swag and a basic stretcher was favoured to keep you off the ground, dry and marginally cooler. You were often serenaded to sleep by the howls of dingoes and invariably woken pre-dawn by the curlew's plaintive cry. Wild animals were never a bother, though it was often apparent that dingoes or wild pigs had visited the camp overnight. Buffalo runs, often in creek beds, were to be avoided as camp spots, and you often heard the buffalo stampede through the scrub if they had been disturbed. Where possible, campsites were beside billabongs or rivers, which meant fishing and often swimming were regular pre and post-work pastimes.

After the wet season, grass was over two metres tall and you couldn't see a thing if you were wandering through it. This got quite uncomfortable if wild pigs could be heard also stomping through. The standard bush working procedure post–wet season was to arrive at your work area and set it ablaze, then adjourn to the nearest watering hole for the rest of the day. The next day there was a clear if somewhat charred work area. With the wonderful attributes of the Top End, it's little wonder that I spent more than 100 nights camping under the stars (both work and pleasure trips) in more than one calendar year.

A Cyclone Named Tracy

After meeting and romancing at the Esplanade hostel in mid-1974 Debbie and I moved in together in a rented duplex unit at 14A Ryland Road, Rapid Creek. It was only a few months later, on Christmas Eve, that Darwin was hit with its greatest modern-day disaster since the World War 2 bombings, Cyclone Tracy. Two weeks before Tracy we sat across the road at Grant and Nellie Unsted's home, happily having an evening drink and anticipating that the impending Cyclone Selma would be an interesting experience to live through, with no sense of the danger it might bring. As luck would have it Selma veered to the west and had no more than a slightly breezy impact on Darwin. A week later Debbie and I set off for Christmas at my parents' home at Bermagui on the NSW coast. Along the way our concerns were more about getting my trusty old Datsun 1600 across the extensively flooded black soil plains on the mainly dirt highway between Mt Isa and Townsville.

We reached Bermagui on Christmas Eve, oblivious to Darwin's impending disaster. After we all enjoyed a great family Christmas lunch at my sister Wendy's home in Bega, it was either my Dad or brother-in-law Bill who decided we needed to watch the afternoon TV news – and there before our eyes was the chaotic scene of destruction that had been Darwin. There was a feeling of helplessness but also of concern for our many Darwin friends, because it appeared that the city had been totally wiped out and fatalities could run into the thousands.

The next few days were worrying times: communication was impossible, as was any immediate return to Darwin. It was just a matter of waiting, and slowly but surely, as some communication became possible and thousands were evacuated, news filtered through. Grant Unsted managed to contact us to say that his family were safe but their home had lost its roof, so they had all moved into our ground-level duplex across the road, which was largely undamaged. We had little choice but to continue with our holiday. Just as our holiday was nearing its planned end Grant called again to say that the army had reroofed his home and to get back to Darwin fast to ensure no squatters took over our place.

Entry permits were quickly obtained in Adelaide, and we headed back to Darwin, the Datsun enduring another 1000 kilometres of the rough dirt road that was the Stuart Highway from Port Augusta north. Leaving Adelaide in the morning, the Datsun overheated at Kingoonya in the blazing summer sun. This necessitated an extended beer stop at the pub before proceeding north in the late afternoon. In the early evening Debbie was driving when we hit a big kangaroo. There was only superficial damage to the vehicle, although the roo didn't fare so well. Arriving at Coober Pedy about 9.00pm and intending to book into a motel, we found that the whole town appeared shut for the night, except the service station. What to do but fill the car with petrol, top up the ice in the beer esky and continue. After an hour or two I asked Debbie to drive for a while, but she soon encountered a rabbit plague near Welbourne Hill, and there was a steady thumping as rabbits were bowled over. After her earlier kangaroo experience this was too much for her, so I resumed driving. We arrived at Kulgera about 4.00am and grabbed a couple of hours sleep before the roadhouse opened at 6.00. From there the trip was uneventful, with overnight stops at Alice Springs and Katherine before negotiating the roadblock south of Darwin with our newly acquired permits.

Driving into Darwin was like entering a war zone, with the level of destruction, even a month after the event, far more intense than any television images could show. Navigating proved difficult with so many landmarks obliterated and wreckage still littering the streets. We arrived at our duplex to find it largely intact, with the power and water reconnected. There was a hunk of timber sticking out of the kitchen ceiling and some broken louvres, but it was otherwise undamaged, and best of all the fridge that had been left empty was filled with ice-cold beer. Water had damaged thousands of cartons of beer, and as quickly as the authorities dumped it there were lines of vehicles recovering the bounty. Grant Unsted later said he got at least four ute loads, so he could afford to be generous. A look out our back door after arrival revealed how lucky or sturdy the little duplex had been: a line of new two-storey houses had been annihilated beyond recognition. Our Cyclone Tracy experience had been unremarkable, but what of other friends who had endured the full brunt?

Gary Fenton, an English born geologist with BHP Exploration and an all-round nice guy, paid the ultimate price and was killed. Many others had the top storey of their homes completely blown away, leaving them clinging to the floorboards for hours with no protection from the lethal sheets of corrugated iron roofing and other debris, not to mention the howling wind and driving rain. John Willis, a work colleague, suffered this fate and clung to floorboards for what he described as an eternity with his wife beside him while they lay on top of their two infant daughters to offer them what protection they could. At least they survived. Another work colleague, Peter Gullefer, was a veteran of World War 2 and the

Korean war. He described the experience as horrendous but felt it didn't come close to 50 hours of continual bombardment which he experienced during the Korean war. Peter excelled himself with the free beer post-cyclone: he managed to fill the cleaned-out shell of a medium-sized caravan with beer he rescued from the dump. A dedicated Emu Export drinker, he was prepared to lower his standards to lesser beers when they were free.

Mike Sanders, still a great mate today, saw out the cyclone in his unit in Stuart Park with several flatmates and neighbours. Mike recalls being constantly in fear of his life, and particularly as the group moved from stairwell to bathroom when the wind direction changed after the eye of the cyclone passed. Recently Mike has recorded his memories of that night with the extreme noises of the cyclone dubbed over his narrative: 50 years on it's absolutely chilling to listen to. A few days after the cyclone Mike, together with an acquaintance who was a local waitress, headed to Perth in his somewhat battered Volkswagen beetle with supplies of tinned food, water, camping gear and of course a beer-filled esky. South of Broome he had a major breakdown when he damaged the front end. He managed to flag down a truckie, who said he'd see what he could do when he got to the Sandfire roadhouse on his way south. Mike and his travelling companion had no choice but to sit out the time. About a day later another semi-trailer arrived from the south and the driver stopped to see what the problem was. When Mike related his problem, the truckie walked Mike to the back of the rig and laconically said, "I just might be able to help you out mate." He then revealed a full Volkswagen front end which the Sandfire locals had managed to extract from one of the sand buggies that they used on the nearby Eighty Mile Beach. The truckie and Mike then proceeded with a lengthy front-end reconstruction, after which Mike and his companion safely continued on to Perth. This act was typical of the kindnesses shown to Cyclone Tracy victims by so many people around Australia.

Lumpy's resurrection

One of the cyclone stories I love relating is that of my very good mate "Lumpy", Lynton Sherry. Lumpy had spent a few days before Christmas in Darwin Hospital and was discharged on Christmas Eve. He slowly meandered home via various pubs and clubs, catching up with his myriads of colleagues and mates and trying to make up for his days of abstinence. Later in the evening, noting the wind was getting up, he managed to reach his unit in Rapid Creek, where he like so many others spent an awful night. (As an aside, Lumpy had earlier borrowed my irreplaceable New Guinea farting competition tape, and it too became a victim of Cyclone Tracy.)

When he emerged from a saturated and largely unlivable unit the next morning, Lumpy and mates decided to take the official advice and evacuate from Darwin ASAP. Arriving to chaotic scenes at the Adelaide River pub, Lumpy managed to get a telegram sent to his parents in Victoria to let them know he had survived – or thought he'd done so. Eventually arriving in Sydney, he holed up with another Darwin mate, Steve Vormister. Serendipitously Steve's father had worked as a manager in one of my Dad's grocery stores many years earlier – it's a small world. Lumpy managed to contact me at Bermagui and we arranged to meet him in Sydney, go to the Test cricket match for a day or two, then afterwards bring him to Bermagui and then ferry him back to his parents' home in Cockatoo.

Our cricket meeting spot was to be outside the entry gates to the Hill on the Sydney Cricket Ground. Lumpy was notoriously always late and so after half an hour or so Debbie and I decided to head to the Hill with several old Sydney Uni colleagues in tow. Having found a suitable space, we kept a close watch on the path below for Lumpy's arrival. Eventually he appeared on the path with Steve and others, so we started shouting "Lumpy, Lumpy" to try to get his attention. The whole Hill took up the chant of "Lumpy, Lumpy, Lumpeeee", so much so that the Channel 9 television cameras panned directly in on Lumpy and that's when his parents watching the TV in Cockatoo finally realised, after more than three weeks, that Lumpy had survived Cyclone Tracy. His telegram had never reached them, if it in fact was ever sent from Adelaide River.

Post-cyclone challenges

Life in Darwin the year after Cyclone Tracy was quite amazing. Many residents, too traumatised by the event left, never to return. At least half the working population had no accommodation and were transferred to and worked from other capital cities, primarily Brisbane, until accommodation became available, while for the remaining population it was one continuous party. People from all walks of life worked at their own jobs until early afternoon then helped friends and neighbours with cleaning-up and rebuilding for the remainder of the day, which regularly ended up with partying well into the night. There was also a pressing need to drink all the free beers recovered from the dump before they went rouey, which in the Top End meant a maximum three-month use-by date. There were some drawbacks: one could expect at least a puncture a day from nails and screws still littering the roads; day-long blackouts were commonplace, so great care and preparation were required to ensure foodstuffs didn't go off; and in many areas three-phase power hadn't been restored, meaning cold showers were the order of the day.

Squatters had moved into many houses post-cyclone, and returning householders had little legal recourse to evict them. Dave Kear, the Hayes Creek publican, came up with an innovative method to move them on: the continuous party. The returning owners/householders would take up residence along with the squatters but they'd bring Dave's party group along with them. The party would immediately start and ran non-stop until the squatters had had enough of the noise and antics. Usually, 24-48 hours of partying was sufficient.

Thunderstorms and dingoes

An unforgettable feature of the Top End is the violent thunderstorms that occur on almost a daily basis in the build-up to the Wet. They're incredibly loud, bright and awe-inspiring. We're all familiar with the very dark blackish-grey clouds associated with thunderstorms, but in the Top End you'd see clouds ranging in shade from dark blue to dark green – the latter shade heralded the most intense storms. Weathering one of these storms with just a swag cover for protection is unnerving, but some storms were outright scary. I remember staying in a house at the Mt Wells battery on my own and feeling ready to crawl under the bed despite being inside. On one of my last Top End field trips we were camped right beside the escarpment at Twin Falls. You could drive right up to the falls in those days. The sound of the storm reverberating off the cliff faces was little short of terrifying, despite a few beers to calm the nerves the two of us eventually evacuated to the canvas-covered rear of the long wheelbase Toyota for the night. Driving out the next day on a beautiful clear morning we came across a very large and very dead buffalo by the side of the track that was almost certainly a victim of the storm.

Another somewhat eerie experience was camping out on your own on odd occasions. The first time, I got back to camp from a day's work, cooked dinner and was happily in the swag soon after dark. This was okay until about 3.00am, when the call of curlews was the early alarm clock. Further sleep was out of the question, so it was then a matter of lying in the swag for three hours listening to the plaintive cry of the curlews and dingoes howling. I adjusted my solo camping procedures after that. Arriving back in camp, it was first a shower or swim, then a few beers and hors d'oeuvres by the campfire before preparing dinner by about 8.00pm, then dining, with an odd red wine thrown in, until about 10.00pm. This routine worked like a charm, always ensuring a sound sleep through till daybreak.

A few colleagues

Some of my work colleagues in Darwin were interesting. Peter Crohn, the Chief Geologist, was born in Germany in 1925 and migrated to Australia in 1940 with his mother and sister. Given what Nazi Germany must have been like at that time their immigration is probably a story in itself. Peter graduated in Geology from Melbourne University and after a few years with BHP joined the Bureau of Mineral Resources (BMR) (now Geoscience Australia) in Canberra. This led to a stint based in Mawson in Antarctica in 1955–56 for which he was awarded the prestigious Polar Medal in 1956.

Peter was transferred to the Northern Territory in 1958 and spent 22 years there until 1979. Among his many activities there with the BMR he was instrumental in demonstrating the manganese potential of the remote Groote Eylandt, off the eastern coast of Arnhem Land. This led to the establishment of the Groote Eylandt manganese mine by a BHP subsidiary in 1961, a world-class manganese deposit. The mine's still in operation more than 60 years later.

In 1970 Peter was appointed Chief Geologist of the newly established Northern Territory Geological Survey (NTGS), a position he held until 1975, when he somewhat reluctantly accepted the position of Director of the Mines Department after an earlier appointment to the position had caused a near-mutiny in the department. Peter held the director's position until 1979, guiding the fledgling department through the transition to self-government on 1 July 1978. In 1985 at the age of 60 he led an Antarctic Research Expedition to Macquarie Island.

Peter was a rather shy and taciturn character, a first-class field geologist and an administrator and manager who probably would have preferred to be out of the office so he could ply his trade in the remote expanses of the Territory. I only accompanied him in the field on two or three occasions, and was highly impressed with the knowledge and expertise he willingly imparted to others.

John Shields, the second-in-charge, was another BMR geologist, who was transferred to Darwin in 1961, fell in love with the Top End and lived there the rest of his life. John was a very capable geologist, but it was his philosophy of work and life that was a standout. He was a great friend and mentor to all, and I recall him telling me soon after my arrival in Darwin that you must always enjoy the work that you're doing or you aren't doing it properly, a philosophy I quickly adopted. "Shieldsy" adored spending his leisure hours sailing on Darwin Harbour as a member of his beloved Darwin Sailing Club, and was known to enjoy a drink or two at the club bar, taking in the magnificent sunsets over the Arafura Sea.

At work he regularly went off on solo field trips with only his cherished corgi for company. His whereabouts on these trips were always a bit of a mystery and in those days although there were regular 11.00am radio schedules, there was no requirement to report in. He held the department record for travelling to Tennant Creek by road: it was five days as I recall – the pubs and roadhouses really were a hazard.

John left the department not long after I did and spent his remaining career as a mining entrepreneur and consultant geologist in the Top End. John's wife Juliet (they were married in 1959) also took to the Territory with gusto. Juliet, a solicitor, quietly worked her way up as a clerk in the Crown Law Department of the Northern Territory Administration and became a senior member of the NT Law Department after self-government.

Berndt Weber was a German-born engineering geologist and an expert in his field. He was a gourmet of some note and at times a somewhat over the top character. He and his wife Gerda loved to entertain, and there were regular visits to their home to sample exotic foods such as smoked camel meat and fine wines. As the evenings progressed and the wine flowed, Berndt had a habit of bringing out his German marching music and playing it rather loudly, I think he was having a lend of his guests, but we were never quite sure. He was remarkably kind and generous, and some years later he visited after we had moved to Adelaide. He arrived laden with a stack of beautiful and I suspect expensive children's books for my five-year-old daughter, Teneille. As I remember, Berndt and I consumed seven bottles of wine over that evening, including a Cullen's rosé which he declared was the best rosé he had ever tasted, it was quite a compliment.

Peter Woyzbun was a Polish-born geophysicist who weathered the Nazi occupation as a youth. He may have had some unofficial involvement with the RAF after his repatriation to England, although he would only have turned seventeen by the end of World War 2. Some more official post-war RAF experience may have ensued, and he went on to graduate in Geophysics in England. On his arrival in Australia, probably in the late 1950s, he became a pioneer in the application of airborne geophysics in mineral exploration. I believe he was also involved as a geophysicist in the discovery of the huge Macarthur River silver-lead-zinc deposit near Borroloola in the NT. Peter had achieved and experienced a lot in life, but like Burge Brown he was a classic bullshit artist. Unlike Burge, however, Peter seemed to have reached a point where he wasn't quite sure which version of some events was the true story, added to which he hated to be bested on any past bush experiences. A case in point: Peter wore a very distinctive black eye patch because of the loss of an eye. (An online photo of Peter in the 1960s when he worked for Adastra Geophysics appears to show him with both eyes intact.) He must have had at least half a dozen stories of the eye loss, some of which dated back to helping Polish resistance fighters, others to later years in Australia.

Sitting around a campfire with a few beers or a rum or two, we used to tease poor Peter mercilessly. One of us would invent a story of working outdoors in 55-degree heat – Peter would soon relate an experience in 65 degrees; or someone would invent a story of catching metre-wide mud crabs – of course Peter had encountered three-metre wide mud crabs – and so it went on. Despite these shortcomings Peter was a pioneering geophysicist, an affable bush companion and a kind and gentle man who remarried and brought up a young family during his DM years.

At one stage both Berndt and Peter had transferred to the Alice Springs office and, while they were cordial drinking mates, their differences occasionally got the better of them on extended field trips together. The story goes that on one trip to the Harts Range region Berndt got so frustrated with Peter's tales that he went to his swag, produced a shotgun and proceeded to shoot all Peter's clothes which had been washed and were hanging on a line.

Paul Le Messurier succeeded Peter Crohn as DM's Chief Geologist at the time of Territory independence. Paul had been geologist-in-charge of Geopeko's Tennant Creek office, but he came with a bit of baggage as he had also been campaign manager for Ian Tuxworth, the Country Liberal Party member for Tennant Creek and NT Minister for Mines and Energy. Paul proved to be a capable manager and a very affable character. I always got on well with him but disliked the way he treated John Shields, whom I think he was trying to pressure to leave the Department. When I was leaving Darwin I couldn't help myself and purchased several t-shirts specially labelled with "I'm ap-Paul-ed ". (Paul Everingham was then the first Chief Minister of the NT.) As fate would have it, I was sitting in the Green Room of the Darwin Hotel having a few drinks with Shieldsy and Berndt, and we were all wearing the t-shirts, which I had given to them. In walks Paul Le Messurier, who greets us in jocular manner but then looks quizzically at our attire. With a bit of Dutch courage I piped up "and we don't mean Everingham". To his credit Paul took it rather well and joined us for a drink.

Peter Crohn, John Shields and Paul Le Messurier should be lauded for their efforts in nursing and developing the NTGS over its first decade, leading to the vibrant organisation it is today, headed by Ian Scrimgour, another man who I know from experience likes a drink or ten and has been charmed by the Territory like so many before him.

Paddy Ryan was a later arrival at the NTGS who certainly provided some interesting moments. He was a very capable geophysical technician and had worked for the BMR in Papua New Guinea for many years, where he obtained a commercial pilot's licence. He loved flying in the mountainous terrain there, and one of his claims to fame was that he joined the mile-high club with his plane on autopilot. Paddy had some strange habits like drinking warm Baileys Irish coffee in the heat of the day when out in the field, but I was somewhat taken aback when I called round to see him while he was home on leave one day. After offering me a beer and pouring a Baileys for himself, he said, "There's something I must show you." Next thing he turns on his stereo and wanders off into another room. Suddenly I could hear a phone ringing through the speakers but the biggest surprise was when I heard Paul Le Messurier answer the call. Paddy had bugged his office, not with any malice intended but simply because he could, with his well-honed electronic skills. While I had a chuckle with Paddy at the time he was strongly advised to remove the bug post-haste.

13

Fieldies, Drillers and Prospectors

Top End, 1973–80

Many of the field trips I undertook were single vehicle excursions with just a geologist and field hand on board. Travelling and camping in remote areas for a week or two at a time, you got to know and rely on your companions.

The old soldier

Over the years, sitting round a campfire or winching the vehicle out of a boggy patch, you develop a strong bond, and none better than that which I formed with the old soldier Peter Gullefer. Hailing from Western Australia, Peter had enlisted as a young lad at the start of World War 2 and served in some of the more bitter campaigns as a "Rat of Tobruk" and later in the New Guinea jungle. He had an extended time in Japan at the end of the war, in repatriation operations. Later he also served in the Korean War, but his military days ended abruptly when the army refused to let him go to Vietnam. He quit and was planning to find mercenary work in southern Africa when his passport was cancelled by the authorities. That resulted in his moving to Darwin with his family, where he settled and later, with its establishment in 1970, found work with the NT Geological Survey.

Peter was an enigma, a man who really loved a battle but was probably born about 200 years too late. He respected his enemy, who in his mind was only doing his job, and postwar bore no hatred for any race, unlike so many of his colleagues. In fact, if battles were fought between nine and five and there was a local down the road I'm sure he'd have joined his enemies for a drink and then continued fighting them the next day. I think Korea may have upset his valorous fighting philosophy somewhat because, as in Vietnam later, recognising friend from foe wasn't clear-cut.

I spent many years around the campfire with a quiet beer discussing Peter's wartime experiences and particularly the fears and expectations you may have when locked in battle. He was always a bit loath to discuss his more harrowing experiences but had some funny stories. The one I loved was when he was stuck in Tobruk or nearby and someone managed to get a supply of Canadian beer through to the troops; however, it had a very high alcohol content and most hadn't partaken for quite some time. They all got stuck into it in one huge binge ending up with most of them lying comatose in the desert sun. If only Rommel had known at the time, the result of the war might well have been different. Peter never liked to make work any harder than it needed to be and had many simple but effective strategies to make life safer and easier while working in the bush, and I was lucky over the years to pick up some of these habits. An example that comes to mind is if you drive off a road/track to find a nice overnight camp spot, to avoid being disoriented next morning always face the vehicle back towards the track. This works a charm especially if a few overnight beers are involved. You did have to watch Peter, as he had a few tricks up his sleeve to maximise his time in the Adelaide River pub on field trips. No matter how early you left Darwin, Peter would find excuses for brief stops, or he simply drove slowly if he ran out of ideas, always arriving at 10.00am just as the pub was opening. I twigged to this one quickly and admit I often joined him for an early beer, but several years later Geoff Lau, who was a very moderate drinker, mentioned one day that it always seemed to take longer travelling from Darwin to Adelaide River than the reverse.

Geoff often went into the field with Peter, and I immediately knew the reason, but never let on to him. For a longer stay at Adelaide River, Peter would announce as we left Darwin that he hadn't been able to get a particular service done or obtain a certain vital part for the vehicle, so he'd phoned ahead and booked it into Jimmy Nichols's Shell garage at Adelaide River. This not only meant a longer stay at the pub, but Jimmy would deliver the finished vehicle to the pub and then join in another round of beers, and often Harry Cox, the local police sergeant, would arrive to join us for yet another extended round.

It was rare to ever to find Peter in the head office at Stuart Park, or later when it moved next door to the Darwin Hotel. He had a novel way of letting us know where he was: "Number Two" office was our drill sample store at Winnellie, but then it got interesting – "Number Three" office was the Green Room in the Darwin Hotel, "Number Four" the Buff Club at Stuart Park, and so on. Amazingly this system worked a treat.

Peter always carried a Brazilian-made three-shot pump action shotgun in the vehicle on field trips – this in itself wasn't uncommon. I often carried a semi-automatic 22. These guns were occasionally used to dispose of injured kangaroos after a collision or sometimes to move wild pigs away from a camp. Peter always maintained that he could, perhaps in a *Mad Max* hypothetical situation, disable an approaching group of up to 50 with his shotgun. His concept was to fire a solid shot Brenneke slug into the leader for effect, for this would annihilate that unfortunate individual, and then cover a 120-degree swathe with his next two pellet shots to disable the remaining group. I was forever skeptical of this claim until the year before leaving Darwin when I induced him to give a bush demonstration. At that time nearing 60, he fired off his three shots faster than I could fire off my semi-automatic 22 and the devastation of the surrounding scrub was little short of amazing. It just makes you marvel that modern automatic weapons can be bought off the shelf in the USA. Johnny Howard did a great service for Australia when he enacted stricter gun laws after the Port Arthur massacre.

Danish Jens

Jens Pedersen was another with whom I spent a lot of time in the bush. Jens was a very laid-back Dane who joined the Department of Mines (DM) out of nowhere – it turned out his partner Marge Higgins just happened to be the Human Resources (HR) officer. Jens took to bush trips like a duck to water and among other things introduced me to the wonders of Danish Esrom cheese. To those who don't know it, it has a wonderful flavour when eaten with a slice of pumpernickel, but it also has the foulest odour, and once you've eaten the cheese that same stench oozes out of your pores for quite an extended period. It's great in the bush but perhaps not so good for social gatherings. Pickled fish concoctions were another regular Jens bush hors d'oeuvre.

About a year after his joining the DM we were heading back to Darwin after a field trip when Jens, who was driving at the time, an essential part of his job, suggested a celebratory drink at Adelaide River. After stopping I asked what the celebration was for, at which he announced he had just got his licence back, having lost it about a year before for DUI. What could I say other than buy him a beer?

Sometime later in Darwin he was exceptionally lucky not to lose it again. Arriving by car one evening at our new post-cyclone home in the suburb of Anula, Jens had visibly had a few too many beers topped up with his beloved schnapps. He partook of a few more and was implored to sleep the night but no, he had to drive home. Of course, he was nabbed by the breathalyzer and taken to the Casuarina police station to be charged, but just as the charges were being laid a major altercation broke out elsewhere in the station. The duty officer took one look at him then said get out of here as he rushed off to assist with the melee.

Jens, who was a master cabinet maker by trade, finally left DM to work closely with Colin Jack-Hinton, the enigmatic foundation-director of the new Museum and Art Gallery of the Northern Territory. Jack-Hinton was an avid sailor and like

John Shields was known regularly to bend his arm at the Darwin Sailing Club, so he and Jens became great companions. One of their major tasks was the opening of a modern museum and art gallery to replace what was destroyed in Cyclone Tracy. Jens's work featured in many display cabinets in the new building, which was opened in 1981. I last caught up with Jens and Marge at Nubeena in southeast Tasmania where they'd moved to, a climate perhaps more suited to a Dane.

South African Harry

Harry Mills, or in full Harold Marmaduke Mills, a somewhat crazy South African, was another interesting field companion. He'd departed South Africa to avoid conscription but loved his home country with a passion and was always quick to point out that he was a South African with English heritage, not a "mad Boer". Harry was loud and boisterous, which in the Top End often meant that some fast talking was needed to get him out of situations, but he was very entertaining to be with. Camped one freezing but glorious starlit night near Katherine Gorge, we'd run out of firewood. There was a 44-gallon drum of rubbish close by so in our wisdom we decided to burn its contents but only had petrol rather than diesel to get it going. Harry filled a plastic container with petrol and as he splashed it on the small fire in the bin also splashed it on his hand. Aflame, in his frenzy he fell back through the lid into our very large foam esky filled to the brim with beer and icy water. It was the one time I saw Harry lost for words as he sat there unmoving for a minute or two. The icy water doused his burning hand and the fire in the drum provided him with much needed warmth for an hour or so.

One of Harry's South African tales was that on their farm his mother used to take in errant young ladies to help them mend their ways and have a better future. Harry, who was a bit of a ladies man, had to pick one of these ladies up while in town but was later apprehended by the local constabulary driving home while in a state of undress. The police let him off but warned him that he could do himself unspeakable injury if he ever crashed while in this state.

Harry also had a near miss with the local constabulary in Pine Creek. He and I had been ensconced in the bar of the Pine Creek pub when we heard news that Bob Krivsky, one of our drillers, had come off his motorbike and had been rushed to the Pine Creek hospital, so of course we headed for the hospital. Harry in his belligerent manner was demanding to see Bob, which somewhat rankled the duty sister who duly called the local policeman, Graeme Browning. Things could easily have been smoothed over, but oh no, Harry continued with his demand, at which Graeme asked which of you two drove here and Harry retorted, I did. At that Graeme invited Harry to hop in the police wagon for a quick trip to and breathalyzer in Katherine. I had no choice but to roll out my swag next to our vehicle and wait for their return. Incredibly Harry passed the breath test, so when they returned a couple of hours later we were able to return to the pub for a few quick drinks before closing. Bob had suffered no major injury but was a sorry sight, missing bark from head to toe, as his riding safety gear had comprised singlet, shorts and thongs.

Harry finally returned to South Africa, reluctantly did his national service and then developed a thriving business in his beloved country, but unfortunately the pressures of modern-day South Africa eventually forced his return to Australia.

Another field officer also deserves a brief mention for his singular act of madness. Brian Atkins was a Cockney Pom, with that distinctive accent, who was constantly on the lookout for that deal which would make him a million. Brian and another were undertaking a survey of the coastline of Groote Eylandt for DM, using a small dinghy with outboard as their transport. Each night they'd moor the boat and camp somewhere along the remote coast. On the western coastline Brian awoke one morning to see their boat rapidly heading out to sea on the receding tide. He raced down the muddy shore in pursuit and without thinking plunged into the murky waters. He figured that he spent the best part of an hour swimming after it and felt in the end if he didn't catch it he didn't have the strength to swim back to shore. In short, he caught it, climbed aboard and survived, and only then remembered the crocodiles and sharks that abound in these waters.

Drillers and "killers"

DM's drilling crews spent most of their time in the bush living in some rugged and remote areas, but they ate well, and a visit to the drillers camp would almost always result in leaving with an esky full of prime steak and/or barramundi that were excess to their requirements. Most landowners were happy to let them shoot and butcher an occasional beast from their herds for a minimal charge, and roaming buffalo were fair game any time as most of the station owners saw them as vermin. In fact, yearling buffalo steak or roast almost became a preference.

The first time I experienced getting a "killer", as the practice was known, was with an old bushy, Harry Barker, who lived at the old Grove Hill pub, in company with the local station owner. It was a bit of a game between the station owners, as you always went onto the neighboring property to get a killer. Once a beast was dispatched with a trusty old 303, the speed with which it was skinned, gutted and dismembered was astounding to a newcomer like me. The meat was quickly laid out in the back of the 4WD, covered and transported off the neighbour's property, after which a fire was lit and the rib bones, still quivering, were barbequed. These rib bones were some of the tastiest meat I have ever eaten.

Back to the drillers, among whom there were any number of characters. Mick Lurch immediately comes to mind, with his enormous beer gut that hung so low it almost covered him like an apron. Mick loved the bush and hated the "big smoke"; even places like Pine Creek were too busy for him. He was a carton-a-day man, with a bottle of Bundy thrown in after dinner, but was also an accomplished diamond driller who choose to work as an offsider to avoid responsibility. He was also just a very nice bloke and a perfect gentleman if ever in the company of the other sex. There were bets laid on whether Mick would make 40 given his lifestyle, and right on cue at age 39 he was admitted to Darwin Hospital where he died a week or so later. I can't help feeling that suddenly taking away his regular daily intake of alcohol may have been a massive and fatal shock to his body.

Mr Unsted-y

Grant Unsted, a one-time Darwin neighbour and subsequently a lifetime friend, was the drilling supervisor for the various DM crews. Educated at the illustrious King's School in Sydney, Grant headed north to see what the Territory offered. Working as a stockman at Willeroo station about 125 kilometres southwest of Katherine, he met the lovely Nellie on one of his rare trips to Katherine. This romance blossomed after Grant became a driller with the DM and Nellie was working as a barmaid at the Pine Creek pub when it was run by the legendary Bogger and Maysie Young. Grant and Nellie subsequently married, and Grant spent his whole working life in the Top End, initially with DM and later running his own water bore drilling business. He became as rough and tumble as any driller of that era but always retained that touch of private school. After retiring and selling his business Grant caught the gold bug and, after a few adventures in the NT and WA, bought property at of all places Beechworth in Victoria, after a lifetime in the tropics. The attraction was that he could pan gold from a creek that ran through the property.

There are so many tales I could tell about Grant, and a few that I can't, but I think his move to Berry Springs post–cyclone Tracy takes the cake. Grant and Nellie purchased a 25-acre block near the popular recreational water hole at Berry Springs. Post-cyclone the NT Government had plans to build a small satellite township based on the acreage blocks developed around Berry Springs. First up Grant and Nellie fenced the periphery of their property before starting construction of a very comfortable own-built house. As they proceeded to build, the NT Government had been busy next door developing infrastructure for the proposed Berry Springs school. This included drilling and pump works and constructing a powerline.

After work one day Grant arrived home to find a bevy of NT Government vehicles parked near his partly constructed home and on closer inspection found downcast senior government officers from several departments in earnest conversation with Nellie. After offering his assembled visitors a cold beer, which was declined, he grabbed one or two coldies for himself and joined the group. He quickly learnt that the contractors for the school infrastructure had assumed that his fence marked the block boundary. When government surveyors were brought in it was discovered that his fence was well inside his property and the school infrastructure had been built on his property without permission. After a couple of hours of serious discussion, a deal was made whereby Grant and Nellie would have free access to the power and water infrastructure for an extended period and the NT Government would purchase about one acre of his property on which the infrastructure had been built. Some very relieved government officers joined him in several celebratory beers once the deal was done.

A few more drillers

Freddy Leonhardt was the drilling superintendent for the DM, spending much time in the field with the various drill crews to provide logistical and technical support as required. Arriving in the Top End from Port Augusta in 1946, aged two, Fred was as rough and tumble as they come, with at least three or four expletives in every phrase he uttered. For whatever reason he attracted the opposite sex, resulting in numerous marriages over the years and many offspring. Fred would always find a short-cut to minimise work effort and was always on the lookout for a good deal, but invariably he came up with lemons. After leaving DM Fred owned and ran several drilling enterprises, which were for a time quite successful, but with each boom and bust (which are part and parcel of the mining industry) Fred seemed to always come out on the wrong side of the ledger. Unforgettable and incorrigible, Fred was still a likeable rogue who was always loyal to his fellow workers, and despite his setbacks he was always one to "get back on the horse" and give it another go. I recently heard that, now nearing 80, Fred is back dabbling in the drilling game once again.

In the Top End you never really knew the background of work colleagues, especially drillers, but the origins of two Czech drillers, Peter Chauvanec and Bob Krivsky, were undeniable. When Peter took his shirt off there for all to see were the numerous gunshot wounds he received while escaping the communist regime in his home country. Bob on the other hand had a price on his head so to speak. A competent marine engineer by trade, one of Australia's waterside unions blacklisted Bob from working in his chosen industry because he had the temerity to escape from a communist regime – such was the power of militant unions back then. The pair were capable, hardworking and very sociable once work had ceased for the day. Bob in particular was a soft-spoken, gentle giant of a man who deserved better treatment from his adopted country.

Prospectors and Miners

Prospectors and small miners were quite plentiful in the Pine Creek region. The small miners gleaned anything from a meagre existence to substantial profits from their mineral prospects depending on the tenor of the mineral deposit and the amount of work put in. The "prospector", however, just wanted to live the dream, the same as people who like to plan how they're going to spend the money from a big future lotto or lottery win. Most prospectors believe there's a bonanza deposit lurking just below the surface of their property but rarely do any genuine work to find out. I was made very aware of this when DM provided drilling assistance to some of these individuals. When the drill rig arrived on their property, they became a little uncomfortable and invariably grew quite agitated as the drilling proceeded beyond the target depth with no tangible results: basically, they didn't want to lose their dream.

Joe Fisher

The legendary Joe Fisher was much more than a prospector, although in his later years when I met him he liked to dabble in the art. Joe was the fourth generation of his family to work in the Australian mining industry, commencing his experience pre–World War 2 in a family-run mine at Wenlock in Queensland. Postwar Joe gained mining qualifications at Mt Morgan Technical College and in the mid-1950s was hired as a field superintendent by a company that became known as United Uranium NL. In this role Joe was intimately involved in exploration for and development of several small uranium deposits in the South Alligator Valley of the NT in the 1950s and 1960s and rose through the ranks to become general manager. He was very much a pioneer of the uranium mining industry in the Top End and a stalwart of the NT mining industry for over 40 years. He was also a member of the NT Legislative Council from 1961 to 1974 and was instrumental in the establishment of Kakadu National Park, which included the South Alligator Valley. Who knows, Joe may have named UDP Falls during mining operations there, a name it retained until the 1980s, when it reverted to its original Aboriginal name of Gunlom.

I met Joe when he was about 60 in the late 1970s, accompanying him on field trips to the Maranboy tin field east of Katherine and later to old gold workings at Mt Ringwood, about 120 kilometres southeast of Darwin. Considering his achievements, he was a very humble and likeable gentleman, but a Territorian through and through. I noticed he had foam-lined metal stubby coolers firmly attached to the dashboard of his old Toyota 4WD, so his beer was never going to get cold. At Maranboy I was doing the overnight camp catering and had brought along the usual steak and vegetables but was delighted when Joe in company with consultant Alan McGain produced some superb avocados to be shared over a few beers as an aperitif after a long hot day in the field. I learnt afterwards that Alan dabbled in avocado farming back on his Sunshine Coast property. At

Mt Ringwood Joe possibly saved my life or at least managed to keep me out of harm's way. About to jump down into some old gold workings we noticed two very large brown-coloured snakes. They were so large that I was quite happy to jump in and proceed with the sampling as I was confident they were pythons. Joe, however, insisted they were king browns and I finally demurred to his superior bush knowledge. Later back in Darwin I checked out the king browns at the local Berrimah Zoo: Joe was right, they do grow very large. As testimony to Joe's dedicated approach to prospecting, in the early 1980s he discovered gold-bearing outcrop to the southwest of Mt Ringwood that had been overlooked by many previous mineral explorers. This was mined by open pit between 1988 and 1993 as the Goodall gold deposit, producing over seven tonnes of gold.

Murray and Elaine

Murray Millwood was another serious miner rather than prospector. Starting I believe as a dairy farmer in Tasmania, Murray got the mining bug and in his early 30s moved to the Top End with his young family to make his fortune. Murray acquired the Rosemary tin mine from the estate of the Touhey brothers; the mine's situated near the McKinlay River and east of Mt Wells. It was then an underground operation with a narrow railway track running through the mine. Murray single-handedly mined the tin ore and then pushed the laden ore cart out through the mine entrance to an ore stockpile perhaps 200 metres from the ore-face. From there he trucked the ore to the Mt Wells battery for processing. Elaine, his dedicated wife, looked after the home and children but would assist him in any way she could. Murray was not only strong but one of the hardest workers I have encountered. He gleaned a reasonable living out of the tin mine, but with the advent of a new Top End goldmining boom in the late 1970s found he could earn considerably more working as a contractor on some of the emerging gold operations.

After 30 or so years in the Top End mining industry, Murray and Elaine needing a new challenge. They bought the Homeward Bound gold mine near Marble Bar in WA, which they've operated, largely on their own, for about 20 years. In 2019 they were featured on the ABC TV program *Back Roads*, with Murray still heading underground each day and Elaine operating the winder to carry him up and down the mineshaft and to lift out any ore produced. At the time of writing, Murray and Elaine, nearing 80, have the mine advertised for sale as "the largest independently owned underground gold mine in Australia".

Others infected with the "mining bug"

Jack Lewis was a Top End bushie from way back. He had family but chose to live the life of a hermit in the bush that he loved. Jack eked out a living from his mining ventures, but it was his self-sufficient lifestyle that most impressed. He was very fond of echidnas as a gourmet delicacy, and wandering round the bush with him it was a bit startling to see him putting his arm in every likely hollow log in his search for them. I asked him if he had ever encountered a snake during his searches; amazingly he never had, though he did admit to getting the odd goanna bite – but the goannas like the echidnas ended up as vital protein in his diet. Jack was lean and wiry, liked a rum or two and smoked heavily. He eventually weakened a tad and moved in with a female companion close to Pine Creek. Apparently when he died many years later, he was buried in his swag.

Merv Lee was another prospector who exiled himself to the Top End bush. Reputedly the Tennant Creek town drunk for many years, he finally gave up the grog and moved to his lovely bush camp on the McKinlay River near Burrundie Siding. Merv too eked a living off his mineral properties and was largely self-sufficient, living off kangaroo and buffalo and a flourishing vegetable and indeed flower garden. His attire was teeshirt and shorts, and he usually went barefoot, so his material needs weren't great. It was always a delight to drop in for a cup of tea and a yarn with a man whose appearance belied his knowledge. I don't know if it related to his garden and the bamboo-backed river setting of his camp, but he seemed regularly to attract visitors of the opposite sex from Darwin and elsewhere.

Paul Porter was a very competent mechanic who ran the local service station in Pine Creek, but he was seriously infected with the mining bug and devoted most of his earnings and a heap of effort to several local mining ventures, where he resorted to the use of heavy machinery, unlike most of the other local miners and prospectors. Paul had boundless energy and unbridled enthusiasm for his mining ventures, but it was only with his untimely death from a heroin overdose at one mining camp that many realised that the energy and enthusiasm together with his forever glazed eyes were products of a drug habit unfortunately picked up living through the horrors of the Korean War. Paul was such a warm and personable character whenever you encountered him that it was hard to reconcile the manner of his demise.

Lastly, I come to Trevor Cole, the epitome of the "prospector" who lived his dream to the utmost. He was a radio operator on ships that plied Australia's coastal waters, and he worked through the warmer six months of the year and then in the Top End dry season headed for his gold mine and camp not far from Grove Hill. Invariably he was accompanied by his cook, Judy, a rather attractive young lady about 20 years his junior. Trevor lived the good life pottering round his gold workings interspersed with fishing trips and generally exploring the idyllic countryside that was the Top End.

If you visited Trevor, you could expect to be harangued for several hours on the riches that lay below his inactive mine shaft. The dream was all in his head, and when he finally approached DM about undertaking some drilling on his property it was with more than a little trepidation. When drilling finally took place and failed to intersect the buried gold bonanza, his enthusiasm continued unbridled – the drillholes sited with his input must have missed the mother lode by inches.

Times spent with the above characters, and others like Snowy Casey and John Crago, were always entertaining as you got to know the backgrounds and varied experiences of these optimistic Territory diehards. Only once did I feel uncomfortable in one of their camps. Peter Gullefer and I ran into three crazy Irish prospectors/miners one day at the Emerald Springs roadhouse We had heard stories of these lads but neither of us had ever encountered them before. After several drinks they invited us back for a barbeque at their bush camp about 20 kilometres away. Foolishly we accepted the offer, thinking it was a good opportunity to inspect their mining activities the following day.

The Irish lads were well under the weather when we reached the camp and served up a decent feed but then proceeded to get decidedly boisterous as the night wore on. When two of them decided to have a punch-up, Peter and I decided it was time to retire to our swags. As we lay there the sounds of the party got louder and more heated, with occasional bursts of gunfire round the camp. I was very thankful that Peter had his trusty pump-action shotgun beside his swag. Eventually the noise subsided, and we got a few hours of uneasy sleep. Next morning we were quick to pack up and when we went to say goodbye found all our new friends comatose but alive. We departed without ever inspecting the mine workings.

14

The Hump Sign and Other Top End Misadventures

Top End, 1973–80

Lord McHugh

Early on in my Darwin life I had a visit from Paddy McHugh, whom I worked with in the Esso days in Yass. Paddy was returning slowly through Asia after a very traumatic experience in Angola. He was in a field crew undertaking geophysical surveys when they were rounded up by Cuban mercenaries who were assisting Angolan resistance fighters in their fight for independence. The crew were escorted by their Cuban captors on a march of several days to the South African border. The Cubans had been friendly and developed quite a good rapport with the geophysical crew. At the border the crew were handed over to South African soldiers and there was a happy farewell with the Cubans. Once the crew had been moved back to safety the South Africans immediately mowed down the Cubans with a barrage of gunfire, much to the dismay and shock of Paddy and his mates.

Paddy was overdue for a bit of rest and relaxation on his arrival back in Australia via Darwin. As Paddy had most of the day to kill before heading back to Perth, he and I, in company with Margaret Falvey (nee Kaye), who was also visiting Darwin at the time, headed down to Howard Springs for the morning to have a relaxing laze in the sparkling waters. Margaret, a delightful young lady, had graduated in geophysics a year before me – sadly she died of cancer only a few years later.

After a most pleasant morning we adjourned back to Darwin for a convivial and rather extended lunch at the Darwin Hotel. Late in the afternoon Paddy casually looked at his watch and realised that his flight to Perth was due to take off in about 40 minutes. This all happened on the same day as the Queen was due to fly into Perth to commence a Royal Tour of Australia. Seizing on this fact I immediately rang MacRobertson-Miller's (MMA's) airport number and advised that I had "Lord McHugh" in tow and that it was imperative that he joined the Queen's Flight in Perth. They advised getting to the airport ASAP. So, it was into the trusty old Datsun 1600 for a speedy drive to the airport. We entered the airport gates to see MMA's Fokker Fellowship just taking off for Perth, so we slowly made our way to the airport counter to try to get Paddy on the next available flight. We noticed some quizzical looks from MMA staff when Paddy breasted the counter a little the worse for wear and dressed in t-shirt, shorts and thongs; could this possibly be "Lord McHugh"? In organising a new flight, the staff were very cool in their dealings with Paddy. We thought no more about it at the time and adjourned back to the Darwin Hotel, as the next scheduled flight was not until the following morning.

It was several years later in a casual bar room chat with an ex-MMA employee that I learned that because of the "Lord McHugh" phone call the Perth headquarters of MMA had been notified and had commenced preparing a plane and requisitioning pilots for an immediate flight to Darwin to pick up our Paddy. It somewhat explains the glum faces of the staff at the time.

The Hump sign

Due to its strategic significance to Australia's defence, Darwin has always had a large RAAF presence. This was nowhere more evident in the 1970s than at Darwin airport, then a joint facility for civilian and RAAF aircraft, where RAAF facilities and accommodation were adjacent to the civilian airport facilities. It was also very apparent to the populace when annual joint exercises with allies were conducted directly over the city, with the scream of jet dog fights, a regular day and night feature for about a week. It was also a common occurrence when working in the bush to have a Mirage jet swoop over at tree top level, its roar shattering the serenity.

The airport essentially bisects the city, and its civilian lounge bar was a drawcard for Darwin locals, as it stayed open long after all other city facilities to cater for the so-called "drunk flights" which departed for the southern states in the early hours of Saturday and Sunday mornings. It was on one of these nocturnal visits that I spied a "Hump" sign dangling precariously from its post on the drive into the airport. This was a souvenir too good to ignore, so we stopped, and I quickly gave the sign a kick, at which it fell off and was quickly lodged in the back of "Tricky" Smith's blue Mazda. We then adjourned to the lounge bar, giving no more thought to the trophy. We were there to farewell one of Lumpy's mates and after a couple of hours were settling in nicely when an announcement came over the PA system "could the owner of a blue Mazda sedan registration number XXX XXX please return to their car". On the second or third repeat Tricky realized it was his car and headed out assuming he must be blocking some other vehicle. He arrived to find two RAAF military police (the RAAF were then responsible for security within the confines of the airport), who asked if he could open his boot. Without a second thought he opened the boot and there was the" Hump" sign. I had neglected to notice that the sign was adjacent to the officers' mess, and some enterprising officer had noted and reported our registration number as the sign was being souvenired. The upshot was that Tricky and I were charged with damaging Commonwealth property. Once this was finalised and the sign recovered, Tricky and I adjourned back to the bar.

A month or two later we were summoned to appear in court, and that was when I quickly learnt that you never ask a favour of a journalist, especially one from the legendary *Northern Territory News*. The day before we were due to appear I very naively contacted a journalist who was an occasional bar acquaintance, asking if media reporting of any outcome could be kept to a minimum. The upshot of the charge was that we were both fined a nominal amount and given a wrap over the knuckles, but the *NT News* couldn't help itself. Next day it wasn't on the front page but there on about page 5 in bold headlines was "HUMP SIGN UPROOTED", followed by the fact that we had been convicted of damaging Commonwealth property, an offence attracting a maximum penalty of up to two years gaol. In very small print at the end of the article they noted that we were fined $20 each. The lesson was learnt, and I've never again approached a journalist for a favour.

Adelaide River fishing safaris

The Adelaide River is renowned for its large jumping crocodiles, which in those days could be viewed on Stefan's Cruises, which were boarded near the Adelaide River bridge on the Arnhem Highway. The muddy croc-infested waters are fairly impressive on the cruise, but the river broadens even further as it heads north to the Timor Sea, where crocs and barramundi abound.

A prominent Darwin construction sand supplier, Neville Wigg (not quite sure of the name), had a sizeable fishing boat based on the river, which I believe he used to access some of his sand leases in the wet season, when vehicle tracks were impassable. Once or twice a year he would kindly invite members of the Department of Mines (DM), principally people who dealt with mining leases, on weekend fishing trips towards the mouth of the Adelaide River. I never got to go on one of these trips, but the stories of the shenanigans and big barra used to do the rounds of the office. It seemed that at least one person fell overboard on every trip, but they were always rescued before the crocs got them. Their clumsiness in falling overboard may have had something to do with the copious amounts of alcohol consumed.

The luckiest of them all was one Russell Hetherington, who had the misfortune of falling overboard while the boat was cruising down the river one evening and worse, no-one on board noticed his departure. As Russell tells it, after a split-second realisation that he was floating in the muddy waters of one of Australia's most croc-infested rivers at night, he believes he literally walked on water to get ashore ASAP. Once there he found a safe perch in a mangrove tree and waited. It must have been some time before his absence was noted; he said it felt like hours before he saw the boat's searchlight combing the banks of the river and heading his way. Fortunately, he was found and rescued. Russell went on to establish arguably one of Australia's most successful mining tenement management companies. For whatever reason Russell also had an uncanny knack of attracting the opposite sex, and there would have been a lot of disappointed ladies if the crocs had got him.

Shooting the rapids

Water sports are a big part of the Top End, and I inadvertently participated on a visit to Katherine Gorge (Nitmiluk). With Tricky, Jan and Deb in tow during a Christmas Break, we headed to Katherine for a weekend of fishing and lazing in the lower reaches of the gorge and the Katherine River. Saturday was just that, but Tricky and I decided to be a little more adventurous the following day, proposing to wade and carry the dinghy and outboard up to the second gorge and beyond. The river was quite high and running fast at that point in the wet season. As Tricky and I were struggling through some fast-moving water with the boat we were delighted when two bushwalkers saw our predicament and came to our assistance. One problem, they were quite tall and I'm quite short. With great enthusiasm they hoisted the boat high in the air, and I immediately lost my grip and the water quickly washed me into the middle of the Katherine River where I managed to hold onto some rocks to stop my progress.

There I was. a long way from shore and looking downstream at about another 50 metres of fast flowing rapids. After some shouting back and forwards it was apparent that there was no way to get a rope out to me so there were just two options, wait for other help to arrive or ride the rapids. I sat there for about five minutes contemplating the options and thinking of the rocks I might encounter and then let go, floating on top of the rapids with only a smooth rock or two encountered, then pitching over a small fall into a deep pool below, from where it was an easy swim to shore – and reputedly there were only freshwater crocs in that part of the gorge. All ended well but there was certainly a brief adrenalin rush. We decided the commercial tour might be the better option for seeing the upper gorges and all four of us booked for that afternoon. The scenery was spectacular, but we hadn't planned on the Wet Season thunderstorm we encountered during the cruise. The crescendo created by the roar of thunder reverberating off the magnificent red crags was both memorable and just a tad frightening.

Watery Mt Wells

If possible, we'd still try to undertake field work during the Wet, but when the monsoon came in properly it was not possible. The government stamp battery at Mt Wells was a preferred camping site, as you could usually stay in an empty house there to get out of the rain. On one occasion I was camped there with Grant Unsted, Fred Leonhardt, Larry Blackmore and another when the rain set in solidly. We had plenty of tinned food supplies and could have obtained more from the battery staff who lived at Mt Wells, but our booze supplies were perilously low, in fact we ran out on the first day of isolation. I was particularly miffed because as I was savouring my last can of beer, Grant managed to distract me and rub a very hot birdseye chilli around the top of the can. I still drank my beer, but the flavour isn't quite the same when your lips are burning.

On the fourth day of isolation, with the rain easing, we'd had enough and decided to make a break for the Stuart Highway, but first we had to ford two deep crossings on the McKinlay River, and I was forever grateful that we had such experienced Top-Enders in tow. At each crossing we'd first seal the lead vehicle as best we could and cover the engine with hessian bags. Two of us would then walk/swim across the river with a heavy Tirfor hand winch. After attaching the winch chain to a big tree and to the lead vehicle, we'd then hand-winch the semi-floating vehicle across. Once this vehicle and its electric components were dried up it started easily, and the vehicle winch could then be used to tow the other vehicles across. The long process was repeated at the second crossing, and after that it was a simple process of negotiating numerous boggy patches before we reached our goal, the Emerald Springs roadhouse on the Stuart Highway. After several days of tinned tucker everyone was ready for a big steak, chips and veggies washed down with a beer or two – except me – for some reason I fancied a heaped-up plate of fried onions, why I'll never know.

On another occasion Grant and I had headed down for a day-trip to Mt Wells to check on drilling progress and collect drill core. On this occasion we'd used a Holden ute so that we could pack on more long drill core trays than in our standard short wheel-base Toyotas. After a few hours at Mt Wells and having loaded the drill core on board, we decided to high-tail it, as a big storm was approaching from the north. In just a few kilometres we were in the thick of it, and by the time we reached the Margaret River crossing near Grove Hill it was running a banker, which the ute could never negotiate. We backtracked a bit and got onto the old Darwin-Larrimah railway line, which the ute negotiated rather well until it got to the disused Margaret River bridge, which it simply couldn't handle. Reversing back down the line we got back on the road and decided to return to Mt Wells, but the first creek crossing, which was dry when we left Mt Wells, was also now well under swiftly flowing water.

It was just on dusk and I was all for spending an uncomfortable night sleeping in the front of the ute, but Grant in his wisdom talked me into hoofing it back to Mt Wells, it was only ten kilometres or so. What a walk it was! With the rain and thick cloud cover it was pitch black; the only time I could see anything was when there was a regular flash of lightning in the distance. We could hear buffalo and pigs in our vicinity, but luckily never bumped into any. We also walked across fast-flowing creeks in water up to my chest – fortunately Grant was a bit taller. More than once I asked Grant, "Why the fuck are we doing this?", only to get the reply "Why not?" It was certainly a relief several hours later when we finally glimpsed a light from the drillers camp and trudged into camp hoping for a beer and a hot meal. The drillers, who had been asleep for some time, were a little underwhelmed by our late-night arrival and weren't that interested in socialising, but did eventually shout us a beer and find some blankets so that we could sleep in the dining area of their caravan. In typical Top End fashion, the next day dawned bright and sunny, and one of the drillers drove us back to the ute, negotiating the now dry creek crossings with ease.

An eventful day-trip

Peter Gullefer and I headed off on another routine day-trip to inspect drilling progress and collect drill core trays from the Princess Louise mine site near Grove Hill. After the obligatory "morning tea" stop at the Adelaide River pub, and on such a delightful Territory dry season day, we took the less travelled Yam Creek Road towards Grove Hill. I'd never been on this track, and it was also quite a while since Peter had, so it was quite a surprise to find a new (and illegally constructed) gate as we were belting round a corner. The gate went flying in the air and, stopping to inspect the carnage, we found our vehicle intact thanks largely to Peter's innovation of having a solid lump of three by four inch hardwood bolted to the front base of the roo bars on our then fleet of SWB Toyotas. The gate was another matter, and all we could do was wire it up to the posts as best we could.

Heading on and seeing a bit of wildlife about, I was surprised when Peter stated that he had never hit cattle or a single roo during all his bush travel. That ended within the next kilometre when he immediately hit two roos at once. Vehicle again okay, roos not faring too well. From there we proceeded to the Princess Louise site without further incident. After a few hours of drill core inspection and loading the core trays on board, we headed off in late afternoon using the more established Grove Hill–Fountain Head Road back to the Stuart Highway. The trip was uneventful until about fifteen kilometres out of Adelaide River, when Peter hit yet another roo near the Robin Falls turn-off. This of course called for some nerve-calming drinks at the Adelaide River pub. After a counter meal there we set off in the dark for the last leg of our now extended journey back to Darwin.

Cruising a little slower than normal because of our wildlife encounters, we had just crossed Stapleton Creek about ten kilometres out of Adelaide River when a big bull suddenly emerged from the long grass on the left-hand side of the road. There was no time to brake, just one hell of a big bang as we collided. The bull flew through the air and landed back in the grass as the Toyota slid off the bitumen on the wrong side of the road. Just as we thought the vehicle was coming to an uneventful stop, we hit a big pothole, and the vehicle gently came to a halt as it tipped on its side. I was dangling in my seatbelt above Peter but we both hastily made an exit through the left door.

While I was trying to assess vehicle damage Peter went looking for the bull, as it could have presented a real hazard in the dark. When he found the carcass, it was apparent that it had probably died on impact, but he still cut its throat to be sure. The Toyota appeared largely undamaged up front but the fiberglass roof was a bit contorted. As luck would have it headlights appeared from the south and when the vehicle stopped we recognised some other travellers whom we had chatted to at the pub. They had a winch and quickly had us upright again. After further assessment of any mechanical damage, we continued on our way but at quite a slow pace for the remainder of the trip.

It was only the next day that we realised just how lucky we had been. On inspection, and while attempting to salvage some of the scattered drill core in the back of the vehicle, we noticed that many sharp missiles of drill core from about 20 to 70 centimetres long had embedded themselves in the vinyl-covered roof above our seats in the collision. I shudder to think of the outcome if the trajectory of those lethal missiles had been a little lower.

"Two Miles to Swan"

In the early 1970s there was just one brewery in the Territory, the Carlton and United Brewery in Darwin, established in 1956 and famed for its manufacture of the 2.25 litre "Darwin stubby". However, Western Australian Swan Brewery products were also still readily available as a legacy of Swan having had a near monopoly on ownership of Darwin Hotels in the 1960s. Probably as a result of the fierce competition between the rival beermakers, impressive two-metre-high signs had been erected two miles either side of every small township on the Stuart Highway between Darwin and Tennant Creek. The signs, with a blue background, featured a huge bubbling glass of beer with the logo "Two Miles to Swan", and many a parched Territorian traveller was delighted when they came into view. It was interesting that south of Tennant Creek, and particularly in Alice Springs, products of the South Australian brewer "West End" prevailed.

You can therefore appreciate my concern when on a day-trip to Pine Creek in the late 1970s I noted with horror that these priceless heritage items were being removed, presumably as a safety issue along with work on a major re-alignment of the highway between Katherine and Darwin. Returning that day and exactly 3.2 kilometres south of Adelaide River, I noticed that one of these signs had been left lying beside the road. In a flash it was tied to the back of my ute and on its way to Darwin. What a trophy, and to add to its appeal it boasted a shotgun hole and "Out of Vietnam" on its back side, which just added to its authenticity.

Back in Darwin the sign was proudly displayed in our post-cyclone home at Anula, although Deb did object to its being a feature in the lounge room. On our leaving Darwin in late 1980, the sign came with us to continue being displayed (outside) at our home in Seacombe Heights, Adelaide, although its significance was no doubt lost on most of the locals. Having helped complete displays at the new Darwin Museum, my Danish mate Jens's next project was to be upgrading the Motor Museum in Alice Springs, and with this in mind he contacted me with a request for the sign's return to the Territory to feature in the display. Jens ultimately decided to move to the cooler climes of Tassie before this took place, so it never happened. There's a happy ending: some years later my brother-in-law Shane Reeves asked if I still had the sign because he had a perfect home for it, so it's now proudly displayed on his acre block near Humpty Doo, that legendary spot just south of Darwin where the nearby pub still serves the coldest beer in the Territory.

The Rhodesian drug baron

I had a wonderful dry season field-trip in 1976 to some of the more isolated parts of the Top End with Ian Ward, an old Papua New Guinea colleague who had also ended up in the Northern Territory. The first week of the trip involved visiting barite occurrences stretching from Dorisvale station, southwest of Pine Creek, then heading further southwest through very remote country to a crossing of the Victoria River, then back onto the bitumen at Timber Creek. The first night out we stayed at Dorisvale and were suitably entertained by the manager, one Leo Whitely. Leo was quite an erudite gentleman who chose to live the outback life.

His occasional travels to Darwin for provisions were legendary, often taking up to three weeks for what could probably have been accomplished in three days. He found taking his leave of the Green Room of the Darwin Hotel very difficult, in fact this is where I first made his acquaintance. After that the trip home would involve a protracted pub crawl via the many watering holes, namely

Berrimah, Noonamah, Adelaide River, Hayes Creek, Emerald Springs and finally Pine Creek. It wasn't unusual for him to spend at least a night at each one (I think John Shield's extended "lost" DM field-trips may have been a legacy learnt from meeting Leo at some stage).

Dorisvale Station was apparently established in the 1920s by the Liddy brothers, and the station buildings, situated not far from Bradshaw Creek, were thought to be beyond the reach of wet season flooding events until the late 1970s, when a sudden but devastating storm blew up. Indigenous inhabitants of the station headed for the nearby hills and warned Leo and others to do the same but, buoyed by 50 years of residents surviving whatever the Wet could throw at them, they opted to stay at the homestead. A huge torrent of water swept down Bradshaw Creek, and Dorisvale homestead along with its residents, including Leo, were washed away. Bradshaw Creek flows north-northeast into the mighty Daly River, and some days later Leo's remains were recovered from the Daly.

Back to our field-trip. After Dorisvale we headed southwest into what was some of the more remote country I encountered in the Territory. There were station tracks, but none looked like they'd been used much and we saw no-one for four days travelling this route. We carried published geological maps with us, and these proved invaluable in guiding us through the maze. Apart from navigation difficulties the trip went without incident, and we visited all the geological features we'd planned to. The only uncomfortable moment was when we camped near Twins Mount. Just waking up at daylight, my reverie was shattered by close gunshots which were very disturbing in such a remote area. As it turned out, Ian had been awakened by one very noisy crow, which he had hastily dispatched. After one uncertain creek crossing on Bradshaw station (we were reluctant to wade through the crossing because we figured that we were in saltwater croc country), we finally reached Timber Creek late Saturday afternoon and adjourned to the pub for a well-earned drink.

The second week of this trip took us on the bitumen back to Katherine then northeast to another remote spot on Eva Valley station (now Manyallaluk). There we were to meet one Gordon Mackie, who believed he had made a major copper discovery while prospecting in the region. Gordon, with obvious Scottish heritage and a liking for scotch whisky to go with it, had spent many years in Rhodesia, but the civil war there in the 1970s (leading to an independent Zimbabwe) saw him move to the safer climes of the Top End. He very much lived the life of a hermit at Eva Valley with occasional drinking sprees in the "big smoke" of either Katherine or Darwin. His humpy at Eva Valley was spartan to say the least, but he did have a very fertile veggie garden and a running creek and otherwise supplemented his diet with a regular bit of roo meat. Living through the wet season would have been a bit damp and breezy, but Gordon was contented with his lifestyle.

After spending a pleasant evening at his abode, we were keen to visit his discovery the next morning. Gordon wanted us to ride horses to the site as he figured it was too rough for a four-wheel drive, but we were insistent on trying to drive there. Driving at a speed somewhat faster than a horse canter completely upset Gordon's navigation, so it took some time before we located the first red volcanic outcrop riddled with a green mineral that looked very much like a copper oxide or copper carbonate mineral. The next few days were spent mapping and sampling these extensive outcrops. It was a case of being too good to be true. How could such a vast and obvious copper deposit go undetected for so long despite its remoteness? The green mineral just wasn't quite right, and I advised Gordon that it probably wasn't copper before leaving camp.

Subsequent assays and microscopic studies of the samples from Gordon's prospect showed there was no copper present and that the green mineral was in fact celadonite, a mica mineral. After informing Gordon of the negative results, little thought was given to Gordon or his Eva Valley prospect. About two years later there was Gordon on the front page of the *NT News* following his arrest for growing one of NT's larger marijuana crops at Eva Valley. I think the arresting officers may have slipped poor Gordon a whisky or two, as he not only admitted to growing the current crop but boasted that he had grown an even more productive one the previous year. I just hope the abysmal failure of his copper prospect didn't lead him in desperation to drug cultivation. If I was a betting man, I'd say Gordon was the scapegoat for a syndicate that got off scot-free.

Gordon was subsequently sentenced to gaol but was released within a year for good behaviour. I ran into him in Darwin just a few days after his release and enquired as to how tough gaol time had been for him. His response was that he was "pissed off" about his early release from the Gunn Point minimum security prison situated on the coast east of Darwin. He'd been having a great holiday; the food and lodgings were far better than Eva Valley and they were free, added to which he had got in some good fishing and learnt to scuba dive during his sojourn at Gunn Point.

Another Top End drug story relates to two public servants, Ric O'Rourke and Jim Mazlin. They were arrested after establishing a sophisticated and automatically irrigated marijuana-growing facility just off the Arnhem Highway near the Mary River, about an hour's drive from Darwin. They were each sentenced to about a year's gaol, but in true Territory fashion were allowed to take leave without pay from their government jobs for the duration of their sentences. Ric, who I knew through my connection to Lumpy (who seemed to know everyone in Darwin), was on release transferred in his job to Tennant Creek, presumably as some sort of departmental punishment. Ric, of course, took to the Tennant Creek lifestyle with gusto and thoroughly enjoyed his time there.

15

Marriage, Birth and Meanderings

Northern Territory 1976-80

In 1976 Debbie and I decided to get married, and we chose Adelaide for the ceremony, as it was her hometown and because it was central to our interstate guests. Debbie's Mum and brothers travelled from Alice Springs while my parents and sisters along with their children arrived from opposite sides of Australia, namely the South Coast of NSW, and Perth, while Neddy Barden, my best man, flew in from Darwin.

The South Coast contingent included my Mum and Dad, sister Wendy and brother-in-law Bill and their five young children. They decided to drive over in convoy, Mum, Wendy and the three girls in the Volvo wagon and Dad, Bill and the two boys in the Holden panel van (usually used for meat deliveries) with the boys settled on a mattress in the back of the van. After meeting up in Adelaide the girls spent their time shopping while the boys amused themselves by visiting the Barossa and McLaren Vale wine regions. In fact, Bill had an ulterior motive for bringing the van: on the return trip the young boys' mattress was elevated by a layer of wine cartons which Bill managed to purchase on our winery excursions.

On the day of the wedding Bill was insistent that I accompany him on a short visit to McLaren Vale to collect just a few more wines. At each winery he was quick to point out that I was getting married later that day, which opened the door to tasting some fabulous shiraz, for which McLaren Vale is renowned. After a pie for lunch, I thought we were on our way back to Adelaide, but no, Bill decided we should have just one more taste, at the d'Arenberg winery. On about the third taste, and with a wedding at 5.00pm, I finally managed to convince my chauffeur it was time to leave just before 2.00pm.

When we got back to the motel at Glenelg, Neddy, my best man, had arrived and was keen to ply me with a few calming ales before the ceremony. Somehow, we got to the historic church at Reynella on time. The bride was radiant, the groom managed to conceal any effects of the wine tasting, and an enjoyable wedding and later reception at Brighton followed. Given that Debbie and I had made all the arrangements by phone from Darwin long before the internet or mobile phones, this all went surprisingly smoothly.

Tanami Desert honeymoon

A day or two after the wedding we said our farewells and Debbie and I flew to Alice Springs and stayed a night with her Mum and partner Harold Drakeford before setting off on our Territory honeymoon. Harold was another old Central Australian character. He'd been the local Alice Springs barber for many years and told many wonderful tales of early life in Alice from information he'd gleaned from his many customers. Harold was now the agent for Hardy's wine in the Alice and a visit to his warehouse was a revelation: neatly stacked around the sides of the interior were a few crates of various Hardy's table wines, but overshadowing all this was a mountain of crates containing flagons of Hardy's port. I believe that at that time Alice Springs was possibly the largest outlet in Australia for Hardy's port sales. Little wonder that the new NT Government banned sales of flagon port in the NT a few years later, only for sales of somewhat less potent cask Moselle to skyrocket.

We headed off on the first leg to Ayers Rock (Uluru) and the Olgas (Kata Tjuta) in our newish but tiny Subaru 4WD (the first model released in Australia), travelling via Hermannsburg, the more remote route. I sought directions at the Hermannsburg store and was assured by a local that it was exactly 100 kilometres to Kings Canyon. After travelling that distance, we were in the middle of the Meerenie oilfield and nowhere near Kings Canyon. I was glad once again to have brought published geological maps with me, which were a great assistance to navigation. When we finally reached a point where the track descended from the plateau to the plain below, it was a case of no turning back as the Subaru could never get back up the rocky track we were descending (today this section of the track is sealed road). From the base of the hill it was a bit unnerving not knowing our location until we reached the old camping area at the entrance to Kings Canyon. What a relief it was to reach that point, as we hadn't seen another soul since Hermannsburg. With little in the way of maps or marked walking trails, we had a good look around the base of the canyon area, then headed 100 kilometres east to the roadhouse at Wallara Ranch, where a track led south to Ayers Rock (Uluru). After a meal and a few drinks at Wallara we camped not far away.

It was only about fifteen years ago that I learned I was related to some of the early pioneers of this region, who were involved in the later development of Kings Canyon as a tourist destination. My great uncle Harry Earwaker had headed north from Adelaide as a young fellow to try to make his fortune mining rubies in the Harts Range northeast of Alice Springs but eventually ended up as the first blacksmith in Alice after also working at the old telegraph station. He married a full blood Arrernte woman and they had two daughters, Mary and Rosa. Harry sadly died in his early 40s in 1903, of typhoid fever, when the girls were quite young. The older daughter Mary married another South Australian lad, Bill Liddle, who became a pioneering pastoralist in the region. In 1929 Bill took up the first pastoral lease in the area, which he named Angas Downs after his hometown of Angaston in South Australia.

Over the ensuing years the property was run first by Bill and then Bill's and Mary's three sons, Milton, Harold and Arthur. Arthur eventually gained full ownership in 1956 and ran it with his wife Bessie for over 30 years. It was Arthur who in 1960 showed budding tourist operators Jack and son Jim Cotterill through the maze of Kings Canyon. Arthur also invited the Cotterills to build a tourist facility on Angas Downs, which in turn became Wallara Ranch. After completing the building and constructing the 100-kilometre track to Kings Canyon, the Cotterills commenced tours in the early 1960s. With later improvements to access roads and construction of other tourist facilities closer to the canyon, Wallara Ranch was superseded and was demolished (burnt down) in 1990.

The next day we drove on to Ayers Rock and stayed at the hotel/motel conveniently located at the base of "the Rock". With no National Park in those days we drove the little Subaru everywhere, right around the Rock and later all over the Olgas, driving between many of the domes and up towards the Valley of the Winds. Thank goodness there's no road access today, allowing people to really appreciate the tranquillity and timelessness of these geological formations, which existed long before humans ever walked this planet.

From the Rock we headed to the Stuart Highway, then on to Alice Springs, where we visited many of the gorges. Happily, we had those west of Stanley Chasm all to ourselves. Finally, we left Alice and headed for Palm Valley, where I got the Subaru hopelessly bogged in the thick sand. We had to sleep in the stranded vehicle that night until a passing station hand pulled us out the next day. From there we went further west, then north, where we had passing glimpses of Gosses Bluff, a huge 22-kilometre-wide impact structure formed about 140 million years ago when a large meteorite or comet struck the earth. We stayed overnight at the indigenous settlement of Papunya to visit one of Debbie's Aboriginal Affairs colleagues. Even then petrol sniffing was rife, and we were warned to lock up the vehicle tank and any other petrol supplies. Next day we headed north again along little-used station tracks until we finally hit the Tanami Track.

Before the revival of gold mining at the Granites and Tanami the track was mainly like a superhighway. In my estimation it was smoother to drive on than the main Stuart Highway between Alice Springs and Darwin. The little Subaru had no trouble keeping up a steady 100km/h.

After a short fuel stop at the indigenous community of Yuendumu (there wasn't much else to keep you there), then a desultory inspection of old mine workings at the Granites, we stopped overnight at Rabbit Flat, purportedly the most remote roadhouse in Australia. The roadhouse was opened by Bruce and Jacqui Farrands in mid-1969 to cater for an increase in tourists and tour operators travelling the Tanami Track between Alice Springs and Halls Creek in Western Australia. It also served as a remote weather station for the Bureau of Meteorology. Bruce, a station hand, and Jacqui, a visiting French tourist with limited English, had met on one of the remote stations in the area, and were married in Perth in January 1968 before returning to the Territory and making the decision to open Rabbit Flat.

The opening of a liquor and fuel outlet led to issues with indigenous groups travelling through the region, and the Farrands had a bit of a love-hate relationship with them. The development of numerous gold mines at the Granites and Tanami goldfields in the mid-1980s saw a sudden boost in business until the companies involved opened their own on-site wet canteens. The Farrands, now in their early 70s, closed the business after 41 years in 2010, but continued to live on-site and take weather observations.

On our arrival we entered the "roadhouse-fort" to find ourselves in a small, barred cubicle about the size of a phone box. After we were inspected through the grid by Bruce, another door was opened, giving access to a pleasant little bar and shop area. When we announced that we wished to camp there overnight, Bruce went out of his way to make us welcome, even lighting fires to warm the hot water in both the ladies' and gents' facilities, which we found somewhat amusing given we were the only guests, but he insisted things had to be done right. On this and later visits Bruce could be a tad cantankerous at times, but he was always the perfect gentleman.

From Rabbit Flat we travelled on to the very impressive Wolfe Creek meteorite crater, then to Halls Creek. At Halls Creek, and later at Kununurra and Timber Creek, we shouted ourselves to more comfortable hotel or motel rooms, which was a blessing after the freezing nights encountered while camping in the Centralian desert regions. We even took a very pleasant scenic cruise on the newly constructed and massive Lake Argyle near Kununurra. From Timber Creek it was just a day's drive before we were home in Darwin. The clear, sunny days on the trip were wonderful, and night skies under the stars were spectacular, but I'm not sure Debbie ever forgave me for that honeymoon as opposed to say a Great Barrier Reef option.

Murgenella Ranger

I first met Frank Woerle at the Border Store, on a field-trip with Peter Gullefer. The store sat above Cahill's Crossing on the East Alligator River and served as a de facto pub for locals, occasional tourists and for residents of the dry indigenous community of Oenpelli (Gunbalanya) some fifteen kilometres to the east. Whatever licence it had, alcohol sales were restricted to beer only. We spent a few pleasant hours with Frank, who was then the ranger at nearby Cannon Hill, as we planned to camp the night nearby. When we finally left to camp that night, I couldn't help asking Peter what was going on, as Frank appeared to be drinking cans of pineapple juice all evening but got more jovial as the night went on. How naïve I was! Whenever Frank ordered a pineapple juice, the barman would wander out the back with the can, empty half and refill it with rum – so much for the liquor restrictions if you were a local legend.

Frank was indeed a Top End legend. Born in Bavaria in 1931, he endured the hardships and horror of the Second World War before arriving in Australia in 1951. Starting first in construction at Morwell in Victoria, Frank variously worked grape-picking, tractor-driving, wood-cutting and rabbit-trapping before arriving by motorbike in the Territory in 1952, where he worked as a uranium explorer and miner, a road surveyor and a pearl diver among other things, before establishing the first ranger station at Cannon Hill in 1970, in the declared sanctuary that was yet to be proclaimed as Kakadu National Park. Apart from a few years in British Columbia in the 1960s, he never left his beloved Top End. After a few years at Cannon Hill, with tourists increasing exponentially and a bevy of uranium explorers traipsing through the Alligator Rivers region, Frank once again sought the solitude of the bush with a transfer to the newly constructed and remote ranger station at Murgenella in Western Arnhem Land. Frank's story, as narrated by him to author Colin Thiele, is told in detail in the book *Ranger's Territory*, published in 1987.

On an environmental assessment field-trip with John Willis, we caught up with Frank and his lovely wife Gwynn at Aurari Bay to the east of Murgenella. Gwynn and Frank had married in the NT in 1959, and Gwynn had shared most of his outback adventures while bringing up a young son who was by then at boarding school. The Aurari Bay location was idyllic, and I remember enjoying some of the best marinated sartees (a Top End specialty) that I'd ever tasted, which Frank had prepared. Only after enjoying them was I told they weren't made of steak but buffalo liver, and a quick inspection of a few leftovers confirmed this. Sitting by the beach in the moonlight and after a drink or two, I was waxing lyrical and raving about this being the best surf I had seen since living in Darwin (the local Casuarina beach near Darwin usually only offered ripples except when there were storms in the Wet, and then you couldn't enter because of sea wasps). What a fool I was.

Rising early the next morning Frank announced the he and I were going to take on that good surf, in the same breath assuring me that the big croc which inhabited the beach was always down the southern end early in the morning. He just dropped his gear and headed off into the surf; assuming this was the norm I did the same, I'm sure Gwynn had seen it all before through her many bush experiences. It was wonderful to catch a few waves, but I couldn't help thinking about that croc (if there was one). At least the water was crystal clear. The northern end of the beach at Aurari Bay I believe is now known as Wunyi Beach. Frank wasn't quite finished with us yet, and after breakfast suggested that John and I accompany him on a trip further along the coast in his small dinghy. In the shallows and a kilometre or two from his vehicle, the outboard broke down, at which Frank announced we'd have to drag it all the way back in the shallows. He also advised us to look out for stonefish, as they were plentiful on the rocky bottom. We all had rubber soled shoes on, but I understand they offer little protection from a stonefish spike, so it was a somewhat uncomfortable wade back through waist to knee-deep water.

In those days it was quite difficult for a member of the public to get a permit to enter Arnhem Land for recreational purposes, and here a friendship with Frank was a great asset. His advice: when you apply for a permit to travel through Oenpelli, just say you're on your way to visit me at Murgenella. We did just that and had some wonderful fishing trips to the coast northwest of Murgenella at Mountnorris Bay, although we never ventured further westward into Coburg Peninsula. After we crossed the East Alligator River, the plains and hill scenery, especially as viewed from Ubirr, were a delight to travel through, before we entered some unique country with very tall palms, then it was on to Murgenella. We'd always call in to see Frank as per permit, but invariably he was out elsewhere in the bush. The coastal area at Mountnorris Bay, with its sandy beaches and great fishing, was an untouched paradise.

On one trip, with Debbie, Tricky and Jan in tow, Tricky and I couldn't refrain from launching the dinghy the moment we got there, leaving the girls to set up camp. A couple of kilometres offshore the outboard motor conked out – in our haste I'd forgotten to fill the fuel tank. Luckily, we'd thrown in the oars, but no anchor and no water (let alone beer). With the tide going out fast it took us the best part of two hours frantic rowing to get back to shore while the girls, oblivious to our predicament, lazed in the afternoon sun with a cool drink. Once we'd rehydrated ourselves with a few cold beers and fully fuelled and equipped, we set off again with the girls in tow. The fish were biting and we caught some nice trevally and cod. Preparing a wonderful fresh seafood barbeque that evening, Tricky and I were a bit dismayed, Jan wouldn't eat the fish because it didn't come from a shop and Debbie, who loved fish, took one look at her plate and was sick. Tricky and I managed to do justice to the feast and cook a steak for Jan. When Debbie repeated the performance the following night she quickly guessed at the problem: our first-born, Teneille, was on her way.

The last time I met Frank he had a huge slash diagonally across his face. It looked like a knife cut, but he assured us he got it walking through mangroves just after the tide had gone out when he inadvertently walked into a sea wasp tentacle caught in mangrove branches. I have no reason to doubt him, though he could spin a good yarn. A man troubled by a society which gave rise to World War 2, he very much sought to escape that way of life and gain solace from and be at one with the Top End bush. Frank died in 2015.

Celebrating a birth

Many months after the Murgenella trip and on a balmy Monday evening, Teneille was showing signs that she wanted to vacate her living quarters of the last nine months, so Debbie was quickly driven to the Royal Darwin Hospital for an imminent birth. Maybe Teneille had second thoughts, as Debbie had to endure eighteen hours of intermittent labour before Teneille finally emerged at 2.00pm the following day. Dr Mounsey, the obstetrics specialist who delivered her, had apparently had some bad experiences with husbands attending births, and it took a lot of cajoling and promising before I was able to be present , for which I'm forever grateful. After staying with Debbie and our new daughter for about half an hour, I was politely but firmly told by the duty sister that I should leave and not return until the following morning, as mother and daughter both needed a good rest. Leaving the hospital grounds, I was both elated and somewhat overcome that I now had responsibility for the welfare of another.

After informing close relatives of the happy event, I decided to call my mate Lumpy at work but was informed that he had the day off and could be found in the Green Room at the Darwin Hotel, where he was celebrating his birthday. This was too good an opportunity, so I soon joined him there for a few celebratory drinks. He was absolutely delighted that he and Teneille shared the same birthday. Before leaving I arranged for Lumpy and a few other friends to come to our house for an impromptu barbeque that evening.

Our next-door neighbour had been away for an extended Christmas break for over two months, as was common in Darwin then. He'd arranged no mowing in his absence so his whole backyard was covered in two-metre-high grass. There and then I formed the idea for a celebratory event fitting such a momentous occasion. Just before guests were due to arrive, I poured outboard fuel all along the neighbour's side of a low wire fence which separated our properties. Once guests had arrived, and ensuring none were too close to the fence, I lit a match with a flourish as if to light the BBQ but instead threw the match into the neighbor's yard. The spectacular results exceeded my wildest dreams: there was a huge thumping bang and suddenly the fence line was lit up by four metre flames over its fifteen-metre length. I'd calculated that the rest of the grass was so wet that it wouldn't burn, so the spectacle was short-lived, but my guests were suitably impressed.

You'd probably have the fire brigade on your doorstep and a huge fine (if not jail time) if you did the same today, but this was Darwin, 1978, and it was a momentous occasion.

Once Debbie and Teneille were home, things slowly settled into a new normality, and I was doing short field-trips, but was now always anxious to get home to my little girl. It was several months before I ventured out on a more extended field-trip to the very remote Birrindudu station, southeast of Halls Creek (see chapter 16), near the WA border.

Ancient treasures

I had the privilege to accompany fellow geologist John Willis and George Chaloupka on a trip visiting incredible cave painting sites in Kakadu National Park and at Mt Borradaile (Awunbarna) in western Arnhem Land. George had fled the communist regime in Czechoslovakia as a seventeen-year-old and migrated to Australia in 1950. Travelling with family in 1956, he lobbed in Darwin and after vehicle breakdowns they decided to stay (indeed, George stayed until he died in Darwin Hospital in 2011). He initially worked with the Water Resources Department, a job that took him all over the Top End, and when he came upon ancient cave paintings in Arnhem Land in 1958 his future was settled. George joined the Northern Territory Museum in 1973 and established himself as an eminent rock art researcher and photographer.

George was a gentle and modest soul who established such trust and rapport with many indigenous traditional owners that he was able to wander freely and unaccompanied through many of their sacred sites. John and I accompanied George on this trip because John was undertaking an environmental assessment of the region prior to any uranium mining taking place at Nabarlek and Ranger, and before the Commonwealth Government took over environmental monitoring and assessment of the Kakadu National Park region through the Office of the Supervising Scientist. I was on the trip to learn a little about environmental assessment.

Some of the sites we visited were quite amazing, and some were in cave systems with little light. Presumably the artists had fires going to provide light when they did their work. The intricate x-ray style detail was amazing, and the unfaded colours were outstanding. Generally, the paintings we saw were better than in any of the publicly available sites in Kakadu National Park, and it's wonderful that George was able to catalogue and photograph so many of these ancient treasures. The feeling as you stood to observe some of these sites was quite mystical, and the quote "and his heart was lost", to describe George as he gazed at the ceiling of a cave covered with art back in 1958, takes on real meaning. I'm forever grateful to have had this opportunity.

Tennant Creek

In 1979 I was seconded to Tennant Creek for about two months while the resident geologist with the Department of Mines (DM), John Howard, was on extended leave. It was an interesting experience to say the least. At the same time a Darwin-based mining registrar, Harry Harmer, was also replacing the local incumbent.

Tennant Creek was a completely different town back then, with little or none of the overt violence that plagues it today, with night-time youth crime and domestic violence rampant, coupled with a culture of alcohol and drug abuse. Tennant Creek in 1979 was a cohesive and friendly community with steady (though winding down) employment provided by the Nobles Knob gold mine and Peko's mining and processing operations. It was so cohesive that on a Wednesday afternoon the whole town almost shut down while the miners, business owners and public servants played golf and then deployed to the bar. There was always some heavy drinking on welfare paydays as is and was prevalent in so many isolated country towns throughout Australia.

The closure of the major mines and the use of fly-in fly-out operators on some newer mid-size mining projects has had a huge impact on the town economy, likewise a major increase in the indigenous population due to their moving from remote stations to settlements both within and adjacent to town precincts. With long-term employment opportunities close to zero it's little wonder indigenous youth despair over their lot in life, giving rise to the social issues there today.

During our stay in 1979 Harry and I lived in the single men's quarters of the government-owned gold battery about a kilometre east of the township. Apart from breakfast we lived largely on takeaway and pub and club meals during our stay. Harry was about my age, but was a long-term Territorian and a most affable fellow, whose family had been among the early settlers of the Territory in the early 1900s. Harry and I both loved a beer, and if I wasn't in the field it wasn't unusual for us to down tools and head to the Memorial Club come noon for a heart-starter.

Harry had joined the army after school and served in Vietnam, and back in the Territory he eventually found his calling as a mining registrar with DM. He died way too early, in 2003, but an extract from his obituary sums him up perfectly: "Harry was well recognised, appreciated and highly respected throughout his public service career, as the font of knowledge, the walking encyclopedia of the ... Mining Act (*NT*). Harry had a good rapport with all clients, even the rogues, for they respected his knowledge and interpretations of the legislation."

The breathalyzer was first introduced into the Territory and Tennant Creek while Harry and I were on our sojourn. This prevented use of a vehicle if one was heading to a pub or the Memorial Club for a counter meal. We adopted a novel approach to getting home late in the evening, simply flagging down the police paddy wagon for a lift home to the battery. They were always obliging, but I think the novelty was wearing a bit thin by the time we left Tennant Creek.

Ron Paterson, the manager of the battery and a long-term resident of Tennant Creek, warrants a brief mention here. Ron was missing all the fingers on one hand, the result of accidentally having his hand crushed while trying to clear some residue, when the heavy stamper designed to crush rock was activated. He said there was little pain at the time because his fingers essentially ceased to exist.

One of my jobs while in Tennant Creek was to assess the mineral potential of an area about five kilometres north of the town, where development of a recreational dam was proposed. This was an interesting exercise where, instead of hoping to find a mineral deposit, one was really hoping that all survey results would come back negative, which they did. Today the area is inundated by the Mary Ann Lake, a delightful oasis in an otherwise very dry, but scenic, environment.

The Territory is not enough

1979 saw the briefest dry season in the Top End during my time there. In other words, it was very hot and humid for most of the year, to the point where Debbie and I started considering a move to cooler climes. I was also acutely aware that the ten-year time span after which the Territory traps you was fast approaching. A field-trip to Alice Springs confirmed my fear that the Territory was just too small.

I was accompanied on this trip by Mike Willick, a born and bred Territorian who grew up around Banka Banka station, north of Elliot. Mike was an NT representative cricketer who had temporarily transferred from Alice Springs to Darwin to further his cricketing career. He was a friendly bloke and a good bush companion.

At every stop we made heading south, at either a pub or roadhouse, at least one of us knew someone at the bar (besides the publican). A stop at Barrow Creek revived memories of Jimmy Hereen, who was once the publican there. Jimmy, a wiry little fellow, joined the Alice Springs branch of DM and worked several years as a roving prospector, spending much of his time west of Tennant Creek and in the remote Tanami Desert. Well, not always. Once Jimmy was supposed to be on a three-week trip in the Tanami in November. At the Melbourne Cup that year, the television cameras zoomed in on this little fellow with a big Stetson hat – yes, it was Jim, his vehicle safely stowed in his brother's backyard in Tennant Creek. There were never any repercussions, and he was never asked to repay the travel allowance he received while attending the Cup – it was just Jim. One day he walked into the Darwin office and announced he was shouting beers at the Darwin Hotel because he was leaving. At that time, retirement at age 65 was mandatory in the NT public service. Later at the bar someone asked why he was resigning from such a cushy job. "The bastards found out my age," he retorted – turns out he was 75. Jim also featured in the Ted Egan classic, "Bloody Good Drinkers".

After completing our work around Alice Springs we decided to return to Darwin via Rabbit Flat and the Tanami to avoid the delays and expenses incurred by socialising with such acquaintances – after all there were only two watering holes before hitting the Victoria Highway, southwest of Katherine. It didn't work: at Rabbit Flat there was one person at the bar beside proprietor Bruce Farrands. This turned out to be an old schoolmate of Mike's who was now managing Mongrel Downs (now Tanami Downs) Station on the NT-WA border. Not only did this result in an extended stay at Rabbit Flat, it also included a 50-kilometre detour and overnight stay at Mongrel Downs.

The only other stop on this lonely route was at the Top Springs Hotel, and once again both Mike and I knew patrons there, resulting in further delays. The following day we made a beeline for Darwin, stopping for fuel only. Demonstrably the Territory wasn't big enough and it was time to move on.

16

Swimming with Crocodiles

Northern Territory, 1973-80

After the discovery of the massive Olympic Dam copper-uranium-gold deposit near Andamooka in South Australia in 1975, information slowly seeped out to the industry regarding the nature of the discovery. Follow-up on large regional magnetic and gravity features defined by the Bureau of Mineral Resources (BMR) in surveys conducted in the 1950s and 1960s had led to the discovery. One such large unexplored magnetic feature (which also sat along an Australia-wide north-northwest-trending linear feature on which Olympic Dam was also aligned) was situated on the very remote Birrindudu Station, southeast of Halls Creek near the Western Australian border. Around July in 1978 we planned a field-trip to locate this feature precisely on the ground using ground magnetic and gravity surveys, with a view to later drill testing to promote company mineral exploration interest in this remote region.

Ma Hawks

I accompanied that old rascal Peter Gullefer from Darwin and rendezvoused with then Alice Springs–based geophysicist Peter Woyzbun ("Woyzie") at the

Dunmarra Roadhouse on the Stuart Highway about 630 kilometres south of Darwin, where we spent a pleasant night. From there we headed west on what's now the Buchanan Highway but was then a mainly dirt track passing through Top Springs. The longstanding and elderly female publican at Top Springs was a legend in these parts: she kept an electric cattle prod behind the bar and was known to have used it from time to time on patrons who got a bit out of hand. Thelma, "Old Ma Hawks", arrived at Top Springs in 1949. She must have been tough as nails to keep the ringers in check, but she did; she was also affectionately known as "leather tits". She had one long-time employee, Norm Douglas. She died on the toilet on 10 May 1981. Legend had it that she had cash stashed all over the pub and the surrounding countryside, and this was borne out when local cop Constable Kevin Dailly and his mate William Purdie were convicted of raiding and stealing from the premises immediately after she died. What an amazing lady she was to run that pub for over 30 years in some of Australia's toughest country.

There are two other yarns about Ma Hawks circulating. Her brother was Paul Anderson, "the Mighty Young Apollo, a famous Australian strongman who performed in circuses and shows from the 1930s right through to the 1970s. Another story goes that Northern Territory government road crews often quenched their thirst at Ma Hawks' pub. On one occasion they informed her that a new road was going to replace the old one, but unfortunately would bypass the pub. Surprisingly, soon after, there was a fire which razed the building. On receiving the insurance payout, Ma Hawks erected a new building, on the new route.

Birrindudu bivouac

On the day we called in we settled for a few quick beers before heading off down what is now the Buntine Highway to camp on the Armstrong River, next day heading further west through Kalkarindji (Wave Hill) towards the WA border. At Inverway station we headed south to Birrindudu. After a chat and cuppa with the station manager, Jim Dooley, we headed 30 kilometres east to our target area near Mosquito Creek, on the northern edge of the Tanami Desert.

Work over the next week or so was uneventful, with warm days and rather chilly nights camping under the stars and, despite the name, no mosquitoes. To counter the cold nights, we had a ration of a bottle of Bundaberg rum each as well as an ample beer supply. After our first night in camp both Peter Gullefer and I noticed that some of our rum had evaporated overnight, so we had the temerity to draw a waterline mark in Texta on our respective bottles. Woyzie was mortified by our actions, but we had no trouble with evaporation after that. Lying in my swag on those starry nights I really missed my new daughter Teneille, an emotion I'd never really encountered in the bush before.

On finishing our work at Birrindudu, Woyzie headed off alone back to Alice Springs via Dunmarra, while Peter Gullefer and I decided to take a detour through Halls Creek and Kununurra before heading back to Darwin. We organised a radio schedule to ensure Woyzie was safely back on the Stuart Highway. As Peter and I headed west from Inverway we noticed that there was no other traffic (not that there was ever much) and the road got progressively wetter and more slippery as we approached Halls Creek. As we reached Halls Creek, we found a "Road Closed" sign. The constabulary wasn't particularly happy when we arrived, but understood the issue when we explained where we'd come from; there'd been no rain at Birrindudu.

After a pleasant night at Halls Creek, topped off by sharing a half-bottle of that ever-so-potent WA rum, we reached Lake Argyle the next day. During our evening there Peter was waxing lyrical about how nice a spot the Victoria River crossing was (about 100 kilometres from Timber Creek) and how some enterprising person should build a pub there. Next day the unbelievable happened: as we rounded the bend before the Victoria River crossing there it was, the brand-new Victoria River Inn. We felt compelled to stop and sample its wares and finally camped a little north of Katherine before returning to Darwin the next day after another memorable but for me homesick field-trip.

The ultimate Gulf trip

In 1976 I was tasked with reviewing the mineral potential of the NT Gulf region and Barkly Tableland as part of a joint Commonwealth/NT/Queensland feasibility study into developing a shorter transport route direct from Camooweal in Queensland, across the vast tableland to Elliot on the Stuart Highway in the NT. This would have cut hundreds of kilometres off the current route, but it never happened. I could probably have effectively done the review as an office study but felt that I needed to inspect many of the potential mineral prospects and the area itself first-hand.

So, in the latter part of 1976, in company with that bombastic South African Harry Mills, I set off from Darwin in our short-wheelbase Toyota in what proved to be a fascinating experience. Trip planning had involved little more than checking with local police that all roads were open in that very hot and stormy season leading into the Wet. Harry and I had never travelled through the Gulf country before so had no idea of what to expect.

After stopping at a few watering holes on the way down the Stuart Highway, with a more protracted stop at Mataranka, we headed east toward Roper Bar. Arriving there late in the afternoon, we had no idea where to camp or what if any facilities were available. Heading down towards the Roper River crossing we passed right beside the police quarters, where a couple of officers were sitting outside having a quiet drink. As we passed, with windows wide open, Harry couldn't help making a remark about "slack coppers". We proceeded to the crossing but had barely stopped when the paddy-wagon came racing down with said coppers on board. They were on a mission and as I hopped out to greet them several empty beer cans fell from the driver's side door; this wasn't looking good and they were fairly belligerent at first, until they realised we weren't boot-leggers running sly grog into the indigenous community of Ngukurr on the other side of the river.

After they calmed down and Harry assured them his comments hadn't been meant for their ears, they shared a beer or two with us as we explained why we were in Roper Bar. Not only did they point us to a lovely camping site perched on a high point well above the river, but they also insisted that we touch base with the police at Wollogorang near the Queensland border when we passed through in a week or so's time to ensure we didn't go permanently missing, as they said "nobody uses that track at this time of year".

After a good night's sleep, we headed for Borroloola with several interesting river crossings to negotiate. The first, the Towns River, gave us no problems, but the next, the Cox River, proved a little more difficult. First, we got bogged in the dry sand approach, but quickly freed ourselves without recourse to the winch; but it was the river crossing itself that was daunting. It meandered over a shallow laterite base for what seemed like 150 metres or so in water up to a metre deep. The concern was deviating from the winding track and ending up hopelessly stuck in deeper water, which was infested with saltwater crocodiles (although we saw none). As it turned out the crossing was negotiated with no further incident and all later river crossings were easier. The track took us through vast cattle station country including one then owned by legendary tennis player Rod Laver, but apart from the river crossings it offered little to talk of. Our stop-off that night was with a Union Carbide exploration crew who were searching for manganese deposits in the area with a camp on Rosie Creek. What a delightful camp it was, with not only the creek but hot springs to boot. I believe the tourist oasis of Lorella Springs now occupies the area. After a long dusty drive, lazing in the hot springs was wonderful and we were then shouted to a great, freshly caught barramundi dinner. Young crocodile was often on the camp menu, but we missed out on that delicacy.

A broken esky

After looking at some of the company's exploration areas next morning, we headed off for Borroloola. Disaster struck on the way when the foam lid of our over-sized esky containing all our fresh food and beer supplies disintegrated when some heavy object placed on top bounced one too many times on the very corrugated track. On arrival in the township, we went looking for a new esky or lid with no success, then headed for the coast at Bing Bong Station, where a port was to be constructed as a loading facility for the McArthur River mine, some 60 kilometres inland, if the mine ever got developed. The McArthur River silver-lead-zinc deposit was discovered in the 1950s, one of the world's larger deposits of these minerals. It was still undeveloped in 1976 but today is a major mine run by the mining giant Glencore. Mt Isa Mines, the then owner, had no staff on site at the time of our visit, so we were unable to inspect it.

Back at Borroloola we set up camp for the night on the banks of the McArthur River and were later joined by three Alice Springs residents who were on a boys-only fishing safari. Over a few beers that night the dilemma of our broken esky lid was discussed at length and it was decided that the only sane approach was to drink all the beer and eat all the fresh food before continuing our journey to Burketown with no beer and only tinned food.

So, a lay day was called and what a day it was. After stocking up with adequate supplies of ice we did a bit of fishing, but it was soon midday (well, somewhere) and the beers started flowing. At the river crossing where we were camped there were regular sightings of large saltwater crocs, so during the morning we were careful not to set foot in the river. By mid-afternoon, with the hot sun beating down and a few beers under the belt, caution went out the door and we all ended up swimming in that river. At some stage I managed to dive in and hit the bottom hard, fortunately not hard enough for any permanent neck damage (probably because of my relaxed state), but it certainly meant that the next few days travelling were extremely uncomfortable. The day/night ended with no further mishap, all personnel accounted for and mission accomplished: there was no more beer in the broken esky.

A little worse for wear, Harry and I set off early the next day, but mid-morning we struck another problem when we got bogged in dry sand on the Robinson River crossing. We easily extricated the vehicle with the winch but then heard strange sounds emanating from beneath. On inspection we discovered that the speedometer/odometer cable had become tightly twisted around the winch driveshaft. It took about two hours working in shifts under a very hot vehicle and laying on very hot sand to cut and remove the high tensile steel cable. This created quite a navigational problem for the rest of the trip. Not knowing our speed – generally slow – wasn't an issue, but not knowing the distance travelled was a major impediment.

We headed on and visited old copper-mining operations at Redbank. These deposits were discovered by William "Bill" Masterton in 1916, and he worked them sporadically using mainly indigenous labour until his death in 1961. For most of this time he lived in a cave/overhanging rock near the mine, and his sparse furnishings, metal bed, stove and cupboards were still in evidence when we passed through in 1976.

From Redbank it was on to Wollogorang and a call into the police station as instructed, then on toward the NT/Queensland border trying to locate a few smaller uranium deposits in this area. Finding a well-used track late in the day, we followed it in for a few kilometres until we came to an exploration camp, but on greeting the occupants we were surprised to find it wasn't the camp we were after and that we were in fact in Queensland and not the NT. However, we were invited to stay the night, so we enjoyed a good meal and discussion about uranium deposits in the general area.

Leaving the next morning we were given directions to the camp we thought we were originally heading to, but on arrival discovered it had already been vacated for the summer months. So, we headed south from the main track towards the Nicholson River, where we knew a team from the Bureau of Mineral Resources

(BMR) were undertaking a dry season geological mapping program. The track, presumably one put in for past mineral exploration, hadn't been used in a long time and was rough and overgrown in part, but we persisted for about 80 kilometres to the distinctive China Wall and an exploration area, which had been extensively sampled and drilled, on Seigel Creek. There was no sign of the BMR camp, so we decided that discretion was the better part of valour and retraced our steps north to the main track.

The bright lights of Burketown

From here we made a b-line for Burketown, stopping to pick up a stray indigenous man soon after crossing the border into Queensland. He appeared quite happy walking the 50 kilometres or so into Doomadgee with no hat or water evident but gladly accepted the offer of a lift. It was dark as we approached Burketown and with no odometer, we really didn't know how far we'd travelled but suddenly this seemingly huge array of bright lights appeared in the distance. We were quite excited, thinking Burketown might be rather larger than anticipated, but were disappointed as we drove into the tiny township (with bright streetlights) with everything shut and not a soul to be seen.

As we approached the pub it too appeared to be in darkness, but on opening the door we found what appeared to be the whole town's populace inside enjoying themselves. We managed to scrounge some rather dry old meat pies for a meal, but at least the beer was cold and the company was merry. As things started getting rowdy around 10.00pm, blinds came down, lights went off and most of the crowd were herded out the door, but we noticed some were lurking at one end of the bar, so we quietly joined them. Immediately the last of the crowd were bundled out the door, the lights came back on, and the drinks flowed freely into the early hours of the morning.

On finally departing we realised that we still needed to find a camp spot, so headed out on this flat plain area on the edge of town and crawled into our swags.

Waking after a peaceful night's sleep and wandering off a little way as nature called, I made a disturbing discovery: the fresh claw of what must have been a very large croc. On further investigation we found we'd camped not far from the large and murky river. Fuelling up a little later we told the service station attendant about our camping spot. He declared that we were mad (or words to that effect).

The road to Camooweal

Our plan from here was to head to Camooweal following the track along the Gregory River but imagine our delight when the Gregory Downs Hotel came into view along this otherwise deserted track, so we decided to stop for an (admittedly somewhat early) drink or two. As we entered the bar there was already a small group quite enjoying themselves. It turned out to be the BMR mapping crew, who had only broken camp the day before and were now celebrating before the long drive back to Canberra. We couldn't help but join them, and there was some meaningful discussion about the mineral potential of the area they were mapping during the afternoon. A pleasant evening ensued and as the jukebox got louder the floorboards were bouncing. On a visit back there in 2019 I noticed they still do. Our campsite that first night was beside our vehicle out the front of the pub. Today you'd probably be run over by a stray cattle train or grey nomad with a ten-metre caravan if you camped in the same spot.

The publican and the BMR boys told us during the evening that we must take a detour and visit Lawn Hill Gorge (Boodjamulla) on the way to Camooweal, so we set off west early the next morning and what a revelation that gorge was, not as extensive as Katherine Gorge but equally spectacular with its red cliffs and emerald waters. Having it all to ourselves, we found the grandeur and serenity of this untouched piece of paradise overwhelming. Revisiting the site in 2018 and 2019 I was delighted to see that it hadn't been overrun by tourism. Camping at the smallish National Parks campsite and walking some of the now-established trails, I found that this national treasure still retained a certain spiritual ambience.

Down the road a little we called in to the Adels Grove (Wugudagi) site, which was then a rather bare bit of ground with the remains of some old buildings still apparent. The site was originally gazetted in 1904 as a Miners Homestead Lease. In 1920 Albert de Lestang developed the property as an experimental botanical garden. Albert planted many species of trees and shrubs over a 30-year period only for a fire to destroy his life's work in the 1950s. The area was redeveloped and opened in 1984 to become the tourist hub for visitors to the gorge and park. In 2020 the site and business were taken over by a commercial entity that fosters the economic development of the local Waanyi people. From Adels Grove we later passed through some scenic river crossings near Riversleigh Station. Although the area north of that station was a known fossil site back in 1976 it has since risen to prominence as Australia's premier site for fossils of rainforest mammals, birds and reptiles.

Rough justice

We finally arrived in Camooweal on what I think was a welfare payday, and adjourned to the pub, where we found ourselves having a beer with the quite jovial police sergeant. A little later he announced that "the natives were getting restless and it was time to do a round-up". We later observed his arresting technique, which was quite brutal. On apprehending the obviously intoxicated and rather helpless individuals, he'd throw them forcefully into the back of his short-wheelbase Toyota with heads often striking the top or side walls of the back door panel. On observing this, Harry and I decided it was time to decamp from Camooweal, so after hastily buying beer, ice, a new esky and some fresh food and fuel, we headed for the Territory.

Before we left, however, Harry couldn't help himself and had a verbal altercation with the ethnic Chinese storekeeper regarding his high-handed approach to his several indigenous customers. Once across the border we set up camp in the first clump of small trees, about 100 metres off the side of the road. We had rolled out our swags, got a campfire going and were sitting down enjoying a beer when we saw a vehicle rapidly approaching from the Camooweal direction. You guessed it, it was our mate the sergeant on a mission. He came steaming into our camp to avenge whatever injustice the storekeeper felt he had endured. When he realised that he'd met us in the pub earlier and that he was now out of his jurisdiction he calmed down and shared a beer or two with us before returning to his fiefdom. I dread to think what the outcome might have been if we'd camped on the Queensland side of the border.

Next day and having no desire to head back across the border to the main track up to Gallipoli Station, we followed a fence line along the border until we intersected the station track. Most of the day was spent inspecting phosphate occurrences in the Gallipoli and Highland Plains station areas. We also came across a minor gorge and waterhole, possibly on the headwaters of the Gregory River. It was teeming with small freshwater crocodiles – possibly it was their last refuge as the extended winter months of little or no rainfall dried out other creeks and waterholes. From there we criss-crossed the flat Barkly Tableland from water bore to water bore until finally near dusk we decided to push on to the Ranken Store on an old stock route. Surely, they served beer there.

A sea of slush

As we approached Ranken, as with Burketown, we were excited to see bright lights in the distance, but on arrival discovered it was just the lights of two cattle trains. The store had been closed for decades. We shared a couple of beers with the truckies before they headed off into the night, then we settled down for dinner and a good sleep. The rain started about midnight and continued through the night. Eventually we had to exit our swags and sit miserably in the front of our vehicle until the rain and storm abated.

We awoke surrounded by a shallow sea extending to the horizon in every direction but decided to have a crack at negotiating the 50 kilometres of mud and slush to the sealed Barkly Highway. After much slipping and sliding and a lot of arm exercise for the driver we hit the bitumen. It was fortuitous that we had pressed on to the Ranken store the previous day, because had we camped further out on the plains I suspect we'd have been stranded for days. After a refuel and some well-earned beers at the now-closed Barry Caves Roadhouse, the plan was to head west then turn north onto the Tablelands Highway (there was no Barkly Homestead roadhouse at the intersection in those days). After that we planned to head west on the Carpentaria Highway to finally hit the Stuart Highway near Daly Waters.

As we headed west on the Barkly Highway, there was suddenly a large thump from the left front tyre. We'd completely thrown the tread. No worries – we still had two spares – but when we started looking, we couldn't find the wheel brace – we either never brought one or mislaid it when bogged on the Robinson River. What total stupidity to travel all that way on some of the more remote tracks in the Territory without a wheel brace! (That story was never told back in the Darwin office.) Eventually the tyre was changed with some difficulty, utilising a large shifter.

Off again and putting the foot down to catch up a bit of time travelling north on the Tablelands Highway, we noticed our fuel was going down at an alarming rate and calculated that we couldn't make it to Daly Waters without making an unscheduled fuel stop at Borroloola, which entailed a detour of 100 kilometres each way. A decision was quickly made to turn left near Anthony Lagoon and follow the Barkly Stock Route for 230 kilometres to Elliot. What a drive into the sunset – with no odometer the drive seemed endless and in the moonlight there was the illusion of constantly travelling up and down hills although we knew we were on an essentially flat plain.

It was with some relief that we finally reached the Stuart Highway, arriving at Elliot about 10.00pm. Mercifully the pub hadn't shut, but all food was off and it had started raining again, so after a couple of beers we decided to press on into the night. Another 100 kilometres up the road the rain stopped so we threw out our swags for a well-earned rest near Dunmarra. The final day back to Darwin went without incident to end what was my most memorable field trip.

Coastal capers

During the late 1960s a small heavy mineral sand deposit was delineated by company exploration at Point Blaze at the southernmost end of Fog Bay on the Territory's west coast. Unbelievably the deposit was washed away in a cyclone which crossed the coast near there a few years later. However, this discovery was motivation for the Department of Mines (DM) to undertake a survey to evaluate the mineral sand potential of the entire Territory coastline, and every geologist in the department wanted to get on board.

I was lucky enough to go out on one of the first field trips to Fog Bay, with fellow geologist Mike Roarty. We drove out via the Finniss River and camped on the pristine sands of Fog Bay. As well as there being no other humans there were also no signs of big crocodile tracks along the beachfront, which was somewhat reassuring. The pastel sunsets over this delightful part of the Territory were mesmerising and sublime, but unfortunately several days of sampling didn't locate any indications of heavy minerals, although the fishing wasn't too bad.

The next phases of this survey were to be undertaken by helicopter, and unfortunately, I missed out on the north and west coast surveys but finally got a guernsey for the east coast survey stretching from the Queensland-NT border up to Nhulunbuy (Gove Peninsula).

With Mike in tow again, we drove from Darwin to Roper Bar to await the arrival of the chopper from Darwin. We'd arranged to stay at police quarters at Roper, and after catching up with the newly arrived policeman, Dick, spent an hour or two fishing on the Roper with no success. The chopper arrived about 5.00pm and after greetings were exchanged the chopper pilot Keith's next words were, "Where's the beer, fellas?" This didn't instil any confidence in his flying abilities. He then managed to deplete our beer supply seriously over the course of the evening.

Next day we headed south and managed to sample any dune sand sites between Booroloola and the border, returning safely to Roper for the night, where Keith once again got stuck into the beers. We were rather glad that we hadn't brought any wine or spirits with us. Next day we were off north to Gove Peninsula. Keith seriously wanted us to pack beers along with our food and water supplies for the trip there and back, but we politely refused. Two pleasant nights were spent at the Walkabout Hotel in Nhulunbuy, and Keith of course excelled himself by being last to bed each night.

A chopper full of barra and beef

After two long days of sampling dunes along the coast with a hand auger to depths of up to ten metres, we tossed our fishing lines in at a very steep-sided sandy river about half an hour's flying time out of Nhulunbuy. Our luck was in, as the mangrove jacks were biting and we caught several big ones, but for every few catches we ended up with broken line as something very big stole our catch, whether shark or croc I'll never know. Dave McMahon, the sole DM officer in Nhulunbuy, was very happy to take the fish off our hands. There was one area we didn't sample, Blue Mud Bay. The crocs sunning themselves on the muddy shore were enormous even from about 100 metres above and even scarier when Keith in his wisdom decided to swoop a couple.

Flying back to Roper after a day's sampling, Keith decided to land the chopper on a sandbank in the middle of the Roper river. The barramundi were biting and it was the best barra fishing I ever experienced in the Territory. We arrived back at the police station with the nose cone brimming with barra. The following day we covered the area between the mouth of the Roper and the coast near Booroloola, and while Mike and I sampled, Keith added to our already bountiful supplies of barramundi.

When we arrived back that evening Dick the policeman asked if it was possible for him to borrow the chopper to shoot a "killer" for his meat supplies. As we'd completed our survey activities and still had a few paid flying hours up our sleeves, we gladly obliged. It was quite surreal half an hour or so later to see a chopper appear in the evening sunset with a large bullock dangling underneath. Once it was unhitched, Mike and I at first watched Dick as he attempted to dismember the animal. He was new to the bush and had no idea, so Mike and I produced a couple of axes and helped him butcher the beast (not that we were experts). Our feast of beef ribs and barramundi much later that evening was well worth waiting for. Next day Keith flew back to Darwin with our Engel freezer filled with frozen barramundi fillets while Mike and I had a leisurely meander back to Darwin by road. It had been another great field-trip.

The tin sample

Working around the Pine Creek area it was a regular occurrence for a prospector to greet you with a rock sample or a tobacco tin full of a sample of mineral concentrate and ask you to identify it. I'm sure they knew exactly what it was in most cases; it was more a case of the prospector doing a check on the geo's knowledge.

At about 9.00pm in the front bar of the Pine Creek Hotel one balmy evening, Freddie Leonhardt and I were suitably under the weather when a part-time prospector/highway grader driver confronted me with a tobacco tin full of tin concentrate for identification. Somewhat miffed to be tasked with this exercise at this time of night I removed the lid and after a desultory inspection proceeded to pour the sample down my throat, washed down with a good swig of my beer and much to the indignation of said prospector. Nothing more was said at the time. Fred and I later left to camp in a nearby creek bed for the night.

I awoke the next morning with a mouth full of grit and asked Fred, "Was I eating sand from the creek bed last night?", before remembering the source of the grit. That should have been the end of the story, but no, on a road trip north from South Australia to Kakadu in 1988, who should I run into at the Wauchope pub but that same prospector/grader driver. I couldn't help but recall the tin sample story to him, at which he flatly denied that it had ever happened.

The story doesn't end there. Attending a mining conference in Darwin in 1994 I got talking to a young geologist with the NT Geological Survey. Over a few beers he began telling this story of a crazy geologist who once worked for the Survey, who had swallowed a tin sample at the Pine Creek pub. I let him continue, although as he proceeded, I realised the story had become somewhat embellished with the passing of time. As he neared the finale, I felt that I had to say, "Would you like to hear the real story?" He hesitated, and then the penny dropped that I was that crazy geo from many years ago. I couldn't contain my delight that I'd achieved Territory legend status (in a minor sort of a way) but also felt that it did vindicate the decision to leave the Territory back in 1980.

17

The City of Churches

South Australia 1980s

I started looking for a move and new job in 1980. As it turned out the pitiful 1979 dry season that was a factor in our decision to leave Darwin was followed by a long and delightful dry season in 1980, but the decision to leave had been made. I'd accepted a job with the WA Mines Department, but another more senior position as a geologist with the SA Department of Mines and Energy came up soon after. Perth, although a large and vibrant city, suffered from the same isolation from the East Coast as Darwin (and at least in Darwin we received free airfares to any Australian city every two years), so Adelaide got the final nod.

With our fairly new Subaru wagon loaded to the gunnels we set off for Adelaide via Perth in mid-December 1980. The last night in Darwin was spent in a motel to avoid the steady stream of drinkers and well-wishers who proved rather a hindrance to our last-minute packing. The trip down the west coast was initially wet and very hot; we had to ford floodwaters between Halls Creek and Fitzroy Crossing, which wrecked the vehicle cooling fan (although we only became aware of this in Perth when the vehicle started overheating in slow traffic). Teneille, our two-year-old daughter, was wedged in her car seat in the back seat, cocooned between piles of luggage, but she proved to be an uncomplaining traveller and camper on this extended road-trip. She picked up one habit on the trip, the necessity of squatting to go to the toilet – it took some months in our new home in Adelaide before she stopped squatting on our back lawn.

After Port Hedland the heat steadily abated and we enjoyed some nice camping stops in Coral Bay, Kalbarri and the Pinnacles before reaching Perth just before Christmas. We stayed there for the Christmas-New Year period with my sister Ann and her husband Peter Burns at Claremont; my Mum and Dad were also visiting from NSW. In fact, it was the last time I saw my Dad, as he died suddenly a week before the following Easter when we were due to catch up. In the New Year we headed down to Margaret River to sample some of the fabulous wines from that region. From there we travelled through the scenic southwest coast of WA to Denmark, Albany, the Stirling Ranges and Esperance. From there we rejoined the Eyre Highway at Kalgoorlie, travelling east through Eucla, the edge of the Nullarbor, the windmill-riddled hamlet of Penong and eventually on to Adelaide.

Settling in at MESA

Arriving in Adelaide we were housed in a motel adjacent to my new office on Greenhill Road, courtesy of my employer with the then rather unfortunate acronym of SADME. The department title often changed at the whim of politicians and senior bureaucrats, but for this and the next few chapters I will refer to it as MESA (Mines and Energy South Australia), a preferred acronym. MESA had paid for our travel, removal and short-term accommodation expenses, but unfortunately someone had forgotten that the Minister needed to sign off on my appointment. Consequently, we spent over two weeks in limbo until the Minister returned from summer holidays. In one way this was fortunate, in that it gave us time to look around Adelaide and purchase a house at Seacombe Heights, just up the road from where Debbie had grown up.

The Minister finally came back from leave and duly signed my appointment papers; as a result I started work with MESA on a Friday. Arriving at work I was greeted by my new boss, Jeff Oliver, the manager of the Mineral Resources Branch, and then introduced to work colleagues who were destined to become good friends. (At this time, I firmly believed that this job would just be a short-term stepping stone back into the mineral industry; little did I realise that this was somewhere I would stay and love for the next 20 years). All the new workmates were so friendly on introduction it was a bit overwhelming, but one, Jack Townsend, resonates in my memory: when I shook his hand he felt like a lifelong friend, and so he proved to be.

The morning was spent finding my way around MESA, but I was beside myself when at midday Jeff announced we were all heading off to the Fountain Inn, a wonderful waterhole about a kilometre up Glen Osmond Road, for the regular Friday lunch – it seemed like Darwin all over again. The lunch proceeded as normal until mid-afternoon, when it was announced that it was time to go back to the office – what was this nonsense? A Friday lunch in Darwin entailed the whole afternoon, in fact a non-return was actively encouraged by the powers that be. I reluctantly returned to the office with the others but spent the next 20 years with MESA discouraging the practice. After any extended liquid lunch, the work efficiency gets close to zero, but worse still the potential to say or do the wrong thing to work colleagues and visitors is greatly heightened.

It was quite an effort to adjust back to working in the temperate zones after eight years in the steamy tropics, and I was on a steep learning curve adapting to the new culture that was South Australia as I interacted with work colleagues and went on initial field-trips over the next few months. The work of our branch was to document and assess the state's mineral resources with a view to encouraging exploration and development of these resources by the private sector. Much of my early fieldwork was done in more settled areas, so rather than always camping out we often stayed in hotels or motels, which provided a more social lifestyle but also a ready temptation to regularly join in with the locals. I knew I could no longer wear thongs as field boots as had become the Territory norm, but getting used to the cooler weather took quite some adjustment. For the first year the concept of putting on more and warmer clothes just didn't gel.

My first field-trip was to Burra, a couple of hours drive north of Adelaide, where the branch was geologically mapping the open pit before the imminent closure of this copper mining operation. Copper was first discovered there in 1845, with significant mining commencing in 1848; it grew to be then one of the world's largest copper mines and is credited with saving the fledgling state from bankruptcy. Miners flocked in from Cornwall and to a lesser extent from Wales, Scotland and Germany, with the initial underground mine operation closing in 1877. It opened again early in the 20th century and later again, with modern operations, between 1970 and 1981. This open pit operation exposed many of the old underground mines, which was quite fascinating to see. Both the mine site and the town include many buildings which are part of SA's unique but understated early mining heritage.

On that trip we stayed at the historic Burra Hotel, which featured in the film *Breaker Morant*, along with several other town heritage sites. The publican was most hospitable as were most "mine hosts" in SA's country towns, but the memorable feature of this pub was catching huge numbers of yabbies in Burra Creek, which flowed beside the pub's backyard. A supper of freshly boiled yabbies after a night of beers and red wine at the bar was marvellous, although they did play havoc with the internal workings. My Territory ways still prevailed on a couple of nights when I needed to throw my mattress out onto the upstairs veranda to get a good night's sleep.

On another early trip to Blinman, an old copper mining site in the Flinders Ranges, out of habit I took my fishing rod with me. Stopping for lunch at Orroroo, I suggested to my companion, Ian Faulks, that we stop by the river so I could drop a line in. Ian gave me a funny look but said nothing. Arriving at the tree line by the "river" I discovered it was just a dry creek bed as are most inland rivers and creeks in SA. It was shattering to realise that I'd moved to the driest State on the driest continent, something I never considered before making the move. On the other hand, these early trips to Burra and Blinman made me aware that many a country pub had a wonderful cellar with a surfeit of excellent aged red wines at very good prices. Blinman was a classic example, where you could climb down into the cellar and pick the wine of your choice with a standard price of $7 per bottle. I suspect that MESA field personnel, among others were heavily involved in depleting these pub stocks throughout SA in the 1980s.

Coober Pedy or the Moon

Another field trip in 1981 was to Coober Pedy to participate in a state government–subsidised drilling program to encourage opal miners to search for new opal fields over the vast prospective areas. Opal was first found in the Stuart Range north of the present township in 1915 by fourteen-year-old Willie Hutchison. Following completion of the Transcontinental Railway in 1917, many fettlers headed for the opal fields followed by an influx of miners after World War 1. Production really took off after World War 2, with the population skyrocketing as returning soldiers and displaced Europeans arrived, particularly Greeks, Italians and Slavic people. The mining community was very multicultural but there was also some deeply ingrained enmity between the various ethnic groups, so much so that bodies are reputed to be hidden down the odd mine shaft.

Mining extends over at least ten percent of the current proclaimed Precious Stones Field area of almost 5,000 square kilometres and at least 30 kilometres north and ten kilometres south along the Stuart Highway from the town centre. It's estimated that there are over 1.5 million open wide-diameter drillholes and shafts extending to depths of up to 30 metres, and the extent of open-pit and underground operations is simply unknown. Conservatively over two billion tonnes of earth have been mined, making it one of the world's larger mining undertakings and making a moonscape of the countryside in the process. Rehabilitation is largely nonexistent, and opal production can at best be guessed at. In the boom years most gem opal was purchased by mysterious overseas opal buyers who flew into town with cases loaded with cash and departed just as quickly with their cases bursting with opal.

Our branch's involvement in the subsidised program included surveying the location of all new holes (no GPS in those days), then on completion being lowered down the newly drilled holes using a hand or motorised winch, to record any known opal-bearing formations and indeed any opal if it was sighted. The holes were up to 30 metres deep and either one or two metres in diameter – going down the smaller size could feel quite claustrophobic.

All branch staff, no matter their specific geological expertise, were expected to be involved in this program, which extended over two to three months. Typically, crews would put in about a two-week stint before returning to Adelaide for a break. Given the generosity of the local opal miners, a two-week stint was about all a body could handle. A typical day would start with breakfast at 6.00am, then a drive out to the drill site by 7.00, a ten-hour day in the field, then back to the Opal Inn for a few drinks with the opal miners. The miners, who can be particularly nasty to their rivals and the dreaded taxman, couldn't have been nicer and wouldn't let us buy a drink, usually producing a large roll of notes from their pockets to shout drinks – wallets weren't in vogue. We'd leave the pub anywhere between 8.00 and 11.00pm, then adjourn for dinner either at the Greek restaurant above the Mobile servo, the Italian club or, best of all, the Acropolis "restaurant". Dinner could end anytime between midnight and 3.00am, then it was home and up at 6.00am for a repeat the next day.

I know that I was totally exhausted after a sixteen-day stint, but one of our number, Peter Crettenden, or "Cretto" as he was universally known, managed a 27-day stint. He was about 24 at the time and there were some bets laid on whether he would make 40 if he continued to live like this. He and I got badly caught out playing 8-ball with the miners one night. It started by playing doubles for a beer and gradually escalated to $10 and $20 as we kept on winning. When the stakes reached $50 a game the opal miners' form suddenly improved dramatically and after losing $50 overall for the night, I called it quits and went home, but Cretto fancied his form and was sucked into several more games of singles. Cretto and I shared a room at the house we were renting for the duration of the drilling program. The end result of the 8-ball evening was starkly evident when he woke in the morning and instantly checked his wallet – the face said it all – the wallet was empty and he'd blown over $200.

Coober Pedy was a wild old town in those days and most vehicles in the town and on the precious stones field were old, unregistered and probably unroadworthy, but the police were either unwilling or unable to take any action on such matters. I suspect half the drivers were unlicensed, and drink-driving was commonplace. The late-night eateries were where you would encounter many of the local characters, such as Crocodile Harry. Some of the proprietors were also notable, particularly Theo, the owner-manager of the Acropolis.

I don't know what the licensing laws were at that time but Theo at the Acropolis had a policy of "if there are customers then we are open" and it wasn't unusual heading to work at 7.00am to see patrons just leaving the premises. Theo was reputed to have been a wrestler on channel 9's *World Championship Wrestling*, which ran through the 1960s into the early 1970s with heroes and villains like Mario Milano and Killer Kowalski (even Andre the Giant appeared at one time), so he was a born entertainer and definitely didn't need to employ a bouncer. What went on within the walls of the Acropolis over the years is anyone's guess, but Theo was always an affable and generous host and the food was first class. Sadly, the Acropolis burnt down some years later, the fate of many a building in Coober Pedy, and was never rebuilt, although "Traces" across the main road took its place as a fabulous venue for Greek food and hospitality hosted by Jimmy the cook and Thelma his wife, who was clearly the boss.

A new family member

On a very warm Proclamation Day in 1983 my second daughter, Emma, was born, and unlike her older sister she was in a hurry. A very pregnant Debbie, Teneille and I had spent the middle of the day at Seacliff beach to gain a bit of relief from one of Adelaide's stinking hot summer days. With a somewhat startled look Debbie announced that we had better get moving as the new baby was clearly anxious to make an appearance. Five-year-old Teneille was enjoying herself in the shallows and was reluctant to leave but was eventually coaxed from the water. After a quick pick-up of an already packed bag on the way, it was off to the Blackwood Hospital maternity unit. Debbie was quickly admitted, and it seemed like Teneille and I had only been waiting outside for a few minutes when I was summoned to the birth. Emma wasn't waiting around. After Teneille was introduced to her new sister and time spent with mother and baby, Teneille and I headed home. Unlike Teneille's Darwin birth celebrations, that evening they were far more muted with a five-year-old in tow. After a few days' rest Debbie and Emma came home, but within an hour of arriving home we had an unexpected visit from an NSW cousin with his wife and daughter. Of course, we invited them to stay, which they did for the next few days, so it wasn't quite the homecoming that had been anticipated.

Lumpy the godfather

After they departed, home life reverted to the new normal for a few weeks. Then I got a call from old Darwin mate Lumpy to say he'd be in Adelaide with a few other Darwin mates the following week. We arranged to meet for lunch the following Friday at "Cobbs", one of Adelaide's topless bars and restaurants. Lumpy duly arrived with his two mates, Robbo and Black Mac, and a good lunch was enjoyed by all. For some reason, perhaps feeling duty bound as a new father again, I returned to work but left the boys in fine fettle after arranging to meet them the next day somewhere on the beach between Seacliff and Brighton.

By the time young Teneille and I headed for the beach in the late morning the temperature was in the forties and the beach was very crowded. Locating the boys on a one-and-a-half-kilometre beach wasn't going to be easy, or so I thought. As I strode along the foreshore, there perched atop a very large esky were what appeared to be two beached whales – of course it was Lumpy and Robbo, but even more to my surprise when I greeted them, there beside them lay a bevy of the Cobbs girls, now dressed more demurely in scanty bikinis. Somehow the boys, who weren't exactly the tall, dark and handsome types, late on Friday afternoon had convinced these delightful ladies to join them on the beach the next day. How they managed this coup is still a mystery to me.

A pleasant afternoon with ample accompanying drinks ensued, although I did find time to ensure that Teneille spent plenty of supervised time in the cooling ocean waters. At the end of the day, I invited everyone back to our place, just a kilometre or two back from the beach, before they all headed back to the city. In they bounced, and the Cobbs girls were soon cooing over and taking turns in nursing baby Emma. It turned out that most of the girls were students or overseas travellers who had simply found an easy way to supplement their incomes. With Lumpy as godfather and the Cobbs girls as group godmothers, it was the closest Emma got to having an official christening ceremony.

Another Lumpy visit to Adelaide five years later also created a degree of mirth. Lumpy was down for the 1988 Bicentennial Carnival, an Aussie rules State of Origin competition which featured every Australian state and the Northern Territory, and he was nominally designated as the NT team chaperone. His role: to keep the younger players out of any after-hours hijinks. Lumpy was hardly noted for his restraint when it came to the amber fluid or a good red, and very late nights were his forte – it was indeed a very strange appointment. As it turned out his services weren't required as the young players were so determined to win the second division of the carnival, which they did, that they imposed their own curfews and alcohol abstention until the final whistle was blown, so the role of chaperone was quite superfluous and Lumpy was able to party on as normal.

Music to the ears

Soon after Teneille commenced primary school at Seaview Downs, she was encouraged to take up a musical instrument. Whether by choice or availability it ended up being a cello, which was both cumbersome to cart around and painful to listen to for the first few months when she practised regularly at home. She improved rapidly, however, and not only became a pleasure to listen to but within a year or two was invited to join the South Australian Primary Schools' String Orchestra (PSSO).

There followed several years of attendance at practice, rehearsals and performances under the tutelage of the affable and sociable Mitch Brunsden, who was also the orchestra's conductor. Considering the ages of the players, from nine to thirteen, many of the performances were outstanding, especially annual events at the beautiful Adelaide Town Hall. Mitch was awarded the medal of the Order of Australia in 2006 for his more than 40 years services to music as a performer, teacher and conductor of student ensembles.

As a result of her PSSO experience Teneille was able to gain entry into the prestigious music program at Brighton High School, but unfortunately her interest waned as she battled through the many distractions of her teenage years. She still retains her cello and, who knows, her interest may rekindle as the years go by.

Good neighbours

The section of Seacombe Heights that we moved to was newly developed, and most of the neighbours had young families and were rather sociable. We lived on the downhill side of Karoona Crescent at the very end of the street and for several years had three vacant blocks beside us. Eventually building commenced simultaneously on all three blocks and new neighbours duly moved in. The people nearest us turned out to be a young couple of Indian descent, Ajit and Sheila Bedi. We greeted each other a few times but, noting that Shelia used to work Friday and Saturday nights, after dinner on one of these nights I casually invited Ajit over to share a wine or two. He turned out to be an engineer who had been educated in Malaysia then moved to Australia where he met and married Sheila. Sheila worked at her parents' Indian restaurant, the Jasmin in Adelaide's CBD.

Opened in January 1980, the Jasmin had quickly established itself as Adelaide's leader in Indian cuisine.

On this night Ajit and I may have indulged in more than one glass (or bottle) so that by the time Sheila arrived home after work we were still at it and she wandered across to find him, bearing the night's leftovers from the Jasmin which were shared around to our delight. From this time on, I regularly invited Ajit over for a wine when Sheila was working and she always reciprocated with little gems from the restaurant when she arrived home. Sadly, they only lived there for a few years before moving, but it was a wonderful arrangement while it lasted. The Jasmin is still operating today and is now acknowledged both in Australia and internationally as one of the world's leading purveyors of fine Indian food. Sheila is effectively the CEO of this wonderful establishment.

Delightful but different

Before moving to Adelaide, I'd only visited the city for brief periods. It had and has the reputation of being the city of churches, but any overly pious religious mores were very little in evidence, unlike the parochial religious attitudes still evident in   Sydney and Melbourne at that time. In fact, Adelaide proved to be a wonderful city with culture, excellent dining and a superb collection of historic pubs with the soul of a large country town. The populace in general was well spoken, caring and friendly without any underlying culture of money being the key to all happiness so prevalent in the Eastern States.

The people of Adelaide did however have one strange quirk: as a group they were rabid supporters of Australian rules football and their respective teams. This was first brought home to me when I attended the SANFL grand final between Port Adelaide and Norwood in 1984 with old Yass mate Gary Colmer. Gary had returned to Adelaide with his delightful, brown-eyed wife Therese, whom he met in Yass, and he was now working in the family real estate business in Adelaide's eastern suburbs. Gary was a dyed-in-the-wool Port supporter.

The first surprise at the final was that as the national anthem was being played a fist fight started between Port's full forward Tim Evans and Norwood's defender Craig Balme. I'd never witnessed this before in any code of football. For the first half of the match, Port, the favourites, seemed very much in control, Gary was elated and in fine form with his aggressive barracking, but in the second half and particularly in the last quarter Norwood gradually gained control, Gary got much quieter, and Norwood ultimately won the first SAFNL final from fifth place by a margin of 100-91.

Post-match, Gary was dumbstruck, so I waltzed him off to the nearest bar in Footy Park to help him regain some equilibrium and composure – he still didn't utter a word. By the time we got home, where Therese had spent the afternoon with Debbie he was still speechless. After a couple of medicinal reds were administered at home he finally spoke, some four hours after the game had ended.

With the advent of the Crows' admission into the AFL in 1991 and later Port in 1997, the whole psyche of the city on a Monday morning was determined by whether the teams had won or lost over the weekend. At MESA, if the Crows had lost, a pall of depression fell on the whole office and rarely lifted before Wednesday. This I believe occurred in all offices and businesses across the city. Adelaideans do take their (Aussie rules) footy seriously.

Passing on the wisdom

Tim Wilson was a young graduate environmental scientist who had just joined the newly formed Environment Branch within MESA. Eager to see mining and exploration activities and their impact on the environment, he headed out on a ten-day field-trip with me as his guide and mentor (the mentoring as it turned out may have been more attuned to a course in "Men behaving badly"). The first few days were spent at Coober Pedy observing the incredible phenomenon of opal mining, which has created a moonscape, but a great tourist attraction. The first evening there we had dinner at the Acropolis and young Tim was introduced to mine host Theo.

A very hot day or two later we were inspecting some company drilling activity for metallic minerals 50 kilometres or so west of Coober Pedy when we were confronted with a rapidly advancing image of what looked like Ayers Rock (Uluru). It was a huge dust storm that had blown up out of nowhere. This was a first for both of us. What to do? – retreat in the opposite direction or drive through the approaching maelstrom? There was no shelter in sight, so we wisely decided to turn the vehicle off, seal the doors as tight as possible and sit the storm out – that is after we retrieved a six-pack of cold beer for each of us, as emergency supplies.

As the storm arrived, we found ourselves sitting in a sea of dark orange with the vehicle shaking and the sound of sand beating against the windscreen quite deafening – we found it thirsty work. After what seemed like an eternity but was probably only fifteen minutes, the back end of the storm reached us with thunder, lightning and a short sharp shower. Beyond that were just clear blue skies with a rapid return to scorching temperatures. What a wonderful one-off experience it turned out to be, although there was some trepidation as the storm first struck. Later back in Coober Pedy the locals were blissfully unaware that a dust storm had passed nearby.

On the Friday afternoon Tim and I headed off for a pre-arranged meeting with some other MESA staff at Tarcoola, about 200 kilometres south. Surprise, surprise, at the tiny bar of the Wilgena Hotel it was very busy and we discovered that tomorrow, Saturday, was the annual Tarcoola Race Meeting. (Tarcoola the township is named after the winner of the 1893 Melbourne Cup.) It was a no-brainer: we'd all take Saturday off and attend the races.

There was no accommodation at the pub in this tiny railway siding hamlet, which boasted a small hospital, primary school, police station and a few railway cottages plus a golf course and a service station of sorts. Gold was discovered at Tarcoola in 1883 and in its mining heyday between 1901 and 1918 the population rose to as high as 2000, with most gold production from the Tarcoola Blocks mine in low hills to the west of the township. According to Wikipedia: "The Trans-Australian Railway was built through Tarcoola in 1915, and in 1980 it became a junction station when the Adelaide-Darwin Railway diverged from Tarcoola to Alice Springs. The link from Alice Springs through to Darwin was eventually completed in 2004."

As luck would have it the very personable Peter Philip Harbutt and his equally friendly wife Pat, who ran the servo, allowed us to roll our swags out and use outdoor showers and toilets in their fenced-off back yard. This had one unfortunate consequence early Sunday morning after the races when their large "roo" dog decided to lift its leg on my swag with me still in it – not a pleasant experience I can assure you. Peter was also obsessed with the thrill of gold prospecting/mining and held the lease over the old Tarcoola Blocks mine, where most of his business profits probably disappeared, although thankfully he did get a reasonable final payout when a junior exploration company purchased the lease some years later.

As an aside, if you're ever lying in your swag near Tarcoola you'll be rewarded by what I regard as one of the brightest and most spectacular star displays I've ever encountered: any cloudless night seems as bright as a full moon even when there's no moon to be seen – a truly gob-smacking experience.

Back to the races on Saturday, which were then about as authentic as a bush racing meeting could be. The track was red dirt and most of the track buildings were thatched in local vegetation to provide a modicum of shade, but the beer was cold and the racing competition between the local landowners was intense. We all had a wonderful day off work, and late in the day proceedings ended with a foot race on the track, which had a significant cash prize. During our travels young Tim had unwittingly revealed that he played on the wing for the Adelaide Uni rugby union club, so he had a bit of speed. After the many enjoyable beers served during the afternoon it wasn't too hard to cajole him into becoming a late entrant. Tim missed the start badly, perhaps due to the afternoon's indulgences, but mowed down the field and was within one stride of beating the long-term winner and odds-on favourite from Port Augusta.

From here the crowd dispersed back to the pub perhaps two kilometres from the racetrack, but we had a problem: one of our number, Steve Ewen, an indigenous man, had had a minor run-in with the local constabulary earlier in the afternoon, where the local boy-in-blue had been embarrassingly proved wrong in his actions. Desiring to regain his authority he walked up to our group and advised if anyone of us dared drive our vehicles back to town we would be locked up for DUI. To his chagrin several locals came to our rescue and ferried our vehicles back to town. I had never seen so many people in Tarcoola. Jam-packed, the little bar could hold no more than 30 souls, so the hordes spilled onto the street outside. I don't think we ate too well that night, but the outside bar service was top-rate and the beers were cold, a great experience.

Next day Tim and I made our way through the picturesque Gawler Ranges down to Port Lincoln, where we were to inspect some local drilling activities and then visit BHP's iron mining operations at Iron Knob, Iron Baron and the South Middleback Ranges. Our first night in Port Lincoln passed quietly after Saturday's race meeting, but after a solid day's fieldwork on Monday we decided to adjourn to the Grand Tasman Hotel for dinner. On entering we noticed the 8-ball table was free and decided to have a game over a quiet beer. We had only been there a short while when two local fishermen came in and asked if they could join us in a game of doubles for a beer, they seemed friendly enough, so we readily agreed. We won the first game, and one chap bought a beer for Tim but the other somehow forgot to get mine, it was no big issue and I said nothing about it, but his partner did. He asked if I had got my beer and when I replied that I hadn't he politely said excuse us for a moment and promptly took his partner outside and belted him. Admonished, the man came back in, bought me a beer and the game resumed. When I got the opportunity I said to Tim, we're going to lose the next game, buy them both a beer and head to dinner. Tim was in total agreement. If these blokes treated their partners like that over a minor matter of honour then what might they do to blow-ins from Adelaide.

We had a pleasant meal and the remainder of the trip proved relatively uneventful, but I think Tim had had a rather eye-opening first field-trip with MESA.

18

The Second Mine that Saved South Australia

South Australia 1980's

In my second year at MESA, I was partly seconded to the Mineral Exploration Branch to monitor all mineral exploration being undertaken on the massive Olympic Dam deposit. Answering to two bosses didn't faze me but didn't last, as it obviously didn't suit either of them. Returning to work on a Monday after a week-long assessment of a silica sand deposit at scenic Black Point on Yorke Peninsula, I walked in to find my desk and belongings missing and an empty space with a pink pay slip stuck to the floor. One of my colleagues had emblazoned the word "FINAL" on the slip. No-one was forthcoming with any information for about half an hour, until I found out that Ian Grant from the Mineral Exploration Branch had decided I was to work permanently for him and he had had my belongings moved to a new office in my absence – it was a *fait accompli*. I spent the next seven years in this position monitoring not only Olympic Dam activities but all private sector mineral exploration throughout the state.

A giant discovery

Situated about 520 kilometres north-northwest of Adelaide, the Olympic Dam discovery on Roxby Downs station in 1975 was an amazing geoscientific achievement, as the resource lay below 325 metres of younger soil and rock cover. The discovery led to the development of a world-class underground copper-gold-uranium mine in 1988 and the definition of what is the Earth's largest uranium resource, third largest gold resource and fifth largest copper resource. With estimated reserves of almost three billion tonnes and a total resource nearing nine billion tonnes, mining should continue for at least a century.

During the 1950s through to the 1970s the Bureau of Mineral Resources (now Geoscience Australia) flew state-of-the-art aerial magnetic surveys, conducted regional ground gravity surveys and undertook 1:250,000 scale geological mapping over vast areas of Australia to better understand the geological structure of the continent and encourage private sector exploitation of its mineral resources.

In about 1971 Reg Nelson, then chief geophysicist at MESA, recommended in an internal memo that MESA drill distinct gravity and magnetic features defined by the surveys, north of Woomera, suggesting that they might indicate metallic mineralisation at depth below these features. At the time the township of Woomera, the operational base for the vast Woomera Prohibited Area, was waning after its earlier glory days of rocket-launching, weapons testing and nuclear experimentation. Reg felt that a mineral discovery could provide a needed fillip to Woomera, but MESA never proceeded.

In June 1975 Western Mining Corporation (WMC), after undertaking various regional studies and research projects, was granted an exploration licence over some of these geophysical features, and within months low-grade copper, gold and silver were intersected below 353 metres in their very first diamond drillhole. It took sixteen months and a further nine deep drillholes before the full potential of Olympic Dam was realised, with a massive 170-metre intersection of ore-grade copper-uranium mineralisation. It took another nine years of evaluation before the joint venture of WMC and the BP Group in December 1985 announced that the Olympic Dam mining project would go ahead. In that decade more than 1600 surface and underground drillholes totalling over 542 kilometres were completed, and the so-called Stuart Shelf region was established as one of the Earth's major copper provinces.

Olympic Dam hospitality

There were some interesting experiences on my many visits to Olympic Dam/Roxby Downs during the 1980s. Early on, I made regular day visits with Keith Johns, the CEO of MESA, and usually one or two others. We'd usually leave Adelaide at about 7.00am on a light plane charter that took about two hours travel. Arriving there we'd be greeted by George White, the very affable geologist-in-charge, and the day would be spent visiting the extensive drilling activities, poring over many geoscientific maps and sections and spending hours examining drill core. It was often a long, hot day. On my first trip I fell for George's departing ploy, hook, line and sinker. Just as we were leaving, late in the day, George ran out to the plane and threw in an icy cold carton of beer – what a generous bloke. Some of us consumed this delight with gusto and were feeling very mellow an hour into the trip home, when nature called and with it the realisation that there was no toilet on the plane, resulting in an interminable hour of suffering before landing in Adelaide.

You only fell for it once but there were always newcomers to be caught out. On one trip we had two visiting Japanese journalists on board who were delighted to partake of the freezing frothies. An Australian colloquialism refers to "Japanese bladders", and these boys didn't disappoint, they were in absolute agony, and a number of emptied stubbies left the flight in Adelaide replete with another amber fluid.

On a later visit the experience of inspecting the newly constructed 500-metre shaft was one I could have done without. Descending 500 metres in a big bucket with just one metal cable supporting your descent and subsequent ascent was a tad unnerving, as was trying to get out of a round bucket in a square hole with a still enormous drop below you.

As the development of the mine progressed, some of my monitoring visits were done in the company of the MESA Mines Inspector, Mike Wilson. By this time Bob Crew, an old hand from Kalgoorlie, was the mine manager and our host, and like George before him he delighted in stitching up MESA people like us. Mike and I would often drive from Adelaide and meet up with Bob at the canteen bar late in the afternoon after our arrival. The bar usually closed at 6.00pm to ensure miners ate at the mess, but you were able to purchase unlimited supplies for later in the evening. Bob's ploy was to drink with us at a furious pace and then purchase a carton for us for the evening, before heading home for a quiet night with his wife and family. Of course, Mike and I would often sit outside the single men's quarters on a balmy evening socialising with the miners and slowly demolishing the carton.

On our first trip together, after we'd fallen for Bob's canteen trick the previous night, he arrived to pick us up for our mine inspection tour, after a brief but hearty 6.00am canteen breakfast. Following a site induction and safety briefing, we had a comfortable ride in the newly installed cage to the 480-metre level near the base of the Whenan shaft. From here the pain began, he walked us along every kilometre of the newly developed drives including access into a zone of very high-grade copper-uranium mineralisation. It wasn't only physically hot but radioactively hot to boot at that spot (though having said that, one would have had to remain in that high-grade zone for about a year to absorb radiation equivalent to having an x-ray). Bob also insisted that we ascend all the safety ladders to access the 420-metre and 360-metre levels before after about three hours underground, we entered the cage again for a brief ascent back to the surface. It was a thorough tour of the mine workings, and any semblance of a hangover had long dissipated, with the most refreshing shower and clean-up at the end. The remainder of the day, spent inspecting processing facilities in various stages of construction and finally drilling rigs and drill core samples, was a breeze after the morning's endurance test.

A beer with protesters

The recognition that Olympic Dam was far and away the world's largest resource of uranium ore, and State Government approval for the project through the passing of the *Roxby Downs Indenture Bill* on 18 June 1982, drew the wrath of the anti-uranium movement and led to large on-site protests in 1983. Remnants of the protest group set up a temporary bush camp on the outskirts of the mining development area, which remained for at least twelve months, but after some of the group resorted to some significant acts of industrial sabotage they were evicted and the camp demolished.

I've never mentioned this to work colleagues, but on one of these inspection trips and very much of my own volition, I grabbed a carton from the canteen and after dinner drove out to the protest camp. I was greeted with some reserve, but the carton broke down a few barriers and it was interesting to spend an hour or so hearing the point of view of these radical protesters. I'm sure WMC's security knew of the visit, but the subject was never raised by any parties, thank goodness.

Tweaking history

After the December 1985 announcement by WMC/BP that they were to proceed with a major mining operation, Keith Johns asked me to compile a ten-year summary of the first decade of operations at Olympic Dam. Various members of the WMC team had already published accounts of the discovery, and I used these together with informal chats to some of the original discovery team, along with details provided to MESA in mandatory (confidential) exploration reports to complete my compilation. On completing a draft, I forwarded a copy to Jim Lalor, the WMC Exploration Manager, for vetting. He called me a few days later, inviting me to come down the road to WMC's offices for a chat. Interestingly, during the chat he said he disagreed with some of the facts as I'd written them and went on to say that WMC relied only on the written word when compiling such discovery resumes. He was a little taken aback when I demonstrated that the facts he was disputing were taken directly from written mandatory exploration reports submitted to MESA. Regardless, it was decided that I'd use WMC's version of events in my compilation. It was a succinct demonstration to me that history is (nearly always) compiled by the victors.

To put all this in context, the WMC geoscientific team had demonstrated remarkable skills with the earlier 1960s nickel discovery at Kambalda in WA, and then with arguably one of the greatest geoscientific discoveries of the twentieth century at Olympic Dam, but like all mineral discoveries it wasn't achieved without a measure of good luck.

Just before the opening of the Olympic Dam mine in 1988 a regular air service utilising a Cessna Citation business jet had been established, and this made visits a joy. Five minutes into the flight from Adelaide you were cruising at 12,000 metres and you arrived within the hour. As in the George White days an esky replete with beverages was slid along the aisle, but there was a toilet on board and it was only a short flight anyway. From memory I didn't go underground in the mine again after its opening in 1988, although I did make a couple of social visits to the township of Roxby Downs when my younger daughter Emma worked there in the mid-2000s.

Give me the bush please

I loved my other work at MESA, which entailed vetting and approving private company exploration activities throughout the state. The job involved reading and evaluating all mandatory quarterly and annual mineral exploration technical reports and ensuring all relevant data and rock/drill samples were submitted to MESA. Additionally, our small branch, comprising only two to three people, was responsible for approving any ground-disturbing activities (track-making, drilling, bulk sampling) and ensuring compliance with rehabilitation of these. As the branch member who most enjoyed being in the field, I got to spend a lot of time in the bush and enjoyed the rapport that I built up with private sector explorers in remote field camps. The work and conditions were never an imposition. As a result, I got to visit most remote areas of the state and had a knowledge of what was happening in mineral exploration in the state, second to none.

A CEO of substance

Keith Johns, MESA's CEO from 1983 to 1992, epitomised the Adelaide/South Australian culture. With a background of Cornish mining heritage, he was destined to join the mineral industry. Keith graduated in geology from Adelaide University under the tutelage of famed Antarctic explorer Sir Douglas Mawson, who was then Professor of Geology, and went on to spend his entire working life at MESA. He rose through the ranks to eventually lead MESA after 35 years and was instrumental in forging a clear path in the development and long-term operation of the Olympic Dam mine among a plethora of other achievements. Keith was the last of the old-school CEOs, a tradition that was largely forged by the longstanding Premier of South Australia, Sir Thomas Playford, and then MESA CEO Sir Ben Dickenson after World War 2. Keith handled his political masters with aplomb and held the respect of the mining industry, but what stood out was his humanity. Within MESA, he knew and greeted every employee by their first name, taking this further even to regularly enquire about family members by their first names. He wasn't a larrikin himself but recognised the need and tolerated the behaviour of those who occasionally played up after extended periods of remote fieldwork.

Keith's humanity rubbed off on the rest of the department and I can say that I've never worked with such a committed and supportive group of people, who were focused on providing the best possible service to the community and the petroleum and mineral industry. Some things disturbed me, particularly the high numbers of staff who spent their entire working lives with MESA, and I was forever urging immediate work colleagues to broaden their horizons, but the work environment was so good that few ever took the advice.

Playing in the parklands

When Colonel William Light planned the city of Adelaide he had the foresight to surround the city on all sides with parklands containing both exotic and native plants. Citizens of Adelaide have now been gaining pleasure from these parklands for almost 200 years. Our MESA office was located on Greenhill Road, beside these parklands, and at every opportunity we enjoyed their pleasures. The MESA Social Club ran monthly Friday barbeques in the park over the summer months, which were encouraged by the CEO provided they finished on the dot at 2.00pm. This generally happened, although the barbeque clean-up group sometimes got waylaid if the keg hadn't been emptied. It was a wonderful way to spend a warm summer afternoon. One parklands gardener seemed to have a seventh sense about these events and would always bring his mowing tractor closer to the action as the sausages and steaks sizzled away. He was always presented with a plate of food and a beer or two for his troubles.

Picking up the keg and other barbeque supplies in a MESA four-wheel-drive, I had the misfortune of having a bucket fall off the back on busy Fullarton Road just as a police vehicle was heading the other way. As we stopped to recover the bucket the police returned to point out that the bucket wasn't properly tied down and could have caused some serious damage. Being the driver and very much in the wrong I answered their questions as politely as I could when one of them picked the bucket up and dropped it on the road to demonstrate the impact. That set off my passenger, Steve Ewen, a normally jovial fellow of indigenous descent. "You could have damaged our bucket then – pick the bloody thing up and put it back on the vehicle," he roared. That set the scene; the officers were going to throw the book at us. Why were we carrying booze and barbeque items in an obvious government vehicle? After much discussion I finally convinced them that use of the vehicle for these purposes was fully sanctioned by the CEO and even offered them Keith Johns's phone number to check. In the end they gave up and waved us on our way, I did at least have the courtesy to invite them to the ensuing parklands barbeque so they could see for themselves, but they failed to appear.

There are many sporting fields in the parklands, and these were regularly used over the summer for after-work twilight cricket matches. Some of these were social games between MESA and the SA mineral exploration industry. There were usually two matches per summer, with regular drinks throughout the game followed by a post-match barbeque. They were a great way of promoting interaction and friendship between the groups. Most games were officially declared as draws, but at times the competition could be quite fierce, with a smattering of good (but past-it) players on both sides. At least there were never any major injuries, although one avid MESA player was known to regularly send down a volley of bouncers to tail-end batsmen as the twilight faded.

Characters

MESA was full of characters in those days, and Ian Grant, my initial boss in the Mineral Exploration Branch, was one, although I only worked with him for twelve to eighteen months. "Grantie" was a Canadian by birth and was reputed to have flown many sorties over Germany and occupied territories during World War 2 as a member of the Royal Canadian Air Force. He was always well spoken and somewhat distinguished, but you were lucky to find him at work most afternoons, his reputed haunt was the Naval, Military and Air Force Club of South Australia in downtown Adelaide. He must have had some agreement with the powers that be because, while his absences were noted, he never seemed to be reprimanded.

He showed amazing foresight in formulating mineral exploration, tenure and royalty components for the *Roxby Downs Indenture Act*, which has worked well over now more than 30 years of operations at the Olympic Dam mine. He seemed to be blissfully unaware of the coming political correctness in the work environment. This was aptly demonstrated to me one day at a meeting with an indigenous native title group, an activity which was to become an integral part of mineral exploration throughout Australia following proclamation of the *Aboriginal Land Rights Act 1976*. During the meeting in his office he went to get a file from his cabinet; the file was clearly labelled "Coon File", and this was apparent to all attendees. I wanted to go away and hide under a table, but he was oblivious to the racist slur – that was just the way things had always been done as far as he was concerned. As it turned out no comment was ever made about the file label, and the meeting ended quite amicably. I can only imagine the consequences of such an action in today's world. Unsurprisingly, when the first MESA voluntary separation packages were offered in late 1983, Grantie was the first to accept one – perhaps his time had come.

Ian Faulks replaced Grantie as my boss, and the difference between the two was like chalk and cheese. Gone was Grantie's flamboyance and regular absence, replaced with a conservative, fair and reasoned, diligent approach. Ian was a great bloke to work for and gave me free rein to conduct most of the fieldwork required to check on company exploration activities. Over a period, we were responsible for approving the construction of literally hundreds of kilometres of exploration tracks in the far western areas of the state, much of the region slated for future national parks and conservation reserves. Approval was given only after extensive consultation with environmental and heritage stakeholders of the areas. Experience showed that rapid natural regeneration of these tracks occurred once exploration was concluded. We hadn't counted on others using these tracks for recreation and access to now proclaimed national parks. Probably even some of the rangers today administering these parks are thankful that this serendipitous access was approved in years gone by.

Ian and I only lived about a kilometre apart so over the years I travelled with him to and from work, paying petrol money in lieu of train/bus fares. Ian liked to hold the stage during our travels, so much so that I learned of another quirk of nature, basically some people don't really listen to you. After years of listening to his discourses, I decided to start giving him the wrong answer to an occasional question he might pose; he never picked it up and would continue unabated. Ian was a good tennis player and not bad at table tennis as well, we played half an hour's table tennis most lunchtimes in the MESA conference room. After initially copping merciless hidings, it took about five years of practice before I could hold my own with him – at least it provided good exercise.

Ian and I did occasional field trips together, and one was quite unique. On a cool midwinter day we set off from Adelaide to inspect a diamond exploration bulk sampling operation in the Springfield Basin between Quorn and Hawker. Neither of us had paid much attention to weather forecasts before departure. In the Southern Flinders Ranges I looked in the distance and said, I think it's snowing. Ian just laughed at the suggestion. A few minutes later as we rounded a bend coming into Melrose, there stood Mount Remarkable covered in snow. From there the ranges all the way to Wilmington, another 20 kilometres away, were likewise covered in snow. What a privilege to have accidentally witnessed such an uncommon event. When we reached the project area it was overcast and blowing a gale. I'm positive that, as we inspected some of the trenches from which bulk samples were taken, these were the coldest field conditions I've ever worked in. We were rewarded, however, when we witnessed real (if very small) diamonds recovered from the processing plant, and later that evening when we sat and had dinner, washed down with a red or two, beside a roaring fire back at one of the historic pubs in Quorn. After a long career working with the Bureau of Mineral Resources and later MESA, Ian took an early retirement in 1993 but sadly died of cancer only a few short years later.

Jack Townsend and Doug Scott were a bit like the "Odd Couple", with a 15-year age difference but an inseparable friendship. Jack was just the all-round

Australian mate to everyone, whose word was his bond. At social events he had a habit of falling deeply asleep after a few drinks, but an hour or so later he would rejoin the party with gusto. He went on to become a specialist, respected Australia-wide, in the study of gemstones and particularly opal – in fact he ended up with the moniker "Gemstone Jack". Doug, or "Scotty" as he was universally known, had worked many years on mines in Canada before joining MESA and adored a drink and a smoke, especially a bottle of port round the campfire. After one of these port episodes near Broken Hill he fell into the campfire and lost his front teeth. Scotty's forte was in creating unique new expressions, with several ultimately taken up by local radio stations to become universally accepted in the local community. Scotty was struck down by a heart attack at just 59, leaving a wife and young child.

Peter Crettenden (Cretto) and Mark Flintoft, two technical field officers, were seen very much as the party animals at MESA, and at places like Coober Pedy they certainly lived up to their reputation. Mark, after he had a few, had the habit of speaking faster and faster until you couldn't understand a word he was saying. Despite their reputation they were both excellent to be with in the field and great company to boot. Cretto, if he had the educational opportunity, would have made a great geologist, botanist, zoologist or whatever; he had a wonderful knowledge of the Australian bush and was a great bush cook. Cretto was also a great learner. When GPS first came to the industry as a navigational and surveying tool, he undertook to learn all there was to know about it and became the MESA specialist in this then burgeoning field. Mark was tops in organising all the logistics for any bush trip whether short or extended over several months: you always knew that vehicles would be in good shape and that all food and equipment for a trip would be there. I always felt incredibly safe travelling with them, although I doubt that the OH&S manual was strictly adhered to. The other skill they both had in spades was public relations: wherever we went they would quickly strike up friendships with pastoralists and other stakeholders and having met would always remember names and maintain good long-term relationships with most. This is a skill so vital in the Australian bush. Both Cretto and Mark feature in further tales in this tome.

Rodney South was another character who can't go unmentioned. Also a field assistant with MESA, he was eccentric to say the least, but delightful company. Rodney was a mad hoarder, he lived in the leafy suburb of Kensington Park and the place looked like something out of *Steptoe and Son*: he couldn't use his front door because he had so much junk piled up, could barely move inside the house and had a massive shed out the back which was also piled to the rafters with what he classified as useful junk. If you asked him if he had a particular item, he knew exactly where every piece of junk was stored.

When I first visited Rodney at home in 1981, he'd just removed the rotting floorboards from his lounge, and his furniture was set up on the underlying clay base. When he died a year or so ago, some 40 years later, the living arrangements apparently hadn't changed. At one time Rodney featured on the commercial television program "Neighbours from Hell". When neighbours and officers from Burnside Council were interviewed on the program, they unanimously agreed that he was a lovely bloke but please oh please could he just clean up the rubbish. His response, "Well I was here before it became a leafy, green suburb, so new neighbours should have known what to expect when they purchased in the immediate vicinity". He received many pointed directives from the council, but nothing ever really changed. Rodney could be a tad frustrating on field trips, all he wanted to do was to collect more junk from deserted buildings and little bush hamlets, but he was always a lot of fun too.

Bob Wildy, one of the senior managers when I joined MESA, was an absolute legend in the department. He joined MESA after a long and successful career as an industrial geologist with ICI in Sydney. Bob was a polite, kind and thoughtful individual who had the ability to be MESA's next CEO, but he loved his Friday long lunch or after work drinks and once he had a few there was no stopping him. He would have had real problems adjusting to the non-touchy-feely mores of the present era, but then again social attitudes were different 40 years ago and there are many of us whose actions then could today land us in a lot of trouble. There are so many legendary stories of Bob's exploits that I choose not to mention here, but the following two short tales give an indication.

Bob often rode his bike to work from his near-city home, usually choosing a pathway through the parklands beside Greenhill Road. One Friday he'd perhaps had one too many at the local Parkside pub conveniently located opposite MESA's building. Donning his helmet but otherwise immaculately dressed in jacket and tie, he set off for home along the Parklands path. A male and female police officer had set up their portable radar device in the middle of the path to make it less visible on Greenhill Road. Yes, Bob never saw them on the path and ploughed straight through the seated police and their equipment, upending them and himself. After they all regained their composure, no real damage had been done, but the officers were keen to arrest Bob for riding his bike under the influence even though he wasn't on the road. In the end commonsense prevailed and he was ordered to ride home carefully and stay off the road. I think the police realised the embarrassment that they'd face from colleagues if the story ever got out.

Bob and his lovely wife Marge were keen bridge players, and another Friday Bob came to work and informed us that he was under orders as he was playing bridge that evening. Marge had allowed him to have a few drinks at lunchtime or a few after work but not both. As some of us walked into the Leicester Hotel after work there was Bob firing on all cylinders, but he informed us that he would be all square with Marge as he had stuck to their deal, because in his mind he was still at lunch. We never heard how bridge went that evening, but there's a suspicion that Bob may have ended up in the doghouse.

James Fraser "Jim" Allender must rate as one of the most colourful characters I met in my work career. A geophysicist with the Santos-Delhi oil exploration group, Jim was a frequenter of the Parkside Hotel after work on a Friday. I don't know whether it was a mutual interest in geophysics, in red wine or in simply having a good time, but we were strangely drawn together and occasionally were even accused of being brothers.

Jim was full of stories and was an incorrigible stirrer and leg-puller, but more than once he'd carry this too far and then need to wriggle out of the odd challenging confrontation. He could be an absolute pest at times. Early in the 1980s Jim left his job with Santos-Delhi and gradually accrued extensive mineral and oil exploration tenements, mainly in South Australia, to become a mining entrepreneur and consultant. Not having the funds to carry out proposed exploration, Jim needed to attract new players to fund the exploration programs, and this was his forte. In this role over more than 30 years Jim has been responsible for attracting more new Australian and overseas investors to fund exploration in the state than any other individual and should be lauded for this.

Jim was dedicated to exploration 24/7 and would often have colleagues round to his home in Unley for a red wine or two. Immediately the first bottle was poured, Jim would rev up his computer and display various geoscientific images and composites from around the state, and discussion and interpretation of these images could go on for many hours and usually six or seven bottles of red. Once his guests had departed Jim often spent all night refining these interpretations, no doubt over yet another bottle of red.

Socialising with Jim meant that I had to be always on guard: he would forever probe me for a bit of confidential exploration information and worst of all, no matter how many bottles of wine were consumed over lunch or at the impromptu evening interpretation sessions, Jim would remember in detail every word of conversation that took place. Going in the field on occasion with Jim could also prove hazardous because of his proclivity to rub up new acquaintances the wrong way, and this will be expanded on in a few anecdotes in the next chapters.

Learning to speak again

At high school I was in the debating team and as school captain was often called upon to give short orations, but in the ensuing fifteen or so years, most of them in remote places, I completely lost this skill and the confidence to go with it. At

MESA we had regular monthly meetings where you presented details of your current projects to a peer group of 60 or so departmental geoscientists. Without doubt this was the hardest audience I have ever had to present to, and some of the post talk questions were harrowing, give me 1000 participants at an industry conference any day.

I recognised that I needed to improve my public speaking dramatically, and around the same time I was also in the process of enrolling in part-time postgraduate studies in mineral economics at Macquarie University. Serendipity played its part, when I was invited by a departing staff member to assume his role as lead lecturer for SA in "Mining Investment", a subject included in a postgraduate diploma course then run by the Securities Institute of Australia. I knew that I was woefully under-skilled for the task, but on the other hand it provided the opportunity to improve my public speaking and advance my knowledge of mineral economics rapidly to a point where I could confidently present it to the students.

So began a most enjoyable part of my working life for the next 15 years. It was only two hours, one night a week for about twelve weeks per year, but it made me lift my game. For the first few years each lecture took about 20 hours to prepare, and for the first few lectures I took a prescribed downer to hide my nervousness, but eventually lecturing became somewhat of a pleasure. It was a new experience working with people from the financial industry, but I was a bit surprised at how people's grasp of the English language had weakened since my time at school and Uni. Some of the assignments presented by students, already tertiary educated, were barely readable.

I made a fundamental error nearing the end of the course one year when I jokingly offered to leak a few national exam questions for the payment of a bottle of good quality McLaren Vale Shiraz. I don't know whether I was being set up but was horrified when one of the students arrived with said bottle the following week. I do know that I emphatically refused the bottle and made sure that the offer was never again proffered.

The course itself was fundamentally about providing the students with the basic skill to evaluate a mining company/project to determine whether a share purchase was viable. I never gave out share tips, but at the end of each course usually provided a list of about ten companies for the students to evaluate and make investment decisions on. There must have been some teaching success as I note one of the ex-students is currently the economic spokesman for one of Australia's largest banks. I never applied the techniques taught to my own investments in the mining/exploration industry, dutifully following the market up in each boom and following it back down in each ensuing bust. After fifteen years I noticed that my educational zeal had diminished. That's no good for the students – it was time for new blood.

19
Replete with Wine, Surf and Safaris

South Australia 1980s

With such a great group of colleagues it's little wonder that the MESA Social Club hosted some wonderful events over the years, including an annual Christmas party, but the wine bottlings that just grew and grew over time were spectacular and attracted many outside guests as well as social club members. The premise of the bottlings was to provide members with good quality wines at very competitive prices.

Wine bottlings

Sample wines were obtained from several wineries each year and then subjected to a critical tasting before a decision was made on the wines to be bottled or purchased. As we could generally guarantee sales of at least 40 dozen on any wine selected, winemakers were quite generous with both the quantity and quality of samples. It wasn't unusual to have 30 to 40 samples, of which maybe five or six would be chosen. It was quite a task for the tasting panel, and as the event grew, judges were required to nominate as either a white or red wine judge simply so they could survive the arduous tasting process (most of us preferred to swallow each wine after tasting rather than adopting the more normal practice of spitting it out). Over the years we had several well-known winemakers join the tasting panel including John Davis of Hunter Valley renown; Michael Potts, winemaker extraordinaire from the Potts family–owned Bleasdale Winery at Langhorne Creek; and a doyen of McLaren Vale, the venerable Brian Light.

One of the earlier tasting panel events was held in MESA's conference room, which was on the top floor, the executive level of the building. It turned out to be a long and boisterous affair and, although it was tolerated on the day, Keith Johns strongly urged the tasting panel to keep well clear of the department when holding such events in future.

We'd purchase white, sparkling and port wines in advance based on members' pre-orders, but to ensure a notable event always liked to bottle at least two 200-litre barrels of red wine on the day. Initially the bottlings were low-key barbeque events at winery venues, but as they grew and the breathalyser had its impact, they became overnight or weekend camping affairs, first on large country ovals but later in Mount Crawford Forest and the Clare showgrounds, where our activities were well out of public view.

Bottling a 200-litre barrel can easily be done in an hour with an experienced crew of four or five. but there was always no end of eager inexperienced participants, who tended to prolong the process. Also lengthening the process was the amount of spillage (into mouths) that took place. A barrel theoretically holds 22.22 dozen bottles, but barrels were usually over-full, we always allowed for a net return of 21 dozen, with the remainder "spilled" in the process. This formula really came to grief one year at Perrini Estate Winery at Meadows. Tony Perrini convinced us to use his mechanised (but very slow) automatic bottling equipment instead of our tried-and-true practice of using two or three siphon hoses. Tony and his lovely wife Connie then produced some wonderful home-made Italian delicacies including his special salami, which complemented all the foodstuffs we'd brought to get through the afternoon. It was a relaxing way to bottle wine, but three hours later, when the first barrel was emptied, we discovered that we only had a net return of nineteen dozen (with orders of 21 dozen already placed). The spillage had been somewhat excessive but most enjoyable. We reverted to an expert siphoning team for the second barrel to try to recover some of the earlier losses.

Mount Crawford Forest and the Clare Valley are two of South Australia's chillier areas in midwinter, when these bottlings were held, so the event was always accompanied by large fires and fine food, which included Stuie Matthews's wonderful pig on a spit together with camp oven delicacies, mainly a variety of curries but also Cretto's excellent mussels in a superb tomato-based sauce and of course Lloydie Sampson's excruciatingly hot chilli con carne. One year we even tried venison on a spit, supplied and cooked by Lloydie Moore. It took a while longer to cook than Stuie's pig and was well worth waiting for, but what we didn't anticipate was next day's after-effect: we all stank to high heaven. In fact, on my way home that year I stopped for fuel at Birdwood. After I had paid the cashier, who was a friend of a friend, he politely asked me to get out of the store as quickly as possible because I was polluting the premises. It took at least a day for the awful odour to stop reeking through our pores, and accordingly venison on a spit was a one-off.

After distribution of wines one year, I got a call from the brother of one of our staff who had shared a bottle of our recent port selection with him, which he said he thoroughly enjoyed. He then quickly came to the point, identifying himself as an inspector with the SA Liquor Commission. His first question was "Does the club make a profit from these annual wine sales?" followed by "Are the wines for club members only?" to which I replied no and yes respectively. He then went on to outline the hefty fines which could be incurred together with the requirement to obtain a liquor licence if I hadn't answered his questions as I did. I think he was just trying to give me a timely warning to be careful. The message was taken on board, and from that time onward we diligently managed to have enough spillage to ensure no profit was ever made on wine sales – and of course who club members might decide to gift wine to after purchase was beyond our control. Over a 20-year period over 5000 dozen bottles were distributed to members, an annual average of 250 dozen. In dollars of today at say an average of $100 a dozen that represents a turnover of $500,000.

Seacliff Surf Life Saving Club

Growing up at Bermagui I'd always been keen to join a surf club but unfortunately in those days the nearest was at Tathra, then an hour's drive away on a rough dirt road. So, when neighbours at Seacombe Heights said their kids were going to nippers we soon after took Teneille along for a try. The first year or so involved two leisurely hours each Saturday afternoon on the beach followed by a drink or two at the surf club with other parents, although Debbie was quickly roped in as junior secretary. Slowly but surely, you were drawn into further commitment supervising children on Saturdays, and as Teneille got older there were also regular all-day junior carnivals anywhere between Grange further up in the gulf and Port Elliot on the southern coast.

To supervise an age group, one had to obtain a surf bronze medallion, which took some effort when approaching 40, and a day at a carnival unloading and loading a large trailer full of equipment as well as traipsing up and down a sandy beach myriad times could be exhausting. Once you obtained your bronze medallion there was also an expectation that you'd attend regular weekend surf patrols over the summer season. Despite this, the joy of seeing children develop their skills and the wonderful life-long friendships made over nearly 20 years were incredibly rewarding. There was nothing better after an afternoon with nippers, followed by the ritual 400-metre surf race at 4.00pm, which usually attracted 70 to 80 senior and junior competitors (often in very cool conditions up until Christmas), than to adjourn to the surf club for a well-deserved beer or two.

My two daughters Teneille and Emma had vastly different experiences at nippers. When Teneille started there were no separate boys and girls events at carnivals or training, so the competition was much stiffer, the annual club championship day was the only time that separate boys and girls events took place. By the time Emma joined, all events were gender specific. Despite this both girls proved highly competitive at the sport though neither continued to senior level, which is the ultimate aim of nippers – to encourage the lifesavers of the future. There's still hope, as my grandchildren Koa and Ochre are currently Noosa nippers.

Seacliff Beach was interesting, situated halfway up St Vincents Gulf, the area is sheltered from large swells, such that waves there are miniscule or nonexistent most of the time except for rough and very inconsistent storm swells. Despite this Seacliff has produced some wonderful athletes, including Dwayne Thuys, a world and dual Australian lifesaving iron man champion, and Di Wallace-Ward, who has competed at world championship level and continues to compete very successfully at Australian Masters events to this day. Due to the lack of surf, much training is done further down the gulf at Southport and Moana, and on the southern coast from Port Elliot to Goolwa, where the swells of the Southern Ocean coming off Antarctica with nothing in between can at times be quite large.

Trembling

Goolwa was then the standard training spot for learning the skills to obtain an inflatable rescue boat (IRB) or "rubber duck" licence. The last seaward break, where most training took place was often several hundred metres out, and you had to battle through myriad lines of breakers to get there. Training was in the winter months and driving there I can remember my pulse rising about five minutes before arriving on the beach. Perhaps the worst experience was being the "patient". Half a kilometre or more out to sea you'd jump into the dark and icy waters and watch the IRB disappear toward shore only to turn 100 metres or so away and rescue you from the waters, hopefully before the next massive wave broke over you. The fact that the Murray River mouth, an attraction to Great White sharks, was nearby added to the imaginings as you floundered in the water waiting. I'll always feel indebted to the trainers, especially Phil Hoff (then a member of the SA Police elite Star Force), for the patience and calmness they showed, allowing the trainees gradually to gain confidence in handling these conditions. I believe in more recent times Goolwa is no longer used for training because of the wear and tear on expensive rescue safety equipment (not to mention on the trainers and trainees).

There were and are so many wonderful volunteers at surf clubs throughout Australia who give their time tirelessly to the cause, and three Seacliff members that I now mention are just a few among many. In the nippers Terry Keefe was a standout. Always happy and adored by children and parents, Terry not only took all his children through nippers over a 20-year period but after a brief respite went back and may in fact still be taking his grandchildren through the same enjoyable process. Glen Patten and Darryl Pope are two senior club members who've devoted their adult lives to the movement after coming through the nippers themselves. Now in their late sixties, they both spend summer weekends as competition judges at club, state and national levels as well as occasionally competing themselves. They've received well-deserved recognition at all levels for their wonderful service.

The general

"Glennie (Professor/the General)" Patten is a particular friend, who has been awarded Australian recognition for his services to surf lifesaving and to biochemistry. His partner, Sue Hicks. has also been a dear friend for over 40 years. (Who knows. they may even marry one day, as Glennie proposed about 20 years ago.) Glen spent his working life as a research scientist with the CSIRO but somehow managed to find time to take on just about every role in surf lifesaving at club, state and national level as well as enjoying a beer (or 20) and a red wine (or two or three bottles).

When I first joined the club I had some reservations about Glen. When speaking at club functions he seemed grumpy and opinionated, coupled with a rather cynical innuendo when speaking of various members. I think it was more that he doesn't suffer fools gladly. As I got to know him better and realised where he was coming from (perhaps it was our shared scientific backgrounds), I grew fond of sharing a chat and a red or two with this character, something I enjoy to this day when our paths occasionally cross.

Over the years there were many funny incidents on the beach and at the club, some of which are better left untold, but a few that can be repeated come to mind now. Wayne and Lorraine Jones were a married couple with young children who often arrived for nippers or club functions in separate vehicles, for whatever reason. However, they built up a reputation for each assuming the other had collected the children at the end of the day/night. As a result the children were often abandoned at the club and a few frantic calls were needed to effect their rescue – but karma prevailed. Wayne was the bar manager at a club function, which he attended with Lorraine without the children. At the end of the night Wayne had the responsibility to ensure no-one was left on the premises and then lock up. Unbeknown to Wayne, Lorraine may have had a drink too many and late in the night visited the Ladies, where she fell asleep. Yes, Wayne forgot to check the Ladies and after locking up drove home assuming Lorraine had got herself home. At about 3.00am a very cold and disorientated Lorraine, in total darkness, managed to ring Wayne demanding, "How the hell do I get out of here?"

On another occasion, following complaints from neighbours about late-night carry-ons, the club had to make a commitment to Brighton Council that it would close and all patrons would be off the premises by an agreed time. On this particular night there was a club function and I'd scored the bar manager role. Attempting to close on time, I was hampered by some of the younger members who wanted to carry on, and one, Bly Bayliss, stood on a large speaker near the bar demanding the bar stay open. What to do? Without much thought I threw him over my shoulder and escorted him off the premises. This worked a treat, and without further ado the remaining patrons left and I was able to close up on time.

It was only later that I found out that Bly was violently ill soon after I put him down. It was a lucky escape.

The mile swim

Apart from our regular late Saturday afternoon 400-metre "surf races", there were annual club half-mile and mile swim events from Seacliff towards Brighton jetty. Glen and I always had a running bet of a pint of beer on who would finish ahead of the other in the mile. In the 1990s I didn't help myself one year when I'd stayed overnight at work colleague Mark Flintoft's home and he then suggested that we have a recovery beer or two with our barbeque breakfast on Saturday morning. It's not the way to prepare for a long swim, which proved to be the hardest ever, but at least I finished. Another challenge involved my younger daughter, Emma. I'd been out of the water for a week or two following a "swimmer's ear" operation, when she announced that she was going to do her first mile but that I had to accompany her. Consulted, my surgeon gave a firm no to the suggestion of getting in the water but then went on to tell me how to seal the ear with Blu Tack if I was stupid enough to swim. Come race day I swam beside Emma to the first seaward buoy, about 70 metres out to sea, but as we rounded it and headed for Brighton she took off, never to be seen till race end – so much for needing an escort.

Having seen both Teneille and Emma right through nippers I continued to train some of the younger groups for a few more years but knew my time had come when I was nominated to take on the Santa role at the nippers Christmas party. It was an interesting task to say the least, first wading into the water at Hallett Cove in bare feet but otherwise full Santa regalia to join the IRB, and then making a dramatic beach entrance at Seacliff, wading through the shallows with a sack of goodies. Once Santa was seated, every kid in the club from four to fourteen came to sit on his lap, mostly in wet bathers. With Santa having a somewhat wet outfit to start with, it wasn't exactly comfortable, especially on a stinking hot December day. There were some nice perks to the job, however: a complimentary six-pack of beer, and after the children had finished with their Christmas requests many of the young mums also sat on Santa's lap to make their Christmas requests.

On a more sombre note, the other event that made me decide to walk away from nippers was the arrest and conviction of a leading Adelaide magistrate, also a nippers carnival referee, on charges relating to sexual abuse of boys from the neighbouring Brighton Surf Club. It put a dampener on my enjoyment of nippers training.

Uluru and Kakadu

Midway through 1988 our family set off on a bush trip to Uluru and Kakadu in the Northern Territory along with the family of another MESA work colleague, Zac Sibenaler. It was a wonderful six-week trip, but quite basic in those days with just tents and swags for comfort. I don't plan to detail the trip but simply relate some of memorable moments.

Uluru itself was the first, it doesn't matter how many times you visit, it's awe-inspiring. We planned to climb it but Debbie's and my head for heights failed us by "Chicken Rock", so we decided to abandon the attempt, allowing ten-year-old Teneille to continue the climb with the Sibenaler family, but insisting four-year-old Emma come back down with us. She was indignant. A few days later we got to Kings Canyon and spent most of the day walking on tracks that were poorly defined by today's standards. At the end of the day a still-miffed Emma, who had taken the precipitous walk in her stride, declared: "See, I could have done Ayers Rock easily." Point taken.

For the trip as far as Darwin I had my old Falcon sedan and Zac was driving his Volvo. Soon after we left Uluru his rear shockers gave up the ghost and he and family had the most horrendously bouncy trip from there to Alice Springs. Rodney South, another MESA colleague, along with his dad, John, and son, Aaron, caught up with us near the Henbury meteorite craters after having vehicle problems before leaving Adelaide. Arriving in Alice early on a very cold Friday morning (maximum 11 degrees centigrade) we were dismayed to find all businesses closed for the annual show day. Ringing around, Zac discovered that the nearest Volvo dealer was in Mt Isa and didn't have replacement shockers in stock anyway. There was nothing more to do that day, so mums and kids joined the locals at the show while the men-folk commiserated over a few beers.

Early Saturday it was straight to Repco (or its equivalent) in the forlorn hope of picking up the Volvo shockers, that was a pipedream, however, a helpful attendant suggested that with a bit of inspiration much cheaper Falcon shockers could be adapted to the situation, and in Rod South we had a master of innovation. Much of the rest of the day was spent outside my mother-in-law's house on Larapinta Drive effecting repairs, but eventually the job was done, and Zac declared later that they worked better than the originals.

Leaving early the next day we were constantly dogged by Rod's ongoing problems with an ever-loosening harmonic balancer. At every stop he'd try for a replacement part, with no success. We ultimately abandoned his party at Elliot, with Rod still scouring the town's vehicle dump for the elusive part (we had a strict timeframe for getting to Darwin). After our arrival in Darwin, we teamed up with my sister Wendy, brother-in-law Bill and their daughter Kristena, who had flown to Darwin and hired a four-wheel-drive and camping gear for our next, Kakadu-Litchfield leg of the trip.

Zac and I had booked two Nissan Patrols for our purposes well in advance, but we arrived at Budget to be told that they only had one Nissan available, and the only other vehicles available were some brand-new soft-top Suzukis. One family of four quickly jumped into the Suzuki and said, "This is great but where do we stow all our gear and supplies?" The upshot, we ended up with the Nissan plus two Suzukis at no extra cost. One problem, all the kids loved travelling in the Suzukis (with soft tops removed), so every day we had to swap vehicles.

Near Ubirr, early on our Kakadu jaunt, Bill managed to lock the keys in his hire vehicle, and repeated attempts to break in were to no avail. A decision was made to break the driver's side little front airflow window. This was unfortunate for Bill, Wendy and Kristena, as from then on they emerged from the vehicle after a hard day's travel looking like dust-covered bulldozer drivers. I guess it made refreshing swims at the various falls just that bit more enjoyable.

Arriving at UDP (now Gunlom) Falls a day or two later, we found the campground empty, so decided to set up base camp there for a few days while we explored surrounding areas. Upon returning after visiting Koolpin Falls the next day we found our camp surrounded by the little tents of a busload of tourists. With so much space why the driver/guide elected to camp on top of us I'll never know. Zac's son Andrew and Teneille had both been given clarinets from their respective schools so that they could keep up their music practice while on the trip. That night they were encouraged to practice well into the night while the rest of our group partied on noisily. The bus was packed and departed early the next morning. I think a point had been made.

We moved on to another campsite for access to Twin and Jim Jim Falls. The first night there we had a midnight visit from a group of wild pigs, I awoke to find Bill throwing beer cans at them, possibly not the best approach when feral pigs are around although in this case it worked. Our camp overlooked two creek crossings, one of which needed to be crossed if heading towards Twin Falls. Before leaving for Twin Falls, I told Bill to always use the shallower crossing of the two as you might have difficulties with the deeper one.

Returning from a wonderful day at Twin Falls we found that some yahoos had blocked off the shallow crossing with their deckchairs and eskies so that they could watch drivers struggling with the deeper crossing. Zac and I, both experienced bush drivers, went through the deeper crossing without difficulty, but when Bill arrived a few minutes later (and not being used to Top End conditions) he heeded my advice and drove up to the shallow crossing and politely asked the yahoos to move. It was a request they chose to ignore so Bill just revved up the vehicle and headed straight into the crossing, I have never seen yahoos, chairs and eskies scatter so fast. Possibly emboldened by a beer or two, I wandered back down from our camp to give the yahoos a bit of friendly advice about Top End behaviour. As I launched into my tirade, I felt one of the young chaps was getting ready to have a go, but then his expression changed, Zac, an Aussie rules full forward, had come down and was standing, towering over me by about a foot. It did the trick.

When we first arrived at the new park information centre near Jabiru I'd enquired about the status of the Rockhole near the Mary River, which we'd visited so regularly when living in Darwin and which was now just in Kakadu National Park. I got blank looks; no-one seemed to know of it. We called in there on the way to Pine Creek, the track was unused, the rock faces and trees were covered in spider webs, but the falls and pool were as delightful as ever, so we all had a wonderful swim, but unfortunately didn't have time left to camp there.

From Pine Creek we drove across to Daly River then up via the Reynolds River into the southern end of Litchfield National Park. The Reynolds River crossing was deep and we were wary of walking through as it was known for the occasional croc, so we towed the Suzukis across with the Nissan, but with motors running in neutral in case we had to try to power through. Arriving at Wangi Falls I was both amazed and saddened. In 1980 we had to drive along a creek bed to access the falls; in 1988 there was bitumen access with buses everywhere. There was a large goanna by the water and I wondered whether it was the same one that had accosted Debbie and Teneille back in 1980. Access throughout Kakadu and Litchfield had changed everywhere in those eight short years: for instance, in 1980 you could drive almost right to Twin Falls; in 1988 it was a kilometre walk from the carpark or a paddle and swim down the creek.

On the last leg back to Darwin we found the Suzukis were overheating a bit and on inspection realised that the plastic radiator fans had been mangled, probably when crossing the Reynolds River. When we returned the vehicles to Budget these defects were noted as they prepared to impose additional charges. Zac took over negotiations (I could never handle this) and convinced them that the fans were Budget's problem as they provided us with vehicles not up to the task in hand, but to add insult to injury he presented them with all the receipts for fuel for the second Suzuki, which they duly refunded. Little wonder that Budget went into liquidation a few years later.

20

Always Face Your Swag Away from the Campfire

South Australia, 1990s

This decade saw significant changes in the way we did business at MESA, and rather more dramatic changes on the domestic front. As a prelude, in the late 1980s I'd somewhat reluctantly returned to the Mineral Resources Branch to head up the Metallics section. I loved my work in the Mineral Exploration Branch, but staying there severely limited promotion opportunities. By this time Ric Horn had succeeded Jeff Oliver as the branch manager. It was business as usual for the first year or so, and I must admit I was getting itchy feet, thinking that a change back to industry looked enticing.

Although in its early days South Australia had been an Australian leader in metal mining, with major copper mines at Burra, Kapunda and Moonta-Wallaroo, and iron ore mining in the Middleback Ranges which supplied the Australian steel industry for over 50 years, by the 1990s it was very much a mining backwater. The massive Olympic Dam discovery in 1975 led to a brief flurry of exploration activity during the 1980s, but this had dissipated by the 1990s. The problem with South Australia was and is that its highly prospective rock formations are for the most part covered by from tens to hundreds of metres of younger soil, sand and sedimentary rock cover. This makes mineral exploration both very expensive and high-risk.

By the early 1990s the State was nearly bankrupt, and the Bannon Labor government was reeling from the State Bank fiasco. The government was looking for a way forward and was very aware of the wealth being generated by the newly opened Olympic Dam mine. MESA was urged to become more pro-active in promoting the potential of the SA mining industry.

A conference in a quarry

In late 1991 MESA initiated and ran the first December industry exploration conference to coincide with St Barbara's Day, Barbara was apparently the patron saint of explosives and mining. The conference was followed by a big industry get-together in an operational rock quarry just up the road from MESA headquarters. The quarry was the ideal venue for such a gathering, with all facets of the industry from executive to driller's offsider in attendance and socialising as one. The quarry venue had to be abandoned several years later due to increasing OH&S demands, but the St Barbara's day event continues to this day, usually at the Adelaide Convention Centre, and is now driven by industry.

At MESA round the same time in 1991, Reg Nelson, then Director, Minerals, came up with a proposal for MESA to fly vast areas of South Australia with state-of-the-art geophysical surveys. Reg's proposal was modified to include regional drilling programs and compilation of statewide geoscientific databases. Keith Johns then took the proposal to the State Government and must have sold it well because they jumped at it. Having achieved this commitment, Keith retired from MESA after 44 years of service and a final job well done.

Making things happen

In July 1992 the South Australian Exploration Initiative (SAEI) was launched by the SA government, with $11 million to be spent in 1992 alone, including the largest airborne regional geophysical surveys ever undertaken in Australia. The culture of MESA was changed completely with the announcement of the SAEI. Overnight the department became entrepreneurial, and staff were mandated to take a similar approach in their dealings with industry clients and in their approach to meeting project deadlines. It was suddenly a joy to work there.

Thirty years on, the success of these ongoing SA Government initiatives can be measured not only in numerous major mineral developments and a quantum leap in levels of mineral exploration but also by the fact that every other State and the Northern Territory, plus several countries, have emulated this approach to encouraging mineral exploration and development. After I departed MESA in 2001 the government also started funding selected company drilling programs (personally I felt this was taking government assistance one step too far). However, this drilling initiative was immediately justified in 2005 when such funding enabled entrepreneur Rudy Gomez to drill a hole 100 metres deeper than his own funds could stretch to, and it was in the final few metres of that hole that a major copper intersection was made. This led to development of and, in 2020, production from the world-class Carrapateena mine, about 100 kilometres southeast of Olympic Dam.

Keith Johns was replaced as the CEO in 1992 by the dynamic and some would say messianic Ross Farden. Ross, a geologist and something of a mining industry legend, was the perfect person to drive the SAEI and convince both the politicians and the public of its importance to SA's future prosperity.

My own situation also changed during the early days of the SAEI. Reg Nelson moved on to head up Beach Petroleum and Ric Horn replaced him as Director, Minerals and in turn I became Manager, Mineral Resources. Also, with the early retirement of Ian Faulks, the mineral exploration function (my real love) became part of the Mineral Resources Branch. Although I could no longer take a hands-on approach, this role was ably undertaken by George Kwitko.

The Branch's main role during the SAEI and later exploration initiatives was to undertake regional drilling programs, which would provide ground-truthing data to assist in interpreting the vast airborne surveys which were being undertaken concurrently. Many of these programs were in remote areas of the state, which entailed camping under basic conditions for extensive periods. There was also a need for these programs to be completed in a timely manner to maintain the SAEI's momentum.

A gee-up CEO

Ross Farden was an extraordinary character. Reputedly a lay preacher in his early days, and later in life obtaining an MBA from one of the top American institutions, he was a man possessed. He walked and talked work 24/7, and I believe he advanced MESA by at least ten years in his two-year stay. He was also instrumental in clearing out some dead wood through so-called "voluntary" separation packages which the government had initiated across the SA public service, although the packages also resulted in the loss of some of our better staff.

Ross liked to socialise with staff whenever he could, graciously inviting many to dinner parties at his home as well as joining the several branches in social drinks of a Friday afternoon after work. When our turn came, he emphasised that staff should feel free to openly discuss the good and the bad things about the current state of the Department/Branch. Personally, I felt that Ross only wanted to hear the positives and didn't really want to dwell on the negatives. Unfortunately, at our branch get-together one staff member, Bob Major, launched into a diatribe of what was wrong with the place. At one point I got behind Ross and attempted to signal to Bob that he should desist, but he either ignored or didn't pick up on my signals and continued to self-destruct. Bob accepted a voluntary separation package just a few weeks later – we'll never know why.

Bob himself was something of an enigma and a loner. He was a first-class geologist and MESA's expert on all things uranium, but he had his foibles. One was wearing a bike helmet for extra safety when driving his own four-wheel drive around suburban Adelaide. Before my time at MESA there was also a story of Bob missing out on a senior position and launching an official appeal against the appointment decision. The story goes that instead of emphasising his own attributes at the appeal he denigrated the appointee and even produced a record of the appointee's regular afternoon absences. The appeal failed, but I always wondered if Bob still took it upon himself to record such absences in our Branch.

Back to Ross. I was lucky enough to go on a week's field-trip with him and two other senior geoscientific staff in the Olary region in the mid-northeast of the state. At one of our first geological stops Ross disappeared, and next materialised running along the crest of a hill at least 500 metres away. Ross must have been in his mid-50s by then, but this was apparently how he always undertook field work. Nights were also interesting: after dinner, there might be a glass or two of red, but discussion of work never let up for a moment – in fact I was often first to bed, a highly unusual occurrence.

Before this trip Ross had been instrumental in setting up formal OH&S procedures for all fieldwork including actions to be put in place if a field party failed to meet a daily radio schedule. On about day three of our trip, radio reception was bad, and according to the new rules we needed to head immediately to the nearest phone to make contact. As this was perhaps 50 kilometres away, Ross decided that we should stick to our work schedule and ring in from a station later in the day. Arriving at a station mid-afternoon, we were greeted with the news that there was already a safety alert out regarding our whereabouts, and this was about to become a full search operation before we phoned in. It was something of an embarrassment.

Ross was well known for his regular and impromptu gee-up speeches at MESA. On the last day of our trip we met up with rangers from Parks and Wildlife to view some new geological signage in the Flinders Ranges National Park. Afterwards they invited us back to their office in Hawker for a cup of tea. Ross at that time was on an executive interdepartmental environment team. He simply couldn't miss out on the opportunity, so he gathered all the rangers and office staff together and delivered his gee-up speech. There was stunned silence in the room, and I didn't fancy our chances of being invited back.

Much later in 2008 there was a large formal dinner at the Adelaide Convention Centre to celebrate the 125th anniversary of the Geological Survey of SA, with politicians, industry and ex-geological survey members all in attendance. Ross Fardon was one of the guest speakers on the evening. As I listened to him, some of the words had changed but I recognised the gist of the oration as a variation on his gee-up speech that he had regularly delivered to MESA more than fifteen years previously. When I mentioned this to him later in the evening, he was a little bemused. Despite the regular gee-ups, Ross probably did more than any other to ensure that the SA Government continues with exploration initiatives to this day.

Early in the 1990s things seemed all right on the home front, and we had another wonderful family trip to the Kimberleys in 1991 (see below). However, Debbie and I had gradually drifted apart since moving to Adelaide. In Darwin we shared friends and interests, and she had an interesting job with the Department of Aboriginal Affairs. In Adelaide she assumed the role of housewife/mother and gravitated back to her old school friends. I think she felt life was passing her by and my regular celebrations with workmates didn't help the situation. We separated in June 1993 but came to equitable arrangements regarding shared parenting and distribution of assets without any recourse to the legal profession, and have in fact maintained an amicable relationship ever since.

Kimberley safari

In June 1991 we set off on another six-week family trip, this time to the Kimberleys in Western Australia, with the same old crew in tow, Zac and family and my sister Wendy and her husband Bill. From Alice Springs to Halls Creek via the Tanami Desert, we also caught up with Rod South and his dad, John, together with their travelling companions, Ken Dickin and his partner. We were a little better set up for this trip with three long-wheel-base four-wheel drives. I had the shell of a large chest freezer on the back of mine with a metal cage built over the top to secure all our belongings. The freezer proved a great success. Filled with ice in Adelaide, we only opened it once each morning and packed smaller eskies with the day's food and drink supplies plus enough ice for cooling. Three weeks later, when we reached Broome, we still had plenty of that same ice on board.

I don't intend to give a running commentary of the trip but will relate a few of the incidents along the way. On our previous Kakadu trip, three years earlier, we ate a lot of vegetarian food, particularly cous cous, which Zac and wife Janice had learned to prepare in all manner of ways while Zac had been working in North Africa some years before. Bill, a butcher and now owner of Milton Meats, a meat processing facility on the NSW South Coast, was a red meat man through and through. He volunteered to provide us with meat for the first few days of the trip, wanting to avoid cous cous too early in our travels. We all met up at Hawker in SA, and on the first night's camp in the Flinders Ranges he produced two very large eskies, one filled with legs of lamb, the other with prime steaks. I later learned that the steaks came from a side of beef he had patiently stored in the meatworks' cool room since the start of the year. One problem: we had no room to keep this supply refrigerated (although the nights were quite cold) so we had no choice but to live on a solid red meat diet for the first ten days. Bill was delighted and I don't think anyone else complained.

I was a bit concerned about Rod South's travelling mate, Ken Dickin. Ken was a popular radio host in Adelaide, and I wasn't sure how I might handle that sort of banter for extended periods. I needn't have worried: Ken's radio persona wasn't the real Ken. He proved a delightful travelling companion and had some wonderful tales to tell around the campfire.

From Alice Springs we passed through the indigenous settlement of Yuendumu, refuelling there, then on to the Granites gold mine, where I'd arranged a brief (and very rare) visit with Trevor Ireland, the company exploration manager. Some of our crew gave the tour a miss and pressed on to set up camp about 50 kilometres north, where the rest of us joined them after the tour. The main Granites mine camp area was a designated dry zone, in line with the wishes of the local traditional owners, but it was amazing how many exploration personnel from there, many of whom I knew, somehow drifted into our less than dry camp that evening.

Reaching Halls Creek a day or two later, Rod South was up to his usual "Steptoe" capers when he found a door that fitted his Toyota 4WD in a station dump just out of town. Despite being loaded to the gunnels, Rod carted that door back to Adelaide, via Perth, where it probably remained in his shed for the next 20 years. We parted ways with Rod and his party at Halls Creek and continued to the Bungle Bungles. Next day our whole party headed off on the Piccaninny Gorge Walk. It was an unseasonally hot day and all the kids plus Wendy and Debbie turned back first, I gave Debbie the car keys so that they could get cold drinks on return (or so I thought). Bill and I turned back an hour or two later while Zac and wife Janice pressed on, completing the 20-kilometre walk and arriving back in camp about 10.00pm that night. When Bill and I got back to Cathedral Gorge the others were lounging in its cool waters, but they weren't happy. I'd only given Debbie the keys to the cab of our vehicle, not the cage on the back where cool drinks, both non-alcoholic and alcoholic, were stowed. The only drink on offer in the cab was a rather warm bottle of port. It took some time to build up brownie points after that.

Our meanderings finally took us to Broome, where we enjoyed motel luxury for a few days before setting off on the next leg, along the Gibb River Road to Wyndham. Leaving Broome, we first headed up the coast, camping at Quandong Beach, a little slice of heaven. We camped on cliffs just above high tide level, an idyllic spot, which we had to ourselves. Three mornings in a row we planned to leave, and each time decided to stay another day. From there we camped at

Bells Gorge, and by a delightful pool on the Prince Edward River on the way into Mitchell Falls, and then headed on to Honeymoon Bay, just north of the indigenous community of Kalumbaru. After always rushing to see every feature on our previous Kakadu trip, we'd learnt to always stop for a few days at any site we enjoyed in the Kimberleys.

Kalumbaru was interesting, and the local kids, seeing my caged vehicle, decided it was a "wally" (police) wagon and proceeded to climb all over it. At Honeymoon Bay we were able to amass a huge stash of fish from a few hours fishing trip, plus oysters aplenty off the rocks. Swimming was the only thing off the agenda, with evidence of some big crocs in the vicinity. With the trusty ice-filled deep freeze working like a charm, we lived on seafood for the next few days and gave heaps of it to other tourists at El Questro. The last camping night of the trip was near Timber Creek, back in the NT, and Bill need never have worried: beside ice we had packed a heap of cryovac-sealed meat into the freezer in Adelaide, and enjoyed a wonderful lamb roast once again, more than six weeks after it had been packed.

It's interesting that after all the grandeur of the Kimberleys, my daughters, Teneille's and Emma's, most vivid memories of the trip were the amount of rubbish floating around Yuendumu, and how on the way home, in Coober Pedy, I casually drove onto the footpath to avoid an indigenous man who collapsed directly in front of us on the road outside the pub. (Yes, I did go back to render assistance, but his mates were already helping him.) Teneille, aged thirteen, had kept a journal of this trip as part of her schoolwork. Her teacher's later comments in the journal were interesting: "Looks like the parents had one hell of a great time" – don't know what she read to get that idea.

Now to a few yarns from the 1990s.

Drilling along the Transcontinental Railway

Our first big SAEI regional drilling program stretched west from Kingoonya to Tarcoola along the Transcontinental Railway, then northwest to the very edges of some of SA's most remote pastoral country. Nearly all of it was on vast sheep properties owned by two long-term family grazing businesses headed up by Hugh McLachlan and Michael McBride. To quote the mcbride.com.au website, "The decade of the 1990s was arguably the low point of wool growing in Australia's history." in that context it would have been understandable if the lessees of these properties hadn't been too keen on having mineral explorers and subsequently miners traipsing around the countryside. Dealing with both, regarding access, use of bore water and location of campsites couldn't have been more different, Michael was intensely interested in what we were doing, was always helpful and provided quantities of bore water essentially free of charge. Hugh on the other hand really didn't want us there and felt we were just wasting his and our time. (Interesting then that the first ensuing mine development, at the Challenger gold mine, was on one of his properties.) Hugh reluctantly sold us bore water at a premium and permitted use of a couple of largely disused outstations as camp sites, but one always thought he felt we were a nuisance at best. At the end of the program, we drilled a gratis water bore on one of Michael's properties in appreciation of his help.

Before the drilling program began there were some reconnaissance/logistical tours of the vast area. It was interesting camping out on Mobella station, which abuts undeveloped lands of the Great Victoria Desert: one felt very remote and alone. By the time the program was nearing completion, driving round the area felt little different to a suburban commute.

On one of these early trips on Mobella I one day elected to undertake a ground magnetic survey while my companions were going to check out some outcrops about a further hour's drive away. While I was safe enough with adequate water, and matches to start a fire if stranded overnight, I have never felt quite so alone in the Australian outback as I watched that vehicle disappear over the horizon. The plan was that the others would return in about four hours to pick me up. As it turned out the others, reflecting on the OH&S implications of our plan, returned about an hour and a half later. I must say that I was a little relieved to see them.

On another of these early trips Mark Flintoft and I called in at Woomera to discuss delivery of goods and perishables to our camps with the store owner, who ran a remote area delivery service. Having come to an arrangement with him, at dusk we decided to press on to Glendambo, about 110 kilometres north, to get an early start heading northwest the next day. We recognised a MESA vehicle heading south just on dark and wondered what part of the state it was returning from. About fifteen kilometres out of Glendambo we were flashed by a vehicle on the side of the road and, on pulling up, realised it was another MESA vehicle with Zac Sibenaler and Patto" sitting on the bonnet with beers in hand. They were returning from a groundwater trip to parts of the Great Artesian Basin and had been pre-warned by radio from the earlier vehicle that we were heading north. After a couple of beers with them we were somehow convinced to return to Woomera for the night rather than travel the distance to Glendambo (how stupid you can be). A great night was had at the Woomera pub. However, there was some poetic justice for Zac. Some years later, when I was talking to his wife Janice, she mentioned that she'd once decided to treat him to a romantic, candlelit dinner on his return from a long field-trip. She also mentioned that after the main course Zac could take no more and headed off to bed exhausted. Yes, it was the same trip, the night after Woomera.

This initial regional drilling program was completed over a few months without much incident (that I can recall). It was the first of many and led to an immediate upsurge of mineral exploration in this remote region.

Barton drilling program

Barton is an old railway siding village on the Transcontinental Railway line not too far from the Nullarbor Plain. In its heyday it boasted several railway families, but by the time we leased one of the old railway houses as our base camp for the drilling program, it was effectively abandoned. The surrounding countryside comprises vast sand dunes, although these are quite heavily vegetated with large trees and shrubs, together with the occasional granite outcrop. The recent advent of reliable GPS technology made navigation in this region far easier; much better than counting sand dunes on an air photograph to determine the location.

The program started disastrously when the truck carrying most of our equipment and supplies rolled over after a blowout about 120 kilometres north of Port Augusta. Mark Flintoft, who was driving, was unhurt, but when he phoned me by "Satphone" I was immediately concerned, as the lads often had a last beer at Port Augusta before setting out for the northern wilderness. I needn't have worried, as Mark registered zero on the breathalyser when police from Woomera finally arrived, although I note that the police, whom Mark knew from earlier Coober Pedy days, stayed and partied with Mark and the crew most of the evening while waiting for a recovery vehicle.

There were many notable stories from this program. The remoteness of the area got to people, in particular some of the TAFE students who were studying to become exploration field technicians, whom we offered paid work experience under an agreement with their institution. Some revelled in the conditions, but others couldn't handle it at all, and one or two had to be sent back on the train within a day or two – at least they realised that this vocation wasn't for them.

At one stage we had a "railway recyclers" group as neighbours for a few weeks. They were tasked with removing most of the old infrastructure from the many abandoned railway sidings, and it was Barton's turn. Our crew thought they were getting rough and bush-happy working in this spartan environment, but they were perfect gentlemen compared with the railway recyclers. They were mostly young fellows from Western Australia who'd had run-ins with the law, and this employment was seen as their opportunity for rehabilitation. At least they were friendly enough towards our crew.

On a Friday night on the eve of my birthday in 1994 I decided to catch the Indian Pacific out to Barton to join the crew for a few days. After a night of train travel and tall tales at the bar, I think some of the passengers thought I'd lost it when I disembarked at this lonely railway siding the next morning. I was expecting to head off to the drill sites straight away but instead was greeted with a cold beer – the crew had decided to have a day off to celebrate my birthday. It turned out to be a great day, with a fair degree of merriment, which was a nice break for the crew. Stuey Mathews, a bush cook whose culinary skills rivalled Cretto's, spent hours shelling quandong nuts (quandongs were plentiful at Barton), and produced a superb entrée of roasted nuts topped off with a great bush barbeque.

Later in the evening a huge feral cat strayed into the house and was somehow trapped in a kitchen cupboard by someone. Feral cats were plentiful out there and wreaked enormous damage on the local wildlife. Charged with overconfidence, I decided that it needed to be dispatched. Donning thick driller's gloves, I managed to grab it, but despite the gloves it managed to inflict some nasty scratches on my arms and legs before succumbing. It's certainly something that I won't try again.

Impromptu firewalking

On another occasion the drill crew had moved to a remote campsite on the Maralinga Tjurutja lands north of the Transcontinental Railway. It was absolutely freezing out there one night when I visited, and driller Lloydie Moore had a huge campfire blazing. On heading off to bed I broke a fundamental rule of camping in a swag: that is, "Always have the opening side of your swag facing away from the campfire." When nature calls in the early hours this rule ensures that you won't stumble into the hot ashes of the remnant campfire, which is exactly what I did. Clad only in jocks, I managed to fall flat on my back before rapidly extracting myself. Not wanting to disturb the camp, I lay in my swag for the next couple of hours until sunrise. Finally examining the damage the next morning, I had two huge blisters stretching from end to end on my feet and some equally impressive ones on my lower back.

Ever the stoic, I decided to soldier on in camp with just some soothing cream for a day or two. Walking around in boots the foot blisters quickly burst and felt more comfortable, but as I got ready to depart the back blisters were becoming more painful. Driving back to Adelaide I called in on the bush nurse at the hospital in Tarcoola. There was no sympathy, just a massive dressing-down for not seeking aid immediately. She did what she could and threw it in a jab of penicillin, then arranged for me to call in at the Port Augusta hospital for proper dressings. The back infection looked dramatic, but amazingly I recovered completely within a couple of weeks and bear no scars from the event. This campfire drama was never reported as an OH&S incident, but I've ever since always faced my swag in the proper bushman's direction near any campfire.

Hot days on the Nullarbor

As the Barton drilling program proceeded, we went from pleasant days and freezing nights to blazingly hot days regularly in the 40s. This is when the kamikaze Japanese motorbike riders come out to play on the Nullarbor. There seems to be some rite of passage with male Japanese to ride across Australia from east to west, mainly on remote tracks beside the Transcontinental Railway line. They seem to have little idea of the lack of fuel and water in this remote area, nor of the extreme temperatures, but they keep coming. It wasn't unusual driving from Tarcoola to Barton to see bike tracks and evidence that the rider had fallen, often more than once. We came across one of these desperates, camped by the side of the track at 4.00pm in the afternoon in 45-degree heat. He was dead to the world, totally exhausted, but determined to ride on. We at least gave him some extra water and fuel and wished him luck.

The heat got to everyone. I'd just arrived on another trip when I encountered one of our female geologists well away from her vehicle. Immediately I pulled up and she asked if I had an esky on board. Of course I had an ice-filled esky, so Joanne, a rather attractive young lady, proceeded to open the esky, then tore her shirt off and threw. I was thinking all my Christmases had come at once, but it was just Joanne's way of cooling down. Much later I learned that two of our crew,

Mark Flintoft and Stuey Mathews, had at one stage resorted to boots and hats only fieldwork. I just hope they applied plenty of sunscreen and can't imagine the reaction if a passing station hand had encountered them in this remote area.

I can't mention Barton Siding without referring to Ziggy, its long-term inhabitant. Ziggy had migrated to Australia after World War 2, and the story goes that at some time in the next few years he was jilted by a lady, so he escaped to the bush to work on remote railway sidings to the west and north of Port Augusta. On retirement from the railways, he set up permanent residence near Barton Siding. He carted used railway sleepers by wheelbarrow over many kilometres along the railway line as the main component of his stockade-like home, with meagre water supplies carted from the railway tanks in Barton together with food and booze supplies purchased from the weekly "Tea and Sugar" train, supplemented by a few home-grown vegetables. It was a spartan life indeed, with his only companions a large group of whippets. He was a nice old fellow who really liked a chat when anybody called in, and he seemed quite knowledgeable considering his reclusive lifestyle. He also used to joke that when he died his whippets would have something to eat for a week or two. When several years later he was found dead, it seems that might be exactly what transpired.

The Centenary Dinner

Back in Adelaide, on 28 February 1994, MESA was to celebrate the centenary of its foundation. Ross Fardon wanted to celebrate in style, so a gala dinner was organised at the Adelaide Convention Centre with politicians, industry leaders from around Australia and business leaders from South Australia in tow. Ross also decided that each table would comprise people with common interests. I don't know if he was aware of my disdain for the legal profession and its place in society, but somehow, I got to host the lawyers' table, which included the attorney-general and other prominent members of Adelaide's legal fraternity. I had one ally at the table, Don Caruthers, then a director of CRA/Rio Tinto, one of the world's largest mining companies.

As it turned out the company was personable enough, and the lawyers did their best to include me in the conversations, but Don scored the major point of the evening. At one stage, with the whole table listening, Don said he was soon to appear as an expert witness in a court case. In seeking a reasonable fee for his services, he enquired of me what was the highest MESA had recently paid for a senior geoscientific consultant. I came back with $750, then a few of the lawyers came into the conversation with comments that the figure seemed fair and reasonable recompense. However, there was a great grin from Don as the penny dropped that I was talking per day and the lawyers were thinking per hour – come in spinner. In retrospect I wonder whether Don was ever really intending to be an expert witness.

With the dinner over, a group of MESA and mining industry people, all dressed in tuxedos for the formal dinner, decided to have a few more drinks at the adjacent Adelaide Casino. On entering one well-lit but empty bar upstairs, we all waited patiently for the bar staff; one of our party even went looking. After waiting about fifteen minutes it was decided we should help ourselves, but as we did, we also laid out cash on the bar to cover each round, details of which were also recorded and placed on the bar. Settling in quite well, it must have been at least an hour later when we were confronted by a troupe of security guards demanding to know what we were doing there. The answer was staring them in the face. They were a bit taken aback by our formal attire, and accepted that all drinks had been paid for, more than adequately, but insisted we vacate the premises. What a Centenary Dinner press story it would have made if charges had been pressed with several senior Australian mining executives in the party.

21

A Dingo Took My Boots

South Australia, 1990s

I had an unusual experience on Tepco Station, south of Olary in northeast South Australia. Keith Yates, Ric Horn and I were on a week-long field-trip compiling a database of mineral occurrences in the Olary region. Keith was consulting to MESA and was a notable figure in the SA mining industry. We had a productive trip and as per standard practice always notified landholders before coming onto their properties. On the last day we went to mineral occurrences to the south of Tepco Station via a gazetted road which bypassed the station and planned to use the same track on the way out. Time got away and our map showed another gazetted road running through Tepco and out to the Barrier Highway near Olary. As it was almost dark, we decided to use this road to save a bit of time, but on reaching a fence line we found a locked gate barring our way. We would have been within our rights to cut the padlock, but our maps showed plenty of other station tracks, so we decided to follow them rather than retracing our route in the dark. After an hour or so we were hopelessly lost, although we knew our precise position per our onboard GPS and could glimpse the lights of Olary in the distance, but the tracks on the map made no sense.

Not everyone likes geologists

At that moment we saw vehicle lights heading our way and assumed it was a kangaroo shooter who could point us in the right direction. The vehicle pulled up and out jumped Jim Sangster, the lessee of Tepco. He greeted us in what seemed friendly fashion but then suddenly reached through the driver's side door and had poor Ric by the throat demanding to know what we were doing on his property. It was a confronting experience; I dare say the three of us could have handled Jim, but you never knew what weapons he might have in his vehicle. When he realised that we had been looking at mineral occurrences he launched into a tirade stating that he would shoot a certain exploration geologist from Mount Isa Mines, who had worked on Tepco more than fifteen years earlier, if he ever set foot on his station again. This wasn't exactly a rational man we were dealing with. After what seemed like forever, he calmed down marginally and indicated the track out to Olary. We reached the highway and had a calming beer at the Mannahill pub shortly after.

Jim haunted us, writing to Keith Johns falsely accusing us of trespassing and knocking down his fences. Keith gave him no comfort, reminding him that we had every right to be on his pastoral lease and when Ric threatened to press assault charges the matter seemed at an end. When Keith retired and was replaced by Ross Fardon, Jim wrote yet another letter, and Ross, without seeking all the facts, sent him a placatory apology. Ric and I were less than impressed.

In retrospect it's a wonder that neither Ric nor I had ever heard of Jim Sangster, because Jim, his father Dick and Tepco Station were legendary in the Olary region. We learnt that he had moved tracks on Tepco, rendering publicly available maps next to useless.

Ted's troubles

During the early 1990s we went on a bonding and mentoring trip which included all branch staff members. It was interesting to see how different people whom you hadn't worked with before acquitted themselves in the field. On this occasion one young geologist, Ted Dubowski, provided something of a stand-out performance. The first day started with a visit to the old Burra copper mine, which after closing had been signposted and fenced to become a notable tourist attraction. The party continued to the Flinders Ranges for an overnight camp.

The next day was spent visiting geological features and old mine sites in the area, and it was at a lunch stop that day when Ted's troubles began. He was always a tad different, and on this occasion, he had chosen to wear bright orange overalls together with a green safety helmet (gear he'd received as a volunteer with the State Emergency Services). As we were leaving our lunch spot, he managed to drive over his green helmet, which disintegrated with a loud bang (strike one). Our next stop was Arkaroola Village in the northern Flinders Ranges, where we were to visit old uranium mines and other fascinating geological features of the region.

That night we had a nice meal at the village washed down with a few red wines, and Ted, who was a moderate drinker at best, decided to take on some of his more hardened colleagues. There could only be one outcome. People sleeping in motel rooms adjacent to Ted were serenaded by the extreme gastrointestinal sounds issuing from Ted's room throughout the night (strike two). He wasn't a well boy the next day, but I must say he soldiered on magnificently through what proved to be at least a fifteen-kilometre walk in some very rugged terrain.

The following day the group headed to the Parabarana-Gunsite deposits to the north of Arkaroola. Many of the tracks in the area had been made by exploration companies, possibly 20 years before in rather rough terrain, and were in poor condition. Ascending one of these we noticed a very large granite boulder to one side of the track, I casually suggested to my driving companion that we should perhaps wait for Ted, who was driving another vehicle, to ensure he didn't collide with it. We continued to some mine workings, where others joined us but not Ted. Eventually we went back to look for him and first saw the two female geologists who were with him now walking up the track, then as we rounded the next corner there was Ted with his vehicle firmly perched atop that granite boulder (strike three). Without too much ado we managed to free him from his predicament with little damage to the vehicle. Heading back to our main party we passed the girls, but when Ted stopped to pick them up they declined, preferring to walk the short distance.

The following day we moved on to a small mining operation on the Mannahill Goldfield, where we camped for the night. The rain arrived about 1.00pm and continued unabated for most of the evening, and with only swags for cover it turned out to be a somewhat uncomfortable night. The highway was only about 20 kilometres away, but we were anticipating a fairly testing drive across the muddy tracks to get there. Preparing to leave next day Ted hopped into the driver's seat of one of the vehicles but was quickly told to move over by Ric Horn. Ric had little confidence in Ted's wet-road driving abilities after his performances of the past few days. So ended what must have been a forgettable few days for Ted.

Tarcoola Races revisited

Another interesting two-week trip with Ric Horn culminated in our attendance at another Tarcoola race weekend. Our first overnight stop was at Arkaroola, where we were to inspect Rio Tinto drilling activities at nearby Mt Painter. Arriving at Arkaroola Village in the early evening I was told that there was a guest staying who wanted to catch up with me. Turned out it was a former Sydney Uni geology student, Andy, who had been a few years behind me. After reacquainting ourselves it transpired that he had just taken a redundancy package from Esso in Sydney and was taking a relaxed holiday in outback SA, or so he thought.

Rio Tinto were undertaking an environmentally friendly drilling program to test a few uranium prospects near Mt Painter in the picturesque Northern

Flinders Ranges. Unlike previous explorers from earlier decades, who cut major exploration tracks through the rugged terrain (today used by the Sprigg family to conduct their spectacular "Ridgetop" tours), Rio were transporting all equipment by helicopter, quite a logistical undertaking. The costs involved in this program must have been horrendous. Ric and I were taken on a "Cook's tour" of the drilling operations by company personnel the next day and were not only impressed by their operations but also by the spectacular views as we traversed the area by helicopter.

Back in the village that night we caught up with Andy and asked what his plans were. He had no set schedule, so we invited him to join us for the next few days, an offer he readily took up. Next night we booked into the William Creek pub, little realising what delights awaited us. I think every male who has worked long periods in remote areas of Australia has dreamt of a miraculous rendezvous with a busload of Norwegian nymphs. Well, they were German, not Norse, but the William Creek bar was filled with a busload of attractive young female backpackers. We were in our element, buying drinks and telling outrageous bush yarns to the assembled nymphs. As night fell the bus driver delivered the dreadful news that they were staying at Coober Pedy that night and needed to get moving. The aura of disappointment at the bar was palpable, Ric was all for booking out and heading off to Coober, and it took much persuasion on Andy's and my part to convince him to stay put.

After a long day in the field next day our overnight stop was in fact Coober. The nymphs were nowhere to be found. Here we were joined by the irrepressible Jim Allender and another older and gentleman-like English-born geologist, Ian Youles, whom Ric had invited to join us on the next leg of the trip. Ian had overseen the exploration program at Mt Painter decades earlier, and apparently, he commuted along the hilly exploration tracks back then in a Toyota Crown sedan, a far cry from the specially equipped four-wheel drives used by the Sprigg family on today's Ridgetop tours. We had one of those wonderful extended dinners at Traces Restaurant, with Jimmy the cook in top form and the retsina flowing freely. Late in the evening Jim decided to shout a round of flaming Drambuies. As he raised his glass with a flourish to propose a toast to the assembled group, he managed to spill the contents on his arm and the tablecloth, both of which instantly burst into flames. I had never seen Jim lost for words before that moment. Luckily Jimmy was quick to douse the flames with little or no damage to Jim or the table. I truly believe that had the fire got out of control in that upstairs restaurant we would have all died of laughter at Jim's antics.

Next day we headed out to Earea Dam, an old goldmining location between Kingoonya and Tarcoola, where one of our drill crews had set up camp. After a delightful camp oven meal washed down with a red or two, it was looking like an early night before a day off for the Tarcoola race meeting next day. Jim and Ric suddenly decided that we should visit the Tarcoola hotel to check on any pre-race festivities. Some of us were reluctant to go but eventually the majority ruled. It was an enjoyable but low-key evening and then the rumour got around that the local teachers, all female, were holding a pre-race party. The teachers' houses were adjacent to the police quarters, and when we got there all was in darkness, Jim, however, just had to give a few blasts on the horn to let them know they had visitors. The response, we were immediately confronted by the local police sergeant who had been roused by the noise. Luckily, we had sober, designated drivers to get us back to Earea Dam, but we had seriously alienated the constabulary for the weekend.

The races next day were as good as ever, and because we had quite a presence with our current drilling operations in the area, MESA field staff had banded together to sponsor one of the main races. The day was uneventful until the post-race gathering outside the hotel. Cretto's second son, Damien, had only been born a few days earlier, but he'd convinced wife Connie that he had a work commitment at Tarcoola which he just had to meet. Feeling very mellow and perhaps with just a little remorse we saw him eyeing off the outside pay phone. He was quickly moved away from the temptation and advised under no circumstances to ring home. Later he disappeared, and where did we find him but in the phone box? His ever more serious facial expression hinted at the strife he was in, and it cost him a mountain of roses to get back in the good books with the lovely Connie.

Late in the day the local sergeant was in dire straits trying to recruit a town team to take on the visiting station people in a social cricket match the next day. When several of us volunteered to play we regained a lot of credibility with him, despite Jim's best efforts. When we won the game, he was even happier.

The next couple of days were spent inspecting other drilling activities while staying at Johns Outstation on Bulgunnia Station. There were also some crazy West Coasters still in tow from the races, who gave poor Andy the fright of his life one morning. Retiring to the corrugated iron outhouse for a morning constitutional, Andy was on the throne when one of these crazies walked up behind the building and gave it an enormous belt with a flat shovel – the noise reverberated round the camp. When Andy hadn't emerged after what felt like at least fifteen minutes, we all became worried. Had he had a heart attack? He did emerge a little later, to our relief.

From here we headed back to the Stuart Highway, where we bid farewell to Andy, who continued north on his ramblings while the rest of the party headed south and home to Adelaide. I often wonder whether Andy regretted his decision to join us or whether he had had the bush trip of a lifetime.

Field-trips with Ric Horn were always interesting, with two recurrent themes: first, he seemed to fall in love with every barmaid in every country pub we encountered, and second, he never seemed to want to come home, despite being happily married to his lovely wife Kath. So very often we'd pack up early on the last day of a bush trip and there I'd be thinking we should be home in Adelaide by early afternoon, but it never happened. Ric would find another interesting outcrop or two we should visit and then stop at a lonely country pub for just one cleansing ale, so that my mid-afternoon expectation was often more like a midnight arrival.

A visit to the Bon Accord

Another interesting overnight trip with Jim Allender and Ric Horn involved an assessment of an old gold-copper deposit near Woolshed Flat, south of Auburn in the Clare Valley, which Jim held title to. It was only two hours' drive from Adelaide, and on reaching the Rhynie Hotel, a few kilometres from our destination, we decided to stop for a coffee. As it turned out we were greatly entertained by mine host, Alan Bond, a real character, who delighted in playing on his more famous namesake's reputation. Alan soon had us tasting more than coffee at ten in the morning. Eventually dislodging ourselves from Bondy's clutches, we spent a long and hot day assessing the mineral deposit. At the end of the day, we headed to the Bon Accord Hotel in Burra, planning to visit some other mineral deposits in that vicinity the next day. However, we couldn't resist a brief return to Rhynie and another short stopover at the Rising Sun Hotel in Auburn – after all it had been a long, hot day.

On reaching our destination, we booked into the Bon Accord and adjourned to the bar. An attraction of this establishment at the time was the rather good-looking mid-forties publican and her very attractive twenty-ish twin daughters. All was going well after a good meal and lots of friendly banter with a few locals, when the publican screamed at Jim (and included Ric and me), "Out, out – I know your type". Ric and I protested our innocence, but she was adamant, so we collected our bags and departed. To this day Jim has never revealed what happened, but we think he somehow implied that there could perhaps be some liaisons later in the evening.

As we parted, we mentioned to the publican that we were heading to the Commercial Hotel, where we had stayed many times before and knew the publican well, but on reaching the Commercial the publican's wife advised that they were booked out (the Bon Accord lady had kindly phoned her already to say some desperates were on their way). At nine o'clock at night we were getting desperate but were delighted when the Burra Hotel was happy to accommodate us. After checking in we again adjourned to the bar where a local 8-ball competition was in full swing. The first person we recognised was the publican from the Commercial, who when he heard we were booked into the Burra asked why we weren't staying at his establishment. We told him that his wife had advised it was booked out. He departed to have his next shot at the table with words to the effect of "I'll have words with that woman when I get home," with perhaps an expletive or two thrown in. So that was our sole experience of the Bon Accord Hotel.

The Tarcoola pub

Built originally to cater for the gold rush of the early 1900s, and the last pub in SA heading west along the Transcontinental railway line, the Wilgena Hotel at Tarcoola was a favourite stop for MESA staff and mineral exploration companies, especially during the 1990s. It just survived into the new millennium, but its total demise was confirmed with the departure of the last permanent resident from the town in 2014. For many years the front bar was minute, but one enterprising publican from the early 1990's (who previously worked at the Glendambo pub) had the wonderful idea of moving the bar set-up round by 180 degrees, a far more salubrious arrangement. One day Ric Horn and I arrived there when that publican's wife ran outside for help: he'd tried to move a very heavy piano on his own and was firmly stuck underneath it. Between the three of us we managed to extract him with no real harm done.

The pub surely had its heyday during the early goldmining days, but it had something of a rebirth in the second half of the 1990s when mineral exploration parties converged on the region. By then Trudy, a 35-plus young lady from SA's Riverland, was the publican, and she really knew how to run a remote country pub. If there were customers, the pub stayed open (liquor licensing inspectors were highly unlikely to pay a night-time visit). How she came up bright and breezy first thing the next morning after some very late sessions quite amazed me. She also ran regular mid-week roast nights, which dragged in the mineral explorers and the station hands in droves.

I always remember a few impromptu rugby scrums that were instigated by geophysicist Alex Copeland and his partner in crime, Mad Dog, who in their spare time still played lower grade rugby for Old Collegians in Adelaide. Mad Dog had apparently been an ear-biter in his rugby past. These scrums or whatever you may want to call them could be intense, and one often left the bar missing a bit of bark, but like most things there, they were always great fun. That iron-clad old pub must hold many secrets, but on a scorchingly hot Tarcoola day it was a perfect oasis.

A near-catastrophe

We very nearly came to grief on one short field trip with Mark Flintoft and two of our female geologists, Joanne Hough and Michelle Bullock. We were heading up to the newly discovered Challenger Gold Mine, where intensive drilling was being undertaken; from there we were travelling on back roads to Coober Pedy to undertake some work there. As we were staying in the Challenger camp quarters, we were carrying very few food supplies for the trip, just enough for lunch while travelling on the first day. The Challenger part of the trip went smoothly, although it started raining heavily the last night there. Heading off the next day we had about a 160-kilometre, three-hour trip ahead of us, but we had no idea just how much rain there had been. As we drove, conditions just got worse, and approaching Lake Phillipson we had to decide whether to take the Lake Phillipson track or a longer route to the west. We chose the latter, arriving late afternoon after a torrid journey. Had we taken the shorter route we'd have been hopelessly bogged south of Coober, where many vehicles remained stuck for up to a week. What we never told the girls was that the only survival supplies we had on board were several cartons of beer and plenty of water, and of course all our swags. We'd have survived easily but the wrath of those girls if they'd been forced to exist for a week on a diet of beer and water doesn't bear imagining. As a footnote to this tale, the lightning display stretching all around Coober the night we reached there had to be one of the more intense ones I've ever witnessed.

The English publican's daughter

This is another tale of lots of rain and closed roads. On this occasion we were accompanying a bus-load of members of the Field Geology Club of SA on a trip to the Willouran Ranges and Peake and Denison Ranges between Marree and William Creek. On the last night we camped at William Creek, where it rained heavily overnight. I set out early the next morning to check the condition of the road to Marree. After slipping and sliding for about fifteen kilometres, I encountered not one but three tour buses with trailers, which were all intermittently jack-knifing across the road in the treacherous conditions. It was time to turn around; our bus was going nowhere.

The three buses somehow reached William Creek, where they disgorged over 100 senior students from a noted Victorian private school. We were in for a long and interesting day. The beers started early, but the tiny bar had been invaded by the very noisy school party. They were treated to some tall tales during the day, especially from a young indigenous Coulthard lad who had them really taken in. When asked about his indigenous name he answered "Dibi". Of course, they then sought the meaning of this name. He managed to carry the façade for quite a long time until he finally confided to a somewhat crestfallen audience that it stood for "dark brown".

By late in the day things were starting to get out of hand, the pub was running out of food and the septic tanks were overflowing. If permitted, we decided it was time to push on to Coward Springs, without our bus travellers, and camp there. There were "Road Closed" signs in place, but we spoke to the roads employee, who agreed to our leaving if it was done discreetly. As we furtively took our leave, we noticed that a lone campervan had decided to follow us. Although road conditions had improved since my early morning reconnaissance, we noticed that the van, without four-wheel drive, was making heavy weather of it, but we all reached Coward Springs, 75 kilometres down the track, without incident. There the van joined us, and we got to know its occupants, an Aussie bloke, his English girlfriend and her sister. The sister had flown from England to Perth just two days before, then on to Alice Springs where she'd joined the van occupants. She was not only a very attractive blonde but impressively the daughter of an English publican. One of our party, Peter Hill, instantly fell in love.

We shared a pleasant evening with a barbeque and beers and went to bed hoping to hit the road early the next day, but that wasn't to be, as a heavy storm hit with soaking rain for the rest of the night. We awoke surrounded by water – at least we'd camped on higher ground. What to do in Coward Springs? There's a hot, flowing artesian bore with an adjacent pool you can relax in for an hour or two, some old railway buildings from the abandoned old Ghan railway line, but not much else. The entrance to the Wabma Kadarbu mound spring conservation park is only about six kilometres down the road, so we convinced our fellow travellers to accompany us on a day's walk to visit the active mound springs, "Blanche Cup" and the "Bubbler" and the extinct but massive spring at Hamilton Hill. Mound springs form flowing springs throughout the vast Great Artesian Basin, but these are some of the more unique examples. In total we must have covered 20 kilometres that day, much of it through knee-deep water, and our newly arrived English companion became concerned at one stage that she might be attacked when a flock of emus decided to join us. Little did she know what nasties were probably lurking in the waters we were wading through, but no one had the heart to point that fact out to her.

We returned to camp a very weary group, but at least the weather had fined up. We treated our new companions to camp oven lamb and even managed to produce a few good reds that evening before we all headed out for Marree the following morning. I always wonder what the publican's daughter thought of her first few days in the Australian outback – I suspect it was a rather unique introduction.

A dingo took my boots

Wherever you may be camping in the outback, you're often aware that dingoes have been through your camp overnight, and it's a good reason not to leave any food or scraps lying around before crawling into your swag. Their plaintive howling throughout the night is another sure sign that there are dingoes nearby. Often, you'll see a wandering dingo or two during daylight, but rarely do you see one at night.

On this occasion Cretto and I were inspecting the rehabilitation of drillholes drilled in the search for diamonds by one of "Diamond" Joe Gutnick's companies. They were in a very remote area over 1000 kilometres north of Adelaide, stretching north from the Lambina Opalfields to the NT-SA border. After a long day when we didn't encounter a single soul and where wildlife and cattle were also something of a rarity, we camped for the night in a grove of light trees by a dry riverbed. The howls of the dingoes were regular as we went through the usual bush rituals of hors d'oeuvres and beers, followed by barbeque and a few glasses of red wine before crawling into our swags. I awoke at daylight sensing that there was something in the camp just in time to see a dingo running off with one of my boots in its mouth. As luck would have it I must have finished the evening with a cleansing ale and the half-finished can was sitting beside me so I hurled it at the dingo and gave it just enough of a fright that it dropped my boot. It ran off but only as far as about 50 metres away where it joined half a dozen of its mates. They weren't intimidated by our shouts or sudden movements, so we had a bit of a Mexican stand-off. Never having encountered this behaviour before, Cretto and I decided on a rapid decamp from the scene after packing up our gear.

After finishing our inspections in the region, we headed off to Alice Springs later that day, where we had a meeting scheduled with our NT counterparts regarding undertaking geoscientific studies in the remote Anangu Pitjantjatjara Yankunytjatjara (APY) lands, which straddle the western border between SA and the NT. In our motel that night the local Imparja TV news featured details of a dingo attack on a remote stretch of the Stuart Highway about 100 kilometres south of Alice the previous night. A lone long-distance walker with a young pup aboard his transport apparatus had been attacked, and his pup had been killed and carried off by a pack of dingoes. With the prevailing dry conditions and lack of bush food, perhaps we were fortunate to only suffer the indignity of a temporarily lost boot.

22

Talking to Traditional Owners

South Australia, 1990s

In 1995 the SA Government entered into an agreement with private companies seeking to open up the vast coal deposits of the Arckaringa Basin in northern SA. Coal mining was intended to power a new process to smelt iron ore, to exploit iron ore deposits in the same broad region. Our task was to define some of these iron deposits, undertaking exploration in similar fashion to private enterprise. This was an unexpected but exciting challenge. We had some very good geoscientists to carry out the task but little iron ore expertise. Mines and Energy South Australia (MESA) had last carried out iron ore investigations in the 1960s concurrent with the discovery and subsequent development of the massive iron ore deposits in the Pilbara region of Western Australia. Before the Pilbara discoveries the Middleback Ranges in SA had been the primary source of iron ore production in Australia for over 60 years.

To bolster our iron ore expertise, we advertised for a senior geologist, preferably with iron ore exploration and development experience. Half an hour before the close of applications, things weren't looking good, when a several-page application scrawled on an A5 writing pad lobbed on my desk. At first, I thought it was a set-up by one of my work colleagues, but as I slowly worked my way through the scrawl, I realised it was from someone who had extensive experience in both Middleback Ranges and Pilbara iron ore investigations. At interview Marc Davies, being a local Adelaide Hills resident, was eager to point out that a job with MESA had been his long-term dream. So, there we had it, MESA had someone with iron ore experience and Marc was following his dream. He was a long-term bachelor and very set in his ways; his workmates in the bush christened him "Soc" (and I won't go into that); but he proved a wonderful, if at times incongruous, asset. At one stage, after spending about eight weeks straight in the field, he went a bit bush-happy, and I had to order him back for a break.

We also needed a local field supervisor for our investigations, which centred around the Coober Pedy region. We had someone in mind, but in fairness had to place a job advertisement in the *Coober Pedy Times*. Out of the blue came another left field application from a local opal miner, Derek "Kiwi" Russell. He had extensive previous experience with mineral exploration drilling and sampling and being a "solo" opal miner he was not only a great self-starter but also very safety-conscious. He got the job and proved another great asset. Kiwi too was a bachelor, but at a dinner party at our home a few years later he surprised the assembled guests halfway through the meal when he dropped to his knees and proposed to his girlfriend Cassie. With such a gesture she could hardly have refused. Kiwi and Cassie remain our friends till this day and now live in Glen Innes with their two daughters.

The iron ore exploration program extended over at least a twelve-month period and included investigations of large but long-neglected magnetite deposits on Eyre Peninsula as well as those in the broader Coober Pedy region.

The integrated iron smelter/iron ore and coal project never got off the ground, but MESA's iron investigations and subsequent publication of a review or iron ore in SA in 2000 resulted in the delineation of several deposits, with subsequent mine development at two sites in the Coober Pedy region and several large-scale developments in the pipeline on Eyre Peninsula.

Lloydie's birthday

During the iron ore investigations, we used both MESA and contractor drill rigs for various programs. Lloydie Moore was the head driller on the MESA drill. I happened to be in camp about 100 kilometres west of Coober on his birthday. Lloydie was a gentle giant, and a top-class bush cook who on an earlier drilling program in the Olary region was catching so many yabbies from the nearby dam that he was providing jars of pickled yabbies to any camp visitors, and at another camp near Burra he caught and then cooked a superb camp oven goat dish. He was known to like a Bundy or 20 and loved a good campfire and barbeque.

On this evening the Bundy was there in spades and Lloydie and his offsider must have burnt at least one and a half tonnes of their carefully stacked wood supply – they burnt the lot. Late in the evening nature called and Lloydie wandered off to the long-drop, where he promptly fell asleep in a rather compromising pose. Kiwi, ever alert to a photo opportunity, in the days before mobile phones had cameras, was quick to capture the scene for posterity.

It was business as usual the next morning and no more was mentioned until the MESA drillers' Christmas party back in Adelaide. Kiwi, utilising MESA's printing facilities, had organised the production of many, many t-shirts and numerous leaflets and posters with Lloydie's compromised long-drop pose adorning each one. As guests arrived, they were each issued with a t-shirt. Lloydie arrived to find the venue adorned with his image. His first reaction was to tear the shirts off guests' backs, but they were immediately replaced with more of the same. In the end he realised his efforts were futile, and after a Bundy or two he was more relaxed about the situation, although he did manage to acquire all the incriminating evidence at the end of the day.

WARWICK NEWTON

Working with Traditional Owners

When Paul Keating introduced the *Native Title Act (1983)* to Federal Parliament on the heels of the High Court's Mabo decision, he opened a can of worms. It will take a century to determine whether the legislation has truly benefited the majority of indigenous Australians, and the net effect on the Australian economy. I believe Keating knew that the legislation would impact most heavily on the mining industry for the first 30 years, making it politically benign for him. When the Act was first introduced there was remarkable goodwill in negotiations between mining companies and indigenous groups, but once the legal profession realised that through the legislation Keating had presented them with a "lawyers' picnic", the confrontational legal approach took precedence, with often unsatisfactory results for all parties, particularly in the way royalty payments have made a few people very rich but haven't flowed on to the majority of indigenous owners.

A *Voice* (to Parliament) I hear you say, little realising that indigenous landowners through this 30 plus year old Act can, and often are, holding nearly all Australian industry to ransom. I rejoice that the burden the mining industry has carried for the past 30 years is now rapidly spreading to all industries and that the implications of the Act are being more widely understood. Enough of this as I'll briefly air my views on indigenous matters in the final chapter: for now, I'll just describe some of my dealings with Traditional Owners.

Besides *The Land Rights Act (1993)*, every state has aboriginal heritage legislation which requires anyone wanting to develop or disturb land to obtain a clearance certifying that no sites of indigenous significance will be disturbed during the process. This requires a survey of the sites, usually by an anthropologist/archaeologist accompanied by several Traditional Owners. Such surveys currently can cost at least $10,000 per day. Problem is, no state has a register of surveys undertaken nor of significant sites identified. As a result, the same area, at a different time and with a different operator, may be "surveyed" multiple times. Sorry, but this strikes me as akin to a form of pointless welfare payments.

My first experience with an aboriginal heritage survey was in the Flinders Ranges area, where MESA was proposing to drill at several sites. The survey was arranged, and the plan was to meet one afternoon at the Blinman Hotel before undertaking surveys over the next two to three days. We booked in at Blinman and waited, but no indigenous survey party turned up. Next day we managed to phone them and were advised that there'd been a death in the Adnyamathana community but that they would meet us at the Wilpena Pound turn-off at 3.00pm that day after the funeral in nearby Quorn. By 5.00pm there was still no sign of them, so we drove into Quorn just in time to see a group emerging from the first pub on the way in. They recognized our vehicle and flagged us down. We produced some site maps of proposed drill hole locations, they gave them a cursory look and then agreed to sign off on the heritage clearance on that basis, outside the pub, without setting a foot on the ground. Everyone was happy, we had our clearance, and they received the survey fee, but it did strike me as a somewhat cavalier approach. The cynic in me was aroused.

At the other end of the spectrum, later surveys undertaken by the Yankunytjatjara people for MESA drilling projects in far north SA were carried out in meticulous detail with all ground within the vicinity of proposed drill holes examined closely by separate men's and women's groups. The organisation of surveys across Australia has improved over time but costs have also gone up exponentially. The other problem is in finding the correct indigenous claimant group to do the survey. Regularly various groups have conflicting claims over the same country, so that an exploration company can pay for a clearance survey in good faith only to discover later that another group doesn't approve. This I believe may have been the case for Rio Tinto when they inadvertently destroyed rock shelters near Juukan Gorge in WA believing the sites had been cleared for mining. The press, rather than highlighting the so-called environmental vandalism by Rio Tinto, might have done well to investigate the dysfunctional organisation of these competing indigenous claimant groups as the root cause of this incident.

The *Anangu Pitjantjatjara Yankunytjatjara Land Rights Act (1981)* (APY Act) gave the indigenous occupants of a 100,000-square-kilometre tract of land in the northwest corner of SA rights of ownership and management of this land but not the rights to veto mining activity. Since proclamation there'd been little or no mineral exploration on the APY Lands, but opal mining at Mintabie and a small chrysoprase mining operation had been permitted. Pre–APY Act mineral exploration and geoscientific surveys had highlighted the potential for the lands to host significant nickel and base metal deposits.

With the launch of the South Australian Exploration Initiative in 1993, it was proposed that the whole of the APY Lands would be flown with state-of-the-art geophysical surveys. The elected APY Council acceded to a request to fly these surveys with few reservations, as the surveys involved very minor on-ground intrusion by survey personnel and only very limited disturbance when the survey plane flew over some of the scattered local communities. Getting access on the ground for follow-up ground surveys and drilling by both MESA and exploration companies was another issue altogether.

For several years I was tasked with negotiating access for such activities with the APY Council and their various advisors. This proved to be a highly frustrating but ultimately rewarding activity, as I gradually came to understand the concerns these people harboured about any kind of intrusion or development on their lands, which they now controlled in perpetuity. The APY Council met one day a month at Umuwa, the administrative centre of the lands, about 1300 kilometres from Adelaide. Flying in wasn't a real option as you never knew when you were on the meeting agenda, so the day usually involved an early three-hour drive from the Marla roadhouse on the Stuart Highway for a 10.00am meeting start. That was after a 1000km road trip from Adelaide. Invariably we'd spend most of the day waiting our turn only to then face a group of people who late in the day just wanted to go home, so patience was vital in negotiations. Just when you felt that you were making progress, the local anthropologist would have her say and set things back yet again. As there was no visitor accommodation at Umuwa, at the end of the day there was always the three-hour drive back to Marla, half of which was usually in the dark. At least when agreement was reached on various access issues, we were able to firm these up with the APY legal representative in Alice Springs. I should also mention that much of the scenery on the way to Umuwa was quite spectacular and an absolute pleasure to drive through. Mt Woodroffe in the Musgrave Ranges, at 1435 metres, is South Australia's highest peak.

Bob Larkins, the MESA aboriginal liaison officer, often accompanied me on these trips and was invaluable in indigenous dealings throughout SA, as he usually knew who the power brokers within the indigenous claimant groups were (often they weren't the people you were directly negotiating with). With a mix of Irish and indigenous heritage, Bob was an Ernie Dingo–like character who was generally a pleasure to travel with on these long bush safaris. Over the years I came to learn that many indigenous Australians have a rather wicked sense of humour just like Bob, but it was also interesting to get an insight into the character of some of these indigenous leaders. Kawaki (Pantju) Thompson was the one who most impressed me. The same age as me, he was a tireless worker not only for his people's land rights but also for their health and welfare. He was a quietly spoken "tjilpi", who not only treasured traditional values but also recognised that some economic development was vital to ensure the future of the APY Lands and their peoples, particularly the younger generation. He ensured that his own children were well educated.

Yami Lester was a Yankunytjatjara man who like Pantju was also instrumental in the development and eventual proclamation of the APY Lands Act. His white father, Dick Lander, was the manager at Mt Willoughby Station, but apparently disowned him at birth. Yami often referred to himself as "half-German, half-Blackfella", so it's assumed Mr Lander had German heritage. Yami in 1953 at about age twelve experienced a "black mist" in the SA outback, which was likely fallout from British atom bomb testing at Maralinga or Emu Junction and went permanently blind not too long after. Many years later, in 1985, his efforts to have the impact of this testing on indigenous inhabitants recognised helped lead to the McClelland Royal Commission into British nuclear testing in Australia.

The media today have set in concrete that his blindness was a direct result of the nuclear fallout, but in his autobiography, *Yami*, he concludes the final chapter, titled "Poisoned Land", with the wry statement "And I never did find out if one of those bombs made me blind." Interestingly my GP in Adelaide many years ago had worked in the far north of SA and had treated Yami at some point. In recalling those days, he unintentionally mentioned that the likely cause of Yami's blindness was that curse of outback Australia, trachoma. To quote part of the Prologue of *Yami* relating to that "black mist" yet again: "People had sore eyes too. I was one of those people and later on I lost my sight, and my life was changed forever. If I had my eyes, I would probably still be a stockman. Because I haven't, I became a stirrer."

Yami was much more than a stirrer, and his contribution to indigenous causes can't be underestimated, but in my several encounters with him the stirrer certainly came to the fore. I recollect one meeting at Umuwa. Yami, not then an APY Council member, was in attendance on the day, and after the meeting he asked Bob and me if we could give him a lift back to his home at Walatina Station, as he knew we were heading back to Marla. We gladly obliged, as he was always great company. Not 500 metres out of Umuwa a voice from the back seat asks, "Well where's the grog boys?" Now Yami was probably one of the original instigators of declaring the APY Lands an alcohol-free zone, even if there was an unwritten tenet that what happened behind closed doors, stayed behind closed doors. Taking a cautious approach Bob and I declared that we had no alcohol on board, and cold water or a soft drink was the best we could offer. Yami wasn't to be placated and persisted, "Cut out the bullshit boys – I'm dying for a cold beer." Eventually we caved in and from deep in the car fridge managed to produce a cold beer for each of us.

For the remainder of the daylight on that drive Yami went on to amaze us with a commentary describing the country we were passing through. Totally blind, he accurately described all the country we passed through whether from memory or some sixth sense and then added dreamtime stories which related to each feature we passed. It was an experience not to be forgotten. Later I asked him whether he had ever run into an old friend of mine who was working in the APY Lands. This fellow's wife was rather on the large size, and next thing Bob and Yami burst out with laughter about the indigenous name she had been given. My Pitjantjatjara lingo was restricted to the odd greeting, so after a while I said, "Come on boys, let me in on the joke." Bob finally relented and provided the English translation "Three Cheeks". Fortunately, the lady in question never got to find out. Yami also went on to entertain us with stories of his travels in Japan and elsewhere, but I suspect they're better left unreported.

There were one or two members of the APY Council who in my view at times let their cause down. One whom I ran into in Alice Springs on more than one occasion would greet you and chat in friendly fashion but then hit you for a $50 or $100 "loan", which inevitably went straight into the poker machines at the casino. Fortunately, I was able to claim these "loans" as necessarily incurred expenses.

When MESA first started negotiations with APY regarding mineral exploration access, there must have been at least 50 outstanding exploration licence applications from over fifteen separate companies, some dating back more than ten years. At one stage an enterprising WA junior exploration company attempted to do a backdoor deal directly with the APY Council. In essence it proposed that APY take control of the administration of all exploration and mining on the lands, with the junior company to act as an advisor to the council but also undertake exploration in joint venture with the APY. The proposal seemed to have the endorsement of the APY Council and had several prominent backers including Charlie Perkins and his son, prominent Alice Springs lawyer, Sean Bowden, and even the ex-premier of WA Peter Dowding (Dowding had replaced Brian Burke as Labor premier after the WA Inc scandal). In hindsight and many years later, after reading the book *Tracker,* the story of Tracker Tilmouth, who was a legendary indigenous entrepreneur, mover and shaker, I realised that it had all Tracker's hallmarks. A radical proposal to improve the fortunes of indigenous people but lacking in practicalities. I may well be wrong about Tracker's involvement, but over the years he often worked closely with Sean Bowden.

Personally I quite liked the idea of APY involving themselves directly in the exploration and mining process with a view to long-term income generation on the lands, but the proposal was doomed to failure, first, because having the rival WA junior as an advisor hardly offered a level playing field to competing companies, but more importantly, no sane State government is ever going to cede the Crown rights to minerals over more than ten percent of its total area. The fate of the proposal was sealed when Yami Lester contacted the Minister to advise that the Yankuntjatjara people weren't a party to the proposal. The furore gradually died down, but not before Neville Alley, then Director of Mineral Resources, and I were subject to threats (from one of the backers who will remain unnamed), a work situation I'd never encountered before or since and not a comfortable one at that.

As an aside, I was rather chuffed by the response I received to a talk I gave promoting the mineral potential of the APY Lands, and I quote verbatim from the journalist's take on it in the September 2000 edition of the *Australian Journal of Mining* "The title of Warwick Newton's speech at the recent South Australian gabfest "Resources Week 2000" sounded like it was lifted from Jurassic Park, or a novel by H. Rider Haggard. "Australia's Last Exploration Frontier" was the tag attached to the session by the South Australian government representative. Evocative and rightly so, for Newton's speech homed in on Australia's most exciting zone of exploration – the Musgrave Block, and the portion of it, in South Australia controlled by its Aboriginal owners – the Anangu Pitjantjatjara (AP) people." On the other hand, the editor, Charles Macdonald, couldn't help himself, with a heading to his editorial "The last frontier? It's the Pit's". I love it.

Today there is limited access for mineral exploration on the APY Lands, unfortunately without a major mineral discovery to date.

Talk work, drink beer

I've very rarely taken family members on work field-trips, but in 1995 an opportunity came up to visit the Dalhousie hot springs, about 1000 kilometres north of Adelaide. Zac Sibenaler and I were to represent MESA at the inauguration of joint management of the Witjira National Park between the National Parks and Wildlife Service, SA and the Traditional Owners, the Southern Arrernte and Wangkangurra people. As it was school holidays it was a great opportunity for my eleven-year-old daughter Emma to join us on a very long drive.

When we finally arrived at the springs, many Traditional Owners were already camped there with their families in preparation for the next day's ceremony. The park area comprises over 100 mound springs of which at least 60 are currently active. The largest spring, where most tourists choose to swim, must be nearly 100 metres in diameter and is up to ten metres deep. The water temperature is around the 40-degree centigrade mark, and I found too much swimming tended to overheat the body, but Emma seemed to have no problems adapting. Emma has quite an olive complexion and was readily adopted by the many indigenous children present – in fact she was quite a bit darker than many of them. It was a great experience for her.

Next day after the inauguration ceremony we headed off on the five-hour drive back to William Creek. Arriving there just on dark I was happy to stay the night, but Zac had other ideas: he'd already organised an overnight stay with a mate who owned Callana Station in the Willouran Ranges, another 200 kilometres and a two to three-hour drive further south. It proved a long drive in the dark, but we were warmly greeted by the station owner and his family – his three boys were particularly pleased to have a good-looking young female visitor for a few hours. After being wined and dined, Emma and I snuck off to the shearers' quarters for a well-earned rest while Zac and his mate chose to continue into the wee hours. The quarters were spartan but comfortable enough, although Emma was a tad confronted by the number of redbacks in evidence.

Next day was just another long drive back to Adelaide, but I think Emma enjoyed her experiences at the springs and the brief taste of station life. When I asked her, she said the swims and play at the springs had been terrific, but it had been a boring drive and "all you and Zac did was talk work and drink beer".

23
Spruiking and Romance

South Australia, 1990s

Mining conferences over the years have always been fun, providing the industry with a chance to catch up on the latest mineral discoveries and mining developments as well as offering opportunities for networking. Once the South Australian Exploration Initiative (SAEI) was in full swing by the mid-1990s, Mines and Energy South Australia (MESA) took every opportunity to promote the new geoscientific data they were collecting and encouraged staff to adopt an entrepreneurial approach when attending, or manning booths at, various conferences.

Livening up conferences

The first conference I attended in this new capacity was the Annual Australasian Institute of Mining and Metallurgy event held in Darwin in 1994, in company with work colleague Nick Dunstan. Conference booths were laid out beside the many swimming pools within the conference facility (only in Darwin!). Besides various geoscientific maps promoting our activities there were many brochures and then state-of-the-art colour laptops on which the geoscientific data could be enhanced. We even had promotional t-shirts featuring some of the geoscientific images. I noted to Nick that all our booth lacked was a few cold drinks, so quickly organised a fridge and a few cold cartons. A bit unconventional in those days, but boy did it attract people to the MESA booth in droves. Later on, I even managed to convince an attractive young research geoscientist from the CSIRO to pose in one of our (wet) t-shirts in one of the pools. I tried something of a similar pose in a shallow spa pool, brandishing an SAEI promotional brochure in one hand and a beer in the other. Later this image lost its appeal when it was photoshopped to include a very large and very naked lady standing beside me.

With Ric Horn I attended an international PacRim conference (a quadrennial conference on mining in Pacific Rim countries) in Auckland a year or two later. This time we came a little more prepared, importing several cases of one of Bleasdale's best reds from Langhorne Creek for the occasion. At that time there weren't many decent reds produced in New Zealand – my cousin, Robert Newton's, "Newton Forrest" label being one of the exceptions. Once word got around that there was a good red wine on offer at the MESA booth we were literally inundated with attendees for the duration of the conference. This was much to the chagrin of the CEO of the NSW Mines Department who had a nearby booth which I would estimate attracted about 20 percent of the attendees at our booth. A business card raffle for two cartons of the Bleasdale also attracted great participation, with a draw being made on stage during the final conference session. A North American winner freighted his booty home; the other, Paul Ashley, an old Sydney Uni colleague, shared his whole carton with friends at a dinner that evening.

Another uranium exploration and mining conference held in Darwin warrants a mention. With uranium as the theme, it attracted a small but persistent group of protesters. They converged on a conference drinks evening, but were quite taken aback when they were invited in for drinks with the conference delegates (at the delegates request). An hour of generally convivial discussion took place, which was far preferable to any confrontation. As they left the protesters chanted a rather half-hearted "No Uranium Mining", but I'd like to think that at least one or two of them left with a little more knowledge of the issue and perhaps a slightly revised impression of the mining industry ogres.

Blackie and the Professor

In later exploration initiative years MESA, the NSW Mines Department and Geoscience Australia jointly funded the so-called Broken Hill Exploration Initiative (BHEI). As part of this agreement there was an annual conference in Broken Hill and a field excursion in the surrounding districts. It was on a pre-conference excursion that I first had the pleasure of meeting two great characters, Professor Ian Plimer and Peter Black ("Blackie"). In some ways they're like chalk and cheese, the urbane and erudite Plimer and Blackie, who at his grossest could be described as a living, breathing Sir Les Paterson; but they shared a great love of geology and the bush and are both inveterate stirrers and skeptics.

Blackie was a very left-leaning high school teacher in Sydney (born in Hurstville, the then heart of the St George Dragons district, as was I). His involvement in many protests and demonstrations of the late 1960s era saw him transferred to Broken Hill in 1969. He took to the union stronghold like a duck to water and remains a long-term resident. Apart from a 30-year high school teaching career, he was Broken Hill's longest serving mayor, from 1980 to 1999, and the State Labor member for Murray-Darling from 1999 to 2007. He even came back for another term as a Broken Hill councillor from 2012–2016, but when accused of bringing the council into disrepute because of a newspaper column he had been writing for decades he abruptly resigned from public office, stating he was too tired to fight the bastards any longer (or words to that effect). Despite some shortcomings relating to alcohol, Blackie's contribution to the city of Broken Hill over nearly 50 years is little short of amazing. Last I heard he was still giving by way of regularly visiting and reading to residents in aged care homes.

Ian Plimer is an economic geologist of international renown who can comfortably sit in industry or academia. He was also a member of Australian Skeptics Inc and has over the years been a vocal critic of the pseudo-science which has often been peddled by creationists and climate change disciples. He proved beyond doubt that so-called remains of Noah's Ark on Mt Ararat in Turkey are geological in nature and converted the perpetrator of that claim to his views. However, he then went on to sue Australian creationists under the *Fair Trading Act* (of all things) for peddling false and misleading information but lost on a technicality in that the actions weren't relevant to the Act. Costs awarded against him nearly sent him bankrupt. Over the last 20 years or so he has devoted many of his skeptical efforts to refuting much of the pseudo-science which is alluded to in today's climate change debate and has published several books on the topic.

I first met these two larrikins just off the Barrier Highway near Olary one morning, as our group from MESA joined the pre-conference field excursion. Blackie greeted me like a long-lost friend – perhaps he sensed we were both long-term Dragons supporters born in Hurstville. At the ensuing morning tea break, Blackie had already opened the esky and offered me an icy cold beer at about 10.00am; at the time it was an offer just too good to refuse. I did decline several subsequent offers, however, until mid-afternoon when the excursion group had about a three-kilometre walk to a particular geological feature. Blackie, in his late 50s, was the oldest of the group but steadfastly shouldered a cold carton of beer as his essential survival supplies for the walk. Despite the warm day he refused offers to share the load. After we reached and extensively perused the geological feature, Blackie offered still reasonably cold beers to the group, most of whom readily accepted. This was just Blackie's way, as I learned over the next few days.

Camping that night, Ian Plimer in true skeptic style introduced the group to the science of hot-rock walking. Some eminent Australian geoscientists as well as many of Plimer's research students successfully took up the challenge, but being neither eminent nor particularly brave I settled for a glass of red beside the glowing rocks. The next day or two of the excursion followed a similar pattern culminating in a gut-wrestling competition in the Olary pub on the last night, which Blackie won convincingly.

On to the BHEI conference in Broken Hill, where it was noticed that Blackie was a notable absentee from the opening ceremony, which seemed a bit odd. Later in the day Ian Plimer let me know that Blackie hadn't been invited to the opening ceremony or conference dinner by the NSW Mines Department, who was the event organiser. Ian and I headed round to the mayor's office to commiserate with him over this oversight. I had never been entertained in mayoral chambers, but after a taste of mayoral hospitality Melbourne University (Plimer) and MESA (me) now officially invited him to the conference dinner. Later in the afternoon we walked Blackie back to his home to tidy up for the evening. There, we were briefly treated to a sneak peek of his magnificent Broken Hill rock collection of over 2500 specimens. Plimer and me then headed back to our respective motels to get ready, after having organised a place for Blackie at the dinner.

When Blackie arrived at the dinner that evening there was a certain hush from some of the attendees. Ian Plimer in his usual fashion gave a wonderful post-dinner oration on Broken Hill geology and mineral deposits, then Blackie decided that he should take to the stage for an equally outstanding piece of oratory, which included a pointed thank you to Melbourne Uni and MESA for having the grace to invite the mayor to this event when his own state counterparts seemed to have overlooked such an invitation. I believe that I may have received a rather surly look at the conference next day from that same CEO of the NSW Mines Department who had witnessed MESA's earlier booth success at the NZ PacRim conference.

As a result of our success with iron ore investigations MESA felt these results needed to be promoted widely, and by default I became the MESA conference spokesman on this topic. My first outing was at an iron ore conference in Scarborough in WA, which felt like trying to sell coal to Newcastle. I was on the same session as one Clive Palmer, who was trying to promote the novel concept (for Australia) of mining and processing magnetite-ore from the Pilbara instead of from the massive, world-renowned hematite deposits in that region. To Palmer's credit he did eventually get this huge project off the ground with Chinese backing, but back then it seemed so implausible that my following talk promoting SA iron deposits suddenly had relative credibility. The second somewhat daunting experience was featuring on the opening session of another iron conference at Darling Harbour beside Colin Barnett, then WA Minister for Mines and soon to become WA Premier. Post-talk he was such a pleasant person to chat with – a good politician, I suspect. I was chuffed later, however, when our own MESA deputy CEO, who was in attendance, came up and said, "Congratulations, you held your own mate." Kind words indeed from the normally reserved Tom Welsh.

I guess I should briefly mention the last conference I attended while with MESA: it was an International Geological Congress hosted by the Geological Society of Australia in Sydney. The conference itself was unremarkable, but I did get into a little difficulty on the final night harbour cruise. Disembarking, very relaxed after a three-hour dinner cruise, a group of us were standing on the wharf when I decided that I'd pretend to give one of them a little shove. Problem was she stepped aside as I was in motion and my momentum projected me straight into the murky and very cold waters of Darling Harbour. I extracted myself post haste but it was a frigid finale to an otherwise pleasant evening – some might say poetic justice.

Beginning of the end

In October 1997 the SA government, in their wisdom, with advice from senior bureaucrats, decided to merge the small and efficient MESA with the very large Department of Primary Industries into a super-department, the Department of Primary Industries and Resources (PIRSA). What possible synergies they imagined existed between the two groups escapes me to this day, but it was a fait accompli. Ross Fardon in his two-year term at MESA had I believe taken it at least ten years forward but in one stroke of the pen this merger took us at least 20 years backward. A close work colleague, Max Pain, put it very succinctly: "I used to hear public service jokes and not quite be able to relate to them, but with the advent of PIRSA I now get the picture." To be fair, many within the old Department of Primary Industries were equally bemused.

For the first time in its 100-year history MESA had a career public servant and not an industry professional in charge. The merger almost brought the exploration initiative program to a grinding halt: where once we could make quick decisions on letting contracts for drilling and aerial geophysical surveys, we were now constrained by all tenders going through a very cumbersome tender committee process. I'm afraid drilling and geophysical survey companies can't wait around for six months or more while tender decisions are being made. Added to the unbelievable bureaucracy it was now the era of strategic planning, interminable meetings and over-the-top OH&S, and countless otherwise productive hours were to be wasted on these pursuits. I was forever in strife for being out in the field when I had been instructed to attend some pointless meeting.

I wear with honour two of my achievements during the PIRSA years. First, being the only senior manager who never attended the newly ordained Friday afternoon get-togethers with other managers across PIRSA, I'm sure my non-attendance was duly noted. The second was my invention of a self-fulfilling key performance indicator (KPI) regarding future levels of company mineral exploration. The politicians liked this one so much that a variant of the same is still in place today.

The writing was on the wall, and the glory days of an efficient MESA were over for now. I'm happy to report that today common sense has prevailed and MESA, now the Department for Energy and Mining, has reverted to a single entity once again, with an industry professional as the chief executive.

Life goes on

Separation and divorce did have quite an impact throughout the 1990s, but life must go on. I think the wonderful work environment created by the SAEI helped greatly in getting through this trying period. Having Teneille, my elder daughter, living with me most of the time and younger daughter Emma most weekends kept me busy, particularly Teneille, who was in her rather rebellious teenage years. There was lots of ferrying around for their various sports: apart from surf lifesaving there was always weekend basketball or netball, at which they respectively excelled, Teneille through sheer toughness and determination, Emma through an innate ability to create space and opportunities for her team. Emma's little netball team won at least seven premierships in a row in their age division before just succumbing to a much bigger adult team in their final year. Easter trips to relatives on the South Coast of NSW also continued unabated.

Emma was determined that she'd attend Brighton High School like her big sister, but living just out of the school catchment area, her cause looked hopeless. Emma had other ideas and applied to gain entry through acceptance into the school's volleyball intake. Though having never played the sport before and being a little vertically challenged for the game, she undertook the necessary trials and tests and was accepted.

Eventually I decided that I should seek some female company again, but where and how to find it in my late forties and working in a predominantly male-dominated industry? The local *Sunday Mail* dating column proved the answer and after a year or two of trial and error I finally met my now wife, Babs. There was an eleven-year age difference, and this was the subject of some discussion at the time, but we eventually got together. An early commitment together was my 50th birthday party at the Seacliff Surf Club. There were a few other interesting engagements over the next couple of years. Babs attended the last St Barbara's Day mining industry quarry get-together, and we were both a little taken aback as we observed the then Minister for Mines and Energy (and soon to be Premier) greet a young lady with a gentle caress of her behind. "Did we really just see that?" said Babs – it was probably her first industry outing. The young lady in question was a vacation student in Mineral Resources at the time, and when I asked her about it later she said the Minister was an old family friend. I think it was rather lucky that there were no mobile phones in those days.

Our respective work took us both to Coober Pedy so on a couple of occasions we timed our visits to coincide. Not such a wise move in a small town. Several of my acquaintances ran into us in restaurants there and to cap it off, as we emerged from the motel one morning Norm Kennedy, an exploration company associate from Meekatharra Minerals, came out of the next room. There was little choice but to introduce him to Babs. We played one on workmate Kiwi while there. At some stage he had cheekily suggested to Babs that if ever in Coober she should look him up. We wandered round to his place one night and I hid while she knocked on the door. He almost took the bait but then turned on all his outside lights bellowing "Where the **** are you Newt!", and much as I tried to stay hidden, he finally found me.

In 1999 Babs and I purchased a house in Hallett Cove on the coast south of Adelaide and moved in together. It was a welcome and stabilising change of lifestyle.

24

Last Dance in the Rain with Jethro Tull

South Australia, 2000s

The new millennium started off with a bit of a whimper: the lights didn't go out; the world's computers didn't self-destruct – in fact it was something of an anticlimax after all the myriad soothsayers' dire predictions. Babs and I saw the millennium in on an upstairs balcony at one of Adelaide's historic pubs overlooking all the festivities on King William Street in the heart of the city. We were joined for the evening by Zac Sibenaler and family, Zac being friends with the publican.

Ten weeks later, on a sweltering Adelaide March day, we held a housewarming in the back yard of our new home at Hallett Cove. Midway through the afternoon Babs disappeared, to return soon after in more formal attire, and then a stranger turned up dressed in collar and tie and proceeded to perform our marriage ceremony in the backyard. Only family, Zac as best man, Bab's cousin Julie, the maid of honour and work mate Stuey Mathews, who was catering – had been pre-warned, so the occasion drew quite a few oohs and aahs. Suddenly I'd gained not only a wife but two sons, and likewise Babs had gained two daughters.

My last days at MESA

On the work front things weren't going quite so well. Coping every day with the new and very cumbersome bureaucracy which was PIRSA was bad enough, but when directors in their wisdom decided to restructure the old MESA, this old dinosaur could see the writing on the wall, so when another round of separation packages was announced in mid-2001 I was quick to put up my hand, along with several other branch colleagues.

Before departure in September 2001 there were just a couple more field experiences. I went on what I thought was my last field-trip, with Mark Flintoft, Marc Davies and Brian Morris. It was to be a ten-day trek covering the state, so it was important to have adequate supplies. Mark convinced the rest of us that our beer stock should comprise only VB (Victoria Bitter), as it was currently so cheap at a bottle shop at Port Adelaide, near where he lived. I was very much against the idea but finally acquiesced when the other two failed to register any protest. By the end of day three, all except Mark were complaining about what a horrible beer it was, but we had to endure it for the duration. Since that time if I'm asked my choice of beer at a bar anywhere in Australia I simply reply, "Not VB."

The first stop on the trek was to be near Ooldea on the edge of the Nullarbor Plain, where we were planning another regional drilling program. After heading across Eyre Peninsula, we reached the Yalata roadhouse, where we were informed that the road north to Ooldea was closed north of the Yalata indigenous community for annual initiation ceremonies. Having travelled almost 1000 kilometres west of Adelaide we weren't about to turn round, so decided to head further west to the Nullarbor Roadhouse, north to Cook on the Transcontinental Railway line then back east along the line to Ooldea. It was only a 200-kilometre detour, but on those outback roads added a good four hours to the trip.

The road heading north from the Nullarbor Roadhouse must be among the loneliest and most featureless tracks in Australia and is notorious for UFO sightings and of course further west at Eucla the hoax sightings of the Nullarbor Nymph in December 1971. While we didn't encounter any UFOs or nymphs on our way to Cook, it was easy to imagine that on that monotonous stretch of the Nullarbor, particularly if travelling alone and at night, it would be very easy to let the mind wander – even more so if one spent much time at the roadhouse before setting off.

Alone at the Ooldea Soak

Having reached Ooldea, the next day the others headed off to check on any vehicle access to the south while I, with plenty of water supplies, took the opportunity to walk into the Ooldea Soak (Yooldil Kapi) area in the Maralinga Tjuruta Lands. The Ooldea Soak with its then permanent water supply had been a trading and ceremonial site for indigenous people of the Western Desert probably for thousands of years. When the Transcontinental Railway was pushed through the region in 1917, a small settlement was established at Ooldea, which is situated about six kilometres south of the soak. A pump was set up on the soak to supply the siding and passing trains with water, and within 20 years the soak had dried up. The eccentric Daisy Bates, a noted author, welfare worker and amateur anthropologist, set up a camp at Ooldea siding in 1919 and lived there most of the time until 1935, tending to the indigenous community at Ooldea Soak. A mission was set up at the soak in 1933 and operated up until 1952, when the remaining inhabitants were relocated to the Yalata indigenous community about 100 kilometres further south.

When I reached the soak area in 2001 there was little left of any buildings or machinery, but relics, both ancient and contemporary, were scattered everywhere. To be on my own in such a lonely place and contemplate the very long indigenous history of the site was a most moving experience and I ensured that nothing was disturbed. The next day we headed east back toward the Stuart Highway, but before reaching Tarcoola were all surprised to see a large group of people wandering along the top of a big granite tor just 100 metres or so from the railway track. First thought was it was a party of geologists, but then the penny dropped: it was the indigenous initiation group from Yalata examining one of their sacred sites. We hadn't expected to see them this far north, and hightailed it out of there, not wanting to disturb their activities. It was a delight to realise that some indigenous groups were serious about retaining their culture.

Our trek then took us north to iron ore drilling sites in the Coober Pedy region and ultimately to the site of our then current drilling activities on Tieyon station near the SA-NT border, but the lasting memories were of Ooldea and the experience of encountering an indigenous initiation activity.

One more field trip

Just when I thought I'd taken my last field trip, Mark Flintoft came up with the ploy that along with himself I was the only other driver available at the time whom he'd trust with towing one of our two very large caravans back south when the Tieyon drilling program was completed. While I didn't quite believe his story, I jumped at the chance.

Our trip north was interesting, especially when we encountered a character, Nobby, from Port Augusta, at the Glendambo roadhouse overnight. Nobby had many years before run the Mintabie store in the Anangu Pitjantjatjara Yankunytjatjara (APY) lands. He told many anecdotes about his time at the store and entertained everyone at the bar with great renditions of Slim Dusty classics. However, his forte now was providing questionable vehicles with bright red painted engines to the APY community – apparently red engines made the cars go faster. Next morning we had to push-start his red-engined Commodore to get it going but I've no doubt he still sold it at a premium when he reached the APY Lands. A real villain but also a very likeable rogue.

It was always a joy to arrive at Tieyon homestead, near where our drilling camp was situated. Approaching from Kulgera on the NT side of the border, as you got into Tieyon station on the SA side you drove through picturesque granite outcrop country with the surrounding paddocks lush green after two to three years of excellent rainfall. The black Angus cattle that roamed the paddocks were then in prime condition because of all the feed available. In 2019 the centenary of the Tieyon Pastoral Company's establishment was celebrated, four generations of the Smith family had owned and operated the property during that time. They first introduced the magnificent black Angus on the property in 1925.

When we were drilling on Tieyon in 2001, Andrew Smith and his son Paul were both living there and operating the property along with their respective wives, who as on many outback stations were probably the mainstays of the operation. Andrew and Paul couldn't have been more helpful to us during a several-month intrusion on Tieyon while extensive mineral drilling investigations were undertaken. If anything, Andrew may have been a little too friendly on occasions. Arriving to help pack up our caravans and field gear we spent most of the following day doing just that before we were ready to roll at about 3.00pm and head to Kulgera for the night.

It would have been very rude not to bid Andrew farewell and thank him for his help during our stay, so our little convoy pulled up beside his large machinery shed. Andrew insisted that we should share a beer with him before departure, which wasn't unexpected, but as the sun was setting around 5.30pm it was looking highly likely that we were going to spend another night there. Just at the critical moment the crusty old head stockman advised that there was a big storm approaching and if we didn't want to spend another week on Tieyon we should leave immediately, so that we did.

It wasn't long before the storm was upon us and the one-and-a half-hour, 85-kilometre route took us the best part of four hours to negotiate as we went slipping and sliding along with the large caravans in tow. I'll always remember one point of the journey where we stopped for a short break on some higher ground. With Jethro Tull blasting from a vehicle, there were about six of us, beers in hand, dancing to "Thick as a Brick" in steady rain while being enthralled by a spectacular 360-degree lightning display. Somewhat incongruous but an amazing, unique and unforgettable bush experience.

Arriving at Kulgera, the first person we encountered at the bar was Paul, Andrew's son, who was returning to Tieyon in a large cattle train after delivering a load of the station's stock. When we described our recent driving experience, he was inclined to spend the night at Kulgera, but after a few more cans of Bundaberg rum and lime, aptly known as "Dark and Stormy", at about midnight he bid us farewell and headed off to Tieyon. I am forever grateful to Mark Flintoft for that last and memorable field experience.

Departing from MESA after 20 years involved a couple of big celebrations, not so much for me as for a few colleagues like Jack Townsend, Max Pain and others who'd spent their entire working lives in the department. Peter ("Cretto") Crettenden was another who chose to take a package to pursue his love of cooking and the Australian outback. He combined providing catering services both in Adelaide and in extended bush camps with a unique outback touring business, "Swagabout Tours". It's hard to reconcile that MESA's Coober Pedy wildman of the early 1980s is now one of Australia's most respected small group outback tour operators.

Early retirement

The first few months of "retirement" at the ripe old age of 54 were most enjoyable and allowed for plenty of reading and wonderful long walks along the spectacular coastal cliff line at Hallett Cove, added to which my blood pressure dropped to acceptable levels, but come early 2002 it was time to move on. Not wanting to get back into the mining industry just then, on a whim I purchased a mobile car cleaning business. Babs was sure that I'd gone stark raving mad; as she rightly pointed out, I never washed my own vehicle. For the next eighteen months or so this was my vocation, and it proved an interesting learning curve in running a small business, in customer relations and in finding my way around the suburbs of Adelaide. In the process I lost over ten kilograms and gained a lot of stamina: although the work wasn't physically demanding it was constant. I learned quite a bit about people too. Most customers were very pleasant and indeed often offered a beer or a wine at the end of the day, but there were always five percent who wanted their pound of flesh and would go over the finished vehicle with a fine-tooth comb to find any shortcomings. Then there was the 0.5 percent you could never please – I learned quickly not to return to such clients.

Sevenhill Cottages

One car cleaning client had a real estate business just beyond the Adelaide parklands, and I'd often pick up one of their brochures with a view to buying an investment property. One evening, scanning through such a brochure, Babs noted that Rosella Cottages at Sevenhill in the Clare Valley was up for sale. We stayed in one of the cottages a year or two earlier and, not having anything on over the weekend, arranged an inspection for the following Saturday. At this point Babs and I had never contemplated, let alone discussed, the possibility of running such an enterprise. Our inspection showed that the business had become somewhat run down since we stayed there, and while the contemporary cottages were passable, the other two conjoined buildings were in a very poor state and were being let cheaply to some of the Valley's younger generation.

It seemed it had been a wasted day, but as always for the Clare Valley a most pleasant visit, so we decided to walk across the road to the adjacent Sevenhill Hotel for a quick drink and snack before returning to Adelaide. At the bar we met the new young publican, Nedd Golding. We could immediately see the positive changes he'd made to the pub since our earlier weekend at Rosella Cottages: the meals were excellent and the bar was buzzing, not at all the sleepy country pub we'd previously encountered. When Nedd advised that the pub had no accommodation and that he wished someone would purchase and upgrade the cottages, his powers of persuasion took over and Babs and I were suddenly listening.

After having Sunday to think it over, we lodged an offer the next day and, once accepted, we were suddenly the proud owners of a business that we had no idea how to run and of buildings that needed more than a little care and maintenance.

The Clare Valley was first settled in 1842, and the township of Sevenhill was surveyed in 1850; the Jesuit-run Sevenhill Monastery and winery about one kilometre east of the township was also established in that year. As the township grew, Irish cabinetmaker Thomas O'Brien built a small stone cottage on the site we'd purchased, and when he became postmaster in 1858, the large front room of the cottage became the township's post office.

Our purchase, covering about one and a half acres, included the original stone cottage and stables, a three-bedroom extension built onto the cottage in the 1940s, plus two contemporary two-bedroom prefabricated cottages added to the property in the 1990s. It also had a profusion of added-on sheds, outhouses, water tanks and a laundry forming a jumbled mess behind the original cottages, which faced onto Main North Road. Everything was run down, and the front cottages were in a squalid state as well as being riddled with salt-damp; the newer cottages only needed a good clean and fresh coat of paint inside and out. The add-on structures simply had to go.

The previous owners had done a wonderful job setting up the accommodation business with the two contemporary cottages back in 1994, but by 2003 they'd simply lost all interest in the enterprise, and a long, cold afternoon spent with them shed little light on the running of the business. There were Babs and I in July 2003 having no idea of the enormity of the task we had set ourselves and only a limited budget to achieve our goals. The very first action was to change the name of the business from "Rosella Cottages", which was now tainted, to "Sevenhill Cottages Accommodation and Conference Centre".

The reno campaign

Getting the contemporary cottages into an acceptable state was our first priority. New bedding and linen were purchased, and we were greatly helped with painting by Bab's aunt and uncle, Arthur and Maureen, who over a period of about a month stayed in each cottage while painting them inside and out. We were also very fortunate to get the services of Suzanne Uppill, a long-time Clare resident, who was contracted to clean and service the cottages as guests came and went. Her knowledge of the industry was incredibly valuable over the years. Although we disagreed on some of the finer details from time to time, we couldn't have successfully run the business from Adelaide, some 130 kilometres away, without her. Babs and I from the outset decided that the cottages must always be prepared to a standard that we'd expect if we were paying customers – I believe this is a vital consideration for all businesses. As a result, over our six-year tenure we personally tested every bed and every other feature in all the cottages.

Once those cottages were up and running, the real work on the older cottages began. Contractors were called in to do the specialised salt-damp treatment and later plastering; a builder and plumber were employed to construct a disabled bathroom and toilet facility, and all the while Babs and I spent our weekends at Sevenhill, cleaning, painting and demolishing most of the unwanted outside "built-ons". Often after a hard day we'd adjourn to the Sevenhill Hotel, where we got to know the locals and what a wonderful community they were. They were delighted that we were renovating what was regarded as a heritage building and would often go out of their way to provide assistance.

Once the cottages were in operation, the working relationship with Nedd was wonderful: he not only kept an eye on the place in our absence but co-opted extra guests for us from some of his weary travellers at the pub. If we had a guest complaint while back in Adelaide, I'd contact Nedd, who'd generally locate a suitable tradesman in his bar to effect an immediate repair. I'd also contact the guest and advise them to head over to the bar and select a bottle of wine of their choice in compensation for any inconvenience caused to them.

While there were setbacks from time to time there were also wonderful surprises. The historic stables were in a state of collapse, and we simply didn't have the funds for proper heritage repair, so a bit of innovation was called for. I called in old mate Kiwi the Coober Pedy opal miner, and we came up with a scheme to build internal retaining walls with sleepers and then pour concrete into the gap. This not only saved the building from collapse but appears to be holding up well to this day, as shown on the "Sevenhill Cottages" website. Kiwi was also a wonderful help to Babs and me with painting the very high ceilings and walls in the 1940s building. A great bonus during renovations was the floorboards throughout the same building. In their degraded state I'd imagined they were just stained pine, but when they were finally sanded and polished, they proved to be stunning dark-red jarrah.

There was a cellar in the front room of the original cottage, although when I first discovered it, it was full of water and needed to have a new pump installed. Nedd also had a wonderful fully stocked cellar and dining area in the pub. With Kiwi, an experienced miner, in tow, I put it to Nedd that we should construct a tunnel under Main North Road between the two cellars. Nedd never came to the party.

To gain accreditation with Tourism SA, we had to submit an extensive strategic plan together with certificates of compliance in all aspects of the business. Our prime key performance indicator was to enjoy the facilities with family and friends, customers and the Sevenhill community, and I believe we achieved this in spades. The original cottage had at some time had a very large Rosella pickles mural painted along one side wall which was a local landmark. When we bought the property, the mural needed some TLC, and in the Sevenhill bar one evening I jokingly said that we were going to paint over the mural as part of our renovations. I was hurriedly taken aside by Richard, a very flamboyant character and long-term resident of Sevenhill, who advised me that Babs and I as proprietors were only short-term caretakers of the property and that we must always look after Sevenhill icons like the Rosella mural. Although the paint-over was said in jest, it brought home to me just how dearly the locals cherished the township's heritage.

Our six years as part of the Sevenhill community were some of our most enjoyable years. Babs worked like a Trojan to get the facilities in shape for the first two years and was then able to relax a bit. I loved every minute of the experience from day one, whether it was chopping a tonne of firewood or fronting my favourite bar, which was unique in having Coopers Sparkling (and Pale Ale) on tap. Nedd ran the pub with aplomb and at that time most of the Clare Valley's vignerons chose it as their watering hole, in large measure due to Cherie, arguably the best barmaid in the world. It didn't matter how full the bar was, Cherie always served customers promptly, in order; no one ever jumped the queue. This same lady could also be very generous on nights when Nedd was absent, serving wine by the brandy glass; on many occasions I was able to ring Babs later back in Adelaide and say truthfully that I'd only consumed two or three glasses of red. I'm not quite sure what this largesse did to Nedd's profits.

Nedd's dad Rob Golding, a part-owner of the pub, had completed some winemaking courses in retirement and managed to negotiate a deal with an elderly ex-seaman and lighthouse keeper to maintain his vineyard at Leasingham for 50 percent of the annual crop. Rob formed a small syndicate which I was lucky enough to be invited to join. Pruning, weeding and picking the crop could be a little demanding at times, but the vineyard was right next door to Claymore Wines cellar door, so after completing a row of vines it was common practice to duck in there for a taste or two before starting the next row. Once harvested we usually had a local winemaker produce the final product, and some of our cabernets and white pedro liqueurs made under Rob's guidance were quite outstanding.

Between the syndicate, mingling with the assembled vignerons at the Sevenhill bar and the fact we were always purchasing wine as part of a complimentary food package provided to guests at the cottages, Sevenhill proved to be six years of wine heaven – added to which most purchases were tax deductible.

Family history discoveries

Before my Mum turned 90 in January 2001, her granddaughter Roslyn Smith sat with her for many hours and compiled a life history, which she presented to Mum in written form on her birthday. There were so many people and events from the past briefly recalled in this that it kindled my interest in family history. Also, sitting in Hallett Cove around the same time, perusing the *Sunday Mail* one weekend, I noticed an ad regarding the 99-year expiry of gravesite leases at the Payneham Cemetery in suburban Adelaide. What caught my eye was the list of names, which included John Scott Earwaker, my great grandfather on my mother's side, who with his wife and two daughters had migrated from Hampshire in England to Adelaide, arriving on 21 July 1854. After visiting the gravesite, I was hooked on researching the Australian family history of John and Mary Earwaker.

This search started to take up a lot of time, but it bore out many facts in Mum's 90th birthday book. This included the fact that one Earwaker granddaughter had married an Afghan cameleer who later was convicted of the shooting murder of another Afghan, north of Marree in SA, and subsequently hanged in the old Adelaide Gaol. It also led to contacts with many long-lost relatives, which culminated in a get-together at Adelaide and Sevenhill in 2004 to commemorate the 150th anniversary of the arrival of John and Mary in Port Adelaide. This was followed by a similar family get-together in Griffith, NSW a year or so later.

At this time one bit of family history remained a mystery, that of the Earwakers' only son Henry (Harry), who had been the first blacksmith in Alice Springs after originally heading to the NT in about 1886 to join the rush to the so-called ruby discovery in the Harts Range. It was known that he died at age 42 in Alice Springs, but he was otherwise a family enigma. Mum thought he might have been murdered – hence the mystery and family secrecy.

Sadly, my Mum died in December 2006, just a month short of her 96th birthday. What a grand old lady she was, humble and kind, with a somewhat wicked sense of humour. She had a fabulous memory and was still a very competitive Scrabble, Rummikub and Uno player up to a few days before her death. She'd also been very much the matriarch of the family since my Dad, Harold's death back in 1981.

It was only a couple of years later that I did an internet search of "Earwaker" plus "Alice Springs", and to my surprise the names Mary and Rose Earwaker emerged from an old census of part-aboriginal people in the NT. Both Christian names were common Earwaker family names, and the surname is so uncommon in Australia that they just had to be Harry's children. Subsequent enquiries revealed that Harry had married an indigenous lady, Alice Ngalia, and they'd lived at the Alice Springs Telegraph Station for many years. Harry died of typhoid fever in Alice Springs in 1903.

We'll never know whether Harry ever told his parents about his family, or whether they knew of the family but didn't publicly acknowledge it, but it seems apparent that Harry was a loving father who instilled the need for education in his descendants. Mary Earwaker went on to marry William (Bill) Liddle, a pioneering Central Australian pastoralist, and from that union there's a very large Liddle family centered in Alice Springs which is arguably one of the most accomplished part-indigenous families in Australia today.

It's been a pleasure subsequently to meet several family members in Alice Springs and Adelaide, and I can only imagine how delighted my Mum would have been to meet her cousins Mary and Rose Earwaker, but it just wasn't to be. I was so pleased to resolve the mystery of Harry Earwaker, and I believe the Liddles were equally pleased to fill a gap in their ancestry. Old Harry the blacksmith would be an incredibly proud man.

Family history activities also extended to the Newton family on my father, Harold Newton's side of the family. In 2010 at Engadine on Sydney's southern outskirts we had a large family gathering to celebrate the centenary of my grandparents', Alfred and Emma Newton's, arrival in Australia from Stockport, near Manchester in England. My then last surviving aunt, 90-year-old Helen Newton, together with two of my cousins, Andrew and Jean Newton, compiled both a detailed family tree and a 200-plus-page book detailing the Newton family history for the occasion.

My aim is to complete a similar compilation for the John and Mary Earwaker family in Australia but completing the book you're now reading has got in the way. What I now realise is that committing to family history research leaves you with a never-ending legacy – the more facts you unearth the more there is to research – but it's a most rewarding pastime.

25

Diamonds are a Boy's Best Friend

South Australia, 2000s

In early 2005, having completed essential renovations at Sevenhill and after selling the mobile car cleaning business a year earlier, I decided it was time to venture back into my real love, the minerals industry. Having prepared a CV, I was about to start looking for work when I got an invitation to lunch from an old industry colleague, Kevin Wills. By the end of lunch Kevin had offered me a job as tenement manager with Flinders Diamonds Ltd (Flinders), of which he was the managing director. After a pleasant lunch and a good red wine, it was easy to say yes.

Little did I know what I was getting into, but over the next six and a half years it turned out to be one of the most enjoyable and rewarding jobs and a great way to finish my industry career. I had a broad understanding of mineral tenure in SA only from my years with MESA, but no hands-on experience, and I'm forever indebted to Teena Coppin, my predecessor at Flinders, who'd set up transparent procedures for many tenement administration activities. My first eighteen months with Flinders was a steep learning curve with a number of glitches along the way.

A "part-time" job

Tenement management is the poor relation in the mineral exploration and mining process. It's vital to maintain secure mineral title over exploration prospects, mineral deposits and mines, but exploration and mining teams simply expect this to happen in the background with a minimum of fuss. Of course, if tenure is in any way compromised, heads will roll. When I arrived at Flinders the company held 50 exploration tenements, mainly in South Australia, with minor holdings in Western Australia and the Northern Territory. At its peak about five years later, Flinders together with a stable of new related companies held almost 250 mineral tenements, including mining production titles in Queensland.

I'd agreed to working just three days per week on tenement administration with Flinders and answered directly to Kevin. It was very satisfying to be able to complete the job in hand each day and head home without any of the worries of management, particularly people management. Little did I realise then that my work would extend beyond tenement management to roles in environmental management, conduct of aboriginal heritage surveys, native title negotiations, preparing draft legal agreements, technical report writing, editing press releases, and to be a father figure to some junior geoscientific staff and sounding-board and occasional Boy Friday to Kevin. All this while eventually reporting to three CEOs. The work was always fun and exciting, and coincided with what was probably Australia's biggest-ever mining and mineral exploration boom as demand from China reached an all-time high.

Flinders was very successful at finding diamonds, particularly in SA, where the company located diamond occurrences on Flinders Island, off the west coast of Eyre Peninsula; Echunga in the Adelaide Hills; various sites in the Flinders Ranges including the Springfield Basin south of Hawker; and at Algebuckina and near the Peake and Denison Ranges in the remote northeast of the State. When Kevin resigned as managing director of Flinders some years later, he handed me a large container to look after and deliver to the new incumbent, saying it contained

$10 million worth of diamonds. What he meant was that it had cost Flinders $10 million to find these diamonds, which were predominantly microdiamonds. They had some residual value as a reference collection but absolutely no gemstone value.

It was only a few months after I joined Flinders that the metallic mineral assets of its exploration tenements were floated off to a new company, Maximus Resources Ltd (Maximus), so named because there was a Maximus coffee poster on the wall of the restaurant where the Flinders directors had recently dined. With a small staff, from Kevin down, we all spent long days for a week or so putting together prospectus material for the impending float. Only a year after the successful Maximus float, a uranium exploration company, Eromanga Uranium Ltd (Eromanga), was also successfully launched in October 2006. Suddenly our delightful heritage office mansion in Norwood housed three managing directors and about 20 geoscientific personnel plus ancillary drafting and clerical staff. With a combined annual exploration budget of about $10 million and still only one tenement officer, my comfortable three-day week was rapidly blowing out to almost double.

Two gold mines

Some challenging projects and experiences arose from these expansions. In the Adelaide Hills Maximus set about reevaluating the historic Bird-In-Hand goldmine near Woodside. An inability to pump water from the underground workings had led to closure of the historic mine, leaving much residual gold in place. By the mid-2000s most surrounding land holdings were hobby farms, plus the immediately adjacent Bird In Hand Winery – a NIMBY paradise. Maximus undertook extensive drilling programs and groundwater studies to prove up a significant gold deposit which could be mined with minimal noise and ground disturbance, and no compromise to the surrounding groundwater table and local environment. This opened a can of worms with the newly entrenched locals;

public meetings abounded and unwanted delays ensued. Maximus eventually sold the property to another mining company, who have persisted to the point where after almost 20 years the grant of a mining lease appears imminent. What other industry faces such never-ending hurdles? Certainly not the scenery-destroying wind farm industry. I note that in the early years Maximus maintained an excellent relationship with the nearby winery, regularly sampling its wares and using its products on many occasions.

Maximus also acquired a small operating alluvial goldmine west of Collinsville in Queensland. The previous owners, Allan Stiff and Colleen Budge, led a rather idyllic existence on the Sellheim mine site, if you don't mind isolation. They gleaned a good living from sporadically collecting near-surface gold nuggets and lived in a comfortable home complete with fruit and vegetable garden perched atop a prominent hill which provided a panoramic view of the surrounding area and also made the most of any cool breezes. The Sellheim river ran through the property, providing a more than adequate source of potable water.

Maximus purchased the property with a view to creating a cash flow to fund ongoing exploration programs, but unfortunately the alluvial mining operation failed to deliver. It was an interesting project while it lasted, with alluvial material scraped and processed, after which a gold detector was used to recover gold nuggets from the soft underlying rocks. This was an exciting process for visitors like me – when handed the detector it wasn't uncommon to quickly locate several good-sized gold nuggets. Maximus decided not to process the nuggets but to market them intact online. This meant transporting them back to Adelaide, and it was quite an experience to carry these nuggets in our hand luggage. I was always amazed at how brightly the nuggets glowed as they went through airport hand luggage detecting devices but was never questioned about my cargo.

Ups and downs

Once the three companies were up and running we instigated annual think tanks involving all staff. The first two were held at Sevenhill Cottages and included some interesting evening sessions at the Sevenhill Hotel and wonderful conference dinners at the Skillogallee Winery. During the daytime sessions there were presentations on all major projects and at the final session participants rated the potential of all projects. The iron ore component of exploration tenements held in the Pilbara region of WA was rated as the poorest project at our first conference. How things can change in the mineral industry due to supply and demand and other factors: at the next annual conference this project jumped to the top of the ratings.

Flinders raised and spent tens of millions of dollars and defined a billion-tonne iron ore resource in the Pilbara over a few short years – they were indeed exciting times. After I'd departed for sunny Queensland, a major Russian steel producer offered to buy the project for a princely sum, but this transaction was subsequently quashed at the last minute by intervention which, who knows, may have involved Mr Putin himself. With a sharp decline in iron ore demand in the early 2010s, a very large family-owned New Zealand company, Todd Corporation, acquired Flinders, now rebadged Flinders Mines Ltd, for a much-reduced sum in a classic case of easy come, easy go. The project remains the largest undeveloped iron ore resource in the Pilbara region, and in 2024 Flinders was rebadged as Red Hawk Mining Ltd. Fortecue Ltd the large iron ore producer acquired the project in 2025.

Three characters

Kevin Wills stands out as the outstanding character from this period in my career. A big man with a few health problems, he was young and fit when I first met him in Darwin many years earlier. Kevin lives geology and mineral exploration, but also knows how to relax when the occasion beckons. I can't think of a better managing director for a company, as he always gave 100 percent for his shareholders. When Flinders was just about technically insolvent Kevin would rush off to Europe and convince certain major backers to invest more. His stamina was incredible, heading off after finishing work on Friday, meeting the European investors and usually returning to the Flinders office by early the next week. He's also a mine finder, having worked with the Argyle diamond discovery team and later leading a team in SA which made the first major gold discovery in that state in the 20th century (apart from Olympic Dam), the Challenger gold deposit.

Bob Kennedy was the chairman of all three companies but was someone that I didn't particularly like. I should have, because it was him taking a dislike to the previous tenement manager that resulted in me getting the job. Bob was an astute accountant and businessman and had a flair for raising funds for new mining floats through his extensive business networking. He was responsible for developing two very successful resource companies, Beach Energy Ltd and Ramelius Resources Ltd. He acquired Beach as a result of protracted litigation and from that seemed to have a penchant for calling the lawyers in whenever disputes arose. It was amazing how easily many of these disputes were resolved over a long lunch or with a phone call or meeting to clear up certain misunderstandings without going down the legal route, saving thousands in legal fees. Likewise, many legal agreements were compiled in house from free online templates and only vetted at the last minute by our legal consultants, again saving thousands. Given my ironic, dry sense of humour and stirring ability, coupled with Bob's somewhat Methodist principles, I chose to be as invisible to him as possible to circumvent any potential confrontations.

Mark Creasy is a WA mining entrepreneur who in the last year or two has reportedly joined the billionaires club. He has stakes in many listed companies and junior mineral explorers. He was a backer and stakeholder in Maximus in those days, and at one time Kevin Wills and I were lucky enough to visit his home, which was set in a beautiful location by the Swan River between Perth and Fremantle. What really impressed me was his collection of minerals and space memorabilia. The mineral collection is world class, and his collection of parts from Skylab, the United States' first space station, which finally crashed in Western Australia and the Indian Ocean in July 1979, is second to none. What Skylab debris Mark didn't collect himself on treks into the WA countryside, he seems to have acquired from other parties subsequently. On our visit Mark struck me as a quiet, unassuming sort of person who like any good Australian shouted us to a beer and a wine or two during our visit.

The 2000s saw an unprecedented mining and investment boom in Australia (one some thought was never ending), mainly driven by Chinese demand for raw materials. This led to the listing of many junior mineral explorers and extremely generous salaries and other perks for many. I'm happy to say that Flinders, Maximus and Eromanga were well managed by their respective CEOs, who ensured the vast majority of shareholder funds were spent on meaningful mineral exploration. In today's mad world of executive salaries and bonuses, the only minor criticism I have is that some share allocations given as bonuses to non-executive directors seemed a bit excessive in relation to their input.

The post-Kevin years at Flinders were interesting to say the least, with the emergence of the very large Pilbara iron project. The new CEO was anxious to make his mark and held a one-day love-in soon after taking the role. I should mention here that while I worked for the Flinders stable I realised that, one, I was getting older and two, I was paid at an hourly rate so long lunches were no longer an option. I was a little surprised at the love-in when the new CEO announced a zero alcohol policy and went on to say, "If you have any alcohol at lunch DO NOT come back to work," while staring directly at me. I couldn't help myself, looking back at him and asking where the innovation was in this as I'd adhered to this policy for the whole of my working life. He seemed a little lost for words.

The Flinders Pilbara iron project had reached the stage where a major pre-feasibility study was required by banks before any project funding was forthcoming. Such studies are by tradition undertaken by large engineering consultants at what

I regard as exorbitant prices. It was interesting then to attend a couple of meetings in Perth with our feasibility study consultants. For each project the consultant company appoints a team of specialists who gradually tick off a project recipe book to complete the expensive study. What concerned me at these meetings was that after 40-plus years in the industry I realised that I had greater knowledge in several fields than these so-called specialists. I suspect that I'd become even more of a cynic and was displaying the first signs of becoming a grumpy old man in those final work years.

26

A Bridge-Playing Grandad; Never a Queenslander

Queensland 2011 to present

Babs and I had a winter holiday in Queensland in 2009 which included a few days at a beachfront apartment at Peregian Beach on the Sunshine Coast. Not long afterwards Babs announced that she was moving to Peregian Beach, and I could come if I wanted. As my older daughter, Teneille, was living there by then and Emma, then in WA, was also planning to settle there, the decision was a no-brainer.

On a Saturday in early September 2010 Babs took off for the Sunshine Coast to look at a house she'd picked out online. It turned out this was not quite up to scratch in real life, but Teneille quickly found another suitable but cheaper option, and a contract was signed late Saturday afternoon. We rented the house out for twelve months while we made our plans to move. By November 2011 we'd sold our Hallett Cove home, Babs had resigned from her position as a kindergarten director and I ceased to operate what had by then become a mineral tenement consultancy.

On our arrival in December 2011, Peregian Beach proved to be a delightful and relatively quiet village just ten kilometres south of the more noted Noosa. Beautiful beaches and coastal walks were the norm and the area was very well serviced with a multitude of nice restaurants and all the facilities of much larger cities. The open surf beaches were more amenable to board riding than body surfing, my great love, which was a tad disappointing.

On the family front, son Ben and his partner had a daughter, Hurley, in November 2011, just before we left Adelaide, which made leaving that bit harder. The following November, 2012, our elder daughter Teneille was married to Tony O'Brien in a most spectacular double temple and sunset beach ceremony on the island of Koh Samui in Thailand, an event thoroughly enjoyed by all attendees. Son Caine, then a novice flier, particularly enjoyed the flight to Thailand, where he was seated between two very attractive young ladies. Turned out they were strippers headed to Thailand for boob jobs; Caine has loved flying ever since, and the ladies serendipitously returned to Australia again on the same flight as Caine and were able to show him the finished work.

Later, in 2015, our younger daughter Emma was married to Grant Fowler on the foreshore of the beautiful Noosa River. The ceremony was originally to be held in the open at Noosa Woods, but a near-cyclonic storm meant plan B, a relocation to a covered outdoor area. Despite the weather gods, the ceremony and subsequent reception at Sunshine Beach were a memorable if somewhat damp occasion.

There have also been some sad times, with the death of my beloved sister Wendy in early 2014 after a courageous battle with lung cancer. She managed a lunch and a riesling or two with her daughters only a day before her death. Her husband Bill followed soon after, worn out but working on his very successful business and horse racing interests until the very end. Later that year Auntie Helen, the last of the second generation of the Newton family in Australia, also passed away, and I should mention that Reg Gasnier, a childhood hero and one of the St

George Rugby League Club's greatest champions, also died in 2014 – it could be described as an "annus horribilus".

So, what did I do in retirement as thoughts of endless bodysurfing quickly evaporated? I continued with a little mineral tenement work gratis for two Adelaide mates who were attempting to launch another mineral exploration company. Unfortunately, after two to three years this project failed, although I did score a couple of nice lunches and an excellent carton of red wine for my troubles. Digitising my photo collection was another early activity, with over 20,000 images scanned and upgraded.

A new addiction

In early 2012 I noticed an advert for Bridge lessons at the Noosa Bridge Club and enrolled. I'd played lunchtime bridge in Darwin over 30 years ago, but new bidding systems meant relearning everything. The two, very good instructors were like chalk and cheese: the older Bev Salter was very schoolmarmish but astute in her approach and had in fact been a schoolteacher. Lizzie French, the tall, blond instructor hailing originally from Zimbabwe, was loud and flamboyant, in fact she forever entertains us with her chic but very colourful outfits and her opinions on all matters.

By mid-year I was hooked and playing bridge at least three times a week. It's a wonderful game where you forever continue to learn and exercise your brain cells. It has also been something of a social institution for me, with over 300 club members of diverse backgrounds from all over Australia and beyond. In fact, that's one of the joys of the Sunshine Coast – no Queenslanders (I jest) – just like Darwin 40 years earlier, everyone comes from somewhere else. It's interesting that the demographic of the Noosa region is rather like that of Sydney or Melbourne in the 1950s – dare I suggest it may be a reason why people are attracted to the area. My wife Babs considers me something of a bridge fanatic these days, with regular sessions interspersed with weekend competitions and an annual week-long congress on the Gold Coast, but I'm an absolute novice compared with a core group of members who regularly play six to seven days a week.

Babs on Great Palm Island

Before leaving Adelaide, Babs had applied for and been appointed as a kindergarten teacher at an elite private school. She quickly discovered that an early focus seemed to be on cultivating the parents rather than concentrating on the children. This was anathema to her work culture, so there was a mutual parting of ways within a few months. After that she had regular but always uncertain work as a relief teacher in the state primary school system. I was somewhat taken aback then on my return from the week-long Gold Coast Bridge Congress in February 2016, when she advised that she'd applied for a permanent teaching position on Palm Island, near Townsville.

Palm Island, or more correctly Great Palm Island (GPI), is the largest of a group of islands named the Palm Isles by Captain Cook in 1770. These tropical islands are idyllic, with Orpheus Island, another of the group, hosting one of the Great Barrier Reef's most exclusive tourist destinations. GPI however has a checkered history, starting with the removal of most of the remaining original Manbarra people to the mainland in the 1890s. The island was gazetted as an Aboriginal Reserve in 1914 and from 1918 through most of the twentieth century it became a dumping ground for indigenous people displaced or forcibly removed from all over Queensland. It's troubled history includes the 1930 Palm Island Tragedy, when the first superintendent appears to have gone berserk in a deadly shooting and burning spree which eventually led to his being shot by his own subordinates; the 1957 strike to protest the working conditions imposed by the Queensland Government on island inhabitants; and the more recent 2004 death in custody. GPI was unfairly labelled "the most violent place on earth outside a combat zone" in the 1999 edition of the Guiness Book of Records.

In accepting the teaching position, Babs had little idea what to expect when she first set foot on the island in March 2016. Housed with two other female teachers not far from the school, her first impressions of GPI were good: it was indeed a beautiful tropical island, the people were generally friendly and helpful, and she loved her new young students. School attendance was a bit sporadic, not surprising when the island offered so many other wonderful outdoor attractions, and students were generally well behaved on campus.

It was the weekends that brought out the problems. Apparently sound systems in many houses were turned to full blast on a Friday night and remained at that level, often for the entire weekend. As weekend parties progressed there was often behaviour apparent that wouldn't be tolerated in normal suburbia. Police only ever interceded if extreme violence was anticipated, preferring to let things (and people) sort themselves out. This is probably a legacy of the 2004 death in custody issue and the very protracted litigation which followed. The problem was, if you didn't own a small boat or couldn't afford weekends in Townsville or further afield, there was little option but to put up with the shenanigans. Despite this Babs never felt personally threatened during her residence there. After just a few short months she managed to get a transfer to Mt Isa, a remote mining city almost 1000 kilometres inland from Townsville.

I never managed to get to GPI while Babs was there but did a little research on the place. Years ago, when living in Darwin there was a bad joke going around about how indigenous issues in the that city could be solved by moving all indigenous people to one of the Wessel Islands, off northeast Arnhem Land and flying in regular loads of grog and metho. One can't help but draw the analogy between this and the situation on GPI, where boatloads of illicit grog and drugs are said to be regularly delivered from the mainland. One can only hope the largely self-run community on GPI can overcome these problems and deliver a more stable life to future generations on this island paradise.

Mt Isa revisited

Mt Isa could also have presented problems given that Babs had never lived in a remote area, but she took to her work and the city like a duck to water. Over her three-and-a-half-year stay, 2016–19, she came to love her students, her school and indeed many of the friendly long-term citizens of this outback mining town. She also became heavily involved as stage manager for the Mt Isa Theatrical Society, which kept her rather busy.

The city has delightful warm weather for eight months of the year but come summer it is bloody hot: in 2018 there were a staggering 67 days where the maximum temperature exceeded 40 degrees centigrade. This record was upstaged by one day in 2019; in January of that year the temperature exceeded 40 for a record 23 days. This was followed by a two-week rain event which led to major flooding and unusually cool conditions resulting in the death of an estimated half a million livestock (mainly cattle) in the northwest Queensland region. Driving south from Mt Isa to Winton soon after, I've never witnessed such death and destruction, with dead animals littering the paddocks. Amazingly there were large herds of very healthy-looking cattle in isolated spots that had survived annihilation, and the countryside was already very green after the deluge.

In the nearly 50 years since I first worked in the Mt Isa region the city has changed considerably. In 1969 the city boasted a population of around 40,000 and had quite a multicultural population, several good restaurants and large clubs which reflected this multiculturism, thriving sporting clubs and a far better daily jet air service provided by Ansett and TAA than is available today. It was also a tad Wild West, and everything was very expensive, especially fresh fruit and vegetables. Today the population has dwindled to under 20,000, the multicultural aspect has largely disappeared with the next generations, and there's now a much larger indigenous population. The latter change is mainly a result of the much-heralded 1968 equal wage decision for indigenous station workers, who were in turn moved off stations en masse to towns and cities like Mt Isa, resulting in major social upheaval and ongoing unemployment and welfare problems.

The reduction in population can almost totally be blamed on workplace policies at Mt Isa mine sites first instigated in the 1990s, where in the name of enhanced productivity daily shift hours were increased to twelve hours and recently shifts increased to a seven-day on-off schedule. This has encouraged many to move to the coast and work on a fly in–fly out basis. Consequently, social and sporting pursuits in the town have been blighted and services in general are much reduced. For example, a Mt Isa rugby league team can field a premiership-winning side one week and struggle to field a side at all the next. One aspect of life that has improved dramatically over 50 years is the price and availability of foodstuffs, also vehicle fuel and servicing. While marginally dearer than capital cities it is no longer two or three times the cost. Despite the reduced population, Babs and I found social life congenial, but perhaps a 20 to 30-year-old would disagree. It was also interesting to note the large senior population of the city today; many long-term residents have opted to stay on in retirement despite the scorching summers.

When I first went to Mt Isa in 1969, I saw some of the local countryside on the drive out to project areas but of Mt Isa itself I mainly saw the various bars of the Barkly Hotel and my motel room with an occasional visit to Lake Moondarra. During the 2016–19 stay I got to see a great deal more of the often-spectacular countryside, which I believe rivals that of Alice Springs and the MacDonnell Ranges. Indeed, the rugged ranges encountered on the highway between Mt Isa and Cloncurry provide what must be one of the most underrated arid scenic drives in Australia, although you do need to keep a lookout for the monstrous B-triple ore road trains which constantly use this road. Some of the man-made and natural water features in the area were also a constant delight, particularly the magnificent Boodjamulla (Lawn Hill Gorge) about 250 kilometres north of Mt Isa. Having first visited the gorge in 1976 when there wasn't another person or vehicle to be seen, it was a delight to return several times during our recent sojourn in Mt Isa and enjoy the serenity of the gorge while staying in the small national park run campsite. Fortunately, most tourists are channelled into the nearby Adels Grove area, which provides more amenities. Unprecedented flooding in 2023 has sadly caused major damage to Boodjamulla, and much of the riverside flora will take years to recover.

The changes since 1976 at the nearby Gregory River on the way into Boodjamulla are a little more disconcerting. The little country pub has changed little, but the riverside itself is overrun every day in the dry season by a plague of tourists in big 4WDs and bigger caravans vying for camp spots. It's such a shame to see an idyllic spot despoiled in such a manner.

Mt Isa is so far away from everywhere else that road distances suddenly pale into insignificance and so during our stay in Mt Isa there were quite a few other trips through northern and central Queensland, with highlights Carnarvon Gorge, the Undara lava caves and Karumba. There were also quick trips to Tennant Creek and Alice Springs, and once again it was interesting to visit old watering holes like the Barrow Creek pub.

Grandad

During our time at Mt Isa things rapidly changed back at Peregian Beach. When we left it was a relatively quiet and laid-back coastal village, but on regular visits home it was apparent that it was rapidly evolving into a bustling township driven by major new land developments at the Peregian Breeze and Peregian Springs estates. A decision was made to sell up and seek a quieter lifestyle in mid-2019. It was hard in some ways for Babs because she saw the house at Peregian Beach as her dream home.

We eventually settled on a smaller, single-storey home in the sleepy little hinterland hamlet of Pomona, about 20 kilometres inland from Noosa. It's still relatively close to Babs's work at Noosaville and only 25 minutes from the Noosa Bridge Club (Wokky's work as grandson Koa calls it). Emma giving birth to Koa in mid-1916 (just as the move to Mt Isa was made), followed three years later by his sister Ochre Kit round Easter 2019, were two of the most exciting events of the latter half of the 2010s for us, though I fear Wokky is going to have trouble keeping up over the next few years. Son Caine, back in Adelaide and his wife have very recently blessed us with another granddaughter, Bridie, this year.

Our home at Pomona is situated on a large suburban block which had bare lawns when we arrived. In four years, Babs has converted it to a lush tropical garden with minor help from me. The lifestyle is fairly laid back but like the rest of the Sunshine Coast it is being loved to death by the influx of new arrivals (including us); the larger towns are becoming nearly as busy as many cities and I wonder if this bit of paradise can retain its unique nature under the strains of massive population growth. Perhaps somewhere like Charleville, 800 kilometres west of here, may have to be our next move to escape the rat race, but we are enjoying it while we can.

Living in Adelaide for thirty years I was largely deprived of watching rugby league for much of that time. Since moving to Queensland my winter televiewing is dominated by the game and particularly the annual "State of Origin" series. This brings out the worst of Queensland parochialism. Born and bred a NSW "cockroach", I can never become a "Queenslander".

Reflections

Dear Reader, you'll have to bear with me through this concluding chapter as I vent my frustrations on issues, many of which have troubled me all my adult life. As a bit of a loner, I'm not one to join mass demonstrations for many of the worthy causes which are espoused; rather I've preferred to goad individuals and institutions off my own bat where I've perceived injustices – in some cases this may have been ill-conceived, for which I offer my apologies. Pomposity, aka arrogance/self-importance/pretentiousness, has been a source of great annoyance. I've always been a bit of a sucker for the underdog, and that, added to an inherent stirring gene and heaps of testosterone buoyed by sexual frustration due to the many extended periods in the bush in my younger days, have led to much of the larrikinism.

The mining industry

Reading this book, you may get the impression that my life and work have been one long bacchanalian orgy, but in fact some hard work has been undertaken. Life in the mineral exploration industry has involved long periods working in some of the more isolated and hostile environments in the country. Many would simply hate such a lifestyle, but I've found that most of my work colleagues, like me, have loved working in such an environment, sleeping and living rough under the stars and at times scorching sun but always delighting in the flora, the fauna and the stunning and subtle changes in the colours of the various landscapes and skies whether they be in arid deserts or tropical rainforests.

While people may be few and far between in many of these places, those who choose to live permanently in the bush, the country, the back of beyond (whatever you want to call it) include some of the great Australian characters, and it has been a pleasure to meet some of these over the years. As for people who work in the mineral exploration industry, they've been nothing but a delightful group to work and interact with over the years. Chance meetings in remote areas with other explorers may have involved a beer or two at the time but have led to so many lifelong friendships. The transitory nature of the industry means you may not catch up with people for years after, but I've always found the comradeship has changed little whenever there's a later encounter. You also come to rely implicitly on your colleagues when in the bush.

I'm delighted and proud to have spent the bulk of my life working in the mining industry. The population at large tend to take it for granted, but I believe the car sticker I compiled in response to a petulant Nimby sticker stating "You can't eat Coal; you can't drink Gas" states the industry's importance emphatically. It was "Can't Eat, Can't Drink, Can't Live without Mining". This is a statement of fact in our modern world.

Despite mining providing so many necessities of modern day life, the industry has and continues to be the "kicking boy" of the media and many uninformed "environmental" lobbyists, and for some strange reason its attempts to portray itself in a good light are generally half-hearted and fall on deaf ears. Perhaps the only truly successful and lasting promotion of mining was De Beers' "a diamond is forever" – and let's face it, diamonds probably aren't a basic necessity of modern life. I'd argue that most people involved in the mining industry are far better informed on environmental issues than the general public, particularly those involved in mineral exploration, who love and care for all aspects of the Australian bush.

To put things slightly in perspective, a north Queensland landowner recently cleared more land in a few months than the total footprint that the Australian mining industry has impacted in the 200-plus years since European colonisation of Australia. Another great example of the rampant clearing going on in Australia right now is evident on the highway between Emerald and Alpha, near the Drummond Range in central-west Queensland, for the sake of running a few extra cattle. The country's already showing signs of major erosion and the impact of this clearing on climate change is probably far greater than the impact of opening and running a new coal mine in the area. Does anyone really question this? Of course not, it's an agricultural pursuit so it must be okay. Likewise, the windfarm industry has been allowed to despoil vast areas of Australian vistas , often with no more than local council approval for their massive and very visual projects. Mining has made mistakes and caused unnecessary pollution and land degradation, but it pales into insignificance compared to the devastation wreaked by uncontrolled farm and land development clearing. Mining is the major contributor to Australia's standard of living today and without it we'd surely have become Paul Keating's "Banana Republic". The industry has very little to apologise for.

Just to finish on this subject I must mention uranium, where the poorly informed efforts of groups of so-called "Greenies", aided by the country's lunatic left, saw a scare campaign against the mining of uranium, the development of nuclear power and the storage of the world's nuclear waste which was so successful that it has deprived Australia of literally trillions of dollars of income over the past 40 years. All I can say to them is Shame, Shame!

Indigenous issues

In more than 40 years of working in the mining industry with extended periods in the outback, I've had many positive interactions with indigenous people. There has been appalling treatment of Australia's indigenous population ever since the First Fleet settled in Sydney Cove almost 240 years ago. We can't change history, but we can improve the lives of today's indigenous population. However, a major stumbling block is that they now represent a small minority group in 21st-century mainstream Australia despite their very long history of settlement on the continent. The result of the recent "Voice" referendum very much bears out their minority status and relevance.

Have things improved much for our indigenous population in the last 50 years? From my observation the answer is a resounding no. Yes, there have been major legislative breakthroughs commencing in 1948 with a right to citizenship, followed in 1962 by a right to vote and later a right to equal pay and in turn indigenous land rights of a sort. These events have resulted in a resurgence of pride in indigenous culture but in terms of material wealth have greatly benefitted a tiny elite group but overall have provided few real and lasting benefits. Visit some of the outback indigenous communities today and you see kids who can observe via media how the rest of the world (supposedly) lives but are themselves condemned to essentially no future if they stay where they are, while with little or no education their prospects of surviving in the larger world are close to zero. I was particularly saddened about 25 years ago when travelling with Mark Flintoft on a work trip west of Coober Pedy. We came across a broken-down cattle truck from Mabel Creek station which had been carrying about 50 people, mainly young children, in the back (cattle) section. There they were stranded, just on dusk, with little food or water and no warm clothing to get them through a cold desert night. Surely, we can do better than this in the 21st century.

A "Voice" is not the answer. Indigenous people are if anything over-represented at the federal, state and community support level throughout Australia, but this hasn't yet provided any long-term solutions. Through Paul Keating's somewhat rushed introduction of land rights legislation we've developed an horrendous "Voice" system where if land rights exist indigenous people have a say in every development proposal throughout Australia. The mining and mineral exploration industry have borne the brunt of this for the past 30 years or so, paying often exorbitant fees for cultural clearance surveys and huge amounts in land rights royalties, so much so that these have almost become de facto welfare payments. As the land rights "Voice" moves into other mainstream projects for infrastructure and non-mining commercial developments, the general public will realise just how powerful and expensive the current indigenous "Voice" is in every aspect of our society.

Encouraging indigenous people to return to living on their lands offers few, if any viable hopes and opportunities for the younger indigenous population. The "Stolen" generation suffered greatly from the usually well-intentioned but ill-conceived and poorly applied integration policies of the past, but the majority survived, and with the benefit of education combined with sheer grit and hard work, many went on to establish themselves as the indigenous leaders of today. I fear today's young indigenous people, with their lack of opportunities, hopelessness, high levels of incarceration, abuse of drugs and alcohol and lack of meaningful education, may become known as the "Dead" generation.

Education is the key to success for indigenous people but it will still be a long and drawn-out process. The critical issue that needs to be addressed with urgency is the appalling racial prejudice of almost all Australians towards our indigenous population. This prejudice was brought home to me at an indigenous culture workshop I attended, again about 25 years ago. The indigenous workshop convenor asked each of the attendees to compile an honest list of adjectives to describe indigenous people. The words drunk, dirty, violent and lazy headed the list. For the next two days she and her associates did their best to convince us otherwise and I think they at least partly succeeded.

If we, as Australians, can't recognise and overcome our prejudices (exacerbated in recent years through an influx of migrants who are even more racially prejudiced) any bright and meaningful future for the majority of our indigenous population is highly unlikely. It's up to every Australian to determinedly show more compassion, understanding, love and friendship to our indigenous kinfolk, otherwise we will deny them a future.

The other huge problem to be overcome by the indigenous community is that of ingrained welfare dependence. Any needy person who has relied on welfare for an extended period understands just how hard it is to break out of the welfare cycle, but in the case of many indigenous communities that cycle is endemic through multiple generations. The Australian community needs to provide every assistance to try and break this vicious cycle.

While I applaud the rebadging of many of Australia's landmarks with their indigenous names, such as Uluru and K'gari, two relatively new established practices, "Acknowledgement of Country" and "Welcome to Country", may prove counterproductive in breaking down prejudices toward the indigenous community. The first is fine when used as a simple acknowledgement of indigenous people's prior settlement in Australia, but when such terms as "we respect all Elders, past, present and future" are used it borders on the absurd. We're happy to denigrate great European Elders such as Captain James Cook but in the same breath respect ALL indigenous Elders – what errant nonsense. Regarding the "Welcome", it's wearing a bit thin for many non-indigenous Australians, who simply do not like being welcomed to their own country, regardless of previous ownership. We're gradually dispensing with prayers, salutes and anthems before many gatherings, and perhaps "Welcomes" should go the same way.

A few social gripes

I've had it in for the legal profession and the clergy for most of my adult life. Over millennia these professions have managed to elevate their standings in the broader community to ridiculous levels, and in the case of the former with exaggerated monetary rewards to go with it. I do acknowledge that they've done an exceptional job in selling their perceived value to society and are ably assisted in the modern world by the film industry's portrayal of their attributes.

With apologies to friends in the legal profession and much of the good done by that profession, I simply fail to understand why their services are so avidly sought when they so often rely on confrontation, and gain results, not based on what is right and just, but on precedent and legal argument. Why do legal professionals always head up commissions of enquiry? Surely in many instances there are much more qualified professionals to investigate and report on specific issues. I could go on but fear it will do little to change the status quo. I freely admit to being in contempt.

Likewise, while many in the clergy carry out lifetime works of wonderful pastoral care, they also rely on horrendous stories of heaven and hell to keep their flock in check, often scaring children beyond belief. Yet these same people are seen as model citizens who are often the first invited to sit on management committees for school and community groups. What special skills do they bring with them I wonder?

The modern American-inspired business world has brought many furphies along with it, and I'd like to address a few. Human Resources is the first of these. When I commenced work the human resources people were there to assist all staff in every way they could, and they did. Forty years later human resources groups are largely a recruitment tool, and a poor one at that, and seem to have a set role of creating conflict among established staff leading to alienation and resentment.

The rise of self-promoters and the ubiquitous MBA – they seem to go hand in hand – is another source of angst. So many of today's CEOs are wonderful at selling their own abilities but have little or no knowledge or experience in the industry they work in and no concept of long-term investment. They generally proceed not only to strip their company of its assets but its very soul, leaving a shattered shell in their wake. They award themselves obscene salaries and bonuses but then abandon the company to move on to their next victim through their MBA-inspired network of colleagues.

Strategic plans have been around a long time and are a vital component of business. However, when the resources used in developing and maintaining a strategic plan lead to shortcomings in day-to-day operations, something is inherently wrong. From my own experiences I believe many institutions, particularly government departments, have gone down this path to their detriment.

As for occupational health and safety, what an incredible growth industry. I accept there was a need for substantial change in past practices, but the industry has gone overboard. This industry attracts the "wannabee policemen" in droves, just as children's institutions have always attracted pedophiles. This attraction to the OH&S industry spawns the classic "big frog" so cogently described in Slim Dusty's song "Big Frogs in Little Puddles". The intent of legislation meant to improve workplace OH&S is no doubt a good thing, but the way it's often put into practice by the "big frogs" at times borders on insanity. Recently I observed a ratio of one machine operator to eight safety officers on a work site – can the country afford such nonsense?

A recent bugbear of mine, reinforced since living in the Sunshine Coast hinterland, is the idyllic five-acre bush block and the hypocrisy that goes with it. I fully understand people wanting to live this lifestyle, and indeed, if I was twenty years younger, I'd be tempted to do it myself. Let's look at it logically. You buy a block then partially clear it so you can build a house, shed and other infrastructure, often together with the planting an expansive green lawn. It looks terrific, but you've destroyed a lot of wildlife habitat in doing so, simply for your own gratification. What you've destroyed is in fact the natural peace and serenity which led you to settle there. The ultimate hypocrisy comes when you put up little green signs outside your property which declare "Land for Wildlife".

The other issue with this lifestyle is bushfire. I've recently read the book "Currowan" by Bronwyn Adcock, which gives an excellent first-hand account of the terror and destruction of the unprecedented bushfires on the South Coast of NSW in the summer of 2019-2020. (The 2019–20 NSW bush fires burnt almost 7% of the total area of the State including 42% of State Forest and 37% of National Park estate and killed billions of the native fauna). The author, with her family, lived on a lifestyle acreage block near native forest.

The NSW Rural Fire Service is the world's largest volunteer fire and emergency service, with over 70,000 members. It has numerous functions, but in the event of a bushfire its priorities are the protection of persons from injury and death and property from damage. Reading the book it's apparent that the service was overwhelmed by dealing with those priorities and could devote scant resources to actual bushfire fighting. The significant growth in lifestyle acreage living was and will be a major contributor to diversion of resources from real bush firefighting.

Alcohol

I've never been into illicit drugs but have had a lifelong love of legal alcoholic beverages and freely admit that I consider myself an alcoholic. Being fairly shy (really) and not much of a conversationalist, I've used alcohol to loosen up some of these inhibitions, and many times they've been loosened just a tad too much. I'm a gourmandiser through and through and love nearly all good food, and I love my beer and wine to go with it. I find alcohol a wonderful boon for socialising, relaxation and for thought stimulation (if you can remember the inspired idea next day), and without it probably wouldn't be quite the laid-back character that I am. Quite interestingly I can go without alcohol for extended periods without feeling any great urge to imbibe, and today usually have several alcohol-free days each week, and fortunately old age also now limits my capacity.

There are, however, many pitfalls in living with alcohol. Very early on I was aware, and still am, that if I have more than one drink a little voice inside me tells me I need to keep drinking more. I truly envy people who can have three or four social drinks and walk away. Fortunately, I'm almost always a happy drinker and would instantly give away the demon drink if this was not so. I found that whiskey and gin in any quantity did somewhat impact my mood and so have deliberately shied away from these beverages. Alcohol has impacted on both my marriages to varying extents and I'm sure it has marginally limited some job opportunities. However, the latter may simply be that I'm a loose cannon with or without alcohol and often say what I think regardless (or even because I simply want to stir up some "big frog").

In society the jury's out on the pros and cons of alcohol – do the social and relaxation benefits outweigh the violence and irresponsibility it can create in many people, leading to injury and family upheaval and of course the proven negative health consequences. The consensus appears to be against alcohol, but I can say on a personal note that the joys and benefits have outweighed the negatives. My concern is for my family who have all been more than touched by the social alcohol syndrome and how they'll navigate their way through life happily and successfully.

Organised religion

On becoming a Church of England altar boy at age twelve I started to delve deeper into the background of the Christian religion with a young scientific mind, and the more I delved the less I liked it. By mid–high school I was excused from what were then compulsory weekly religious sessions run by ministers of each major Christian denomination. I suspect the questions I used to ask were often not greatly appreciated by the clergymen.

Organised religion has dominated the world stage for many thousands of years. For so many it has provided hope and comfort through the ages. Unfortunately, it has also been used as a means of control and power over the populace by ruthless, tyrannical and often sadistic people.

Many people need belief in a god to get them through life. I fully respect their need, and there's no doubt that myriad disciples of religion have carried out wonderful acts of kindness through the ages and continue to do so today, to relieve the pain and suffering of so many. Organised religion has also spearheaded so many of humankind's incredible achievements in the arts, humanities and sciences through millennia.

However, all that's good about organised religion pales into insignificance when the pain and suffering it has caused through endless war and persecution in the name of one god or another is considered. Surely any just god wouldn't want to be a part of these actions – nor I'm sure would it support one footy side over another as many modern players seem to think, as they give recognition to their god whenever they score a goal or try.

What disturbs me is that most organised religions' gods seem to have been created by man, and some of the stories in religious tomes such as the Christian Bible reach far beyond any credibility. That Bible is full of horror stories and ideas on creation which defy logic; by comparison indigenous Dreamtime legends at least give a more interesting and colourful interpretation of creation. The scientific and atheist alternatives to creation espoused by people such as Stephen Hawking and Richard Dawkins offer far more satisfactory explanations of the universe, but to me still fall short of an irrefutable answer.

I think Einstein nailed it in response to a the question of whether he believed in God when he noted "That deeply emotional conviction of the presence of superior reasoning power, which is revealed in the incomprehensible universe, forms my idea of God". If there is some ultimate entity I'm sure it would in no way be a part of the ongoing pain and suffering inflicted on the world by organised religion. Perhaps if we ever got to know the meaning of life, then life would have no meaning.

Despite the nonsense and evils associated with organised religion, it still holds enormous sway in Australia today. It pays no tax because of its supposed charitable nature, and its schools are heavily subsidised by government, allowing children to be brainwashed through their formative years. In fact, almost any lunatic can set up a religious organisation which will pay no tax and reap enormous profit for the founder. The untoward influence of organised religion in our society is still all-pervasive despite an increasing number of Australians declaring they have no religion in regular censuses.

I just wish for the day when the wonderful lyrics of my favourite song, "Imagine" by John Lennon, become a reality. It's still a long way off.

The human race

I get on well with most people whom I encounter and marvel at the achievements of humanity over past millennia. As individuals we're for the most part a kind and gentle race, but as a species we're probably one of the most abhorrent that has ever existed on the planet. What we don't eat of the other species we continue to destroy and exterminate at an increasingly rapid rate in the name of development. It needs to stop – but how? We're a species out of control.

Population growth must be halted now if other living beings on earth are to have any chance of survival. Forget the pathetic current efforts to slow or halt global warming: if the root cause, overpopulation, isn't recognised and addressed, then increased demand for all things will override these futile endeavours.

Is there any chance this ultimate environmental imperative will be addressed? I think not. Modern economic theory is based on continual growth; this is fundamentally unsustainable on planet earth but politically it's death to oppose it. Politicians, for the sake of their own political survival, will never address the issue of overpopulation, and even the most ardent environmentalists seem loath to broach this topic. China, the one major country that has seriously attempted to address the issue, is now thwarted by the economic implications as it tries to compete in a so-called free market (growth) economy. Regardless of the political factors, there's little chance that any legislated curbs on population would be heeded, particularly by citizens of Third World countries where procreation is an imperative.

Population growth is out of control. Perhaps a nuclear war or a new virus will decimate us, or artificial intelligence will recognise that the human race is the real threat to sustaining life on planet earth and devise some method of extermination. In terms of geological time, the reign of humans as the dominant living species on earth will almost certainly be short. Perhaps many indigenous peoples recognised the planet's limited resources and practised population control, albeit unknowingly. Indigenous Australians in particular, have existed for at least 65,000 years while curbing population to what local resources could sustain (or has nature itself simply done the curbing?).

One can only hope that as the human race self-destructs it doesn't take the atmosphere, the oceans and all other living creatures with it, thus creating a Mars-like environment for our beautiful planet.

Conclusion

If I have a major regret in life it's about leaving the planet in a much worse state than it was. Conflict on various scales continues unabated round the Earth. Overpopulation as already mentioned has contributed to massive pollution and global warming issues, but the wonderful technical innovations of the past 70 years or so have also contributed to a massive redistribution of wealth such that about half of the world's wealth is now owned by one percent of the population. Something needs to change but I can foresee no instant solutions. With such inequality, do we have another "French Revolution" about to happen on a world scale, or will technical mind control innovations keep the populace brainwashed and in virtual slavery if not exactly unhappy.

All that aside, I've always considered myself incredibly lucky to have lived at all. The odds of being the single sperm that conceives are akin to winning a major lottery, so life is there to be enjoyed while we have it, not to hope for some eternal existence to follow. What a horrible concept if you think about it!

I don't take life too seriously. I've lived a very comfortable and contented life, never having any great wealth but equally having no great need or desire for material items or social climbing. Skills both sporting and otherwise have come fairly easily, and I've been blessed with a degree of intelligence even though some of the antics described in this book may suggest otherwise. Consequently, I'm rather complacent and have never been particularly motivated for high achievement. Money has been a case of easy come, easy go, and if I or my younger wife, Babs, should live to a ripe old age I or more likely she may come to regret that attitude.

I've travelled overseas infrequently, but frankly I'd rather be catching a wave, paddling through the Noosa everglades, enjoying a timeless outback sunset or wandering through the Australian bush than taking on the hordes of civilisation to visit cultural and historic sites in which I've only a passing interest. In terms of gourmandising, the Sunshine Coast offers all I could reasonably desire and sinking a cold Coopers Pale Ale at a country pub, tucking into oysters by the Noosa River or simply partaking of a good Tilba vintage cheddar, washed down with either a McLaren Vale shiraz, a Clare Valley riesling or a Bleasdale sparkling shiraz is more than adequate.

I've been blessed with a very loving, close and extended family, although there have been times when Geoffrey Blayney's tyranny of distance in Australia has meant we haven't caught up as regularly as I might have liked. On my Mum, Kitty's 95th birthday (her last) she was presented with a quilt compiled with squares containing messages from her children, grandchildren and great grandchildren (and their partners). Mine thanked her in particular for her sense of humour and caring nature, two attributes that I believe are vital for navigating through life and ensuring a life well lived.

What more can I say.

Sunshine Coast Hinterland, Queensland

Acknowledgements

Thanks first and foremost to my very patient editor, Kai Jensen, poet and author, who has diligently worked through my manuscript over an extended period, making numerous corrections and amendments without altering my rambling, laid back and understated style. Kai also provided sage advice on chapter length and titles which has seen a dramatic improvement in the manuscript. I would also like to thank him and his wife (my niece), Rajni, for allowing me to mimic the cover style of his recently published book of poetry.

I am also much indebted to author Kimberley Barden, who not only agreed to format my manuscript for publication, but has also led me by the hand through the processes and pitfalls of self-publishing, thank you Kim.

My daughter Teneille Newton, utilising her wonderful marketing skills, has been responsible for the cover design using as background, images of a quilt designed by my wife Babs Newton (on the occasion of my 70th Birthday) and a contemporary dot painting by my other daughter, Emma Newton. My love and thanks to them all.

Fellow bridge player and retired Noosa columnist, Susie Osmaston, read my original manuscript chapter by chapter and her positive feedback encouraged me to persist through to publication, thanks Susie.

Then there are the many people who have read selected chapters and provided feedback and factual corrections, thank you one and all and apologies to those I have surely missed. They include Sue and Brian Gullefer, who provided me with insights about long term Top End issues and residents and constantly encouraged me to publish; Bev Keenan, who refreshed my recollections and provided new revelations of high school days; South Australian work colleagues, Mark Flintoft, Peter Crettenden, Ric Horn, Jim Allender, Zac Sibenaler and Kevin Wills who all feature in the book; and to my three Darwin mates from the early 1970's, Lynton Sherry, Neddy Barden and Mike Sanders, who have all miraculously survived those heady days.

I must also thank my niece Ros Bulloch. Ros sat and talked with my Mum, Kitty Payne, for endless hours before her 90th birthday in 2001 and then produced a wonderful book of memories on the day. I realised then how important it is to write things down, otherwise the stories are lost forever.

Finally, my love and commiserations to my dear wife Babs, who has suffered over a decade of keeping bread on the table only to arrive home from work to find me sitting at the computer working on this book or playing online bridge or solitaire. Then again, perhaps another story is brewing.

Bibliography

Barnes,L.C. and Townsend, I.J., 1982.Opal-*South Australia's Gemstone*. South Australian Dept. of Mines and Energy, Handbook No.5

Chaloupka,George, 2023. *Journey in time: the world's longest continuing art tradition: the 50,000-year story of the Australian Aboriginal rock art of Arnhem Land.* Published by Reed New Holland Publishers, Sydney ISBN 9781760793630. First published in 1993 by Reed Books.

Collins, Major Frank James "*Bob*", 2016. *Keepers of the Gate; personal stories by NGVR soldiers (chapter 9, Lega Lt Thomas William James "Tom").* Published by New Guinea Volunteer Rifles/ Papua New Guinea Volunteer Rifles Ex-Members Association Inc. ISBN 9780992585570

Eupene, Geoff; April 2009. *Obituary William Joseph (Joe) Fisher AM.* The AusIMM Bulletin, Australasian Institute of Mining and Metallurgy: 91-92 ISSN 1034-6775

Isaacson,Walter, 2008.*Einstein: his life and universe.* Published by Simon & Schuster Paperbacks, New York. ISBN 13:978-0-7432-6474-7

Johns, R.K.,2010, *A mirage in the desert? The discovery, evaluation and development of the Olympic Dam ore body at Roxby Downs, South Australia, 1975-88,* O'Neil Historical and Editorial Services, Adelaide. ISBN 9780980520118

Moreman, John, 2003. *Wau-Salamau 1942 Australians in the Pacific War.* Published by Department of Veterans Affairs, Canberra. ISBN 1 877007 18 8

Newton, A.W., Wilson,M.A. and Harris,J, 1988. *Olympic Dam – The First Decade* in Mineral Resources Review, S.Aust. No. 156 (pp 5-26). Department of Mines and Energy, South Australia

Wikipedia: *GeorgeChaloupka/ Imperial Hotel, Ravenswood/ Various Other*

Woerle, Frank and Thiele, Colin, 1987. *Ranger's Territory.* Angus & Robertson Publishers. ISBN 0 207 15541 0

Wright, Alexis, 2017. *Tracker.* Giramondo Publishing Company. ISBN 978-1-925336-33-7

Music Lyrics:
Anderson, Ian, 1972. *Thick as a Brick (Jethro Tull).* Chrysalis/Reprise
De Sylva, Buddy and Meyer, Joseph, 1925. *If You Knew Susie.* Shapiro, Bernstein Co.
Driftwood, Jimmy, 1936. *The Battle of New Orleans.* Unknown.
Dusty, Slim, 1971. *Big Frogs in Little Puddles.* Columbia.
Egan, Ted, 1969. *Drinkers of the Territory.* Unknown.
Hairston, Jester, 1956. *Mary's Boychild.* RCA Victor.
Humphries, Barry, 1965. *The Old Pacific Sea.* Bulletin Records
Lennon, John and Oko, Yono, 1971. *Imagine.* Apple.

www.ingramcontent.com/pod-product-compliance
Lightning Source LLC
Chambersburg PA
CBHW060346080526
44583CB00014B/1081